BUILDING A
Latino Civil Rights
MOVEMENT

BUILDING A

Latino Civil Rights

MOVEMENT

Puerto Ricans, African Americans,
and the Pursuit of Racial Justice
in New York City

SONIA SONG-HA LEE

The University of North Carolina Press
Chapel Hill

The paper in this book meets the guidelines for permanence and durability of
the Committee on Production Guidelines for Book Longevity of the Council on
Library Resources. The University of North Carolina Press has been a member
of the Green Press Initiative since 2003.

Library of Congress Cataloging-in-Publication Data
Lee, Sonia Song-Ha.
Building a Latino civil rights movement : Puerto Ricans, African Americans,
and the pursuit of racial justice in New York City / Sonia Song-Ha Lee.
pages cm. — (Justice, power, and politics)
Includes bibliographical references and index.
ISBN 978-1-4696-1413-7 (cloth : alk. paper)
ISBN 978-1-4696-1414-4 (ebook)
1. Puerto Ricans—Civil rights—New York (State)—New York—History—
20th century. 2. Puerto Ricans—New York (State)—New York—Politics and
government—20th century. 3. Puerto Ricans—New York (State)—New York—
Social conditions—20th century. 4. African Americans—Civil rights—New
York (State)—New York—History—20th century. 5. African Americans—New
York (State)—New York—Politics and government—20th century. 6. Civil rights
movements—New York (State)—New York—History—20th century. 7. African
Americans—Relations with Hispanic Americans 8. New York (N.Y.)—Ethnic
relations. 9. New York (N.Y.)—Race relations. I. Title.
F128.9.P85L44 2014   323.1168'729507471—dc23   2013047867

18 17 16 15 14   5 4 3 2 1

Contents

Figures and Maps

Acknowledgments

This book has been written through the generous and steadfast support of many colleagues and friends. My undergraduate adviser, Leon Litwack, sparked a love of history and an appreciation for those who came before me. My graduate adviser, Evelyn Brooks Higginbotham, served as a model of academic rigor and compassionate collegiality. She affirmed the development of my intellectual life when my ideas were most unformed. Lizabeth Cohen provided a wonderful support structure by organizing a reading group and teaching us how to engage with each other's work critically. I also received invaluable feedback from James Jennings, Susan O'Donovan, Mark Sawyer, Carol Anderson, and Vincent Brown during my days in Cambridge. My colleagues and friends Sara Schwebel, Judy Kertész, Erin Royston Battat, Suleiman Osman, Kim Sims, and Louis Hyman provided steadfast support and humor during graduate school.

Colleagues that I met through Centro de Estudios Puertorriqueños (Center for Puerto Rican Studies) and the Schomburg Center for Research in Black Culture provided a wealth of knowledge and support. Miriam Jiménez Román, Juan Flores, Ismael García-Colón, Andrés Torres, Anthony De Jesús, Jorge Matos, Pedro Juan Hernández, Félix Rivera, and Lillian Jiménez connected me to key sources—the archival collections, as well as the oral history interviewees. Their intellectual and personal investments in this research project were crucial to helping me write this book.

At Swarthmore College and Washington University in St. Louis, I found colleagues who gave me insightful comments and a nurturing intellectual community. Rafael Zapata, Marjorie Murphy, Pieter Judson, Sarah Willie-LeBreton, Keith Reeves, Cheryl Jones-Walker, and Lisa Smulyan cheered me on as I learned to link my teaching with research interests. Members of the History Department at Washington University provided me with a vital support system through which I could revise my manuscript. Special thanks go to Iver Bernstein, Yuko Miki, Andrea Friedman, Jean Allman, Andrea Campetella, Sowande' Mustakeem, Shefali Chandra, Derek Hirst, Lori Watt, and Nancy Reynolds, who read my work and gave me valuable feedback. Margaret Garb went above and beyond the call of duty by reading multiple drafts of nearly every chapter. Her intellectual generosity will continue to inspire me throughout my career. Colleagues that I met through conferences and other intellectual circles also enriched my work in countless ways: Ande Diaz, Frank Guridy, Jesse Hoffnung-Garskof, Lorrin Thomas, Cary Fraser, Dan Berger, Lisa Ramos, José Cruz, Mérida Rúa, Aldo Lauria Santiago, Craig Wilder, Johanna Fernandez, Scott Kurashige, Brian Purnell, Daniel Widener, and Tamar Carroll. Their kindness and enthusiasm have been contagious. Toward the final stages of revision, Iliyana Hadjistoyanova helped me gather important research material. Students from Swarthmore College and Washington University energized me and reminded me that ideas matter—that every good book can have a lifelong impact on the way that we treat each other and build our world. These students are too numerous to name, but special thanks go to Grace Kaissal, Isabel Rivera, Diego Menendez, Toby Wu, Karen Mok, Olamide Abiose, and Andreas Mitchell.

Many thanks go to my editors at the University of North Carolina Press, David Perry and Brandon Proia; the academic editors of the book series Justice, Power, and Politics, Rhonda Williams and Heather Ann Thompson; and the two anonymous readers of the manuscript. Their careful and insightful comments helped me write this book more clearly and accurately.

Archivists and librarians from multiple institutions provided me with generous assistance. I am indebted to the staff at the Kheel Center for Labor-Management Documentation and Archives at Cornell University, the Tamiment Library & Robert F. Wagner Labor Archives at New York University, the Schomburg Center for Research in Black Culture, the Rare Book and Manuscript Library at Columbia University, the La Guardia and Wagner Archives, the New York State Archives, the Lyndon B. Johnson Library, the John F. Kennedy Library, the Library of Congress, the Center for Puerto Rican Studies, and New York City's Municipal Archives. I also received generous funding for this book from Harvard University, the City University of New York Caribbean Exchange Program, and Washington University in St. Louis.

The heart of this book comes from the voices of the many people who opened up their homes and allowed me to share their personal stories with the larger public. They picked me up from Greyhound bus stations, cooked and bought meals for me, and generously shared their memories and insights. Were it not for their willingness to trust me with their documents and memories, this book would not have materialized. Words cannot express my deep gratitude to them.

I have been blessed with a group of loyal and fun-loving friends who helped me remain enthusiastic and hopeful about my work through the long years of research and writing: Ellen Chi, Grace Bucci, Cathy Glanzman, Malia Villegas, Jackie OldCoyote Logan, Yoojin Janice Lee, Shauna Miller, Sung Mee Kim, Sheri Shepherd-Pratt, Audrey Lee, Camille-Kay Brewer, Helen Moon, Jane Hong, April Bang, Melody Boyd, Jane Horton, Jessamine Lee, Emy Chen, and Irene Li Barnett.

My family has been the anchor that grounded me throughout my intellectual journey. My parents, Yeong Dai and Ai Rim, immigrated twice to provide the best education they could for me. They also gave me the freedom to pursue my passion in my own ways. The extravagant love of my sisters, Lydia and Christine, sustained me during the hardest times. Finally, I owe my deepest gratitude to my husband, Jason Peifer. His humor brightened my days in ways that I did not imagine possible before. His steadfast support helped me keep my sanity and enjoy all of life's big and small blessings.

BUILDING A
Latino Civil Rights
MOVEMENT

Introduction

In the mid-1970s, even as President Richard Nixon's "law and order" and anti-busing campaigns signaled to many the decline of the civil rights movement, Evelina Antonetty was beginning to reap the fruits of her organizing work in the South Bronx. Antonetty, a Puerto Rican, had been training Puerto Rican and African American mothers to fight for their children's education in New York City schools since 1965. Standing at the forefront of the bilingual education movement for Spanish-speaking children, she was at the peak of her political activism. Crucially, she was forging national networks with African American, Native American, and Mexican American parents interested in community control of education. She believed that her political work reflected a broader political transformation among Puerto Rican New Yorkers. Borrowing parts of a speech delivered by the Reverend Martin Luther King Jr. at a Young Men and Women's Christian Association meeting in 1957, Antonetty expressed her own desire to reclaim her dignity in the face of a racist society:[1] "Maladjusted is a word used perhaps more frequently than any other in modern psychology, and I am calling on the people of this city to be maladjusted. There are many things in this social system to which I am proud to be maladjusted. I can never adjust myself to the evils of segregation and discrimination. . . . I am sure history has a place for those who have the moral courage to be maladjusted. . . . Maladjusted like Don Pedro Albizu Campos who believed that [if] even the birds are free, why not Puerto Ricans?"[2]

Puerto Ricans' claim to being "maladjusted" represented a profoundly new relationship with the North American racial system. Anthropologists and sociologists had used the term "cultural maladjustment" since the 1930s to refer to a temporary stage of adjustment experienced by European immigrants and black southern migrants alike.[3] High crime rates,

1

family breakups, and economic dependency were assumed to reflect temporary modes of adjustment rather than innate inferiorities. Advocates of the cultural approach believed that their studies would improve the lives of poor migrants and immigrants, since a focus on culture rather than biology emphasized the capacity of the poor to change and assimilate to white middle-class norms. However, even as northern urban centers like New York City underwent significant changes in their racial demographics—with European immigrants and their descendants moving to the suburbs and black and Puerto Rican migrants replacing them in significant numbers—the term "cultural maladjustment" became a language of racialization. It began to represent poor migrants' permanent inability to incorporate themselves into white middle-class society. Black and Puerto Rican migrants' high rates of unemployment and low academic performances became increasingly interpreted as features of black and Puerto Rican "inferior" cultures, which were supposedly fixed and static.[4]

Antonetty's use of the term "maladjusted" indicated Puerto Ricans' new stance in dealing with their position of racial subjugation: rather than avoiding associations with African Americans, they began to align themselves more closely with black leaders' confrontational political methods. Modeling themselves after Martin Luther King Jr. and other black civil rights leaders, Puerto Rican leaders reclaimed the literature of "cultural maladjustment" and used it to create a new vocabulary of racial pride. Puerto Ricans had not "argue[d] or f[ought] back" in the past, Antonetty asserted, but they were "no longer content to exist in a minor role." They were now "determined to be self-determined." Just as Black Power leaders reimagined blackness as a basis for cultural renewal and political mobilization, so too did Puerto Rican leaders reconstruct Puerto Rican-ness as a basis for their political empowerment.

Antonetty's strategy of being "maladjusted" to segregation included establishing close collaborations with African American leaders as well as creating Puerto Ricans' own independent political organizations. Together with black leaders such as Milton Galamison, Babette Edwards, and David Spencer, Antonetty established the People's Board of Education in 1967 to promote an educational reform campaign in the city's public schools. She also began to connect with educators interested in black education reform across the nation through publications in *Foresight*, a bimonthly journal produced by the Black Teachers Workshop. Sharing ideas with writers like James and Grace Lee Boggs from Detroit, she contributed to a national conversation about the implications of Black Power in urban education. Even as Antonetty forged vital links between Puerto Rican and black activists, she also remained committed to the development of independent Puerto Rican and Latino organizations. She utilized United Bronx Parents, an organization she founded, to address the specific needs of Puerto Ricans living in the South Bronx. In the late 1970s, as New York's Dominican population was increasing, she also took part in efforts to create partnerships with other Spanish-speaking groups through the Coalition in Defense of Puerto Rican and Hispanic Rights.[5] By creating such multiple and overlapping political networks, Antonetty took part in a broader political movement in which black and Puerto Rican activists forged a common struggle toward racial justice.

Identity Formation within Civil Rights and Black Power Studies

This book analyzes the political world in which Puerto Ricans and African Americans conceptualized their racial and ethnic identities in overlapping ways to build a common civil rights agenda. In order to trace the construction of these racial and ethnic identities, I look at the formation and dissolution of mass social movements built by African Americans and Puerto Ricans in the post–World War II era. Numbering close to 613,000 and making up 7.9 percent of the city's population in 1960, Puerto Ricans were the second-largest minority group in the city after African Americans, who composed 14 percent of the city's population, at 1,088,000. These numbers increased in the following decades, with Puerto Ricans and African Americans making up 12 percent and 24 percent of the city's population, respectively, by 1980.[6] Puerto Ricans, I argue, were as vital as African Americans in shaping New Yorkers' notions of "race," "ethnicity," and "minority" in the civil rights and Black Power eras.

My study engages a recent trend within civil rights studies, which goes beyond analyzing the formation of racial and ethnic identities in isolation from one another. A number of civil rights studies focused outside of the South have analyzed the multiple Latino and Asian American social movements that overlapped with black freedom struggles in the 1940s through the 1960s. The histories of African Americans' collaborations with other people of color have indicated that dreams born out of the black freedom struggle impacted not only African Americans and white Americans but also other people of color.[7] Similarly, recent studies within Puerto Rican history have explored the development of Puerto Rican politics alongside parallel developments within black politics. Works from the 1980s had analyzed the formation of Puerto Rican political structures solely through the lens of Puerto Ricans' relationships with white Americans and other Spanish-speaking groups, but more recent works have paid greater attention to the ways in which Puerto Ricans' political, social, and economic conditions increasingly resembled those of African Americans in the postwar era.[8]

My book links these parallel developments within civil rights histories with critical race theory to understand how the meanings of "blackness" and "Puerto Rican-ness" changed over time as a result of the social mobilizations that took place between the two groups in New York City. Not only were Puerto Ricans and African Americans racialized as "nonwhite" in parallel ways, but they also utilized their racial and ethnic identities as sites of political mobilization through mutual collaborations and contestations of power. The remaking of "blackness" and "Latinidad" in the postwar era thus took place not as separate movements but as intertwined and mutually reinforcing historical processes. Taking to heart Rogers Brubaker and Frederick Cooper's critique that previous scholarship on "identity" has placed too much focus on "boundary-formation rather than boundary crossing, the constitution of groups rather than the development of networks," I look at the formation of Puerto Ricans' racial and ethnic identities as an interplay between their sensibility as a people of color with African Americans, their self-understanding as Hispanic with other Spanish-speaking groups, and their identity as members of a distinct Puerto Rican nation.[9] The boundaries between these subjectivities were never fixed but constantly shifting. Although most racialization studies have explained the establishment of those boundaries largely as a top-down process, whereby a dominant group imposes essential markers of indelible inferiority upon another, I argue that African Americans and Puerto Ricans themselves were pivotal actors within the racialization of "blackness" and "Puerto Rican-ness."[10] They helped delineate the boundaries of these categories and the permeability between them.

Recent works on the Black Power movement have described the cross-fertilization that took place across various black, Latino, and Asian American social movements. A growing literature on the Third World Left brings to light the Black Panther Party's particular influence on Latino and Asian American political mobilizations in the late 1960s.[11] These works reveal the ways in which cultural nationalism and class struggle provided common inspiration for young Chicanos, Puerto Ricans, Asian Americans, and African Americans who were in search of liberation from multiple systems of oppression. Breaking through the old myth that Black Power is segregationist, these scholars show the tremendous life that black nationalists breathed into the world by creating multiple circles of racial, class, and gender solidarities with other "oppressed nationalities." As Jeffrey Ogbar put it, the Black Panther Party was popularly known as a "black hate group," but its slogan "all power to the people" allowed the organization to transcend race and to serve as a paradigm for revolutionary movements across different ethnic groups.

For all the celebration of Third World unity that these works emphasize, however, many historians who have analyzed the implications of Black Power in more reformist civil rights organizations have come to different conclusions. Looking at black and Mexican American activists' efforts to secure better opportunities for their communities through various arenas, such as school desegregation, bilingual education, fair housing, and the War on Poverty, some historians argue that black and Mexican American activists found it politically expedient to forge separate civil rights struggles.[12] The reasons for the political separation vary. Some scholars take a top-down approach, demonstrating that the different forms of racialization imposed on each group necessitated different avenues of redress; others focus on the bottom-up agency of blacks and Chicanos themselves, emphasizing that their own formulation of cultural nationalism encouraged separatism and friction.

Third World and civil rights studies' disparate conclusions hinge on how they treat cultural differences between blacks and Latinos. Many scholars working within Third World studies assume that blacks and Latinos have historically shared a sensibility as "people of color." They emphasize blacks' and Latinos' shared position of racial and class subordination while minimizing cultural clashes between them. Meanwhile, those working within civil rights and antipoverty studies take those clashes at face value, assuming that black and Latino cultures are naturally fixed and in conflict with each other. Neither approach, however, adequately addresses how black and Latino activists deployed their cultures as political tools to achieve different purposes. They could be imagined as mutually inclusive or exclusive according to each group's assessment of the political benefits attached to multiracial organizing. For example, many have evoked Latinos' cultural identity as mestizo (racially mixed) as a static construct that makes them naturally incompatible with African Americans' mono-racial identity as "pure" blacks. Yet, mestizaje could conflict or overlap with "blackness": while Mexican Americans in the West and the Southwest argued in the 1970s that *mestizaje* reflected Latinos' Indian and Spanish heritages, Puerto Ricans in the Northeast and Midwest claimed that it reflected their Indian, Spanish, *and* African heritages.[13] Just as *mestizaje* could include or exclude "blackness," "blackness" could also be imagined as uniformly North American, or as ethnically heterogeneous. While West Indian immigrants in the Northeast constructed a common political identity with African Americans as "black" throughout the early part of the twentieth century, they adopted a more distinct ethnic identity as "Caribbean" in the 1970s and 1980s. As a result, "blackness" was constructed as an ethnically homogeneous, North American identity.[14]

If we understand race and culture as political categories, where lines of inclusion and exclusion are constantly shifting, then we must recognize that people of color constructed their racial and cultural identities through a political process.[15] The final outcome was not predetermined by fixed cultural differences or by a natural shared sensibility as "oppressed nationalities," but it was contested and negotiated as various groups of people weighed the costs and benefits of representing themselves in particular ways. Historian Mark Brilliant, for example, argues that bilingual education inherently necessitated separate battles because it reflected Mexican Americans' needs as different from those of African Americans.[16] Language, however, marked only one of the many ways in which Mexican American children had become racialized. Their racialization as a "colored race" and as those who were assumed to possess a "culture of poverty" placed them in the same category with African Americans. Yet Mexican American leaders chose to prioritize their distinctiveness as a language minority group and to see bilingual education as an issue that was incompatible with school desegregation. This move by Mexican American activists did not reflect fixed cultural incompatibilities but was a strategic political decision to create a political base separate from African Americans. Mexican American activists themselves played an important role in delineating the boundaries between "blackness" and "Latinidad."

The Political Deployment of Race, Ethnicity, and Minority Status

Most scholars of Puerto Rican identity formations have framed their analyses around the question of whether the term "Hispanic/Latino" constitutes a "racial" or an "ethnic" category.[17] According to this literature, the majority of Latinos themselves insist that they compose an "ethnic" group. This position is viewed as advantageous because it allows Latinos to resist the imposition of North American racism by claiming an identity as neither "black" nor "white" but "other." This self-preference makes sense, given the more positive connotations that the term "ethnicity" carries over "race" today. Whereas being "ethnic" indicates the possibility of becoming American, being "racial" signals an identity that is unassimilable (for example, Jewish ethnics assimilated into a "white" American culture, whereas African Americans are perpetually imagined as "unrepresentative" Americans). An "ethnic" category tolerates multiple and flexible identities, whereas a "racial" identity is exclusive (one can be half Irish and half Italian, but one cannot be both "black" and "white"). Finally, an "ethnic" difference does not carry moral connotations, but a "racial" one implies distinctive ability and moral worth (for example, immigrants are celebrated for carrying cultural traditions that are morally neither good nor bad, but "black culture" is imagined as inherently violent).[18] Despite Latinos' insistence that "Hispanic/Latino" signifies an ethnic identity, however, scholars have argued that it tends to operate as a racialized category in daily life. No matter how "blonde or blue-eyed" an individual is, the moment that individual self-identifies as a Puerto Rican, he or she enters the category of racial "Otherness." In the words of anthropologist Virginia Dominguez, "People may talk culture, but they continue to think race."[19]

What becomes clear from this debate, then, is the fact that the categorization of Latinos as ethnic or racial does not depend on an objective conceptual differentiation but on a highly contested negotiation of power. While the dominant society has sought to impose notions of permanence and inferiority upon Latinos' cultural differences by imagining them as a racial group, Latinos themselves have sought to defend themselves from such racialization by calling themselves an ethnic group. Latinos were not the first group of migrants to use this political tactic. Jewish immigrants had used a similar strategy in the 1920s when they sought to legitimize their cultural differences without running the risk of being placed on the "wrong side of the racial divide."[20] As philosopher David Theo Goldberg has argued, we must look at the formation of racial ideas "historically" rather than "conceptually," by "laying out how the terms have predominantly been used, the sorts of effects they have had, and how these have transformed over time."[21]

If we move away from simplistically categorizing Puerto Ricans as either ethnic or racial, we can see that they straddled the worlds of the racially "in-between" European immigrants as well as the Afro-Caribbean diaspora prior to the postwar era.[22] The majority of Puerto Rican migrants portrayed themselves as an "ethnic" group, even as others imagined them as a "racial" group not too different from African Americans. When a sixteen-year-old Puerto Rican boy named Lino Rivera triggered the 1935 Harlem riots, for example, most of the city's media referred to him as a "Negro" and failed to mention the fact that he was Puerto Rican. Members of the Puerto Rican elite distanced themselves from the riots. They emphasized that, although Puerto Ricans faced issues of discrimination similar to those of African Americans, they faced entirely different problems from the latter due to their "ethnic characteristics." Middle-class Puerto Ricans went to great lengths to avoid being included in discussions related to "minority groups," fearing that they would be associated too closely with "American Negroes."[23] Instead, they emphasized their ethnic identity as *hispano* or Spanish American, imagining themselves as a group more similar to European immigrants. Puerto Ricans, after all, shared many of the experiences of the Irish, Jews, and Italians: they spoke a foreign language and were considered foreigners, and their poverty conditions were assumed to be temporary by many public officials. Although contemporary observers might look at this association skeptically—given the rigid boundaries that we have created between "whites" and "Hispanics" today—such a view would miss the fact that the terms "ethnic" and "racial" were used interchangeably in the first half of the twentieth century, and both terms were used to describe European immigrants and Puerto Rican migrants.[24]

While some Puerto Ricans identified themselves with European immigrants, others emphasized their membership in the diasporic world of "nonwhite" Afro-Caribbeans. By living in Spanish Harlem, a neighborhood adjacent to Central Harlem, Puerto Ricans came into close contact with people of African descent who belonged to a cosmopolitan black world. The United States' imperial project in the Caribbean had brought tens of thousands of Afro-Caribbean migrants to Harlem in the 1910s and 1920s.[25] Harlem thus became the home of political giants such as Malcolm X, whose mother was Grenadian, and Kenneth Clark, whose parents were Jamaican. It gave birth to musical productions that reflected the hybridity of Afro-diasporic cultures, such as the *mambo*, boogaloo, and the Cubop.[26] The population of black foreigners in New York City was significant enough—they composed 17 percent of the city's black population in 1930—that "blackness" in New York was much more ethnically heterogeneous than it was in cities like Chicago or Detroit.[27] Artúro Schomburg, as historian Jesse Hoffnung-Garskof has ably demonstrated, was only one out of many Puerto Ricans who maintained "black" and "Puerto Rican" identities simultaneously.[28] As co-inhabitants of an international black Harlem, Afro-Caribbeans from Puerto Rico, Cuba, Jamaica, Haiti, and other Caribbean islands came to share an antiracist sensibility with African Americans. Although Afro-Caribbeans had not experienced Jim Crow segregation, they belonged to nations that had been viewed by U.S. political elites as "racially mixed" and "inferior."[29] These individuals viewed themselves as members of the "colored race," even as they agitated for their citizenship rights as members of nation-states across the Americas.[30]

Puerto Ricans occupied a middle space between European "racially in-between" immigrants and the "colored race," but several factors led them to identify more closely with the latter in the post–World War II era. America's rise as a global superpower after the war demanded the construction of a new national identity pinned to a culturally pluralist ethos. Since the United States marked its global political legitimacy in opposition to Nazi Germany, Americans sought to erase their history of racism and replace it with a narrative of universal assimilation and racial democracy. Scholars and government officials began to refer to European immigrants and African Americans alike as "minorities" and "ethnics," erasing differences between those who were considered to be racially "other" but nevertheless "white" and those who were considered to be "nonwhite."[31] Puerto Ricans' position of racial ambiguity was also made irrelevant as they too came under the general category of being "minorities." Various groups that had formerly occupied different locations within the American racial spectrum were generalized as minorities and were expected to experience the benefits of assimilation, regardless of skin color. American social reformers, who were especially invested in buttressing America's global image as a racial democracy, dedicated themselves to fostering racial harmony among whites, blacks, and other minorities.[32] African American civil rights leaders were critical of the distance between America's rhetoric and its practice of racial democracy. Nevertheless, they capitalized on this ethos to draw broad linkages between their struggle for civil rights and those of other minorities. In New York City, black activists ranging from the president of the local branch of the NAACP, Ella Baker, to East Harlem social worker Preston Wilcox began to include Puerto Ricans in their discussions of racial discrimination faced by "minority groups."[33] By creating a common political identity between themselves and Puerto Ricans as "minorities," African Americans saw that they could legitimate their political struggle as a universal fight for human rights rather than a competition for political power based purely on self-interest.

African American leaders also drew linkages between their domestic struggle for civil rights and Puerto Ricans' anticolonial struggle. They recognized that the processes of racialization and colonization of people of color all over the world were entangled. The black struggle for racial equality was only part of a broader global fight against the advancement of Western capitalism and imperialism.[34] Many black intellectuals came to share the view of W. E. B. Du Bois, who argued in 1945 that "groups like Negroes in the U.S. who are segregated physically and discriminated against spiritually in law and custom; groups like the South American Indians who are the laboring peons, without rights or privileges, of large countries; and whole laboring classes in Asia and the South Seas . . . all these people occupy what is really a colonial status."[35] Some black journalists, such as George Little from the *Pittsburgh Courier* and Denton Brooks from the *Chicago Defender*, took a particular interest in comparing African Americans' second-class citizenship status with that of Puerto Ricans. In their view, Puerto Ricans' colonial status highlighted the role of the U.S. government in perpetuating Western imperialism since Puerto Ricans were legally under the jurisdiction of the United States.[36] By the 1960s, political texts ranging from Harold Cruse's *Rebellion or Revolution?* (1968), to Stokely Carmichael and Charles Hamilton's *Black Power: The Politics of Black Liberation in America* (1967), to even the reformist Kenneth Clark's *Dark Ghetto* (1965), posited that African Americans' racial subjugation represented a form of "domestic colonialism."[37] By emphasizing the multiple overlaps that existed between the world's racial and colonial subjects, African American leaders opened up a way through which various groups of people could create a common language of protest with them. Identifying with the black freedom struggle did not require a primordial link to an African ancestry but only a broad political orientation opposed to America's capitalist and imperialist practices.

Forging Common Coalitions and Overlapping Identities

Many Puerto Rican leaders initially hesitated to identify too closely with African Americans. But they gradually became convinced that they had more to gain by linking themselves to the black freedom struggle than by dodging their status of racial subordination. Chapter 1 analyzes the historical process through which the culture of poverty discourse, deindustrialization, and urban renewal convinced Puerto Ricans that they could not overcome their racialization unless they publicly acknowledged it. The culture of poverty discourse had originated from the cultural pluralist ethos, which had initially predicted that African Americans and Puerto Ricans would assimilate into mainstream American society. As deindustrialization and urban renewal increasingly locked poor blacks and Puerto Ricans into economic marginalization in the 1950s and 1960s, however, more and more New Yorkers came to view "black culture" and "Puerto Rican culture" as permanently damaged. The writings of sociologist Daniel Patrick Moynihan and anthropologist Oscar Lewis regarding the cultures of African Americans and Puerto Ricans, respectively, became self-fulfilling prophecies.[38] Moynihan's and Lewis's claims that the "culture of poverty" operated in a "self-perpetuating cycle" became a justification for less government intervention for people of color since their "pathological" cultures were viewed as intractable. As blacks and Puerto Ricans fought against the racializing impact of the "culture of poverty" discourse, they developed a common antiracist sensibility.

The fact that black and Puerto Rican New Yorkers developed a common antiracist sensibility, however, did not mean that they automatically adopted a common political identity as people of color. In order to express their racial grievances in a meaningful way, they needed to access political vehicles through which they could collaboratively effect change. Chapter 2 analyzes black and Puerto Rican workers' expressions of political dissent within a context that did not facilitate cross-racial collaborations. This chapter functions as a contrast to the subsequent chapters of the book. The leadership of the International Ladies Garment Workers' Union (ILGWU) actively impeded the mobilization of black and Puerto Rican union members as racialized minorities. Despite the similar experiences of the two groups, black and Puerto Rican workers did not form cross-racial collaborations within the ILGWU due to white labor leaders' overall resistance to race-specific political organizing and Puerto Ricans' own lack of access to political networks in comparison to African Americans.

The civil rights movement and the War on Poverty, however, catalyzed Puerto Ricans' political association with African Americans. Chapters 3 and 4 analyze the ways in which reform organizations, antipoverty programs, and school desegregation initiatives provided vehicles through which blacks and Puerto Ricans could fight against racial discrimination collaboratively. White reformists envisioned their programs as social service agencies that would attend to the needs of the poor, but Puerto Rican and black activists used the political dynamism unleashed by the national civil rights movement to turn those programs into sites of independent political organizing. They refused to limit their roles as mere recipients of social services, insisting that they fight against their racial and economic marginalization on their own terms. Puerto Rican women emerged as new power brokers for their communities through their credentials as social workers and mothers. Puerto Rican activists forged an overlapping identity with black activists as "minorities" and used such an identity as a tool of grassroots mobilization.

Puerto Ricans' self-identification as "minorities" in the 1960s signaled their assessment that a political association with African Americans would result in many more opportunities than liabilities. The term "minority" had connoted victimization in the 1930s and 1940s, and it had become firmly attached to African Americans and other "nonwhites" since the late 1950s.[39] Despite the risks involved in associating themselves with African Americans, however, Puerto Ricans embraced this designation because their inclusion in the War on Poverty depended on it. The Johnson administration had initiated antipoverty programs specifically in response to demands being made by African American civil rights leaders across the nation. Even though antipoverty programs were officially racially neutral, most Washington officials admitted that the rising significance of the black vote had been a significant part of the calculus when Congress passed the Economic Opportunity Act of 1964 and made large pools of federal funds available for poor communities.[40] As representatives of a much smaller group of migrants mostly concentrated in the Northeast, Puerto Rican activists realized that they would have a difficult time claiming their share of antipoverty funds unless they aligned themselves with African Americans as members of another minority group. Most Washington officials did not know much about Puerto Ricans' particular conditions of poverty or their specific racial status. But they were willing to include Puerto Ricans within antipoverty programs by considering them another group of "minorities" in need of government intervention.

Critics at the time claimed that Puerto Ricans' willingness to self-identify as minorities in the 1960s reflected their interest in attaching themselves to a black civil rights agenda purely for opportunistic reasons.[41] Claiming a minority identity, they argued, allowed Puerto Ricans to access material rewards. But Puerto Ricans' association with African Americans through a shared minority status resulted in much more than access to federal resources. Puerto Rican and black antipoverty leaders certainly competed for antipoverty funds, but they also experienced an internal transformation of political consciousness by participating in this federal program. As both groups came to recognize the slow pace and limited parameters of the War on Poverty and civil rights programs, they adopted a common resolve to achieve the "maximum feasible participation" of the poor on their own terms. They embraced the empowerment of their own local communities rather than racial integration as their preeminent political goal.

The community control movement emerged out of black and Puerto Rican activists' frustrations with the War on Poverty and racial integration plans. Chapter 5 analyzes the ways in which activists involved in public school reform utilized the concept of self-determination to organize one of the most vibrant cross-racial movements in the city. Rather than relying on the help and expertise of middle-class white professionals and political leaders, they began to value working-class parents' own knowledge of their children's educational problems and ability to find solutions. Parents and teachers of color drew upon black and Puerto Rican nationalism as tools of grassroots mobilization and education reform. They believed that they could rekindle black and Puerto Rican youth's hunger for learning by designing a pedagogy focused on black and Puerto Rican culture and history. The Young Lords Party and the Black Panther Party, which became the most well-known Puerto Rican and black nationalist organizations, were only parts of a broader mobilization of people of color who deployed black and Puerto Rican nationalism to mobilize their communities.[42] Bilingual education emerged out of Puerto Rican activists' efforts to build a pedagogy centered on Puerto Rican culture, but African Americans equally embraced it as a pedagogical tool useful in the creation of a multicultural, antiracist world.

As these nationalist movements emerged in the context of Third World decolonization movements, some Puerto Rican activists linked their local civil rights struggles with a renewed call for the island's political independence. Activists from the mainland and the island began to think of political change in transnational and cross-racial ways. Juan Mari Bras, the founder of Movimiento Pro Independencia (MPI), who had previously organized a small group of island *independentistas*, began working closely with Puerto Rican and African American activists from the mainland in the late 1960s. During a visit to Puerto Rico in 1967, Student Nonviolent Coordinating Committee (SNCC) leader Stokely Carmichael posited that the goals of attaining Puerto Rican political self-determination on the island and black liberation on the mainland were mutually dependent and reinforcing since the black population functioned as a "colony" within the United States.[43] One could argue that such radical activists helped create a "black Atlantic," which, in Paul Gilroy's words, represented a "global, coalitional politics in which anti-imperialism and anti-racism might be seen to interact if not to fuse." They understood "blackness" not so much as the color of one's skin but as a shared history and perception about the world.[44] Not all Puerto Ricans claimed to belong to this "black" world, but many found it useful to compare their own experiences with those of blacks, and vice versa. Blacks and Puerto Ricans bound by the concept of self-determination could thus create separate identities as minority competitors for antipoverty funding, as well as overlapping identities as working-class parents and colonized subjects.

The era of black and Puerto Rican nationalism was stymied by white backlash in the early 1970s. Chapter 6 analyzes how external repression and internal class divisions fractured the movement. As black and Puerto Rican activists tried to institutionalize power by translating grassroots organizing into electoral seats, school board seats, federal funding, and job security, they began to seek the development of separate bases of political power. The increase in the numerical proportion of Puerto Ricans and African Americans in the city provided new political possibilities. With each group composing a majority in certain districts, some electoral leaders came to believe that the two groups no longer needed to collaborate. Assured that black political candidates could rely predominantly on black voters and Puerto Rican candidates on Puerto Rican voters, they began to carve out separate black and Puerto Rican political agendas and territories.

In this process, it became politically expedient for them to engage in a process that I call "bifurcated racialization," whereby the cultures of subjugated groups are cast not only as fixed, but also as exaggerated opposites. Puerto Rican elites saw black "militancy" in contrast to Puerto Ricans' "patience," just as black leaders saw African Americans' racial identification as "black" as politically more radical than Puerto Ricans' ethnic identification as "Puerto Rican." Within this configuration, Puerto Rican elites constructed "Hispanicity" as an ethnic identity that was mutually incompatible with "blackness" to justify their desire to organize separately from African Americans. Such a construction had been used as a political strategy of racial elevation by previous generations of Puerto Ricans prior to the 1960s. But Puerto Rican elites from the 1970s had to assert it all the more aggressively at this time since Puerto Ricans' political identity had become considerably entangled with that of African Americans as a result of their civil rights and antipoverty collaborations. They had to go to great lengths to portray bilingual education as a separate issue from racial discrimination in schools, even though language and racial discrimination were intricately connected. Puerto Rican elites claimed that their "Hispanic" identity represented a natural incompatibility with "blackness," but it actually represented a political strategy born out of their middle-class sensibility. Their strategy intersected with that of white politicians who sought to co-opt the black freedom struggle by positioning themselves as the advocates of the "more worthy" minority group—the more "docile" and "less angry" Latinos.[45] White leaders like Mayor Edward Koch helped break the coalition of African Americans and Puerto Ricans by portraying the city as a myriad of ethnic interest groups rather than as one divided between "whites" and "minorities." According to his political framework, Jews, Italians, Puerto Ricans, and West Indians would each create shifting alliances with whichever group was willing to make a deal with them, with no ideological commitment toward dismantling or reproducing white political dominance.[46]

The Hispanic ethnic strategy had mixed results. While creating coalitions with Mexican Americans under the Hispanic umbrella gave Puerto Ricans the opportunity to secure federal funds for bilingual education and bilingual ballots, their desire to disassociate themselves from African Americans did not necessarily succeed. The term "Hispanic" became associated with the characteristics of the "black underclass" in the 1970s. Low-income Puerto Ricans and Mexican Americans were increasingly seen through the lens of negative stereotypes, such as high crime rates, drug addiction, out-of-wedlock childbearing, and welfare dependency. In the words of sociologist Martha Giménez, the term "Hispanic" both "falsely upgraded" Chicanos and Puerto Ricans by linking them to Spain and "falsely downgraded" them by stigmatizing their cultures as the source of their economic problems.[47] Ironically, even as Puerto Ricans' stigmatization under the term "Hispanic" reflected their common racialization with African Americans, Puerto Rican elites tried to paint "Hispanicity" as at odds with "blackness."

This is not to say that Puerto Rican elites monopolized the political leadership of their entire community in the 1970s. Many working-class Puerto Ricans continued to see "Puerto Ricans" and "Latinos/Hispanics" as political groups compatible with the black working class. Rank-and-file groups led by Puerto Ricans and African Americans in Local 1199 of the Hospital and Health Care Employees Union, Local 6 of the Hotel, Motel and Club Employees' Union, and Local 3 of the International Brotherhood of Electrical Workers' Union continued to push for the political representation of black and Hispanic unionists simultaneously throughout the 1970s.[48] To some labor leaders, the decision to adopt a Hispanic constituency reflected not so much a disregard for black workers as their growing awareness of Spanish-speaking immigrants and their needs for labor representation. According to Eddie Gonzalez, founder of the Hispanic Labor Committee (formed in 1969), labor leaders needed to develop "an internal communication [and] network capability" among new Latino immigrants living in New York City, such as Hondurans, Dominicans, and Colombians. The name "Hispanic" allowed Hispanic Labor Committee leaders to include these more recent immigrants in their organization.[49] However, the voices of Puerto Rican electoral leaders who used "Hispanicity" in a more racially exclusive manner more strongly influenced the meanings that the term bore in the 1970s and onward.

Implications for Latino Civil Rights Narratives

There are certain particularities that led Puerto Ricans to form a common identity with African Americans in New York City more easily than Mexican Americans who lived in different regions of the United States. First, although Puerto Ricans' national folklore often privileged its Spanish roots over its African and indigenous roots, it acknowledged the presence of an African heritage at the very least. Certainly, the overwhelming majority of the Puerto Rican intellectuals on the island had adopted a Eurocentric view of Puerto Rican culture, assuming that the island was in its essence "white, Western, Catholic and Spanish."[50] Puerto Ricans' notion of mestizaje was heralded insofar as it predicted that the nation was "whitening" itself and its "blackness" was disappearing. To the extent that blackness was celebrated within Puerto Rican nationalist narratives, it was limited to the cultural realm. Popular musical traditions like bomba and plena, for example, have often been heralded as indicative of African contributions to Puerto Rican culture. Notions of high culture, civilization, and upward mobility, however, have been linked to Puerto Ricans' Spanish heritage.[51] Nevertheless, the fact that blackness was not completely denied meant that Puerto Ricans could politically deploy it as a vital part of their culture when it became politically expedient to do so. Puerto Ricans seeking to revitalize the commercial and residential life of the Lower East Side in the 1970s, for example, renamed their neighborhood Loisaida, partially because it sounded like Loíza, the region of Puerto Rico that is remembered as a historic site of slave resistance.[52] In this context, Puerto Rican activists attached new meanings to Puerto Rican "blackness," linking it to notions of political empowerment and collective upward mobility. Puerto Ricans' celebration of *mestizaje* was thus malleable enough to elevate blackness as a positive aspect of Puerto Rican culture, even though it had been historically degraded as "backward." In contrast, Mexican history has rarely even acknowledged the presence of Africans in the population. Despite the growing scholarly literature on African slavery in Mexico in recent years, Mexicans have historically denied that Africans represented a significant part of the nation's population.[53] Not surprisingly, the making of a Chicano identity in the 1960s came without references to the African part of Mexico.

Second, New York offered a world with rich traditions of political radicalism. With a long history of black-Jewish coalitions rooted in the labor movement and the Communist Party, New York had plenty of interracial organizations through which African American and Puerto Rican workers could find a common consciousness as workers. Although many of these organizations had gone through a time of silencing and repression in the 1950s, individuals who were members of such organizations in the earlier period carried their ideas and experiences with them into the civil rights movement and the War on Poverty. Tenant activists, for example, had carried the Communist Party's tradition of organizing tenant strikes from the 1930s into the 1960s, whether organizing poor white tenants or poor tenants of color.[54]

Third, Puerto Ricans and African Americans shared physical spaces in neighborhoods and the workplace, making the joint political mobilization of their communities possible and desirable. Although they did not choose to live in neighborhoods concentrated with public housing projects, nor did they choose to work in garment factories and hospital kitchens, they utilized these physical spaces to forge, in the words of sociologists Aldon Morris and Naomi Braine, "free spaces where resistance can be contemplated, acted out, and condoned."[55] These spaces were concentrated in two particular neighborhoods in the city: East Harlem, which was approximately 39 percent Puerto Rican and 32 percent black in 1960; and the South Bronx, which was 39 percent Puerto Rican and 16 percent black. The percentage of both groups in each of these neighborhoods would only increase a decade later.[56] Puerto Rican–black mobilizations took place in other neighborhoods of New York City (such as the Lower East Side, Brownsville, and Williamsburg), but these two neighborhoods demonstrated the most visible and successful coalitions. In unions where blacks and Puerto Ricans composed significant portions of the overall membership—such as the Drug, Hospital, and Health Care Employees Union (Local 1199) and the Retail, Wholesale and Department Store Union (District 65)—they also used union halls to call for racial parity in wages, working conditions, and promotions.

Some might argue that these factors make this black–Puerto Rican history exceptional rather than representative of other black-Latino histories. Those who have been invested in elevating "Hispanicity" over "blackness" have certainly argued that Puerto Ricans are an "exceptional" group of Latinos because they do not fit into the otherwise consistent pattern of Latino assimilation. Linda Chavez, who served as a consultant to President Ronald Reagan, argued that Puerto Ricans' consistent high rates of poverty reflected the fact that they are U.S. citizens by birth, and that this citizenship "became a liability in the welfare state." Tacitly linking them to African Americans, Chavez claimed that Puerto Ricans have sunk into state dependence because they have been "smothered by entitlements."[57] Such statements, however, are more indicative of an ideological commitment to Hispanic "respectability" than an honest assessment of income variance among Latino groups. Although Puerto Ricans currently represent the poorest group of Latinos residing in New York City, their rates of poverty bear more resemblance than difference to other Latino groups.[58]

Furthermore, Puerto Ricans have played a significant role in shaping Latino politics in New York City because their material conditions parallel those of other Latino groups. Puerto Rican leaders had formed *hispano* groups long before the 1970s, but their political activities since then highlight their strong influence on the mobilization of a broad group of Latinos in the city. A predominantly Puerto Rican leadership formed the Hispanic Labor Committee in 1969; Puerto Rican representatives Robert García, José Serrano, and Nydia Velázquez have served as chairs of the Hispanic Congressional Caucus since the 1980s; and more recently, the Puerto Rican Legal Defense Education Fund was renamed Latino Justice in 2008. Throughout these efforts, Puerto Rican political leaders have positioned themselves as representative not only of Puerto Ricans, but also of Dominicans, Mexicans, Colombians, and Ecuadorians, among others. Even as interethnic tensions among these groups have grown recently, Puerto

Rican politicians have been at the forefront of shaping a coalitional, inter-ethnic Latino politics. In places like New York City, as well as Philadelphia, Hartford (Conn.), Dover (N.J.), and Chicago, Puerto Ricans shaped a co-alitional Latino politics that was distinct from, but mutually supportive of, black politics.[59]

Conclusion

This book draws from a combination of archival and oral history sources. By interviewing more than thirty-six individuals and using oral history ac-counts gathered by others, I have been able to uncover the historical nar-ratives of many who were previously considered insignificant to the civil rights movement. Mindful of the highly subjective and performative na-ture of these interviews, I have tried to provide the context for the histor-ical moment in which my interviewees' memories were evoked. I began conducting interviews in 2003, soon after the media reported that Lati-nos had surpassed African Americans as the largest minority group in the United States. I understood that many of my interviewees' memories were influenced by mainstream media's often exaggerated accounts of black-Latino conflict. Not surprisingly, many of them constructed their stories as a counternarrative, emphasizing the history of political unity between blacks and Puerto Ricans and at times romanticizing each group's respect and admiration for the other. Many others, however, spoke openly about conflicts, disagreements, and disappointments between the two groups. They believed that the black–Puerto Rican coalition had been success-ful despite the existence of conflicting interests. To be clear, the group of interviewees analyzed in this book consists primarily of political activists. The ideas that percolated in their midst at times seeped into the broader Puerto Rican community through music and other types of popular cul-tural productions, but their ideas reflected a group of people who saw themselves distinctly as political leaders.

The story that unfolds in this book reveals Latinos' pivotal presence in the freedom struggles of the United States in the 1960s and 1970s. Just as they had the power to broaden or constrain the black freedom struggles by embracing or rejecting their common association with African Americans at the time, they now have the power to influence how the memory of this movement is used to steer contemporary narratives of American history. African American history has disrupted the writing of American history since the 1960s as it challenged historians to consider the meaning of race in our national narrative. Did African Americans' experience of enslavement, segregation, and racial subjugation rupture the American narrative of progress, liberty, and equality for all? Or did it simply present an *exception* to an otherwise triumphal narrative of inevitable progress, as available to most Americans? As Latinidad gains increasing political salience in the twenty-first century, historical scholarship must explain where Latinos fit within these two divergent narratives. Will Latino history be written as a history of "ethnicity" and "immigration" that supports fundamental beliefs about American "freedom"? Will it be used to demonstrate the availability of equality and upward mobility for every immigrant group in the United States? Or will it be written as a narrative of colonialism, conquest, racialization, and racial struggle? Philosopher Linda Alcoff argued that Latino ethnicity is considered more threatening than European ethnicity precisely because Latinos "invoke the history of colonialism, slavery, and genocide," and these histories present a "thorn in the side of . . . 'manifest destiny,' 'leader of the free world,' and other such mythic narratives that legitimize U.S. world dominance."[60] This is a reality that we can obscure or we can illuminate.

As calls for racial equality get dismissed as "racism-in-reverse" and demonized as "balkanizing" in the twenty-first century, we have an opportunity to write Latino history as a narrative that has not only parallels with the African American narrative but also many overlaps. Just as the black freedom struggle presented much more than a single trajectory of black exceptionalism, so too did the Puerto Rican freedom struggle create more than a single path of political empowerment for Puerto Ricans. Together, these two struggles presented an alternative political vision, where individuals could fight for their rights, not to the exclusion of others, but through multiple solidarities with them. Puerto Ricans and African Americans inspired coalitions that were based on the principles of inclusion and self-determination, allowing individuals to express their political allegiances flexibly through multiple identities—as "black," "Puerto Rican," "colored," "Third World," "working-class parents," and "colonized." They constructed notions of "blackness" and "Puerto Rican-ness" that imbued a distinct political commitment toward antiracism and coalitional politics. If we can understand how such racial and ethnic identities evolved out of particular historical contexts, we may gain the boldness to imagine how our own contemporary notions may become more oriented toward justice and equality.

CHAPTER ONE

Puerto Ricans, Race, and Ethnicity in Postwar New York City

When Armando Boullon walked into a barbershop in Fort Greene, Brooklyn, on February 19, 1958, he expected to spend an ordinary afternoon getting a haircut. He had been to the same barbershop three months earlier and had gotten a haircut from the owner himself, Frank De Bello, an Italian man. He was shocked that day, however, when he was refused service as soon as he entered the premises. "What do you want here? We don't cut colored people's hair," De Bello told him. When Boullon reminded him that he had gotten a haircut from him before, De Bello insisted that he was not telling the truth. This could have simply been one of the many racial confrontations that Boullon experienced as a second-generation West Indian immigrant living in New York City, but what aggravated him this time was that this Italian man seemed to arbitrarily choose when he would treat another man as a "colored" person. Boullon then remembered that, during his first visit, De Bello had initially asked him, "Porto Ricano?" Boullon had nodded affirmatively, not caring whether being a Puerto Rican should determine his ability to receive a haircut. When Boullon later brought this case to the New York State Division of Human Rights, however, he learned that De Bello based his rationale on this perception. When questioned by Commissioner of Human Rights John A. Davis, De Bello argued that he had been willing to cut Boullon's hair at first because he thought Boullon was a Puerto Rican. He could cut "Puerto Rican hair" because Puerto Ricans had "very soft hair," whereas he could not cut "Negro hair" because he had "botched up a mess" the last time he had tried to cut such hair. Upon further questioning, he admitted that some Puerto Ricans have "hair like a Negro," but not in general. Still, he never explained how this "Porto Ricano" became a "colored" man in his eyes from one day to another. In his mind, there were clear and fixed boundaries between Puerto

Ricans and "colored" people. When the commissioner recommended that he send a letter to Boullon telling him that he would cut his hair in the future, De Bello simply refused to do so. Left with no power of enforcement, the commissioner simply dropped the case.[1]

Puerto Ricans occupied a racially ambiguous place in New York City in the first two decades of the postwar era. Their "soft hair" and "light skin" marked their similarity in physical appearance to Europeans and their potential to pass as "white." Yet they could also be indistinguishable from West Indians and the broader Afro-descendant population of the city. Puerto Ricans, however, came to occupy an increasingly similar location to African Americans in the racial spectrum in this era. This chapter examines the racial discourses and structures that shaped the lives of Puerto Rican migrants from the late 1940s through the 1950s. The rise of Nazi Germany in the 1930s and 1940s demanded that Americans conceptualize a way to understand group differences apart from notions of biological inferiorities. Leading American scholars and public figures thus adopted the "cult of ethnicity" as a way of portraying America as a racially democratic and egalitarian nation. According to this discourse, Puerto Ricans and African Americans were no different from European ethnic groups. Their high rates of poverty and cultural marginalization reflected rural migrants' general difficulty in adjusting to an industrial, urban center. With time, however, they would form their own cultural and political organizations that would help them assimilate into the broader society. Their ability to integrate would prove not only their individual capacities, but also the flexibility and pluralistic nature of American democracy. Although sociologists from the University of Chicago had first developed the ethnic framework in the 1910s, government officials tapped into this concept in order to galvanize civilian morale primarily during World War II.[2]

The postwar era, however, also saw the rise of another discourse that was much more ominous for "nonwhite" Americans. The "culture of poverty" literature predicted that migrants of color were much less likely to assimilate into mainstream American society than former European immigrants. It shared a focus on culture with the "cult of ethnicity" discourse, but it adopted a much more pessimistic outlook on racial minorities' capacity to overcome poverty. Propagated by social scientists and public policymakers in the 1950s and 1960s, this literature argued that poor environments, such as high rates of female-headed households and high unemployment rates, produced psychological pathologies among the poor, such as self-hatred and defeatism. Some policymakers believed that such pathologies were fixable through government intervention in housing and schools, but others claimed that they were permanent deficiencies that would be transmitted from one generation of the poor to the next.[3]

As deindustrialization and urban renewal increasingly constrained African Americans' and Puerto Ricans' access to good jobs and housing in the 1950s, the more ominous predictions of the "culture of poverty" discourse came to prevail over the more optimistic tone that had inspired the "cult of ethnicity." Puerto Ricans, though occupying a racially ambiguous position of being neither "white" nor "black," came to be increasingly associated with African Americans as a result of their presumed "culture of poverty." Puerto Ricans were thus racialized alongside African Americans in the postwar era. Puerto Ricans struggled to defend themselves against the stigmatizing impact of such a discourse. But their desire to find their own voices and create independent political leadership often went unheeded in this period.

Placing Puerto Ricans within the U.S. Racial Spectrum

Since invading the island of Puerto Rico in 1898, North Americans had had difficulty assigning Puerto Ricans a place within their racial spectrum. The United States had strategic reasons for colonizing the island: the island provided a military outpost; islanders provided a larger market for U.S. products and cheap labor for U.S. corporations; and the island provided a laboratory to test new economic and political arrangements between the United States and Latin America.[4] According to the interests of American capitalists who sought to exploit cheap Puerto Rican labor, Puerto Rican workers were imagined as in need of discipline and order. American traveler and entrepreneur Alfred G. Robinson noted that Puerto Ricans, who were "lazy, easy-going and . . . idle people," would transform themselves "into active and energetic workers" when infused with North American capital and governance.[5] Puerto Ricans' racial inferiority also justified their subjugation to American rule. Whitelaw Reid, a member of the U.S. delegation that shaped the Treaty of Paris, claimed that Puerto Rico was made up of a "mixed population, a little more than half colonial Spanish, the rest negro and half-breed, illiterate, alien in language, alien in ideas of right, interests, and government."[6] Spain itself, which symbolized the "white" heritage of Puerto Ricans, was imagined as an inferior type of the West. "Spain . . . was the Turk of the West," claimed journalist A. D. Hall in *Cuba: Its Past, Present, and Future* (1898). "Spain is an obsolete nation. Living in the past, and lacking cause of pride today, she gloats over her glorious explorations and her intellectual prowess of the middle ages when much of Europe was in darkness," argued Hall.[7] At the same time that Puerto Ricans were viewed as racially impure, however, they also ranked somewhere above the people inhabiting other territories the United States acquired at this time. North American legislators extended U.S. citizenship by birth to Puerto Ricans in 1917 partly because they considered Puerto Ricans to be the "whitest of the Antilles." Such a status would not be granted to Filipinos, whom Americans considered too "Oriental" to be assimilable to American values and norms.[8]

As Puerto Ricans began to migrate to the mainland in the early part of the twentieth century, the label of "Hispanicity" partially shielded them from becoming racialized as "Negro." "By insisting that he is Puerto Rican and Spanish," wrote Claude McKay in 1940, a Puerto Rican could, "like the swarthy Sicilian, escape a little from that stigma which fixes the American Negro in a specific position in the social set up."[9] The Puerto Rican and the general Latin American populations in New York City were relatively small at the beginning of the twentieth century—the Hispanic population composed only .7 percent of the population of the city. There were about 41,094 Spanish-speaking individuals living in New York City in 1920, of whom 17.9 percent were Puerto Rican, 35.7 percent were Spanish, and the rest were Cuban, West Indian, and Central and South American.[10] Situated within a small Hispanic population composed mostly of Spanish immigrants, Puerto Ricans blended in as an inconspicuous "semi-white" group of Spanish people. This privilege paid them some dividends. For example, in the 1920s, the majority of Puerto Ricans shared buildings with European ethnic groups, such as Italians, Jews, Russians, and the Irish, rather than with African American residents. Jewish and Italian neighbors still expressed their distrust of Puerto Ricans—especially during violent street confrontations—but their suspicions did not lead them to actively block Puerto Rican settlement in their neighborhoods.[11]

Due to their position of racial ambiguity, Puerto Ricans helped break the color line in certain neighborhoods of the city. Once light-skinned Puerto Ricans entered East Harlem sections below 116th Street, which had been mostly populated by Italians and Jews, their darker-skinned compatriots and African Americans followed.[12] Like European immigrants, Puerto Ricans were also relatively successful at creating small businesses, such as bodegas, restaurants, cigar stores, and bookstores. In the 1920s, they had organized the Liga Puertorriqueña e Hispana partly to protect Puerto

Ricans from Jewish attacks motivated by their competition for small businesses in East Harlem.[13] Although the majority of Puerto Rican jazz musicians became famous by performing with African American musicians in Harlem clubs, Latin relief bands made up of Puerto Ricans and Cubans of "light complexion" performed in elegant hotels and clubs in downtown Manhattan to a mostly white clientele. Their status as relief bands allowed club owners to pay them less than union wages—relief bands only played when the headliner bands were on break—but the fact that they could perform at such clubs indicated the privileges their light skin could bring.[14]

At the same time, though, Puerto Ricans were not able to overcome the economic and political marginalization that many African Americans suffered. Most Puerto Ricans in the 1920s, whether possessing "white" or "Negro" features, worked as factory workers or rural farmers, often enduring low wages and poor working conditions. Close to 60 percent of the Puerto Rican population in the city was made up of tabaqueros (cigar workers) at this time.[15] Puerto Rican low-wage workers, along with African American, Cuban, and other Afro-Caribbean workers, were seen as "exploitable" by their employers. In the 1930s, Puerto Rican workers became particularly vulnerable when First Lady Eleanor Roosevelt spread fears among New Yorkers that Puerto Rican restaurant, hotel, and domestic workers could spread tuberculosis to other employees and customers. According to Puerto Rican migrant Bernardo Vega, the First Lady's portrayal of "Puerto Ricans as a racial group with contagious diseases" significantly jeopardized their chances of securing good jobs.[16] Puerto Ricans were also racialized as intellectually inferior and born with criminal tendencies. In a 1935 study commissioned by the New York State Chamber of Commerce's Special Committee on Immigration and Naturalization, Puerto Rican children were depicted as worsening the "problem of intellectual subnormal school retardates of alien parentage, whence are recruited most delinquents and criminals."[17]

New Yorkers' inability to place Puerto Ricans in a specific place within the white-black binary became more confounding to them in the postwar era, when the black and Puerto Rican populations in the city increased dramatically. Southern black and Puerto Rican migrants began to reside in New York City in large numbers due to the postwar prosperity in the North and the shortage of jobs in their home regions. Between 1950 and 1970, the black population in the city increased from 748,000 (9.5 percent) to 1,668,000 (21.1 percent), and the Puerto Rican population increased from

246,000 (3.1 percent) to 846,700 (10.7 percent). Meanwhile, the white population in the city shrank considerably. Between 1940 and 1960, 1,698,200 whites left New York City and settled in the suburbs. New York's suburban population exceeded its urban population for the first time in the 1950s—the suburban population increased by 2,180,492 and the urban population decreased by 109,973.[18]

When Puerto Ricans were counted officially for the first time in the U.S. Census of 1960, they were counted neither as a "race" like African Americans nor as a "foreign stock" like European immigrants. While there were three categories for races ("white, "Negro," and "other races") and thirteen categories for "foreign stock" (such as from the United Kingdom, Germany, Italy, or Mexico), the category of those "born in Puerto Rico" or of "Puerto Rican parentage" was entirely separate. The census did note that 4 percent of Puerto Ricans in New York City were "nonwhite" (24,871 out of 612,574), but it did not have a separate count for "white" Puerto Ricans, signaling that census takers considered the majority of Puerto Ricans neither "white" nor "nonwhite."[19]

Puerto Ricans themselves hesitated from categorizing themselves as either "white" or "nonwhite." Many recounted experiences of coming to the United States and being "shocked" at North Americans' practice of strictly dividing people into two racial groups. Antonia Pantoja, who migrated to New York City in 1944 at the age of twenty-two, described how surprised she was when she saw passengers being segregated by race in the train she took from New Orleans to New York City. The group of Puerto Rican friends that accompanied her—a "black man," "a white man with reddish hair," and another "white-complexioned woman with wavy black hair and thick lips and nose"—did not know how to follow the rules on the train, given their "combination of color and facial characteristics." To her, the whole experience felt like "the raping of our innocence." Against the backdrop of an unpretentious, cordial group of racially mixed Puerto Ricans, she painted North Americans as cold, calculating, and harsh. Although she admitted that "race was a source of problems" on the island, she claimed that Jim Crow segregation was an entirely foreign practice for her since Puerto Ricans "never denied entry or were separated by race."[20] Robert De León, a Puerto Rican born and raised in East Harlem, recounted a similarly jarring experience during his first encounter with Jim Crow segregation in the South. While he was in military training for World War II in Columbus, Georgia, he encountered a cop who would not let him drink water from the "white" fountain. After De León moved to the "colored" water fountain and drank from it, he told the cop, "You know, it tastes the same." While realizing that he needed to somehow survive in this Jim Crow environment, De León emphasized the difference between his response and those of southern blacks who were subjected to the same forms of exclusion. "What bothered me the most were the 'Negroes' who did not understand why I was behaving that way." De León's reaction likely reflected his racial sensibilities as a New Yorker. Many African Americans born and raised in the North also had narratives of shock and dismay during their first visits to the South. Yet De León distinguished himself as a Puerto Rican confronting the realities of a U.S. racial hierarchy.[21]

Puerto Ricans' emphasis on the "foreignness" of North American practices of racism was often exaggerated. As historian Miriam Jiménez Román argued, Puerto Ricans often claimed that they were not "racist" because they did not display North American patterns of racism, but such a claim was based on the assumption that there was only one kind of racism, with the North American kind being the main standard.[22] Puerto Ricans' claim to "racial exceptionalism" was based on two notions: that racial mixture in Puerto Rico naturally produced racial equality and that notions of racial hierarchy were fluid because they were inflected with class qualifiers rather than biological markers. Both notions, however, hid the deeper foundations of racism that grounded Puerto Rican society. Racial mixing was celebrated in Puerto Rico not so much because it reflected the Spanish, African, and Native ancestries of the people equally, but because it was assumed to be a stepping-stone toward the "whitening of the race," or in other words, the disappearance of blacks. A system of color prejudice with gradations therefore did not substitute for, but was interwoven with, a highly unequal racial hierarchy.[23] The importance of intelligence, cultural refinement, and education as markers of class also did not function to cancel the power of race, but instead to reinforce it. In Puerto Rico as in the United States, race and class worked in tandem, so that "whiteness" was equated with the elite, and "blackness" was equated with poor people. This racial hierarchy reflected the history of slavery and racial discrimination in Puerto Rico, which shared more similarities with North American history than differences. Slave masters punished their slaves with impunity, and slaves organized slave insurrections along with free blacks and pardos (racially mixed). Although the large population of black freedmen in Puerto Rico—around 43 percent of the island's population throughout the nineteenth century—prevented a total association between Africans and enslavement, Puerto Rican society nevertheless ordered their primary institutions along a racial hierarchy. Church-based *hermandades* (brother-hoods), sections of the colonial administration, and the military all barred blacks and *pardos*.[24]

Puerto Ricans' claim to "racial exceptionalism" vis-à-vis the United States was not based on a systematic analysis of differences and similarities between the two places but on Puerto Rican elites' nationalist project. In the face of North American imperialism, Puerto Rican elites who sought to create a distinct Puerto Rican identity against their colonizers constructed the notion of a "benign, innocent Spain" counterpoised to a "cold, calculating" United States. The history of Spanish colonialism and slavery on the island, which was as brutal and harsh as the British system in North America, was manipulated to create the notion of a "benign slavery" where slave revolts did not occur and slaves easily earned their manumission. Tomás Blanco's *El prejuicio racial en Puerto Rico* (1942) argued that there was no racial prejudice in Puerto Rico and that the individual social status of islanders was determined by "wealth, prestige, culture, education, etc.," rather than "skin color or purity of blood." Blanco's assessment, however, was based on the simple assumptions that North America's de jure segregation defined racism and that the absence of such a system in Puerto Rico made it prejudice-free.[25] Such logic was used by not only Puerto Rican elites but also elites in many other countries in Latin America and the Caribbean, such as Brazil and Mexico—nations also invested in creating a nationalist discourse against a growing U.S. empire.[26] Puerto Rican elites constructed this mythic national image, but this image percolated through cultural productions at every level, so that ordinary Puerto Rican migrants who came to New York City also used it to explain their journeys of migration and adjustment. Focusing on the "foreignness" of North American racism became one way in which they could express their experience of displacement.

Puerto Rican migration narratives contained a dramatization of dislocation within the North American racial system, but these narratives were interwoven with accounts about migrants' relative ease in coexisting with African Americans as well. Manny Diaz, who was born in Puerto Rico in 1922 and migrated to New York City at the age of five, recounted that he had felt comfortable socializing with people of light skin and dark skin since his childhood. His hometown, Humacao, had been an important sugar cane–growing area of the island since the nineteenth century and had thus been populated by a large number of African slaves. Having grown up in an area of the island with an especially strong African presence, Diaz claimed that "at the age of five, my mental set was already that . . . there's nothing wrong with being black."[27] Frank Torres, whose father came from Salinas, also remembered that he felt comfortable going to school with black children while living in Spanish Harlem. When his father, Felipe Torres, became a lawyer in 1927, he set up an office at 116th Street and Fifth Avenue, which was the dividing line between Spanish Harlem and black Harlem. Although he was not familiar with any specific rule of exclusion within the American Bar Association, he had an "understanding of separation, of not being invited," and thus he joined the Harlem Bar Association instead. While living in a neighborhood adjacent to black Harlem, Frank Torres remembered that his family "didn't stop being Puerto Rican. We didn't start being American black, but there was a mixture that was taking place, which we were very comfortable with."[28] Felipe Luciano, who later joined the Young Lords Party, claimed that African Americans and Puerto Ricans were members of his most intimate group of relationships. Growing up in Brownsville, Brooklyn, Luciano explained that "my best friends were black and Puerto Rican. . . . I grew up eating some of their chicken, collard greens, fried pork chops, and *arroz con habichuela* [rice and beans]; dancing to Tito Puente, Johnny Pacheco and Machito, Frankie Lymon and the Teenagers, Johnny Ace and Little Willie John, so that the blues were not something esoteric to me."[29]

Belonging to a world in common with African Americans did not mean that Puerto Ricans became "black"—they insisted that they were neither "white" nor "black" but a culture set apart. They neither absorbed white supremacist values, nor did they completely reject them. This racial ambiguity persisted through much of the early part of the twentieth century, but events following World War II created new pressures to define Puerto Ricans' racial status more clearly.

Overcoming Racism through the "Cult of Ethnicity"

Puerto Ricans' uneasy census categorization as neither "foreigner" nor "nonwhite" reflected the contradictions of American conceptualizations of race, ethnicity, and culture in the postwar era. Beginning in the 1930s and 1940s, American intellectuals and political leaders looked at relationships between various groups through the lens of "ethnicity" and "cultural pluralism." Theories about "cultural pluralism" had been introduced to the American public through intellectuals like Horace Kallen and W. E. B. Du Bois since the 1910s. In Kallen's original formulation of cultural pluralism in 1915, the United States was a federation of ethnic nationalities rather than a country with a uniform culture. Rejecting the assimilationist vision of America as a "melting pot," Kallen conceived the nation instead as "an orchestration of mankind," whereby different cultures would coexist and create a unified harmony.[30]

A few years later, sociologist W. I. Thomas from the University of Chicago produced, with the assistance of Florian Znaniecki, the first writings of what would later become known as the "cult of ethnicity." Published at the height of American nativist campaigns, Thomas's The Polish Peasant (1918–20) portrayed Polish immigrants' differences from the dominant population as reflective of temporary cultural adjustments rather than biological inferiorities. He acknowledged that the migration from rural Poland to modern cities like Chicago had broken down Polish traditional customs and social controls, producing patterns of "social disorganization," such as high rates of crime, sexual promiscuity, family breakup, and economic dependency. But he documented the ways in which Polish immigrants gradually reorganized themselves into a stable social group through cooperative economic institutions, the press, and education. There was no need, therefore, for reformers to worry about racial conflict or immigrant poverty since such problems indicated only temporary stages of adjustment and would naturally subside when immigrants reached the stage of full assimilation.[31]

Sociologist Robert E. Park took up Thomas's framework in the 1930s to develop a theory about ethnic adjustment called the "race relations cycle." Park's four stages of adjustment—contact, conflict, accommodation, and assimilation—cast a sympathetic view on European immigrants. Significant in the formulation of Park's ethnic framework was the notion of a linear and inevitable progression, so that groups that had been previously marginalized and deemed as naturally inferior "races" were now assumed to progressively adapt and assimilate into the broader society. This formulation was primarily used to interpret the immigration histories of Europeans, but the optimism that grew out of the first Great Migration—during which, between 1910 and 1930, more than 1.6 million blacks moved out of the rural South to cities in the North—also inspired a few African American intellectuals to use the same model to interpret the experience of southern black migrants. E. Franklin Frazier's The Negro in the United States (1939) argued that African American southerners distributed themselves along class lines in the northern context, such that they were making a transition from being a "racial caste" to being an "assimilationist minority."[32]

As Americans observed the gruesome practices of white supremacy in Nazi Germany in the 1930s, notions of cultural pluralism and ethnicity became popular beyond academic halls. Americans began to emphasize the benefits of intergroup relations and cultural tolerance in an attempt to distance themselves from beliefs about biological inferiority that had fueled the ghastly persecution of Jews in Europe. The U.S. Office of Education sponsored a series of twenty-four radio broadcasts in 1938–39 entitled "Americans All . . . Immigrants All," propagating the notion that America was made up of not one, but many nationalities and cultures. Ruth Benedict, an anthropologist who had stressed the importance of cultural tolerance over genetic hierarchies, was invited by agencies of the government to apply her skills to maintain civilian morale during World War II.[33]

Confident in the power of social science to change American race relations, some scholars began to use the ethnic framework to reverse America's history of racism. They suggested that the words "ethnicity" and "minority" should replace the word "race" entirely. According to sociologist Donald Young's *American Minority Peoples* (1932), "Negro-white," "Jewish-Gentile," and "Oriental-white" relations should all be studied under the term "minority" so as to move the focus away from biological factors and into intergroup relations instead. Scholars believed that a shift in vocabulary could turn Americans' attention away from the "exaggerated emotional content" of racial attributes and toward a more objective study of human difference. "Because the conventional stereotype of 'race' is so erroneous, confusing, and productive of injustice and cruelties without number," said anthropologist Ashley Montagu, it would be "better to drop the term 'race' altogether from the vocabulary" and use instead "some noncommittal term like 'ethnic group.'" Although the terms "ethnicity" and "race" both carried connotations of primordial linkages of descent and homeland, "ethnicity" focused more on a common culture, history, and values and less on biological characteristics.[34] The term "minority" was also favored because it focused on the common forms of victimization that many different groups suffered as objects of collective discrimination. The experience of World War II had taught Americans that minorities across the world—whether Jews in Europe or African Americans in the United States—could become invested in a common fight for racial democracy. As sociologist Louis Wirth saw it, people from everywhere recognized that the world was "shrunken and interdependent" and believed that "internal disturbances in any one country became a threat to the peace of all." Since the problem of each minority group in various parts of the world rested on the shoulders of all people, it was only fitting that the same word be used to describe all of them.[35]

This ethnic model, or the "cult of ethnicity," embodied a political strategy more than a lived reality. Although the concept of cultural pluralism celebrated difference, it was predicated upon an ideology of consensus— the notion that America was supreme in its practice of democracy and harmonious intergroup relations. Any ethnic group that would challenge the dominant view that the United States was a country that respected self-government, equality before the law, and individual rights for minorities would not be celebrated but ostracized. Thus, this great celebration of cultural pluralism went hand-in-hand with a heavy hand of political conformity.[36] The most glaring contradiction in the "cult of ethnicity," however, was the assumption that African Americans experienced a process of migration adjustment similar to that of European immigrants. As a scholar who was active in interracial labor and socialist organizations, E. Franklin Frazier was well aware of the fact that black migrants in the North were subject to institutionalized forms of racial discrimination that European immigrants never experienced. He knew that high rates of juvenile delinquency, crime, welfare dependency, and female-headed households among lower-class black families reflected the impact of slavery and contemporary practices of segregation—which indicated the uniqueness of African Americans' experiences. There was also little indication that the black middle class had attained full assimilation as U.S. citizens. Still, Frazier's incorporation of black migrants into an otherwise European immigrant model allowed him to argue that black migrants too would assimilate and culturally adapt to white middle-class norms rather than remain as a permanent racial "other." Franklin, after all, viewed assimilation as the one and only way for African Americans to attain full racial equality in this time period.[37] Despite its internal contradictions, the cult of ethnicity was thus embraced by many white and black Americans since it served the needs of the nation-state as well as African Americans' specific strategy of inclusion.[38]

With time, however, it became clear that the cult of ethnicity elevated the interests of the nation-state above those of its citizens of color. According to this discourse, the heart of democracy tended to rest more in the hands of white liberals who "rescued" minorities from their plight than in the hands of the minorities who fought for their rights themselves. The film *Twelve Angry Men* (1957), which received three Academy Award nominations, including Best Picture, illustrates this tendency.[39] The film featured a youth "born in the slums" who was accused of committing first-degree murder. His verdict was to be determined by a jury of twelve white men. The young man was clearly not the main character of this film—his character came with no lines, and his face was shown for only a few seconds. The fact that he did not speak English well and that he had light skin indicated that he could be a European immigrant, a light-skinned Puerto Rican, or any number of possibilities. The ambiguity of his ethnic background implied that the young man's life would be the same regardless of the specific ethnic group he represented.[40] The principal characters of the film were twelve white men who sat on the jury and who delivered him out of a death penalty. Despite the initial belief among some of the jurors that the boy was guilty because "these people [who live in the slums] lie" and they "are by nature, violent," the opinion that won the day came from the juror who looked at the boy more sympathetically. "This kid's been kicked around all his life, born in a slum, mother dead since he was nine, lived for a year and a half in an orphanage, when his father was serving a jail term for forgery," said Davis, the juror played by actor Henry Fonda. "He's a wild, angry kid, that's all ever he's ever been, and you know why? . . . Cuz he's been hit on the head by somebody once a day everyday." Davis embodied the new American ethos, which recognized that the boy's guilt should not be determined on the "personal prejudices" of the jurors but on factual evidence. Although the boy's criminality was highly likely given the environment in which he grew up—characterized by "filthy neighborhoods" and "broken homes"—his potential individual innocence was to be considered. Yet at the heart of the message of the film was not the innocence of the boy but the strength of a prejudice-free nation. The supposed virtues of the American legal system were most clearly articulated by one of the jurors with a heavy accent, an immigrant who vouched for the exceptional nature of American democracy: "This is what I always thought was remarkable thing about democracy; we . . . come to this place to decide on the guilt or innocence of a man we have never heard of before. We should not make it a personal thing. This is one of the reasons why we are strong." As the immigrant saw it, America was a great nation because it graciously offered equal justice to all of its citizens regardless of their ethnic background.

The cult of ethnicity also carried a number of flawed notions about the economic status of racial and ethnic minorities. Much of the optimism that fed the cult of ethnicity was the economic and political growth of the United States as a global superpower rather than the economic advancement of racial and ethnic minorities themselves. In New York City, historian Oscar Handlin and sociologists Nathan Glazer and Daniel P. Moynihan popularized the notion that southern black and Puerto Rican migrants represented the "newest immigrants" who would follow in the footsteps of the Jewish, Italian, and Irish immigrants of the early twentieth century. According to Handlin's *The Newcomers* (1959), the problems of "substandard housing and juvenile delinquency" associated with "Negroes" and "Puerto Ricans" in the postwar era were the same as those faced by European immigrants of an earlier generation. New Yorkers should therefore expect these problems to be "temporary" and "soluble."[41] Although acknowledging that the "newcomers" differed from the European immigrants in that they faced "color prejudice," Handlin did not believe that this difference made their problems "radically new." Glazer and Moynihan disagreed slightly from Handlin's assessment, acknowledging that blacks had experienced more frustration, more prejudice, and more "personality damage" than any other immigrant group in America. Still, they believed that postwar developments indicated new possibilities for black economic advancement. Given black women's recent breakthrough into professional and white-collar jobs, they surmised that black workers would attain racial parity with whites in the labor economy in the near future.[42]

As Glazer and Moynihan later explained in the 1970 edition of their book, part of the optimism of their original study in 1963 was based on the real improvements that African Americans had experienced in employment during wartime production.[43] Their claims were not entirely unfounded—the formation of the Fair Employment Practices Commission and the wartime boom had resulted in some increase in black employment in the 1940s. Between 1940 and 1950, the proportion of black male workers classified as operatives (semiskilled industrial workers) increased from 12.6 to 21.4 percent, and the proportion of those in manufacturing industries rose from 16.2 to 23.9 percent. The Negro Labor Victory Committee alone, organized through the leadership of the Communist Party and many American Federation of Labor (AFL) and Congress of Industrial Organizations (CIO) unions, had placed 15,000 black men and women in war-related industries.[44]

By the late 1950s and early 1960s, however, it was clear that whatever gains had been made in the 1940s had been minimal. There had been no advancement in black employment overall, and especially not in the skilled trades and white-collar positions.[45] Meanwhile, the national economy continued to grow. The nation's total economic output increased by 25 percent in 1952–60, and the use of goods and services for consumption increased 30 percent. By 1965, the gross national product was increasing at a rate above 5 percent per year. The steady economic growth of the postwar era brought such a sense of optimism that, according to journalist Theodore White, "Americans were brought up to believe either at home or abroad, that whatever Americans wish to happen, would happen."[46] Glazer and Moynihan's assumption that African Americans and Puerto Ricans would soon follow the economic mobility of white ethnics was therefore nurtured more by the national mood of prosperity than by a precise knowledge of black and Puerto Rican employment patterns after the 1940s.

Advocates of the ethnic model also held notions of cultural inferiority that were only slightly different from nineteenth-century notions of biological inferiority. Glazer, Moynihan, and Handlin all claimed that African Americans and Puerto Ricans lacked political and business leadership because they did not have the "tradition of philanthropy and communal solidarity" that Italian and Jewish immigrants had created in earlier decades. African Americans had "no values and culture to guard and protect," said Glazer and Moynihan, and thus did not create "massive self-help efforts." Glazer and Moynihan ignored, however, the hundreds of self-help organizations that blacks and Puerto Ricans had created in New York City, such as Puerto Rican mutual aid societies, the National Association for the Advancement of Colored People (NAACP), and, most important, the hundreds of black churches spread across the city. Glazer and Moynihan reduced blacks and Puerto Ricans to a people with "no culture to protect" simply because the cultural institutions of people of color were invisible to the mainstream. Handlin even made the mistake of ignoring Puerto Rico's long history of colonialism under U.S. rule and claimed that the primary factor driving heavy Puerto Rican migration in the postwar era was a culture of high fertility and "overpopulation."[47]

Puerto Rican Postwar Migration and Operation Bootstrap

Advocates of the cult of ethnicity used the model of European immigration as a universal template to interpret the histories of all Americans. Robert Park's theory about immigration adjustment became, in their eyes, inevitable forces that would determine the integration of all racial and ethnic groups. Yet they paid little attention to Puerto Ricans' colonial relationship with the U.S. government. As colonized migrants, Puerto Ricans were incorporated into American workplaces and neighborhoods in an entirely different fashion from European immigrants. Advocates of the cult of ethnicity believed that "overpopulation" provided a scientific explanation for Puerto Rico's poverty and the postwar migration to the mainland. But the root causes of the migration stemmed from the island's economic instabilities wrought by U.S. capital investments since 1898. The "overpopulation" debate was a political discourse meant to justify the increasing intrusion of U.S. capital into the island at a time when Puerto Rico was facing greater economic hardships. By the 1940s, the U.S. political and business elite had had control of Puerto Rico's main economies of sugar, tobacco, and needle industries for almost half a century. These interventions had been conducted in the name of progress and economic development but had actually made the Puerto Rican economy uniform and hyper-dependent on the United States. This instability became only too obvious when the unemployment rate on the island reached 60 percent during the Great Depression in 1929. With financial difficulties on the mainland, the U.S. Congress passed the Costigan-Jones Act in 1934, which further handicapped Puerto Rico's sugar production by giving it a quota far below those assigned to Cuba, the beet states, and Hawaii. President Roosevelt commissioned the Puerto Rico Policy Commission to design an agricultural reform program that would deal with the "chronic maladjustment of a land-hungry and sugar-dominated economy." The Chardón Plan, as it became known, did propose radical structural changes, such as the diversification of agriculture and the enforcement of the 500-Acre Law, which prohibited companies from holding more than a certain amount of land. Yet the U.S. government provided no real means of enforcement, letting the noncompliance of powerful sugar growers undermine the intent of the law.[48]

It was at this time that leaders from the Partido Popular Democrático (PPD), led by Luis Muñoz Marín, came to rely heavily on the "overpopulation" discourse to understand Puerto Rico's economic problems. Muñoz Marín had founded the PPD in 1938 with the motto "Bread, Land and Liberty." He had created a campaign of political reform that included socialists, trade unionists, non-nationalist *independentistas*, professionals, and small farmers. The more left-leaning constituents of the PPD reflected the origins of Muñoz Marín's political genealogy, which had overlaps with the socialism and anti-American nationalism more commonly associated with Pedro Albizu Campos. In a 1929 article in the *American Mercury*, Muñoz Marín bemoaned that Puerto Rico had become "Uncle Sam's second largest sweatshop," a "factory worked by peons" and controlled by "absentee industrialists."[49] Muñoz Marín believed that political and economic independence was possible for Puerto Rico at this time. But the economic hardships of the 1930s led him to rely more heavily on the advice of U.S. analysts and their prescriptions for the island. Bolstered by the pseudoscientific claims of Thomas Malthus, a group of American population control advocates replaced eugenicists as the creators of postwar theories of "desirable" and "undesirable" groups of people. According to these demographers, Puerto Ricans were poor because their overproduction of babies strained the "natural" balance between resources and consumption. This discourse explained the island's poverty by blaming Puerto Rican women's high fertility rates. In 1946, the U.S. Tariff Commission's chief economist, Ben Dorfman, submitted a report titled "The Economy of Puerto Rico," which predicted that Puerto Ricans as a population would soon die of starvation due to the overpopulation problem. Muñoz Marín believed Dorfman's conclusions only too easily and concluded that overpopulation replaced colonialism as the main challenge facing islanders. He argued that Puerto Rico had reached its maximum sugar production in 1934, but that this production could not keep up with the population growth of the island, which had added 270,000 more mouths to feed between 1934 and 1940.[50] The problem with Muñoz Marín's seemingly scientific calculation was that Puerto Ricans did not live by eating sugar. They ate corn, beans, and other goods that were imported from other countries. Puerto Rican survival never depended directly upon the output of their labor since labor and resources were not distributed evenly but were mediated by authority figures, who determined which needs would be prioritized over others.[51] At this time of great chaos, however, Muñoz Marín came to rely on the authority of new American "science" to explain the island's predicaments.

With the economic recession triggering labor strikes, ineffective agricultural reform programs, and rising unemployment rates, Muñoz Marín planned a road map for Puerto Rican economic recovery based on the prescriptions provided by U.S. analysts. This plan ultimately privileged the interests of U.S. corporations and burdened Puerto Rican workers with the responsibility of bearing the island's troubles. Workers would serve their nation by engaging in 1) factory work under strict labor repression, 2) emigration, and 3) reduced fertility. Rushed by a desire to reach quick and measurable success, the PPD's chief economic architect, Teodoro Moscoso, designed *Fomento* as an industrialization program driven primarily by U.S. capital. Muñoz Marín appealed to the U.S. Congress for support of this industrialization program by calling it "Operation Bootstrap," the program that would allow Puerto Ricans to "lift ourselves by our own bootstraps." Yet, Moscoso decided that waiting until Puerto Ricans could lift themselves up by their own bootstraps would take too long. The initial Puerto Rican–run factories designed to produce rum bottles, clay products for home construction, and shoes/leather goods did not produce profits quickly enough for him. Impatient with the meager and slow results, Moscoso convinced PPD leaders to pass the Industrial Incentives Act of 1947, which granted private firms exemption from insular income and property taxes and license fees until 1957, as well as exemption from federal minimum wage laws. This gave U.S. companies a tax-free environment—a gigantic economic incentive for the companies that chose to relocate their factories to the island. By 1960, only 10 percent of *Fomento* firms represented local investment; the rest were tied to foreign capital.[52] Most important, Moscoso indoctrinated workers with calls to not go on strike, because "a low wage was better than no wage" and disruptions caused by labor strikes would be "tantamount to treason."[53]

Puerto Rican political leaders' adoption of Operation Bootstrap came with the full support of the island's labor leadership. Unlike the Confederación General de Trabajadores (the General Confederation of Workers), which had modeled itself after the Industrial Workers of the World, the main labor organization of Puerto Rico at this time, the Federación Libre de los Trabajadores (the Federation of Labor in Puerto Rico) willingly ceded control to U.S. labor unions. Its leaders agreed to abide by rules determined by U.S. industries and U.S. labor leaders.[54] As historian Miles Galvin explained, the appeal of the "Yankeephile short circuit" corrupted Puerto Rican labor leaders as much as it corrupted politicians. The AFL-CIO's offer was too tempting to reject: it guaranteed support in Washington for the island's commonwealth status as well as a "flexible wage system." American labor leaders would set wages in Puerto Rico at a level "not so high as to curtail local employment nor so low as to give Puerto Rico a 'competitive edge' over the mainland."[55] Puerto Rican labor leaders were convinced that everybody would win.

The final policy that would seal Puerto Rico's status as a modern, industrializing nation was the reduction of its population through state-generated emigration and birth control. PPD leaders never forced anyone to leave the island, but they certainly encouraged and facilitated emigration by establishing Migration Division offices in cities like New York and Philadelphia and agricultural labor programs in rural areas such as Hamburg (Pa.), Riverhead (N.Y.), Camden (N.J.), and Cleveland (Ohio). These offices functioned as labor recruitment agencies, providing information about Puerto Rican workers' education and skill levels to U.S. employers.[56]

Puerto Ricans who migrated to the mainland in the postwar era were therefore driven by forces much larger than their fertility patterns. The decrease in airfares in the 1950s (from $180 to $35 for flights between San Juan and New York) certainly made migration easier, but Operation Bootstrap had primarily determined the work choices available for islanders. Puerto Rican farmers had little choice but to relocate to either the major cities of the island or the mainland in search of factory jobs. The industrialization program set in motion a massive outmigration of Puerto Ricans, causing what demographer José Vázquez Calzada called "one of the greatest population exoduses registered in contemporary history."[57] The outmigration of Puerto Ricans, which had varied between 11,000 and 42,000 per decade from 1910 to 1940, jumped to 151,000 in the decade from 1940 to 1950 and 470,000 in the decade from 1950 to 1960. It remained high, at 214,000 in 1960–70, dropping down to lower numbers only in the 1970s. From 1940 to 1970, more than a million people left the island's rural areas, causing the rural population to decrease from 70 percent to 42 percent of the total population of the island during those years. Through these years, the majority of Puerto Rican migrants (68.6 percent in 1960) went to New York City, although many others went to California, New Jersey, Florida, Pennsylvania, Illinois, and Ohio.[58]

Similar to the state-induced emigration, Puerto Rican women's sterilization programs were never conducted through state coercion, but the state provided women with plenty of incentives. Moscoso persuaded the U.S. Senate Foreign Relations Committee to sanction the first State Department–financed birth control effort in Latin America by using mathematical formulations that equated reduced populations with economic and political stability: PG/(E+SD) = PI ("Population Growth" divided by "Economic and Social Development" equals "Political Instability").[59] With the vast financial support of the Rockefeller and Ford Foundations, as well as the U.S. Department of Health, Education, and Welfare, PPD leaders offered free sterilization to Puerto Rican women, $50 to physicians for each operation, and reimbursement for 90 percent of hospital costs. Between 1947 and 1968, the percentage of Puerto Rican women who were sterilized grew from 6.6 percent to 35.5 percent, making Puerto Rico the country with the highest proportion of its reproductive population sterilized in the world.[60] As historian Laura Briggs argued, this was by no means a single-handed state imposition on the female Puerto Rican body—as many feminists claimed in the 1970s. Many middle-class Puerto Rican feminists themselves had laid the groundwork for the birth control movement in the 1930s much before the U.S. government began to fund it in the 1940s.[61] Yet, the mass sterilization program did create the notion that the nation's viability in the modern world depended on women's loss of control over their reproduction.

Operation Bootstrap brought about a significant increase in the national economic output of goods on the island. The average real weekly salary in manufacturing increased on the island from $18 for men and $12 for women in 1953 to $44 for men and $37 for women in 1963. Life expectancy increased from forty-six to sixty-nine years of age between 1940 and 1960.[62] This national performance earned Puerto Rico the reputation of being a "showcase of democracy" for the United States and the rest of the world. According to Clarence Senior, a native of Missouri and director of the Migration Division of the Department of Labor of Puerto Rico (more commonly known as the Commonwealth Office), the island's accomplishments helped "the United States prove to the world that democracy holds real promise for the 'underdeveloped' two-thirds of the world."[63] For U.S. government officials, these national results indicated that their investments in Puerto Rico had paid off and that they could use the island as a "laboratory for democracy" during the Cold War. The U.S. government increased its support for the island's economic development in the 1950s, recognizing that Puerto Rico's example could win Americans legitimacy within the rest of Latin America and the Caribbean. Under President Truman's Four Point Program, and later under President Kennedy's Alliance for Progress program, the U.S. government transferred billions of federal dollars to aid the colonial administration in Puerto Rico. In the 1960s, Puerto Rico received more than $3.3 billion in federal aid to improve its infrastructure and standard of living, with no other country in the Western Hemisphere matching such a massive foreign aid package.[64]

In spite of the spectacle of Puerto Rico's national economic growth, however, the lives of many individual Puerto Rican workers did not improve during this period. The unemployment rate stayed within the double digits (13 to 16 percent) between 1950 and 1960. The lives of rural farmers suffered the most, as the industrialization program drove a massive outmigration to cities, with little provision for the sustenance of agricultural production on the island.[65] Puerto Rico's economic development, based on unrestricted foreign investment and minimal labor intervention, had produced quick results that the Puerto Rican and U.S. elites could boast about, but income inequality increased. The island's political leaders could do little to slow Puerto Rico's path toward becoming a hyperdependent nation.

"The Culture of Poverty": A Common Language of Racial Domination

New Yorkers who witnessed the massive migration of Puerto Ricans into their city in the 1940s through the 1960s had little knowledge about the structural factors that had unleashed this migration. To understand their new neighbors, they relied instead on accounts provided by journalists, social scientists, and reformers who saw Puerto Ricans through the "Puerto Rican problem" debate. Although postwar Puerto Rican migration had been triggered by the economic instabilities wrought by Operation Bootstrap, the "Puerto Rican problem" debate portrayed Puerto Ricans as a people possessing a culture of "overpopulation" and other psychological "pathologies." City newspapers gave exaggerated reports about the large exodus of Puerto Ricans into the city in 1947, claiming that there were more than 600,000 of them in the city; Puerto Rican leaders argued that they numbered no more than 300,000 or 400,000. The 1950 U.S. Census later indicated that there were in fact 254,880 Puerto Ricans living in New York City.[66] National periodicals such as *Time* magazine claimed that, just as "Okies were mainly California's problem," "the problem of Puerto Ricans is chiefly New York's."[67] Newspapers ranging from conservative tabloids to the most liberal dailies portrayed Puerto Ricans as "welfare cheaters" who went back to the island after collecting relief money. Their large families were blamed for causing the growth of slums.[68] Social and health experts spread fear about Puerto Ricans' weak health conditions. The *New York Times* reported that Puerto Ricans had high rates of tuberculosis and pulmonary diseases and syphilis and other venereal diseases that originated from "hereditary factors" and "physical apathy," as well as "food deficiency" and "ignorance of hygiene."[69]

The focus on Puerto Ricans' deficient habits, such as "ignorance of hygiene," reflected New Yorkers' tendency in the 1950s and 1960s to view racial minorities through the "culture of poverty" discourse. Although this discourse shared many similarities with the "cult of ethnicity," it emphasized racial minorities' cultural handicaps much more than their ability to overcome racial discrimination. Michael Harrington, a political scientist and activist, for example, argued that residents of the slums of New York City in the postwar era lacked a "culture of aspiration" and lived in a culture of "pessimism and hopelessness." He made a stark contrast between these new slum residents—who were mostly racial minorities—and those of older slums from the early twentieth century—who were mostly European immigrants. A national culture or a religion had fostered a "vital community life" in the ghettos of Little Italy, South Village, and the South Bronx in the past, Harrington argued. Additionally, residents of older slums had not been "defeated by their environment" even though they had lived in run-down, dilapidated tenements. In sharp contrast, Harrington argued that poor black residents in Harlem suffered from a "psychological depression" brought about by a "long history and the tremendous institutionalized power of racism" in addition to "simple material want."[70]

Part of Harrington's pessimism stemmed from his ignorance of African Americans' organized social life. In contrast to the residents of old slums, who were organized through unions, fraternal organizations, and political parties, Harrington claimed that residents of new slums were not organized into any type of social or political institution. Instead, they were "atomized." Even the "Negro Church," which Harrington acknowledged was the "one really Negro institution that developed under slavery," provided only a "moment of release [and] ecstasy" rather than any form of social organization.[71] Harrington dismissed the black church as an institution of escapism, but he had little knowledge of its significance as the center of black social and political life. Congressman Adam Clayton Powell Jr., for example, had been able to outwit his adversaries from Tammany Hall in part because he had a solid political base among his congregants at the Abyssinian Baptist Church.[72]

More important, Harrington's pessimism reflected the political assumptions that many postwar social scientists carried. With the growth of the postwar American economy, many Americans celebrated the affluence experienced by large sectors of the nation. Rising incomes, higher rates of homeownership, and increasing mass consumerism indicated that America had entered an age of political stability and ideological consensus. American prosperity became the social norm and poverty became a "paradox."[73] Immersed in this "culture of affluence," social scientists who still sought to draw public attention to the poor adopted an unusually pessimistic tone in their writing. Harrington believed that middle-class America needed to be jolted out of its apathy in order to understand the "other America." He himself acknowledged that his description of the "culture of poverty" was slightly exaggerated. "If my interpretation is bleak and grim, and even if it overstates the case slightly, that is intentional," he claimed. To him, these overstatements were necessary to create a sense of "outrage" among readers so that they would be "shock[ed]" into action—lest "optimism" lead to "complacency and the persistence of the other America."[74]

Despite his best intentions, however, Harrington did not foresee that a pessimistic tone could create apathy as much as it could foster outrage. Harrington believed that the "uniqueness" of black poverty demanded more government intervention. As Chapter 3 will demonstrate, such an interpretation was indeed taken up by the many public policymakers who framed the War on Poverty as a program designed to improve both the material and the psychological conditions of the poor. But others believed that black poverty was so all-encompassing that it was beyond repair. Such a belief became more prominent with the publication of Daniel Moynihan's The Negro Family: The Case for National Action (1965) and Oscar Lewis's La Vida: A Puerto Rican Family in the Culture of Poverty—San Juan and New York (1966).[75] Both authors argued that the pathology fostered by the "culture of poverty" was "self-perpetuating." Lewis claimed that structural changes, such as developing the economy, redistributing wealth, and organizing the poor on the island of Puerto Rico and in New York, could change the culture of poverty among Puerto Ricans. Nevertheless, Lewis argued that such interventions would not put an end to the culture of poverty. It would still be absorbed by young children, who would not be "psychologically geared to take full advantage of . . . increased opportunities which may occur in their lifetime."[76] By arguing that the "culture of poverty" was unresponsive to government intervention and automatically transmitted from one generation to another, Lewis changed the political connotations attached to the term. Rather than indicating the changeability of poor people—as studies on European immigrants had indicated—it sealed their "pathological" behavior as static.

Writers who constructed the "culture of poverty" discourse did not intend to harm racial minorities, but their ideas nevertheless became convenient tools of justification for those who sought to exploit them. The discourse thus became a tool of racial domination—a language used to blame the economic and social struggles of racial minorities on individuals rather than the sociopolitical structures that framed such conditions. Several factors facilitated this process of racialization. First and foremost, the incorporation of Puerto Rican workers into the lowest sectors of the New York labor economy alongside black workers demanded a justification for their labor exploitation. Just when black and Puerto Rican migrants took up the manufacturing jobs that had previously afforded upward mobility to European immigrants, these jobs began to disappear. The deindustrialization of the city was set in motion after World War II, as automation and the relocation of manufacturing industries began to shrink the pool of jobs available for migrants with little education and few job skills.[77] As historian Carmen Whalen has shown, the economic devastation that black industrial workers suffered in cities like Chicago and Detroit in the postwar era was similar to the experience of Puerto Rican workers in the urban centers of the Northeast.[78] African American workers were slightly shielded from the devastating impacts that deindustrialization had on Puerto Rican workers, but not by much. Puerto Ricans were hit the hardest by the relocation of the garment industry because a large proportion of the Puerto Rican working force depended on it. Over 57 percent of Puerto Rican New Yorkers in 1950 were employed in manufacturing jobs, most of which were related to the garment industry; meanwhile, only 6 percent of black New Yorkers were employed in manufacturing.[79] Black New Yorkers found more job opportunities in municipal jobs, such as public works, the post office, hospitals, and sanitation. In 1963, they occupied 23 percent of all city jobs, whereas Puerto Ricans had 3 percent of them.[80] Especially in public hospitals, which became a growing industry in the postwar era, black workers found plenty of jobs as cooks, laundresses, and kitchen help. Such an advantage was evident in the unemployment rates among minorities: in 1960, the unemployment rate among Puerto Rican males in New York was 9.9 percent, while for black males it was 6.9 percent.[81] Despite black workers' slight advantage over Puerto Rican workers, however, neither group was able to enter the highest-paying sectors of the labor economy that became accessible to white workers. Professional and managerial jobs, which emphasized office work, education, and theoretical knowledge, remained largely restricted to white workers with academic degrees and networks established through generations of privilege.[82]

Black and Puerto Rican workers' inability to get better jobs reflected the impact of deindustrialization on the city's poorest residents, but it became convenient to blame the workers' low salaries on their cultural "pathologies." Puerto Ricans were especially stigmatized as those who possessed a culture of "dependency." According to sociologists Nathan Glazer and Daniel Moynihan, one-half of all families in the city receiving welfare were Puerto Rican, and one-quarter of all Puerto Rican children in the city received some form of public assistance. Such a widespread reliance on public aid indicated Puerto Ricans' "cycle of dependency" and a "culture of welfare," which was passed down from one generation to the next.[83] Glazer and Moynihan did not go so far as calling Puerto Ricans "welfare cheaters"—as many other New Yorkers had. But their portrayal of Puerto Ricans as a people suffering from a "culture of dependency" allowed the city's employers and officials to believe that offering any kind of job to Puerto Ricans—no matter how low-paying—was an act of benevolence rather than exploitation.

The shortage of housing in the city also exacerbated Puerto Ricans' public image as "poor" people. Puerto Rican and black migration into New York City coincided with urban renewal, which displaced the poorest residents of the city into neighborhoods that became increasingly poor and "nonwhite." It was not that urban renewal advocates intentionally targeted racial and ethnic minorities. At its core, urban renewal represented a redevelopment program that envisioned the rise of New York City as a global economic, cultural, and political capital through the presence of a dynamic middle-class resident and working population. It included a coalition of housing reformers committed to providing public housing with modern amenities to poor residents at affordable rates and business developers eager to use government subsidies to minimize financial risk and maximize profits. The federal government had begun subsidizing housing construction since the formation of the Federal Housing Administration (FHA) in the 1930s. But the "politics of growth" of the postwar era, as sociologist Alan Wolfe called it, dictated that the federal government could stimulate national economic growth and serve the needs of its individual citizens simultaneously by pumping millions of federal dollars into urban redevelopment.[84]

At first, the interests of housing reformers and business developers looked compatible. Urban renewal projects would replace dilapidated slum buildings, which lacked hot running water, plumbing, private bathrooms, and flushing toilets, with new buildings equipped with such modern amenities. At the same time, new luxury apartment buildings, offices, medical hospitals, research universities, and highways would serve the needs and tastes of middle-class residents and workers. With time, however, it became obvious that the priorities of business leaders and their middle-class clientele would prevail over those of the working class. Title I of the Housing Act of 1949 mostly funded projects that benefited middle-class individuals, such as Lincoln Square and the United Nations headquarters complex.[85] The 1956 Federal-Aid Highway Act provided ample funding for the construction of highways, such as the Cross-Bronx Expressway. With the construction of the latter, City Planning Commissioner Robert Moses and city officials sacrificed a stable community of more than 60,000 working-class families in the Bronx in order to facilitate the commute of middle-class suburbanites. Marshall Berman, from the Bronx, recounted in *All That Is Solid Melts into Air* that, "at first, we couldn't believe it. . . . Hardly any of us owned cars; the neighborhood itself, and the subways leading downtown defined the flow of our lives. . . . Could a fellow Jew really want to do this to us?" Berman focused on his sense of ethnic betrayal by a fellow Jew, but the highway construction displaced Bronx residents across race and ethnic lines, destabilizing the lives of Irish, Italian, black, and Puerto Rican residents alike.[86]

Robert Moses's cavalier methods disturbed the lives of many working-class New Yorkers, but black and Puerto Rican residents facing removal found themselves in the most vulnerable position. According to a 1953 report conducted by the New York State Committee on Discrimination in Housing, more than 55 percent of the residents displaced by Title I developments were black and Puerto Rican. Only a third of the displaced tenants had been relocated to public housing; another 10 percent of them found housing in areas slated for redevelopment and clearance. For a large number of the displaced (42 percent), the New York City Housing Authority (NYCHA) did not have records for their new housing arrangements.[87] Blacks and Puerto Ricans who found alternative housing often ended up paying more for rent than white residents. A survey of Puerto Rican tenants in the mid-1950s revealed that Puerto Ricans paid more in monthly rents ($49 on average) than blacks ($43) and whites ($37).[88] Moving from neighborhood to neighborhood and transferring their children from one school to another, poor black and Puerto Rican migrants began to refer to "urban renewal" as "Negro removal."[89]

Once black and Puerto Rican tenants were forced to relocate, they had to move into neighborhoods that became increasingly occupied by public housing projects. Robert Moses targeted black- and Puerto Rican–dominant neighborhoods such as East Harlem, Brownsville, and the South Bronx as "ideal" for public housing construction. Between 1941 and 1961, NYCHA put up 10 percent of all of its public housing projects in East Harlem, which added up to fifteen new projects that housed an estimated population of 62,400 individuals. By 1959, one out of three East Harlem residents became tenants of public housing. In the South Bronx, a total of eleven public housing projects were built in the first half of the 1960s.[90]

The selection of black and Puerto Rican neighborhoods for public housing construction was based on the real estate industry's perception that racial and ethnic minorities presented financial risk. As early as 1937, the Home Owners Loan Corporation had given the Manhattan area above 96th Street a "fourth grade" or "D" rating, characterizing the area as mostly filled with "low grade tenements" and unfit for investment as a result. In the 1940s, this low rating was compounded by East Harlem's reputation as a neighborhood with high rates of crime and juvenile delinquency, populated mostly by "hordes of Italians, Puerto Ricans, Jews and Negroes."[91] To Robert Moses, these factors made East Harlem an area entirely unfit for private redevelopment and useful only as a dumping ground for public housing projects. In his calculation, public housing projects and profitable commerce did not coexist. His assessment of East Harlem, though completely flawed, became a self-fulfilling prophecy. The construction of public housing projects in the neighborhood throughout the 1950s and 1960s drove out the commercial establishments that had thrived in the past, as well as middle-income residents who were not eligible for admission to the new public housing projects. As a result, an increasingly poor black and Puerto Rican population came to reside in the neighborhood. Between 1950 and 1970, the white population of East Harlem shrank from 50 percent to 22 percent. By 1956, only 7 percent of the families in the neighborhood earned more than the $4,000 income limit for admission to public housing.[92]

With time, public housing projects became physical embodiments of black and Puerto Rican poverty. Whereas public housing had primarily housed poor whites before the 1950s, poor black and Puerto Rican residents made up the majority of public housing tenants from the 1960s and onward. In 1959, blacks constituted more than 39 percent and Puerto Ricans 17 percent of the public housing tenant population. By 1971, the public housing tenant population had become 48.5 percent black, 21.7 percent Puerto Rican, and 29.1 percent white.[93]

Public housing projects had not always carried notions of social stigma. In the 1930s and 1940s, public housing was mostly restricted to working-class white families with a steady income and a two-parent composition—a husband and a wife. It was understood that these were respectable families who had fallen into financial difficulties but would soon recover by living in healthy, clean environments.[94] Working-class blacks in New York

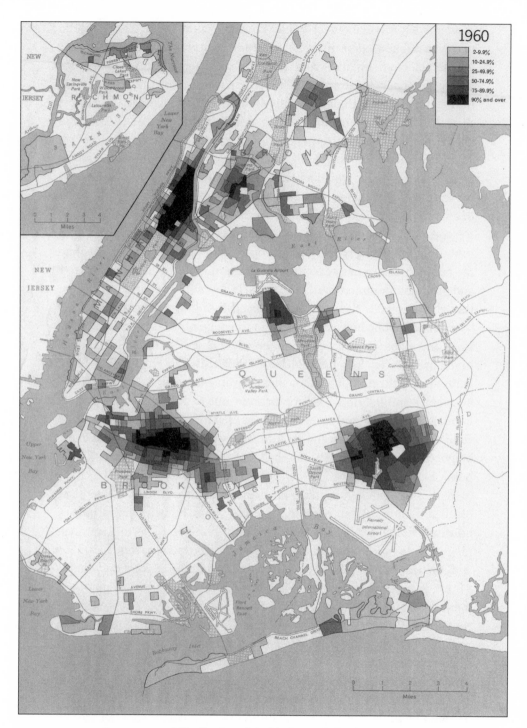

MAP 1.1 Percentage and distribution of the black population in New York City, 1960. Reprinted from Nathan Kantrowitz, *Negro and Puerto Rican Populations of New York City in the Twentieth Century*, 1969. (Courtesy of the American Geographical Society)

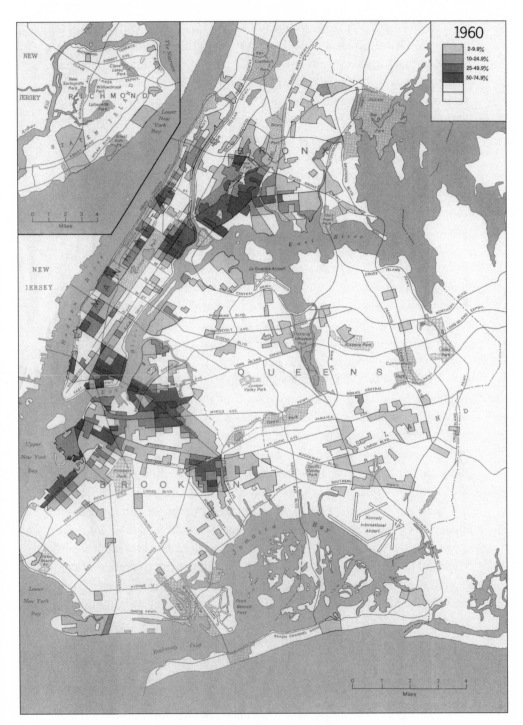

MAP 1.2 Percentage and distribution of the Puerto Rican population in New York City, 1960. Reprinted from Kantrowitz, *Negro and Puerto Rican Populations*. (Courtesy of the American Geographical Society)

had fought to gain access to public housing at this time, associating public housing with the kind of social engineering that would cure "the evil of the slums," such as crime and disease. In the 1950s, however, just as desegregation campaigns opened public housing to people of color, the projects came to be associated with the cause, and not the cure, of the slums' moral decline. Just two years after the opening of the Brownsville Houses in Brooklyn in 1952, for example, local residents began to blame the increase in crime and drug rackets on the new public housing residents. White families who were displaced by the construction of public housing chose to buy houses in nearby areas like Sheepshead Bay or Canarsie, leaving areas like Brownsville to become an increasingly segregated neighborhood of blacks and Puerto Ricans.[95]

Many New Yorkers attributed the "moral decline" of the projects to the "cultural problems" of rural migrants from the South and Puerto Rico. But much of the negative connotations that became attached to public housing in the 1950s and 1960s stemmed structurally from housing policies. Due to funding cuts and increased costs, the height and density of pubic housing grew significantly. NYCHA spent less money and housed more people by constructing high-rise buildings, paying little attention to the impact that such structures would have on the physical landscape of the surrounding neighborhoods. The racial segregation brought by white flight was also aided by housing policies. Working-class white families were able to access the private housing market only because the FHA provided extremely affordable mortgage rates for them. Meanwhile, working-class black families could not access such state-subsidized private housing. The 1958 Sharkey-Brown-Isaacs Law prohibited discrimination in private homes built with government-guaranteed mortgages, but the weak enforcement apparatus of the law allowed mortgage lenders and realtors to continue restricting FHA-subsidized private homes to white families exclusively. Black and Puerto Rican residents who had no choice but to remain in segregated neighborhoods tried to maintain racial and economic diversity in their neighborhoods by demanding the construction of middle-income housing, but with little success.[96]

As Puerto Rican families had little choice but to be displaced into neighborhoods filled with public housing projects, they became known as a people who had a "propensity" to live in overcrowded conditions. New York's newspapers had already described Puerto Rican migrants as those coming from an "overpopulated" island even before they became subject to urban renewal policies. "These refugees from an overpopulated tropical island . . . are the displaced persons of the Western Hemisphere," commented a 1949 *New York Times* article.[97] Puerto Rico's image as an "over-populated" island was also related to its reputation as an "over-diseased" island. In a letter that Robert Moses wrote to the president of the Federation Bank & Trust Company, Thomas Shanahan, in 1953, Moses revealed his fears regarding Puerto Ricans' contagious diseases. "As to the Puerto Rican problem," Moses urged, "federal and state governments, if not the city, could insist upon examination . . . which would screen out people who almost instantly land in our hospitals with diseases which could not possibly have been picked up here."[98] Coming from an "overpopulated" and "over-diseased" island, Puerto Ricans seemed unable to escape congested living conditions in the metropolis. In New York City, Puerto Ricans came to occupy a disproportionate percentage of tenants living in overcrowded apartments. In 1950, at a time when Puerto Ricans made up only 3 percent of the city's population, they made up as many as 53 percent of all households living in apartments and brownstones converted into single room and rooming-house units.[99] Tenant relocations triggered by urban renewal policies had been the primary factor determining Puerto Ricans' overcrowded living conditions, but New Yorkers viewed such conditions as reflective of their culture. A Bronx building inspector commented that, "in the sense of actual crowding, I'd never seen anything like it. On one floor you'd have ten families, young couples with small children. They [Puerto Ricans] had community kitchens with six women. What a tough way that was to live."[100]

If deindustrialization and urban renewal sealed the image of Puerto Rican adults as an "exploitable" group of poor New Yorkers, juvenile delinquency debates marred the image of Puerto Rican youth as "menacing" and prone to "criminality." Irish and Italian gangs had been viewed as commonplace and reflective of a healthy level of male adolescent boisterousness in the early twentieth century. But youth gangs became a social menace when they became racially distinct and more violent in the post-war era. As the number of black and Puerto Rican migrants coming into the city increased, Irish and Italian youth gangs began to defend their turfs along racial and ethnic lines. Simultaneously, as World War II veterans returned to their old neighborhoods, they introduced youth gangs to more sophisticated weaponry, allowing the youth to replace sticks, stones, and bottles with knives and homemade revolvers and rifles. The increased violence in gang conflict intensified racial fears among white families and community leaders. The use of more sophisticated weaponry was prevalent among Italian, Irish, black, and Puerto Rican youth alike, but the media often focused attention on the violence of black and Puerto Rican youth gangs.[101]

Black and Puerto Rican youth became subject to intense analysis by journalists and film directors who exploited their audience's racial fears to dramatize their stories. Journalists often exaggerated Puerto Rican youth's use of drugs. They repeatedly approached East Harlem community leaders to write stories about narcotics use among Puerto Ricans. "The streets of El Barrio . . . harbor the city's highest rate of juvenile delinquency," and "it is . . . one of the most heavily hit by juvenile narcotics addiction," reported the New York Times in July 1960 in an article titled "Night Cloaks Crime in City's Toughest Block."[102] Leaders from the East Harlem Protestant Parish and Union Settlement Association protested to the New York Times, arguing that the article was "inaccurate" and "seriously misrepresented our community." The article exaggerated the narcotics problem and ignored East Harlem's thriving community organizations, businesses, schools, and cooperative apartments, they claimed.[103] Their letter, however, fell on deaf ears. The newspaper continued to report on the problem of narcotics and the "self-destructive" nature of El Barrio throughout the 1960s.

Movie directors and producers also contributed to the growing fascination with the black and Puerto Rican juvenile delinquent. In movies such as Knock on Any Door (1949), Blackboard Jungle (1955), Rock, Rock, Rock (1956), Cry Tough (1959), and The Young Savages (1961), white urban missionaries, such as teachers, doctors, nuns, priests, and police officers, were portrayed as those who would save black and Puerto Rican "urban savages." In these films, white urban missionaries were initially rejected, often raped, assaulted, and denigrated, but eventually they saved the delinquents of color from their miserable lives.[104] By the time West Side Story came out as a film in 1961, white Americans had seen urban youth of color playing violent characters on movie screens for more than a decade. As the image of the violent and drug-addicted Puerto Rican juvenile delinquent became increasingly pervasive in New York circles, New Yorkers began to see the entire Puerto Rican migrant population as problematic and threatening.

The public school system also reinforced the view that black and Puerto Rican youth were incapable of learning due to their psychological troubles and mental inferiorities. When 600 "special" schools were set up after World War II for socially and emotionally maladjusted students, a disproportionate number of black and Puerto Rican students began to populate these schools.[105] The New York City Board of Education's 1955 report, *The Puerto Rican Study*, revealed that, although Puerto Rican students made up only 12 percent of school enrollments, they made up more than 20 percent of the students in these 600 schools. According to journalist Dan Wakefield, an assistant principal in East Harlem revealed that many Puerto Rican students were considered "holdovers" because they had trouble with reading tests or IQ tests.[106] By the early 1960s, some educators began to question the validity of using IQ tests to assess the intelligence level of students of color, given that they were administered by white educators and designed for middle-class white students.[107] They demonstrated that the IQ test constituted a social situation and that the attitude of the children toward the examiner was more important than the content of the test. Yet, for the most part, IQ tests were considered fair and objective tools of assessment.

Black and Puerto Rican students who attended regular public schools also demonstrated lower academic performance than white students, but most white educators believed that such a disparity reflected their inferior cultures and psyches as well. In 1960, while 40 percent of white New Yorkers had completed high school, only 31 percent of blacks and 13 percent of Puerto Ricans had done so. According to a 1960 study conducted by the New York Urban League, black and Puerto Rican students composed as many as 23 percent and 20 percent, respectively, of the city's vocational high schools, but only 11 percent and 5 percent of the academic high schools, respectively.[108] Most white teachers attributed such statistics to black and Puerto Rican children's "broken homes" and "maladjusted" cultures. "Things just don't make an impression on these [black and Puerto Rican] children," noted a white teacher in East Harlem. "The reason is that their whole culture is different. The only way to teach them is to repeat things twenty-five times. . . . They are not motivated at home."[109] Many white teachers assumed that their Puerto Rican students were addicted to drugs. According to Suki Ports, a Japanese American member of the Harlem Parents Group, a teacher in West Harlem assumed that her student had a drug addiction simply because he slept in class. "The kid that she was calling a drug addict was delivering newspapers. He got up at four in the morning, and delivered newspapers, so by the time he got to school, he was sleepy so he would put his head down sometimes, but she was calling him a drug addict."[110]

White educators saw black and Puerto Rican students through the lens of the "culturally deprived child" discourse. This discourse was yet another part of the "culture of poverty" literature, whereby New York liberals tried to explain differences between whites and nonwhites through an analysis of their cultures rather than their bodies. Broken homes, malnutrition, drug addiction, the absence of a male figure—these were the various cultural and psychological factors that explained minority children's lower academic performance. Initially, educators believed that the term would equalize public education for children across race. It was considered to be a racially neutral term that referred more specifically to the socioeconomic backgrounds of the children, including poor white children. Since "cultural deprivation" was believed to stem from material deprivation primarily, educators believed that the educational prospects of "culturally deprived children" could easily be improved by supplementing academic programs with job opportunities.[111] With time, however, the term became synonymous with black children. In 1963, Nathan Glazer noted that terms such as "culturally deprived" and "disadvantaged" had simply become "euphemisms for the Negro child."[112] According to social psychologist Frank Riessman, white teachers and guidance counselors began to adopt an "environmentally determinist" and "fatalist" point of view toward the "culturally deprived." They began to suggest that "we 'accept' [the underprivileged] and their culture; that we 'understand' their deficiencies as natural." Just as black children's intelligence was viewed as innately inferior in the past, their lack of motivation for learning also became a feature of a fixed, inferior culture.[113]

By being categorized as "culturally deprived" and relegated to an inferior education, black and Puerto Rican students became racialized within the public school system. A 1954 report from the Board of Education tried to use a racially neutral language to describe its student population, noting that the majority of black and Puerto Rican children attended "X" schools, which were 90 percent or more black- and Puerto Rican–populated, while the majority of white children attended "Y schools," which were 90 percent or more white. Despite the Board of Education's attempt to skirt the racial element of the public school's unequal system, it was clear that black and Puerto Rican students were receiving an inferior education. "X schools" had buildings that were older and less equipped than "Y schools," and teachers in "X schools" did not meet even the minimum qualifications established by the Board of Education.[114] Although black and Puerto Rican students' inability to access a better education system reflected white educators' prejudiced view toward them, they were nevertheless blamed for their academic failures.

By the mid-1960s, most white New Yorkers came to see the "culture of poverty" as resulting from permanent cultural flaws rather than temporary conditions of social disadvantage. They attached a new level of permanence to the notion of psychological dysfunction as they used the "culture of poverty" label to racialize blacks and Puerto Ricans. Daniel Moynihan's *The Negro Family* (1965) and Oscar Lewis's *La Vida* (1966) received the most public criticism for racially stigmatizing blacks and Puerto Ricans under the "culture of poverty" literature, but the foundations of their theories had been articulated for more than a decade prior to the publication of their works.

Negotiating Ethnic Representation within the "Cult of Ethnicity"

Puerto Rican New Yorkers attempted to capture their own political voice within the "Puerto Rican problem" debate, but they found it difficult to do so through electoral politics. When Oscar García Rivera was elected as the assemblyman of the 17th Assembly District in Spanish Harlem in 1937, he was hailed as the first Puerto Rican to be elected to public office on the mainland. But his political career proved to be short, as the Republican Party refused to support him for reelection when his voting patterns aligned him with the American Labor Party and Communists.[115] During the 1930s and 1940s, Puerto Ricans relied on the steady support of Congressman Vito Marcantonio, an Italian American. As a former vice president of the International Workers Order, he was committed to labor unions and had developed ties with Puerto Rican labor leaders. When the predominantly Jewish and Italian population of East Harlem became home to more Puerto Rican migrants during his administration, he became a fierce advocate for issues pertaining to his Puerto Rican constituents. Whether fighting for Puerto Rican independence, acting as legal counsel for Albizu Campos and other incarcerated Puerto Rican nationalists, or pushing for the reinstatement of Spanish as the language of instruction in Puerto Rican schools or for Puerto Rican migrants' access to public housing in New York, Marcantonio stood as a consistent advocate of Puerto Ricans. A 1939 editorial in *La Voz*, the Spanish language newspaper of the Communist Party, claimed that "no man could be a better candidate in the 20th District than Vito Marcantonio, friend of the poor, of the Puerto Ricans and of Puerto Rico, as well as all the Spanish-speaking community."[116] The 1940s and 1950s, however, did not welcome a political figure like Marcantonio. The rise of the Partido Popular Democrático

(PPD) made the Puerto Rican nationalist cause seem too radical, and Cold War politics made his prolabor allegiances seem "communistic."

In 1949, Mayor William O'Dwyer made the first concerted effort to bring Puerto Ricans into a broader coalition of liberals composed of white ethnic Democrats in the city. He founded the Mayor's Advisory Committee on Puerto Rican Affairs (MACPRA) as a government agency that would facilitate the adjustment of Puerto Rican migrants in the city. MACPRA leaders tried to help Puerto Rican migrants by viewing them within the ethnic framework. They portrayed Puerto Ricans as another immigrant group that currently faced economic difficulties but that would soon be upwardly mobile through hard work and education. Commissioner of Welfare and MACPRA member Raymond M. Hilliard argued in 1949 that New Yorkers need not worry about Puerto Ricans overwhelming the city's social services because very few of them actually took advantage of their welfare eligibility. The majority of Puerto Ricans, Hilliard claimed, were "self-supporting, hard-working citizens of New York City," and only 10 percent of them were dependent on welfare. Puerto Ricans' 10 percent may have represented a higher proportion compared to the 4.2 percent of the total population of the city that received public aid, but this disproportion only reflected their more recent arrival into the city, claimed Hilliard. "Language handicap," "lack of seniority" in securing employment, and lack of "well-established community groups" made it difficult for many Puerto Ricans to have their own sources of income, but these were temporary conditions typical of the immigrant experience.[117] Following MACPRA's lead, many city officials began to similarly portray Puerto Ricans as the "last immigrants" who would follow in the footsteps of European immigrants and their upward mobility. Hilliard's successor, Commissioner of Welfare Henry L. McCarthy, predicted in 1952 that "if the Irish, Germans, and Italians can make it in one generation, the Puerto Ricans can too."[118] In 1957, the New York Planning Commission predicted that Puerto Ricans would easily access upward social mobility, given all the signs that pointed to "continued assimilation with further education and job experience, with consequent gains in rent-paying ability."[119]

MACPRA leaders' efforts brought about some gains within the Puerto Rican community. Through Hilliard's initiative, the Welfare Department suspended the three-year minimum residency requirement for social workers, allowing more Puerto Rican social workers to serve the increasing Puerto Rican welfare clientele. Recognizing the tremendous poverty conditions from which the migrants came, MACPRA also convinced Congress to extend federal welfare benefits to Puerto Ricans on the island. These policies seemed to reduce the rate of Puerto Ricans on welfare rolls in New York City to a certain extent. Commissioner of Welfare McCarthy at least boasted that the percentage of Puerto Ricans relying on welfare decreased from 10 percent in 1949 to 7.5 percent in 1953. MACPRA leaders also cooperated with the Migration Division of Puerto Rico's Department of Labor in marshaling city services in housing, education, and recreation for Puerto Rican migrants.[120]

Despite these efforts, however, there was no significant breakthrough in Puerto Ricans' political relationship with the city's electoral leadership. Tammany Hall took some steps to bring Puerto Rican constituents into its fold in the 1950s. Its leaders had been gradually losing their power since federal investigations in the 1930s had uncovered a number of corruption cases among party leaders, and civil service bureaucrats of the New Deal had taken over control of public assistance distribution.[121] Tammany leaders tried to deal with these challenges by tapping into the voting potential of the growing black and Puerto Rican populations in the city. The boss of the Bronx County Democratic organization, Ed Flynn, selected Felipe N. Torres as a candidate for state assemblyman in 1953, a seat that Torres won. In the following year, Tammany boss Carmine DeSapio selected Antonio Méndez as district leader for the Democratic Party in East Harlem.[122] Despite Democratic leaders' attempts to appeal to a Puerto Rican constituency, however, it was not clear that Puerto Ricans' alliance with party leaders resulted in any material benefits to Puerto Rican migrants themselves. Puerto Ricans continued to be relegated to the most menial jobs in the city, and the increasing segregation of Puerto Rican children into 600 "special" schools effectively closed their path toward any type of career advancement. Worse yet, some believed that party leaders intentionally selected Puerto Rican individuals with little political ambition as candidates in order to limit the growth of Puerto Rican political leadership. According to journalist Dan Wakefield, the selection of district leader Méndez was partially based on DeSapio's perception that Méndez had "no recognizable ambitions of a political future beyond the one assigned him by DeSapio."[123]

Seeking to find their own political voice within the various political realignments taking place in the city, a few Puerto Rican leaders made their grievances known to city officials. Ruperto Ruiz, president of the Spanish American Youth Bureau, released a public statement in October 1953 excoriating MACPRA for its limited political efficacy. Ruiz criticized MACPRA for placing Puerto Rican leaders as members of the committee simply "as a front." Rather than providing a real vehicle of political empowerment for Puerto Ricans, Ruiz felt that the committee served simply as a "buffer between City Officials and representatives of the Puerto Rican community." The fact that Puerto Rican members of MACPRA could not exercise much authority through their position reflected the committee's lack of authority itself since it came with no power of enforcement and functioned only as an advisory agency to the mayor's office. Yet, given the mayor's claim that MACPRA would facilitate Puerto Rican migrants' adjustment in the city, Ruiz felt that the committee had misled Puerto Ricans by giving a semblance of political representation. Furthermore, Ruiz felt that the committee actually impeded the development of independent Puerto Rican leadership. While "imposing itself as a super-agency in charge of Puerto Rican Problems," Ruiz claimed, MACPRA did not "permit the Puerto Ricans to develop responsible leadership on their own, free of political influence." Lastly, Ruiz claimed that the committee jeopardized Puerto Rican interests by singling them out as the only minority group in need of help. Ruiz complained that "the establishment of the [Mayor's Advisory] Committee has created the belief and resentment . . . among a large group of the citizenry, that the Puerto Rican group is the favorite political expedient of the City administration."[124]

With this last statement, Ruiz zeroed in on an important and difficult tension that Puerto Rican leaders faced during the postwar era. Although they needed to publicly address the specific kinds of abuse that Puerto Ricans suffered in the city in order to seek redress for their grievances, they feared being stigmatized as "dependent" and "needy." Joseph Monserrat, director of New York's Migration Division of Puerto Rico's Department of Labor, shared Ruiz's fears. When Mayor Robert F. Wagner offered him a position within his administration in 1954, Monserrat declined, choosing instead to play a more low-key role as a member of Wagner's advisory council. Monserrat also advised Wagner against appointing a Puerto Rican assistant commissioner in the Department of Welfare, arguing that such an appointment would "stir up public anxiety" and imply that the Puerto Rican welfare problem was so considerable that it required a staff member dedicated solely to solving this problem.[125] Given the potential advantages and risks involved in being recognized as a group in need of help, Ruiz demanded that MACPRA be abolished and that a new municipal agency be established to address the needs of Puerto Rican migrants. He argued that this agency should foster the development of "strong, independent, responsible" Puerto Rican leadership, but with the focus on building "intergroup relations" and investigating "violations of minority rights" broadly, without singling Puerto Ricans out as the only group in need of help.[126] In sum, there was a delicate balance that Puerto Rican leaders and their political allies needed to strike: while Puerto Rican leaders needed to be given enough political authority to make institutional changes on behalf of their constituents, their positions could not be so conspicuous as to indicate Puerto Ricans "special" need for political representation.

Ruiz's words did not go unheeded. Mayor Wagner, who was eager to capture the black and Puerto Rican vote, listened carefully to the criticisms being made against MACPRA. Soon after becoming mayor, Wagner reformulated the Unity Committee, a municipal agency with little enforcement apparatus, and renamed it the Commission on Intergroup Relations (COIR). He significantly increased the apparatus of the organization—between 1956–57 and 1959–60, COIR's budget grew from $120,000 to $370,525, and its staff expanded from twelve people to fifty-three. COIR was vested with the responsibility of overseeing housing discrimination, as the Sharkey-Brown-Isaacs Law of 1958 gave it power to investigate, and hold hearings on, allegations of discrimination in private housing. The ethnic membership also changed. The Unity Committee had been composed exclusively of African American, Roman Catholic, and Jewish members, but COIR included Antonia Pantoja, a Puerto Rican, who became the agency's chief of the Community Relations Department.[127]

For all of the increased investigative and advisory powers that COIR possessed, however, it still did not carry the kind of enforcement power necessary to enact broad changes in housing patterns. Mayor Wagner advised COIR staff to adopt a conciliatory and cooperative relationship with city bureaucrats, so that education and public pressure rather than legal enforcement would bring about change smoothly. The commission could thus expose racial inequalities brought about by the city's Housing Authority policies, but it could not change those policies. It also did not serve as a vehicle for the expression of political grievances for Puerto Ricans, since 85 percent of the complainants of housing discrimination in 1958–60 were African American and only 9 percent were Puerto Rican.[128] In 1964, the staff membership of COIR, which was renamed yet again as the Commission on Human Rights, was 42 percent black and 7 percent Puerto Rican.[129] Within a municipal agency focused on "inter-group" relations, Puerto Ricans were able to escape being stigmatized as an exclusive group of needy citizens, but they ended up having their interests subsumed under a larger black constituency.

Conclusion

Puerto Ricans migrated to New York City in large numbers at the same time that the postwar economic boom led many New Yorkers to adopt an optimistic outlook on immigrants' assimilability. They adopted the "cult of ethnicity" and predicted that Puerto Ricans, though presently facing conditions of poverty and overcrowded housing, would soon be upwardly mobile like other immigrants had been in the past. Advocates of the ethnic framework, however, did not foresee that automation and the relocation of factories would erode the blue-collar job base that had been so crucial to European immigrants' economic advancement in the first half of the twentieth century. Facing a shrinking labor economy and low wages, it seemed that Puerto Rican migrants, along with black southern migrants, would not be able to find an easy escape from their status as the poorest residents of the city. Urban renewal, which forced black and Puerto Rican migrants to repeatedly move from one poor neighborhood to the next, reinforced their public image as those who naturally belonged to an environment of chaos. Their "cultural adaptations" to conditions of poverty, which were initially viewed as temporary and prone to change, became fixed in the New York imaginary. The "culture of poverty" discourse, although written by those who saw themselves as advocates of Puerto Rican and black migrants, ended up racializing blacks and Puerto Ricans into a permanent group of poor people. Puerto Rican leaders tried to protect their communities from such stigmatization by making alliances with a few of the city's electoral leaders, but with little success. Within this context, Puerto Rican labor organizers made limited gains in developing independent political spaces for their community in New York. Although small in numbers, and not always in sync with the organizing efforts of black labor leaders, Puerto Rican labor leaders tapped into various vehicles of political expression to make their demands known to the New York public. We turn our attention to their efforts in the next chapter.

CHAPTER TWO

We Were Walking on Egg Shells

Puerto Rican and Black Workers' Political Dissent in the International Ladies Garment Workers' Union

Herbert Hill appeared before the House Committee on Education and Labor in New York City on August 17, 1962, to testify against the leaders of the International Ladies' Garment Workers' Union (ILGWU). As labor secretary of the National Association for the Advancement of Colored People (NAACP) and as a special consultant to Congressman Adam Clayton Powell Jr., he had accumulated ample evidence from the 1940s to the early 1960s to prove the union's racial discrimination against its black and Puerto Rican members. His actions surprised many since the ILGWU had a very progressive record of recruiting black union members at the height of the Great Depression. Hill's testimony, however, unequivocally blamed ILGWU's racially discriminatory practices for the poverty of the union's black and Puerto Rican members. According to Hill, the ILGWU had become a two-faced institution that maintained a "public image of a union fighting against sweatshops, bringing stability to the industry, securing educational and recreational services for its members," while in reality working as a "trade union controlled by a rigid bureaucracy that long ago lost contact with its rank and file members." He characterized the union as a "bureaucracy that has more in common ethnically and socially with the employers than with the workers it is supposed to represent." Hill left no room for the public to wonder about union leaders' responsibility in creating such a bureaucracy. He claimed that ILGWU leaders intentionally kept union leadership and certain locals "lily-white" by allowing union business agents (representatives of local unions) to maintain personal control of admission into training programs. Such a system left high-paying jobs such as tailors, cloak-makers, and cutters to an exclusive circle of Italian and Jewish garment workers, while black and Puerto Rican garment workers remained in low occupations such as shipping clerks.[1]

President of the ILGWU David Dubinsky furiously defended his union, reminding House Committee members that "I and my union have established a record for the labor movement . . . as a union that fought discrimination and fought against sweatshops."[2] He claimed there was nothing he could do about garment workers' low salaries since they were caused by the relocation of garment factories to the South and the Caribbean, which he felt was completely outside of his control as a union leader. In an autobiography written in 1977, Dubinsky dismissed the congressional inquiry as nothing more than Powell's act of retaliation for Dubinsky's support of Powell's GOP opponent Mae Watts in the 1962 elections.[3] Charles Zimmerman, manager of ILGWU's Local 22 Dressmakers' Union, did not dismiss the accusations as easily as Dubinsky—he acknowledged that no one should be "immune from criticism" when it came to fighting against discrimination since no one had done "enough." Yet he was still shocked that Hill had failed to "distinguish between allies and antagonists" and hurled such a "malicious" and "anti-Semitic" attack against one of the most racially progressive unions in the nation. He could not have been surer of his own credentials as a political ally of African Americans. He had served as an active member of the NAACP Legal Defense and Education Fund, the National Urban League (NUL), and the Congress of Racial Equality (CORE) and as manager of a local whose membership was overwhelmingly black and Puerto Rican. Eager to prove the union's standing as an ally of civil rights organizations, he convinced A. Philip Randolph, the nation's most prominent black labor leader, to defend the ILGWU. To Zimmerman's delight, Randolph promised House Committee members that he would not allow "any witch hunt against a bona fide labor union such as the ILGWU" to bring unnecessary divisions within a civil rights–labor coalition.[4]

Zimmerman further justified the lack of black and Puerto Rican leadership in the union by attributing it to the dominance of women among them. He acknowledged that the growing numbers of minority workers in the union demanded a greater level of participation within the union. Whereas Puerto Rican and black workers had made up only 2 percent and 3 percent of the garment industry in 1940, respectively, the percentages increased to 40 percent for Puerto Ricans and 10 percent for blacks by 1960.[5] Within the ILGWU, Puerto Ricans composed 24 percent of the union membership in 1962, while blacks made up 16 percent.[6] Yet, according to Zimmerman, the fact that only 1 percent of the union's paid officers were black or Puerto Rican did not reflect a willful practice of racial exclusion. Instead, he believed that most of the union members themselves chose

FIGURE 2.1 Black and Puerto Rican members of Local 10, ILGWU, before the public hearing at the New York State Commission for Human Rights, May 15, 1962, A. Philip Randolph is in the middle of the front row. (ILGWUR, Kheel Center, Cornell University)

not to get involved in union organizing because "most of the members are women who must get home right after work to prepare meals and take care of household duties."[7] ILGWU labor organizer Tom Brooks supported Zimmerman's reasoning, claiming that "the girls, as any ILGWU leader will tell you . . . are great on the picket line, on a shop or a price settlement committee. But the women in most cases do not care for the long haul of trade union leadership."[8] In a union whose membership was 80 percent female, male union leaders found it strategic to justify racial inequities by focusing on the gender particularity rather than the racial status of the rank-and-file members.

While ILGWU leaders denied charges of racial discrimination, black and Puerto Rican workers' responses reflected disagreement. Black union members Florence Rice and Helen Green gave harsh testimony against union leaders at the congressional hearings. When she first began serving as the chairwoman of Local 105, Rice claimed that she thought the union was "the greatest thing." She slowly became disillusioned, however, when she noticed that white employees received higher salaries than black and Puerto Rican employees, all under the tacit approval of ILGWU leaders. "Eventually you begin to recognize that all this that glitters is not gold,"

Rice claimed. "Underneath the whole damn thing is ugliness, because you begin to see, whites are in control." While white employees were constantly "given preference," "Negro and Puerto Rican girls . . . could not . . . produce enough work for a minimum day's pay" because they always got "the cheaper work." ILGWU leaders were complicit in maintaining such a pattern of discrimination, Rice claimed, because business agents were informed of the situation, yet "nothing was ever done."[9] In a more recent interview, Rice revealed that she and Green were the only two union members who showed up at the congressional hearings, out of an original group of five who had committed to testify; the rest backed down when union leaders intimidated them. "I was intimidated. They called me the whole night. . . . They told me that if I testified, I wouldn't work again. So that makes people stop and think." Not surprisingly, Rice and Green immediately lost their jobs after they testified.[10]

Meanwhile, Puerto Rican workers' responses ranged from equivocation to unwavering support of union leaders. Modesto Garcia and Angel Luis Navarro had both worked as cutters in different shops and had attempted to become members of Local 10 in order to receive higher salaries. They were refused membership by Local 10 leaders, however, and simply told to wait. When asked by chairman of the House Committee Herbert Zelenko the reason that they were refused union membership, they simply answered, "I don't know."[11] Several Puerto Rican ILGWU members expressed their opinions on the charges made against the ILGWU more clearly in a series of articles written in El Diario, the largest Spanish-language newspaper in New York City. Dismissing Congressman Powell's committee charges as "disgusting," the business agent of Local 62, Julio Ramirez, claimed that race had no impact in determining the leadership of the ILGWU: "In our union, we do not see Hispanos, we do not see Negroes, we do not see Jews, we do not see Italians. We see only people." Puerto Rican members like Ramirez used the same kind of "color-blind" rhetoric that white union leaders used to justify their domination over Puerto Rican members. Furthermore, Carmen Morales, chairwoman of another ILGWU local, echoed Dubinsky's suspicions by stating that the only reason that the Powell committee had brought these charges was that an election was coming up.[12] These Puerto Rican union members interpreted Powell's hearings as a politically motivated scheme. Rather than seeing Powell as a potential ally in their struggle against labor exploitation, Puerto Rican ILGWU members defended their white labor leaders and rejected a black civil rights leader's assumed position as a Puerto Rican spokesperson.

Why did black and Puerto Rican ILGWU members respond to the congressional investigations so differently? According to Hill, these two minority groups suffered the same forms of labor exploitation and racial discrimination by their white employers and labor leaders. Yet their official response to their conditions of subjugation could not have seemed more different. This chapter uses the events that took place within the ILGWU in the late 1950s and early 1960s as a case study to analyze black and Puerto Rican workers' political responses to the different forms of racial and class subjugation that shaped their workplace experiences. It looks at minority workers' articulation of grievances through *public transcripts* and *hidden transcripts*, paying attention to their ability to disclose their sentiments toward their employers and union leaders through official and unofficial vehicles of political expression. I argue that, although the congressional hearings could have indicated black and Puerto Rican union members' differing opinions toward their labor leaders, the hearings obscured the real similarities that existed between the two groups. The difference in their testimonies did not so much reflect a dissimilar racial consciousness between black and Puerto Rican workers as it did Puerto Ricans' relative lack of access to political power in comparison to African Americans. Such a structural disparity created political tensions between the two groups, but it did not reflect irreconcilable differences between them.

Black and Puerto Rican Workers' Racial and Gender Subjugation

Puerto Rican members of the ILGWU shared many experiences with black union members as victims of racial discrimination. The majority of black and Puerto Rican garment workers were in fact concentrated in the same locals: Local 22 (dressmakers), Local 25 (blouse and waist makers), Local 60 (dress and waist pressers), Local 102 (cloak and dress drivers and helpers), Local 132 (button and novelty workers), and Local 142 (ladies' neckwear workers).[13] Within these locals, the majority of black and Puerto Rican union members were relegated to the lowest-paying jobs and could participate in the union only as rank-and-file members. Some ILGWU leaders portrayed both Puerto Rican and black workers as difficult to organize because they were "backward" and "distrustful of people" and "they know nothing about unions."[14]

Puerto Rican and black garment workers were certainly conscious of their victimization as racial minorities, and they made attempts to express their grievances.[15] Although their testimonies differed greatly at the 1962 congressional hearings, individual complaints filed with the New York State Division of Human Rights reveal that they were subject to similar forms of abuse. From 1945 through the 1970s, New Yorkers of various racial, ethnic, religious, and age backgrounds filed complaints with the State Division when they felt that they were victims of discrimination. Aida Iglesias, a Puerto Rican worker at a button factory, submitted an individual complaint to the State Division in 1951. "I was discharged by the foreman who had repeatedly abused and insulted me because of my Puerto Rican birth," claimed Iglesias. In a detailed report written by a field representative from the State Division, Iglesias complained that she had been "subjected repeatedly [to] statements . . . by Mr. Klein [her employer] that all Puerto Ricans are immoral and lewd." She added that "the foreman . . . also abused me by stating that I should 'go to the corner like all Puerto Ricans of mixed sex and hustle.'" When Iglesias sought counsel from Mr. Horowitz, the manager of ILGWU's Local 9, she received further verbal abuse. Mr. Horowitz argued that Iglesias's complaint was invalid because she suffered from "persecution phobia," which was "characteristic of Puerto Ricans." The abuse, Horowitz claimed, was of her "own imagination." A field representative of the Division of Human Rights, Robert Cotter, concurred with Horowitz's assessment of Iglesias's mental health condition. He claimed that she had indeed been the "unfortunate victim of hallucinations" and that Mr. Klein did not practice discrimination against his Puerto Rican employees.[16]

Iglesias's experience of being dismissed by the State Division of Human Rights was no different than that of African American garment workers who found themselves in similar situations. Elsie Hunter filed complaints with the State Division against two of her employers in 1946 and 1949. In 1952, she filed a complaint against the ILGWU for firing her as a punishment for the two complaints she had previously filed. According to Hunter, an ILGWU business agent named Marinello advised her current employer, Lena Piscitello, to discharge her because she was a "troublemaker." Marinello claimed that her actions were "detrimental to the interests of the ILGWU" because she had turned to the courts for redress of an alleged wrong "before exhausting all the rights and remedies provided by the constitution and by-laws of the ILGWU." Division investigators responded to Hunter's charges in a way that was similar to the way they had responded to Iglesias—rather than assessing the validity of Marinello's claims by examining what forms of redress were actually available to union members like Hunter, they took no action until Hunter withdrew her complaint because "she was sick and tired of it all."[17]

Puerto Rican and black female workers also shared similar pressures to fulfill their responsibilities as the main caretakers of their children and as workers. Despite Florence Rice's willingness to risk losing her job by exposing the ILGWU leaders' racist practices at the congressional hearings, she explained in a recent interview that her decision was determined by the particular condition of her life at the time. "My daughter was already married then. . . . If I [had] had to raise my daughter during that period, I don't know whether I would have spoken up." In 1962, Rice was a forty-three-year-old woman whose only daughter was already married. She no longer bore the financial responsibility of providing for her children. Thus, Rice had been able to fight for black women's economic and civil rights insofar as she felt that she did not violate any gender expectations. She explained the general rule that "black women always thought of their children first. They will subject themselves to anything just so they can take care of their children," she noted. Not only did black women generally not have time to organize, they also would not "allow themselves to get involved in discussions" because dissenting often meant losing their jobs and risking their ability to sustain their families.[18]

The same held true for the majority of Puerto Rican women in the union. Carmen Quiñones, a Puerto Rican member of Local 23, claimed that she did not get involved in union leadership because "I have my daughter, and I don't want to be too . . . involved. I just want to work and come home to take care of my daughter." While living in East Harlem and working in the garment district on 9th Avenue and 34–40th Streets, Quiñones rushed to the train station after work but still barely made it to the day care center by closing time. There was no time to go to union meetings in the evenings.[19]

Those who chose to fulfill their child-rearing roles at home while sharing men's outside world of labor activism lived under severe external and internal pressures. Ida Torres, a Puerto Rican ILGWU member, chose the unusual path of pursuing a career in labor activism. She joined the Retail, Wholesale and Department Store Union (RWDSU) in the 1960s and became president of the union's Local 3 in 1998. She revealed how difficult this process had been for her: "My family thought I was terrible because I was out working and should have been home taking care of my children. That was the whole community. When I went to work . . . and I asked my aunt to take care of my children, she said, 'stay home and take care of your own children, welfare will take care of you.' I'm separated from my husband; I want to go to work because I feel like I'm drowning. The only way I can get a divorce is if I'm finally independent. She thought it was the improper thing to do, however."[20]

Forty years later, despite her career success, Torres still felt ambivalent about her decisions: "I'm torn inside, even to this day, did I do the right thing? Should I have stayed home and taken care of the children? Would [my daughter] have been a better, smarter person? Bullshit. But you are indoctrinated a certain way and that guilt never leaves you."[21]

Black and Puerto Rican women came under similar attacks when their greater levels of participation in work outside their homes threatened men's sense of patriarchal authority in the postwar era. Increasing patterns of urbanization and corporatization in America, industrialization in Puerto Rico, and the rise of psychology as a scientific field led African American and Puerto Rican male writers to blame men's threatened sense of masculinity on their mothers' and wives' psychological instabilities. From E. Franklin Frazier's Black Bourgeoisie: The Rise of a New Middle Class in the United States (1957) to René Marqués's novel En una ciudad llamada San Juan (1960), black and Puerto Rican men argued that "over-domineering" black and Puerto Rican mothers and wives created feminized men with low self-esteem.[22] Marqués explained that the main problem that Puerto Rico faced with the introduction of U.S. industries to the island was the beginning of matriarchy: "It was in the forties that Puerto Rican society made a rapid turn toward the Anglo-Saxon matriarchy. The cultural and ethical patterns of a social structure based on the tradition of the pater familias rapidly deteriorated." In novels such as Marqués's and José L. González's El hombre en la calle (1948), Puerto Rican women were characterized as figures who contaminated and destroyed the idyllic traditions of the island by absorbing American cultural values. They either prostituted themselves after moving into the city in search of jobs or they ruined their husbands' lives by demanding material goods over meaningful lives. Since these Puerto Rican writers associated women's empowerment with U.S. industries, they held onto a mythic notion of Puerto Rican machismo as a way of dealing with the changes that industrialization brought them.[23]

The battles that black and Puerto Rican women faced against a patriarchal labor leadership were not new historical phenomena. Gender prescriptions had historically constrained the activities of ILGWU's female members and leaders. It was the leadership of 20,000 women from the dress and waist-makers' industry, most of whom were Jewish, that had led

FIGURE 2.2
Even as union leaders
encouraged women to
participate in strikes, they
argued that their children
should be their main
concern. (ILGWUR, Kheel
Center, Cornell University)

to the spontaneous strike of 1909 and the founding of the ILGWU. Yet gender prescriptions had led the majority of the female strikers not to involve themselves in labor leadership. Jewish women who became prominent ILGWU leaders, such as Pauline Newman, Rose Pesotta, and Fannia Cohn, revealed through personal memoirs that Jewish women who became labor leaders chose political careers at the cost of traditional marriage. They believed that a dual commitment to the union and their individual families would inevitably create tension.[24] By the time the union's racial composition changed in the postwar era, Jewish women's position was still highly controlled by men's paternalistic attitude toward them. In the early 1960s, Rose Pesotta was the only female member of the Executive Board of the ILGWU. Jennie Silverman, one of the few female organizers in the ILGWU, argued that the union's sexist practices included putting pressure on female union officers to retire sooner than male ones.[25] Gender subjugation had thus shaped power relationships within the ILGWU from its formation through the 1960s.

Puerto Rican Workers' Public and Hidden Transcripts

The fact that black and Puerto Rican female garment workers did not voice their criticism of ILGWU's gender discrimination at the congressional hearings does not mean that these criticisms did not exist. Neither does the lack of Puerto Ricans' articulation of racial grievances indicate their lack of racial consciousness. If we place Puerto Rican ILGWU members' congressional testimonies in the context of the complaints submitted to the New York State Division of Human Rights, we begin to understand the risks that workers of color took when they decided to publicly divulge information regarding their racial and class subjugation. Being fired from their jobs, being diagnosed as mentally disturbed—these were a few of the negative repercussions that workers of color could face if they revealed their sentiments in places where their perspectives were not respected. It is likely that Modesto Garcia and Angel Luis Navarro were selected as the two Puerto Rican witnesses at the congressional hearings because their testimonies revealed so little about Puerto Rican ILGWU members' status in the union: although their experiences indicated the possibility that Local 10 leaders had discriminated against them, they had little evidence to prove such an argument. Their pithy answer to Chairman Zelenko's question about the reasons why they were denied union membership by Local 10 ("I don't know") also suggested Puerto Rican workers' unwillingness to enter into a heated racial confrontation between white union leaders and black civil rights leaders.

Puerto Rican workers' testimonies at the congressional hearings, therefore, cannot be interpreted as indicative of their actual sentiments toward union leaders. Such public transcripts need to be read against the backdrop of their more hidden transcripts. As political scientist James C. Scott has argued, subordinate groups cannot always "speak truth to power."[26] In other words, Puerto Rican workers could not oppose union leaders directly because their survival depended on the concealment of their real feelings. If they revealed their grievances at the congressional hearings too openly, they risked losing favor with a powerful union that wielded a great amount of influence over the lives of Puerto Rican garments workers in New York City and on the island. Therefore, their public transcripts, which Scott defines as "the open interaction between subordinates and those who dominate," cannot be taken at face value. Ramirez's and Morales's statements of praise for their union leaders in El Diario can be read more as examples of Puerto Ricans' "art of dissimulation" than reflective of their true opinions. In addition, their *hidden transcripts*, expressed by "daily acts of resistance and survival" through more unorganized and less official venues, need to be considered.[27]

We must first analyze the structure of the labor economy that employed Puerto Ricans on the island and in New York City to understand the constraints that shaped Puerto Ricans' public transcripts. In comparison to African Americans, a disproportionate number of Puerto Ricans depended on the garment industry as a source of employment. Over 57 percent of Puerto Rican New Yorkers in 1950 were employed in manufacturing jobs, most of which were related to the garment industry. Meanwhile, only 6 percent of black New Yorkers were employed in manufacturing.[28] Puerto Ricans from the island were also heavily dependent on U.S.-based garment industries, as they employed one-fourth of all workers in manufacturing jobs on the island and 45.5 percent of the island's female workers in 1952.[29] The concentration of Puerto Rican labor in the garment industry resulted from the long relationship that U.S. employers had built up with island women involved in home needlework since the 1910s.[30] As Puerto Rican women built a reputation for having "agile hands" and providing a cheap source of labor, and as white workers began to move to the suburbs in the postwar era, U.S. garment industry employers readily replaced their former employees with Puerto Rican migrants. They also took advantage of exemptions from taxes and license fees on the island and moved their factories there. Puerto Ricans on the island and on the mainland were therefore highly dependent on the goodwill of their bosses in the garment industry.

Due to Puerto Ricans' colonial status, they were also dependent on the favor of ILGWU president David Dubinsky for the stability of the garment industry on the island. The ILGWU was the largest union in New York City, with a membership of 200,000 in the early 1950s and 180,000 in the early 1960s. Its financial assets included sixteen medical clinics, a resort in the Poconos, and four radio stations.[31] By the early 1960s, Dubinsky had also become a power broker whose influence reached the lives of garment workers in Puerto Rico. Hipólito Marcano, president of the Federación Libre de Trabajadores (the main labor organization on the island), maintained close ties with several U.S. labor leaders, such as Ralph Helstein of the Packinghouse Workers and Paul Hall of the Seafarers International Union. But Dubinsky was by far the most influential American labor leader on the island due to the island's new dependence on the garment industry. Luis Muñoz Marín and AFL-CIO president George Meany unofficially delegated organized labor's position on the island's wage policy to Dubinsky. The minimum wage in Puerto Rico needed to be kept low enough to incentivize the relocation of garment industries from the mainland to the island but not so low as to curtail mainland production entirely. According to historian Miles Galvin, Muñoz Marín was thus "very anxious to cater to Dubinsky to work out the best arrangement possible for Puerto Rican development."[32] As a result, the Puerto Rican leadership in New York also felt the pressure to accommodate Dubinsky.

Given Puerto Ricans' structural dependence on the garment industry and U.S. labor leaders, Puerto Rican leaders' response to the 1962 congressional hearings was highly constrained. The Migration Division of the Department of Labor of Puerto Rico (more commonly known as the Commonwealth Office) was the main agency of the Puerto Rican government charged with facilitating migrants' adjustment to their new surroundings on the mainland. Joseph Monserrat, the national director and director of the New York office of the Migration Division, made sure that Puerto Rican speakers at the congressional hearings would support the union. He sent Eddie Gonzalez, a former ILGWU organizer and co-director of the Migration Division, to defend the union. In recent interviews, Monserrat and Gonzalez have revealed the severe constraints on their public responses at the congressional hearings. "I was working for the government," Monserrat claimed. "I was a radical myself. I was for unions, and I wanted my people to know what it was about, but I had to do it in a subtle way." Advocating on behalf of Puerto Rican workers in a "subtle" way meant that Monserrat would pick his battles strategically. In the case of the congressional hearings, he decided that "Hill and Powell had their own agendas," but he would "not complain . . . and just move ahead."[33] More than forty years after the events took place, Monserrat was willing to reveal the fact that his governmental position constrained his stance with the ILGWU leadership, but the bureaucrat who had surreptitiously worked as an advocate of workers still did not fully explain the rationale behind his public defense of the union.

Eddie Gonzalez was more explicit. He knew that there was no "real Puerto Rican leadership" in the ILGWU, but he also "didn't know the A. C. Powell agenda, and didn't think the Puerto Rican community understood it" either. He did not feel the need to give his support to a congressman and a civil rights organization when he and other Puerto Rican leaders were not privy to their political intentions. More important, he revealed how much the Commonwealth Office depended on ILGWU leaders. "The Commonwealth of Puerto Rico was being carefully watched by the unions," Gonzalez testified. "We were walking on egg shells. Monserrat didn't want to say, 'Yes, the ILGWU is racist' because we had a relationship with the ILG[WU] to unionize workers in Puerto Rico. That was the deal."[34] Puerto Rican leaders like Gonzalez and Monserrat could have tried to defend the rights of Puerto Rican workers by attacking ILGWU leaders' racism in public or by appealing to their goodwill through more private negotiations. Given the highly public nature of the congressional investigations and Puerto Ricans' great dependence on the garment industry, they chose the latter.

Puerto Rican workers gave a highly scripted narrative of support to the ILGWU at the congressional hearings, but their hidden transcripts reveal a more accurate expression of grievances. In 1957, Puerto Rican workers brought their case to the Association of Catholic Trade Unionists (ACTU). They had signed collusive contracts with independent unions with criminal elements and locals affiliated with the AFL, and they hoped that ACTU leaders could take their case up with more powerful labor and city officials. In August 1958, Puerto Rican workers at a garment factory in Brooklyn organized an unauthorized stoppage, threatening to get rid of the entire ILGWU leadership. Two months later, 200 Puerto Rican ILGWU members of the Local 132 Plastic, Moulders & Novelty Workers' Union organized another strike. They protested their substandard wages and working conditions, as well as the fact of English being spoken at ILGWU meetings, holding up signs that read "80 percent of our members speak Spanish. A meeting conducted in English is a farce."[35] After they returned to their jobs, they continued to make contacts with various institutions that could give them support, such as the Commonwealth Office of Puerto Rico, the NAACP, Congressman Adam Clayton Powell Jr., and District 65 of the RWDSU.[36] In an individual letter written to Dubinsky in 1960, Puerto Rico's ILGWU Local 600 member Maria Rodriguez also complained about the lack of Puerto Rican leadership in her local. Despite the workers' legal right to choose their own local manager, ILGWU leaders had chosen a non–Spanish-speaking North American to succeed Robert Gladnick as manager of Local 600 in Puerto Rico. "We are entitled to a Puerto Rican leader in our union. This is Puerto Rico, 100% Puerto Rican members, and you must regard us . . . as brainy and capable people here too," Rodriguez claimed.[37] Through wildcat strikes, individual letters, and appeals to various kinds of institutions, Puerto Rican garment workers took measured risks in making their demands known. These were vehicles through which they could make potential gains, but if authorities were to meet their demands with repression, they would not risk jeopardizing the political standing of the entire Puerto Rican community in New York City.

Puerto Rican workers also found creative ways to walk the fine line between confronting and coaxing their union leaders through articles in El Diario and La Prensa. El Diario was the main Spanish-language newspaper in New York City, and it was owned by Roy Chalk, a Cuban American who often adopted a more elite perspective. As the main Spanish newspaper of the city and the most widely read paper among Puerto Ricans, however, it also included wide reportage regarding the garment industry and Puerto Ricans' general employment conditions. Within this venue, Puerto Rican union members expressed their concerns while adopting a highly conciliatory and deferential tone toward their labor leaders. For instance, a 1957 El Diario editorial protested "the lack of Spanish elements in high circles of the ILGWU" and suggested that Dubinsky, Gus Tyler, and others "must examine . . . their conscience." But the editorial also affirmed the ILGWU leadership, stating, "But we are patient—because we know that [ILGWU leaders] are men of good will."[38] Another writer in La Prensa explained the vicious cycle that confined Puerto Ricans to lives of poverty while exonerating labor leaders' role in perpetuating such conditions. "When [the Puerto Rican worker] comes home after a hard day's work, he's tired. His salary does not permit him to live well. During his free time very often he does other jobs or dedicates his time to his children. So he can't rise in union ranks." While revealing the harsh realities of the life of the Puerto Rican worker, the writer did not blame union leaders for maintaining this situation, stating that "this is not a result of discrimination."[39] He blamed low wages on the competitiveness of the garment industry instead. This type of ideological switching reflected the mask of dissimulation that Puerto Rican workers had learned to put on as they made demands based on a highly unequal power structure. Such a nuanced articulation of criticism, however, would not be tolerated at the congressional hearings, where speakers were required to be either for or against the ILGWU leadership.

Puerto Rican Labor Organizing

Puerto Rican migrants did not always operate in such a politically constrained environment. In the 1920s and 1930s, the small group of Puerto Rican migrants residing in New York City had formed several political groups that reflected the working-class backgrounds of the majority of the migrants. Founded in 1922, Alianza Obrera Puertorriqueña created

a forum where Puerto Rican workers could forge links with the Socialist Party. Jesus Colón, who was a founding member of the first New York
Committee of the Puerto Rican Socialist Party, served as the secretary of
the Alianza Obrera in 1922.[40] The Porto Rican Brotherhood of America
(Hermandad Puertorriqueña), founded in 1923, maintained a political
platform that included the working-class interests of the members, a system of mutual assistance and ethnic defense within the city's ethnic politics, the cause of Puerto Rico's independence, and the autonomy of Latin
America in relationship to the United States.[41] Such a broad political platform reflected the multiple class, nation, and anti-imperial critiques that
Puerto Rican workers nurtured among themselves. Puerto Rican *tabaqueros*
(cigar makers), who composed 60 percent of the Puerto Rican migrant
population in New York City in the 1920s, also brought the tradition of
la lectura (the reader) to New York. According to Bernardo Vega, a Puerto
Rican *tabaquero*, cigar makers paid fifteen to twenty-five cents per week to
a reader, who read books by writers such as Zola, Balzac, Hugo, Kropot-
kin, Malatesta, and Karl Marx, while cigar makers rolled tobacco leaves
into cigars.[42] Such organizations had allowed Puerto Rican migrants to
politically organize themselves as workers and as Puerto Ricans throughout much of the first half of the twentieth century.

The "cult of ethnicity" that pervaded New York City political debates
in the 1940s, however, demanded that Puerto Ricans display their ethnicity to demonstrate political unity with other Americans, not dissension.
Within the ILGWU, this discourse dictated that their ethnicity would be
celebrated insofar as it built the union's reputation as a culturally pluralist
organization but was strictly rejected if it created tension between Puerto
Rican unionists and their white leaders. The fact that the union was made
up of people of various ethnicities was a source of pride for ILGWU leaders. For example, the manager of Local 22 Dressmakers' Union, Charles
Zimmerman, argued that "the Spanish workers are just as good, efficient,
and industrious as the former waves of immigrants who have come to New
York in previous generations."[43] The successful ethnic succession of workers indicated the union's role as an equalizer for the city's many immigrant
populations. ILGWU leaders' appreciation for Puerto Ricans' ethnic particularity led them to actively support Puerto Ricans' cultural and social
life. For example, ILGWU leaders offered English classes in locals that had
a heavy concentration of Puerto Ricans beginning in 1949. Lois Gray, extension director of the New York State School of Industrial and Labor Relations at Cornell University, noted that ILGWU leaders catered to Puerto

Ricans' language needs exceptionally well as a union.[44] ILGWU leaders also conducted orientation classes in Spanish and published a Spanish version of their union publication, *Justicia*. They fostered the development of social programs for Puerto Ricans, such as Local 22's Festival Bailable (Grand Dance), which featured "Latin American tunes, Spanish *danzas*, and plain American jazz."[45] They also sponsored tours to Puerto Rico in collaboration with the Commonwealth Office to help bridge the cultural gap between Puerto Ricans and other New Yorkers.[46] These programs reflected ILGWU leaders' sensitivity to the fact that Puerto Ricans made up a specific ethnic group, a people possessing a distinct language and musical traditions.

Nevertheless, ILGWU leaders flatly opposed the formation of Spanish locals within the union. Zimmerman argued that such a local would be a form of "reverse Jim Crow."[47] The ILGWU's Skirtmakers' Union, with a membership that was half Puerto Rican and a quarter Jewish in the late 1950s, was led by four Spanish-speaking business agents—all of whom were Sephardic Jews.[48] ILGWU leaders tacitly justified their desire to maintain a Jewish leadership within an increasingly Puerto Rican union membership by using Sephardic Jews' ability to speak Spanish as a measure of their ability to represent Puerto Ricans. While claiming to uphold a "colorblind meritocracy," ILGWU leaders actually thwarted the development of Puerto Rican leadership in the union. They felt no qualms justifying the lack of black or Puerto Rican leadership in the union by stating that "Negroes and Puerto Ricans are not ready for positions of leadership in the union."[49]

Within such a paternalistic framework, the ILGWU provided enough space for Puerto Rican workers to learn the ABCs of labor organizing but not enough to become leaders with real authority within the union. The path that Frank Perez took exemplifies the experience of many Puerto Ricans in the ILGWU. Perez had been "a little to the left" all his life. His father had fled from Puerto Rico to New York City as a result of his activism as a socialist *independentista* in Santurce in the late 1940s. When Sam Isenberg, a Jewish ILGWU labor organizer, recruited him in 1955 to become an ILGWU organizer, he felt fortunate that he would be able to work with the poor while receiving a decent salary. Perez knew that Isenberg recruited him partially because he was a Puerto Rican, but also because "of my ability to impress people. He saw that right away. I was a natural."[50] His success in recruiting Puerto Rican members into Local 132 led him to be elected as an executive board member of the local. Through Isen-

FIGURE 2.3 ILGWU's Training Institute, June 8, 1960, Frank Perez is standing on the far left; Kathy Andrade is sitting second from the right. (Courtesy of Frank Perez)

berg's recommendation, Perez attended the ILGWU's Training Institute, where he met Kathy Andrade, a Salvadoran organizer who recruited many Puerto Ricans into the union as well. Eager to foster greater democracy within union ranks, Perez also began to collaborate with others in forming a union of organizers, which became known as the Federation of Union Representatives (FOUR).

It was at this juncture that Perez saw the level of bureaucracy and rigidity that shaped the ILGWU's structure of leadership. From the perspective of labor organizers like himself, FOUR reflected the essential spirit of the union itself. Labor organizers felt vulnerable as workers who could be appointed and fired according to the whim of top leaders, and they sought to be recognized as an official union so that they could negotiate with leaders like Dubinsky from a position of power.[51] For example, Perez felt that the number of organizers needed to increase in the union since the number of members was increasing. Yet these decisions were entirely in the hands of Dubinsky and the union's Executive Board. To Perez's dismay, ILGWU top leaders refused to recognize FOUR as a union, even though many other labor unions—the Electrical Workers, the Oil and Chemical Workers, the Newspaper Guild, and the Airline Pilots—had accepted them within their ranks. ILGWU leaders even fired those involved with organizing FOUR.

This was an insult to all of the FOUR organizers.[52] But for Perez, such a forceful use of power confirmed his view that ILGWU would not tolerate the growth of Puerto Rican leadership within the union. He knew that ILGWU leaders saw Puerto Ricans as a people who had "'agile' hands . . . but there was no recognition for the person's mind," Perez believed.[53]

Perez was disappointed with the ILGWU's top leadership, but he took full advantage of the connections he made through ILGWU's Training Institute before leaving the union. Through Martin Forester, an African American organizer he met at the Training Institute, he joined Local 144 of the Hotel Trades Council. Founded in 1950 and led by Peter Ottley, a Grenadian immigrant, Local 144 was much more open to the leadership and empowerment of organizers of color than was ILGWU. Perez worked for Local 144 for more than twenty years, becoming a member of the top executive board before he retired in the 1980s. Although Local 144 was smaller than the ILGWU—it had a membership of 45,000 when Perez retired, compared to ILGWU's membership of 180,000 in the early 1960s—it provided a much more flexible leadership structure for up-and-coming labor leaders of color.[54]

Labor leaders Eddie Gonzalez and Kathy Andrade saw similar limitations within the leadership structure of the ILGWU. Gonzalez worked as an ILGWU organizer from 1955 to 1960. He too attended the Training Institute and found union activity in the ILGWU to be a rewarding experience for a time. He taught literacy classes to Puerto Rican ILGWU members in preparation for voter registration. While working as an ILGWU organizer and co-director at the Office of the Commonwealth at the same time, he used networks from both organizations to educate the Puerto Rican community about broad political issues. In 1960, however, he decided to work full time at the Office of the Commonwealth. When he left the ILGWU, he said he did not leave out of "anger," but it was "the opportunity" offered by the Office of the Commonwealth that pulled him there—he used the extra time to take evening classes at City College of New York, eventually earning a bachelor's degree. Through the education and political skills he gained through the Office of the Commonwealth, he was able to become one of the founding members of the Hispanic Labor Committee in 1969. Kathy Andrade worked as an ILGWU organizer much longer. From 1958 through the 1980s, she worked as the business agent of the predominantly Puerto Rican Local 23-25. She found her career as an ILGWU organizer gratifying, but she too recognized that the ILGWU leadership maintained discriminatory practices against Puerto Ricans.

"[ILGWU leaders] were very open-minded about [Puerto Rican] needs, except they wanted to control everything. They wanted to polish us, offering scholarships."[55]

Puerto Rican labor organizers' experiences in the broader labor movement were not too dissimilar from those in the ILGWU. Puerto Rican members were allowed to participate in union activities but were not given the power to develop their own leadership capacities or to create their own civil rights agenda within union halls. When the director of the Migration Division of the Department of Labor in Puerto Rico, Clarence Senior, suggested in 1954 that a Puerto Rican Labor Committee should be set up similar to the Jewish Labor Committee, AFL leaders opposed such a plan. According to labor scholar Lois Gray, they argued that "separate organizations would divide the labor movement, accent nationality and ethnic differences, and lead to separate unions or power blocks within existing organizations."[56] Due to outside pressure coming from the Migration Division, the ACTU, and Puerto Rican workers themselves, the AFL consented to the formation of the Labor Advisory Committee on Puerto Rican Affairs (LACPRA), but only as a voluntary organization. Testimonies that the ACTU gathered regarding the exploitation of Puerto Rican workers by racketeer unions eventually led to the formation of the Committee to End the Exploitation of Puerto Ricans and Other Minority Groups as an official wing of the AFL in 1959. This committee was much more effective than LACPRA, since its recommendations carried more weight with AFL-affiliated unions and staff representatives included Puerto Ricans themselves. As a result, Paul Sanchez became an important bridge between Puerto Rican leaders and labor spokesmen. Through the active support of Harry Van Arsdale, the business manager of Local 3 of the International Brotherhood of Electrical Workers, Puerto Rican members also formed the Santiago Iglesias Educational Society in 1958. They aimed to directly target the discrimination and exploitation that Puerto Ricans suffered within the electrical industry.[57] Puerto Rican workers certainly benefited from the existence of such organizations. Investigations undertaken by these organizations led to the expulsion of racketeer unions, and Puerto Ricans' membership in legitimate unions led to the improvement of their working conditions and wages. Nevertheless, Puerto Rican labor leaders still faced difficulties in finding a place for themselves at the top levels of union leadership. They also did not have the freedom to craft a civil rights agenda of their own within union halls.

A few labor unions stood apart from this pattern. Leaders from the

Local 1199 of the Drug and Hospital Employees' Union and District 65 of the RWDSU were exceptional in their willingness to support a civil rights agenda in the 1960s.[58] Local 1199 made recruiting workers of color and fostering leadership of people of color a priority to such an extent that Martin Luther King Jr. referred to it as his "favorite union."[59] Gilberto Gerena Valentín's collaboration with District 65 of the RWDSU was by far the most fruitful Puerto Rican–labor alliance in the city of New York. Gerena had worked as a labor organizer with Local 6 of the Hotel and Club Employees' Union since 1947. Although he was suspended from the union for having ties with the Communist Party, he continued to work with labor organizers interested in recruiting Puerto Rican workers—whether they were Communist or not.[60] By 1956, he had organized a vast network of Puerto Rican migrants through El Congreso del Pueblo (Council of Hometown Clubs), which gathered Puerto Rican migrants according to the Puerto Rican towns from which they came. Although the hometown clubs started out simply as gatherings of friends and family interested in providing shelter, jobs, emergency financial aid, and other social benefits, they quickly developed into political units of organizers committed to fighting police brutality, racial discrimination, and labor exploitation.[61] After being elected president of Congreso in 1956, Gerena further expanded the network of Puerto Rican migrants by forming the Puerto Rican Parade Committee the following year. In 1958, this event brought together more than 20,000 Puerto Ricans and 125,000 spectators to celebrate Puerto Rican culture.[62] Gerena became known as one of the most effective grassroots organizers of the Puerto Rican community.

Gerena was able to use his labor connections to mobilize Puerto Rican civil rights leaders. During the 1963 March on Washington, Gerena collaborated with various labor leaders and helped bring more than 2,000 Puerto Ricans to the march. In 1965, Gerena convinced District 65 leaders to use union headquarters at 13 Astor Place to conduct the first meeting of the National Association for Puerto Rican Civil Rights (NAPRCR). With the full support of District 65 president David Livingston, more than 620 Puerto Ricans enrolled to become members of the NAPRCR.[63] Although Gerena had the mere title of being a District 65 labor organizer, he was able to influence the union's top leaders so that District 65 provided a space through which Puerto Rican leaders could develop a civil rights agenda of their own. Using the institutional resources of District 65, Puerto Rican members of NAPRCR had the chance to discuss issues such as police brutality, the housing shortage, and public school education—

issues that were not necessarily related to Puerto Ricans' work conditions but were important to the broader Puerto Rican civil rights agenda. Such a fruitful labor–Puerto Rican civil rights alliance, however, was rare in New York City at this time.

Black and Puerto Rican Workers' Access to Political Power

Given Puerto Rican workers' constraints in mobilizing themselves within the labor movement, the 1962 congressional hearings still beg the question of why black and Puerto Rican leaders' responses differed so much. Did the political and economic structures that governed the lives of black and Puerto Rican workers differ significantly? If so, why?

Despite the bold accusations that NAACP labor secretary Herbert Hill leveled against the union, black labor leaders as a whole did not wield that much more influence within the labor movement than did their Puerto Rican counterparts. A. Philip Randolph's support of the ILGWU during the congressional hearings reflected black workers' overall dependence on white-dominant labor unions. Although Randolph publicly stated that the ILGWU did not practice racial discrimination, in a private letter sent to Dubinsky in September 1962, he criticized Dubinsky for intentionally preventing blacks and Puerto Ricans from taking positions of leadership as business agents or vice presidents in the union. He also felt that Dubinsky did not provide vehicles through which black and Puerto Rican workers could air their grievances within the union.[64] As president of the Negro American Labor Council (NALC) and the Brotherhood of Sleeping Car Porters (BSCP), he was well aware of the working conditions of black garment workers. James Haughton, an NALC organizer, had reported about such matters to Randolph. But Randolph had chosen to make the organizational ties between the NALC and the ILGWU a priority at this critical juncture. According to Haughton, when he brought a group of black garment workers to the office of the BSCP after the congressional hearings, the workers said to Randolph, "Brother Randolph, have you ever worked in the garment industry? Do you know what women have to put up with, the conditions in which we have to work? How could you . . . say that there is no discrimination in the ILGWU?" Randolph did not respond with any justifications to the workers—he was simply "dead quiet." Florence Rice interpreted Randolph's actions by claiming that "sometimes people get attached to people. One way I find that people get attached to people—I ask, who gives the money?"[65]

Rice was correct in her assessment of Randolph's attachment to the ILGWU, but Randolph relied on the union for much more than money. From Randolph's viewpoint, as well as that of many black civil rights leaders, the labor–civil rights alliance was an essential ingredient of the leadership buttressing the civil rights movement. The half million black workers who joined CIO-affiliated unions had created the vanguard of the civil rights leadership in the 1930s and 1940s. Industrial citizenship had fostered a rights consciousness among black workers, catalyzing social changes much more sweeping than those brought by the NAACP's and the National Urban League's (NUL's) prior legal approach. Furthermore, labor-based organizations like the Highlander Folk School in Tennessee had catalyzed the first voter registration drives in the South through citizenship classes. Subsequent civil rights marches and boycotts in the South also relied on the support of labor unions from the North.[66]

Randolph was well aware of labor's long history of racial discrimination against black workers. By 1962, he had been battling against AFL-CIO president George Meany's policy of condoning racist practices within labor unions for decades. Unions such as Local 2 of the Plumbers Union, the Brotherhood of Railway and Steamship Clerks, and the United Brotherhood of Carpenters and Joiners operated segregated locals. More progressive unions like the United Automobile Workers (UAW) had integrated locals, but, like the ILGWU, UAW leaders refused to admit black workers into apprenticeship programs so that they could join the skilled labor forces. Due to the intransigence of white labor leaders, Randolph founded the NALC in 1960, claiming that the "leadership of the AFL-CIO . . . cannot be expected to move voluntarily and seriously to take positive and affirmative action for the elimination of race discrimination unless they are stimulated, prodded, and pressured to do so, both from within and from without."[67] Meany continuously opposed Randolph's efforts, referring to the NALC as an illegitimate organization that fostered "racism in reverse." Despite such a history of conflict, however, Randolph insisted that labor and civil rights leaders find common ground, arguing that their alliance had a "natural basis." Fighting against poverty, wage freezes, racial discrimination, and right-to-work laws were all essentially tied to each other, and he did not believe that either civil rights or labor leaders could succeed without the support of the other.[68] Given the precarious line that Randolph walked as both public ally and critic of labor unions, he made the tactical decision to protect ILGWU's reputation at the congressional hearings.

Just as black and Puerto Rican labor leaders dealt with similar difficulties within labor leadership, their position of power within electoral politics was equally constrained. The Republican Party had paid minimal attention to potential black and Puerto Rican constituencies. The Democratic Party had begun making inroads into earning their votes in the 1930s, but mainly through a patronage system in which votes were exchanged for jobs, with little recognition that the black and Puerto Rican leadership could benefit the Democratic Party itself. From the beginning, black New Yorkers had entered the Democratic Party under a position of subjugation—African American leaders were incorporated into Tammany Hall through a segregated auxiliary called the United Colored Democracy in 1898. Conscious of Tammany Hall's own need to regain their votes in the 1930s, West Indian immigrants had spearheaded efforts to integrate Tammany Hall. These efforts had resulted in a significant increase in the number of black leaders in the Democratic fold, who entered electoral campaigns alongside white candidates on an equal level. Herbert L. Bruce, a native of Barbados, won the election in the 21st Assembly District in 1935 after gaining the Democratic Party nomination. Raymond Jones, a native of St. Thomas, helped William O'Dwyer's 1945 mayoral campaign and became one of the most powerful black Democrats in the city as a result. Bertram Baker, a native of Nevis, became the first black state assemblyman from Brooklyn in 1948. Hulan Jack, born in British Guiana and raised in St. Lucia, became a state assemblyman in 1940 and Manhattan borough president in 1953. Such electoral gains reflected the rising importance of the black vote in New York City, as the black population increased from 4.7 percent to 9.4 percent of the city's population between 1930 and 1950. Yet with a few exceptions—such as Ben Davis and Adam Clayton Powell Jr., who relied on independent constituencies from the left and the black church—the political leadership of most black electoral leaders remained dependent on the support of white Tammany Hall leaders. When Hulan Jack was convicted of obstructing justice and of three city charter violations in 1960, for example, he could do little to protect himself when Tammany leaders chose not to defend him.[69] The position of Puerto Rican politicians sponsored by Tammany leaders, such as East Harlem district leader Antonio Méndez and Bronx state assemblyman Felipe Torres, was similar to that of most African American electoral leaders. Their electoral titles had gained some jobs and a modicum of political connections with city officials but had brought minimal political influence for the Puerto Rican population as a whole.[70]

Despite blacks' and Puerto Ricans' overall dependence on white electoral leadership in the city, however, the forcefulness of the 1962 congressional investigations reflected a change in the political terrain that was sweeping across the United States. Cold War politics created a new moral and political ground in the nation. African Americans and international media brought pressure against America's racial politics. Domestic and international media coverage of the Montgomery bus boycott, the confrontation between Governor Orval Faubus and the National Guard in Little Rock, and the sit-ins taking place at lunch counters all across the South made it virtually impossible for American politicians to continue ignoring the voices of the black electorate. Decolonization movements in various African and Caribbean nations also led many African Americans to believe that political self-determination was possible and feasible in the near future.

In New York City, no one reflected and used the rising importance of the black vote better than Congressman Adam Clayton Powell Jr. Before entering electoral politics, Powell had developed his political radicalism as the assistant minister and business manager of the Abyssinian Church in Harlem in the 1930s. He organized picket lines to demand better health care at Harlem Hospital and jobs for Harlem's homeless and unemployed, and he directed rent strikes and public campaigns to promote the hiring of black workers. From the time he became a Democratic congressman from Harlem's congressional district in 1945, through the mid-1950s, he continued to carry his unrelenting commitment to end racial discrimination into Congress. In 1956, he shocked the white political establishment by outwitting his political opponents in the Democratic Party. Dissatisfied with the party's nomination of Adlai Stevenson for president, he broke ranks with the party and endorsed the Republican Party candidate, Dwight Eisenhower, instead. When Tammany Hall leaders in New York City decided to punish him by denying the party's nomination for reelection to his congressional seat in 1958, Powell made himself a national folk hero by crushing the Tammany-backed candidate, Earl Brown, by a vote of 14,837 to 4,935. Powell's victory represented not only his own personal victory against Tammany Hall chief Carmine DeSapio, but a victory of all black people against white bossism. His campaign aides, led by Raymond Jones, painted Powell's political struggle against Tammany leaders as a racial struggle between African Americans and "plantation" owners and "Uncle Tom Negroes." His electoral victory thus became a source of pride among all African Americans who yearned to see black leaders act independently from the control of white leaders. By the time of the presidential elections of 1960, campaign managers from both the John F. Kennedy and the Lyndon B. Johnson teams courted him, recognizing that Powell's endorsement was essential to capturing the national black vote and the presidential victory as a result. His enormous popularity among black voters, coupled with his seniority in Congress, earned him the chairmanship of the Education and Labor Committee in 1961.[71]

Riding the wave of the black freedom struggle and the growing influence of black voters, Powell took all opportunities that came his way to create an all-out assault on racial discrimination. As chairman of the Education and Labor Committee, he hired Herbert Hill to conduct extensive investigations into discrimination within labor unions. Congressional hearings were held on many other topics as well, such as racial discrimination in the performing arts, on television and radio, and in large advertising agencies.[72] Just as he had not shied away from challenging Tammany Hall leaders, he did not hesitate from publicly humiliating ILGWU, the largest union in the city, in order to further racial equality in the lives of garment workers. Powell's political boldness certainly reflected his maverick personality, but it revealed African Americans' mounting political influence more than anything else. President Harry Truman's adviser Clark Clifford had argued as early as 1948 that the black vote would be an important determinant of presidential elections. By 1960, 90 percent of African Americans residing outside the South were concentrated in ten states—California, New York, Pennsylvania, Massachusetts, New Jersey, Ohio, Michigan, Illinois, Indiana, and Missouri. Since these ten states accounted for 239 of the 537 national electoral votes, winning the black vote became an essential component of winning the presidency.[73] Political journalist Theodore White asserted that "to ignore the Negro vote and Negro insistence on civil rights must either be an act of absolute folly or one of absolute miscalculation."[74] Buoyed by this historic change, Powell felt emboldened enough to confront a powerful union in public.

Powell proved to be an astute politician capable of manipulating various circumstances to his own advantage, but he made a political miscalculation when he assumed that he could be a spokesperson for Puerto Ricans. Despite his many visits to the island and his recent marriage to Yvette Flores Diago, a Puerto Rican woman, Puerto Ricans did not expect him to know much about their history or their political priorities. He had never made efforts to collaborate with Puerto Rican leaders in the city. Powell thus made a fatal error when he decided to take up the issue of Puerto Rico's political status by supporting statehood and the imposition of English as the main language on the island. In February 1962, only six months before the congressional hearings, Powell proposed that instruction in all Puerto Rican schools be conducted in English to ensure "American loyalty" among Puerto Rican children. Powell hoped that his position would reflect his opposition to U.S. colonialism on the island, but his insensitivity to the importance of the Spanish language as a cultural marker for Puerto Ricans made him seem like a nativist and a "carpetbagger." In July 1962, Puerto Rican nationalists attacked Powell's home on the island, throwing rocks and shouting, "Yankee, go home!"[75]

The different responses given by Puerto Rican and black ILGWU members at the congressional hearings thus reflected the distinct economic and political conditions that shaped each group: Puerto Ricans' particular dependence on the garment industry, African Americans' growing political power, and Powell's political disfavor among Puerto Ricans. To the extent that black garment workers and leaders more freely expressed their complaints against union leaders than did their Puerto Rican counterparts, their testimonies reflected the rising significance of the black vote in New York City and the nation. Aside from this fact, however, Puerto Rican and black leaders shared more commonalities than differences in the way they went about solving the problems that plagued each of their constituencies.

In fact, the 1950s and early 1960s marked a pivotal period in which black and Puerto Rican leaders began forging a common ground through which they could build cross-racial alliances. The Communist Party and other left-leaning organizations had initiated black–Puerto Rican coalitions in the 1930s, but more reformist organizations like the New York Urban League (NYUL) and the Commonwealth Office of Puerto Rico began to view black–Puerto Rican unity as a desirable political goal in the 1950s. In 1952, Puerto Rican and black leaders from the Spanish American Youth Bureau, El Diario, La Prensa, the NYUL, and the NAACP organized two conferences, adopting "Negro–Puerto Rican unity" as the main conference themes. Addressing "common problems of discrimination faced by Negro and Puerto Rican citizens in various fields and the need for common action to combat such bias," leaders such as director of the Office of the Commonwealth Joseph Monserrat, president of the Spanish American Youth Bureau Ruperto Ruiz, and Councilman Earl Brown tried to forge a common political agenda for the two groups.[76] NYUL in particular took proactive steps to forge links with Puerto Rican migrants. In 1954, its leaders collaborated with leaders from the Office of the Commonwealth and the ILGWU to organize trips in which New York City officials would visit Puerto Rico, learn about Puerto Rican society and culture, and serve as cultural bridges between New Yorkers and Puerto Ricans.[77] NYUL leaders also set up Urban League branches in East Harlem and the South Bronx with the specific goal of "facilitating the adjustment of Negro and Puerto Rican" migrants. According to the 1955 New York Urban League Annual Report, such efforts were set up because NYUL leaders realized that, although "Negroes and Puerto Ricans . . . both similarly face discrimination in employment, housing and education . . . they were also victims of some serious misunderstandings about one another." NYUL sought to "bring about greater understanding and coordination of activity" between black and Puerto Rican leaders.[78]

Constructions of Black–Puerto Rican Unity and Conflict

As talks of black–Puerto Rican alliances spread, New Yorkers raised questions about cultural compatibilities between the two groups. Some tried to portray African Americans and Puerto Ricans as inimical to and essentially different from one another. Sociologist Shirley Jenkins's 1957 study contended that Puerto Ricans and African Americans harbored much resentment against each other. Several of her Puerto Rican respondents said they believed "American Negro people looked down on them because they are 'foreign,' [they] came from a colony and didn't speak English." Meanwhile, Puerto Rican respondents also revealed their racial stereotypes of African Americans. "They drink too much, they take dope, and they are too aggressive," said several Puerto Rican respondents. According to Jenkins, the topic of Puerto Rican racism raised the most hostile feelings between the two groups. The majority of Puerto Ricans stated that they were not racist because they did not discriminate against African Americans. "The feelings of the Puerto Rican are not against the Negro but against being called Negro because of the way it is used in this country," stated a Puerto Rican union organizer. "The Puerto Rican Negro doesn't feel he is a Negro because to be a Negro is to be a servant and he does not feel he is a servant." Despite Puerto Ricans' claim of innocence, African Americans felt that Puerto Ricans' belief that one could refuse being given the status of "servant" betrayed their ignorance about American race politics. They also felt that Puerto Ricans' refusal to call themselves "Negro" or "colored" betrayed their own racism. "The trouble is that the Puerto Rican regards himself [as] a third race," said an African American respondent. "They won't call themselves colored and we won't call them white." African Americans' resentment toward Puerto Ricans' sense of racial superiority aggravated their sense of competitiveness with them: "We have been here so long, and have so little. The Puerto Rican people move in and get everything." Another black respondent said, "The Negro knows the Puerto Rican has the advantages in the white world, and asks why he should help the Puerto Rican when it is easier for him than for the Negro." Jenkins's study made the relationship between Puerto Ricans and African Americans seem bleak. Notwithstanding the title of her dissertation, "Intergroup Empathy," her findings focused on the two minority groups' racial and nativist prejudices against one another.[79]

Reportage from the *Amsterdam News*, New York's black newspaper, however, contained much more optimistic predictions about African Americans' and Puerto Ricans' ability to coexist. In a 1950 article titled "Harlemites Help Puerto Ricans Battle Slums," reporter Randolph White argued that "much evidence is found in the 'fringe' neighborhoods where Puerto Ricans and American-born Negroes live side by side to support the theory that Harlem is capable of uniting to fight its common enemies." Although the two groups lived in a neighborhood where police brutality went unchecked, landlords failed to make repairs, and garbage piled up in vacant lots, White found that Puerto Ricans and African Americans had the potential to thrive as neighbors. Unlike Jenkins, White found that the two groups held very positive views about each other. "I deliver ice in Puerto Rican houses. I don't have a thing against them. I notice that sometimes Puerto Ricans and Negroes share the same apartments," said a black interviewee. Another black interviewee said, "The Puerto Ricans are the most polite people you would want to meet." Adding to the flurry of positive statements compiled by White, a "dark-skinned Puerto Rican mother" also stated: "I don't object to being called a Negro because I think I understand the difference between the meaning of the term 'Negro' in Puerto Rico and in the United States."[80]

Jenkins's and White's accounts both contained overstatements and false stereotypes. Jenkins's African American respondents exaggerated Puerto Ricans' ability to gain upward mobility through their "whiteness." White's interviewees overestimated the two groups' ability to thrive together simply because they were neighbors. Realizing the difference between the usage of the term *negro* on the island and "Negro" in the United States certainly would not ease tensions between the two groups, as the term carried social stigma in both places. Puerto Rican and African American migrants had as much in common as they had differences. Thus, the two groups could be seen as capable of building a politically unified bloc of minorities or as endlessly fighting against each other, depending on the viewer's perspectives.

Notions of black–Puerto Rican unity or conflict were carefully constructed by different groups of New Yorkers according to their views on the political utilities of cross-racial alliances. Some felt that cross-racial alliances were an extension of black politics and thus argued that any narrative focused on black–Puerto Rican conflict could only be a fabrication of white racists. "If there is anything which the white politician fears more than Negro unity, it is Negro–Puerto Rican unity," claimed a 1960 *Amsterdam News* editorial. The editorial referred to the spate of articles that were featured in the city's newspapers about Puerto Rican leaders' conflict with Manhattan Borough president Hulan Jack. Jack had endorsed black candidate Ivan Michael instead of the Puerto Rican incumbent, Garcia Lopez, for the 14th Assembly District in Harlem. The editorialist claimed that white politicians controlled the press so much that "today we can't pick up a daily paper without reading some story which is slanted toward making Negroes and Puerto Ricans jump at each other's political throat."[81] According to the editorialist, jeopardizing black–Puerto Rican political unity could give whites another tactic through which they could undermine the political potential of people of color.

The editorialist's assessment was not entirely incorrect. White Americans were invested in constructing "black–Puerto Rican conflict" as a natural and inevitable historical fact. In contrast to the editorial in the *Amsterdam News*, the *New York Times*' reporting of the Hulan Jack conflict with Puerto Rican leaders indeed dramatized the story with ominous language. The *New York Times* article claimed that Puerto Rican district leader Antonio Méndez denounced Jack "as an enemy and traitor to the Puerto Ricans" and that other Puerto Rican leaders believed Jack and his colleague Congressman Adam Clayton Powell Jr. "wish[ed] to impose a Negro supremacy in New York City." Puerto Rican leaders were so enraged by this betrayal that they felt this would create "a wave of general antipathy against Negroes solely for being Negroes."[82] Hulan Jack's decision surely disappointed Puerto Rican leaders, but the *New York Times* seemed eager to magnify the significance of this incident, using it to fuel antiblack sentiment among Puerto Rican readers.

Mainstream media also seemed eager to exaggerate the nature of intimate relationships between Puerto Ricans and blacks. The first generation of migrants of color had in fact preferred to date and marry within their racial and ethnic groups. But the media continued to report about Puerto Rican families' opposition to African American male suitors in the 1950s and 1960s, when the second generation of migrants of color had already begun courting across racial and ethnic lines more frequently. "For all the color the Puerto Ricans got in their race, they act strictly like white people about their women," noted Charlie, an African American youth featured in a 1951 *New York* magazine article. Charlie elaborated that "they're Jim Crow just like down South that way. A Puerto Rican girl's family will whip her if she's going out with a colored boy, even if he's three shades lighter than her."[83] A *New York Times* article in 1960 reported on a shooting incident in the Bronx with an opening paragraph that read, "Resentment about Negro girls' dating Puerto Rico boys was said by the police to be the possible reason for a shooting in the Bronx Wednesday."[84] The article gave few details about the confrontation between Carlos Rosario and the off-duty patrolman who killed him during the incident. Instead, the story was centered on the impudence of young men and women of color who dared violate racial boundaries in their intimate engagements. Certain Puerto Rican and African American youth indeed dated secretly against their parents' wishes in the 1950s and 1960s. According to interviews conducted in the first decade of the twenty-first century by Frederick Douglass Opie and Mark Naison, however, many of them interacted more openly with each other as they began attending the same colleges, living in the same public housing complexes, and frequenting the same jazz clubs and theaters in Harlem and the Bronx.[85] Naison claimed that intermarriage between Puerto Ricans and blacks was "quite normal" in neighborhoods as "multiethnic" as the Bronx.

Given the popularity of multiracialism in the period in which the interviews were conducted, it is possible that Opie's and Naison's interviewees exaggerated the normality of Puerto Rican–black intermarriages. Imagining a past in which Puerto Ricans and African Americans effortlessly entered each other's worlds could certainly provide a road map for a future they desired in the twenty-first century. The dramatic contrast between their memories and the accounts of white journalists of the 1950s and 1960s, however, highlights the constructed nature of each narrative. Each group of narrators recounted the version of history that seemed most palatable and believable. For white observers in the postwar era, it was difficult to believe that anybody—even people of color—could associate dark skin tones with notions of desirability.

White Americans possessed an investment in overplaying black–Puerto Rican conflict, but they did not invent it. Puerto Ricans' and African Americans' notions of race did often clash, and these clashes posed real and ongoing challenges for those who sought to build political alliances between the two groups. Puerto Ricans' attempts to escape being racialized as "black" certainly alienated the two groups from one another. According to Piri Thomas's autobiography, *Down These Mean Streets* (1967), Puerto Ricans exaggerated their Spanish accent in order to avoid being associated with African Americans. In his old age, Thomas's father felt shame and guilt about having done so but explained that this was the only way he could find "value" for himself. "I saw the look of white people on me when I was a young man, when I walked into a place where a dark skin wasn't supposed to be," Thomas's father confessed. "I noticed how a cold rejection turned into an indifferent acceptance when they heard my exaggerated accent. I can remember the time when I made my accent heavier, to make me more of a Puerto Rican than the most Puerto Rican there ever was." Thomas's father explained to his son that he felt he had to do so because he was "not a stupid man," and he "wanted a value."[86]

Puerto Ricans' tendency to name their social, cultural, and political organizations "Hispanic" or "Spanish" rather than "Puerto Rican" also suggested that some used "Hispanicity" as a tactic of racial self-elevation. Puerto Rican leaders formed the Spanish-American Youth Bureau in the 1940s to deal with juvenile delinquency among Puerto Rican youth in East Harlem.[87] In 1952, Joseph Monserrat founded the Council of Spanish American Organizations to deal with issues of housing.[88] In 1954, a group of young Puerto Rican social workers interested in community development formed the Hispanic Young Adult Association (HYAA).[89] In 1956, a group of Puerto Rican educators led by Hernan LaFontaine founded the Hispanic Association for Higher Education to foster higher education for Puerto Ricans.[90] Puerto Rican leaders indeed preferred to identify themselves publicly as "Hispanic" rather than "Puerto Rican" for much of the 1950s.

Some New Yorkers interpreted Puerto Ricans' "Hispanic" self-identification as an indication of their desire to be set apart from African Americans. Sociologist C. Wright Mills argued in 1950 that Puerto Ricans strategically used the term "Latino" to "borrow prestige from some larger and more favored minority" because their self-image was "better served as Latinos than as Puertorriqueños."[91] This interpretation was valid in some ways. Prior to the postwar migration of Puerto Ricans, a significant portion of the Hispanic community in New York was composed of a group of intellectuals and middle-class professionals from the Caribbean and Latin America, such as Pedro Henriquez Ureña, Erico Verissimo, and Eduardo Hamuy.[92] Some New Yorkers therefore associated the term "Hispanic" with a small group of elites who were not quite "Anglo-Saxon" but belonged to some form of a "white" group. Jesus Colón, a Puerto Rican migrant, also indicated the vastly different connotations that the terms "Hispanic" and "Puerto Rican" carried in New York City in the 1950s. The mainstream media associated "Puerto Ricans" with criminality, but they associated "Hispanic" or "Spanish" with noteworthy accomplishments. In a 1956 book review published in the Herald Tribune, for example, Louis Agassiz Fuertes, a Puerto Rican professor at Cornell University, was described as a "Spanish-born professor of civil engineering at Cornell" and his Puerto Rican identity was not mentioned at all. "It never fails," Colón lamented. "When the person in question has been involved in any recriminatory act and he happens to be a Puerto Rican, the fact of his country of origin is conspicuously printed. . . . But when the person has done . . . something worthwhile, the papers seem to conveniently forget if he or she is a Puerto Rican."[93]

New Yorkers' association of the term "Hispanic" with an elite "white" class, however, did not mean that all Puerto Rican migrants attached the same meaning to the term. According to Jesus Colón and Bernardo Vega, Puerto Rican and other Hispanic readers of Spanish newspapers in the city shared a hispano identity grounded in a working-class and anti-imperialist sensibility. Gráfico, for example, frequently addressed local problems of housing, crime, civil rights, culture, and the arts related to all Hispanic people, as well as political struggles taking place in Venezuela, Cuba, and Puerto Rico against the forces of U.S. imperialism.[94] Puerto Ricans also shared the world of entertainment with other Hispanics, as they watched the same comedies, melodramas, and musicals produced in Argentina and Mexico. Rhythms such as bomba, plena, aguinaldo, seis, danza y danzón, coming from Puerto Rico, Cuba, Mexico, and Venezuela, also led Puerto Ricans to share cultural affinities with other Hispanics.[95] Puerto Ricans' preference for publicly self-identifying as "Hispanic" in the 1950s therefore may have reflected a political strategy aimed at avoiding racialization, but it may well have also revealed a working-class sensibility that had little to do with the desire to be treated as "white."[96]

Given the many overlapping and clashing experiences that defined black–Puerto Rican relationships in New York City, some New Yorkers acknowledged tensions between the two groups but did not portray them as insurmountable problems. Claude McKay's study of Harlem in 1940 revealed that many conflicts existed between African Americans and other Afro-Caribbeans, such as West Indians and Puerto Ricans. Although he acknowledged that the "Spanish element" presented the most "provocative bloc of people in relation to the Negro group," he claimed that Puerto Ricans' claim to superiority in regard to African Americans was not too different from West Indians' and African Americans' banter about who was better off than the other. "The natives call the West Indians 'monkey-chasers,' and the West Indians call them 'coons' and they fight or laugh over it," but both groups were "subject to the same discriminatory practices as a minority group." The "educated American Negro" could dismiss West Indians as "outsiders," and West Indians could pretend that social conditions for "Negroes" were better on the islands than in Harlem, but both groups suffered from conditions of poverty and low wages. Similarly, the Puerto Rican could try to "escape a little from that stigma which fixes the American Negro in a specific position in the social set-up" by "insisting that he is Puerto Rican and Spanish," but such pretenses did not erase the reality that Puerto Ricans' "avenues of employment are limited, as are the Negroes in the same field."[97] To McKay, Harlem was a "Negro Metropolis" made up of many clashing ethnic groups, but whose experience of racial victimization bound them into a common world. Attempts to exaggerate black–Puerto Rican tensions as insurmountable and inevitable therefore reflected a desire to overstate the "problem" of racial minorities and their "incapacity" to build political power.

Conclusion

The ILGWU provided an important space in which Puerto Rican and African American workers learned about the challenges of organizing politically as people of color in New York City. Although their racial and ethnic differences were celebrated as reflective of the union's "racial democracy," they were not allowed to develop their own political leadership within union halls. According to each group's level of access to political networks of influence, Puerto Rican and black workers protested against their poor working conditions and racialization through different political venues. Ultimately, however, the ILGWU and other labor unions did not serve as vehicles through which Puerto Ricans and African Americans pursued racial equality in the city. With the exception of District 65 and

Local 1199, the highly rigid and bureaucratized nature of unions' leadership structures impeded racial and ethnic minorities' efforts to build a grassroots protest movement through labor unions in the 1960s.

Labor leaders' refusal to adopt civil rights as a political goal of their own represented a missed opportunity for workers across race and ethnicity. It was not simply Puerto Rican and African American workers who were dependent on ILGWU leaders for their economic advancement. The ILGWU itself depended on the cooperation of garment workers of color to retain some form of a garment industry in the city and their own institutional survival in the era of deindustrialization. The 1950s and early 1960s presented the historical conditions under which Puerto Rican and black workers could have joined forces with white labor leaders to fight against automation and industry relocation. But few labor leaders seized such an opportunity. Furthermore, black and Puerto Rican leaders did not develop a joint, coordinated political agenda of their own. Had Congressman Powell's political influence been combined with a well-organized coalition of workers and leaders of color, ILGWU leaders might have been forced to reconcile the discrepancies between their rhetoric and the practice of racial equality more readily. Not all was a waste for labor leaders of color, however. They carried the lessons that they learned from labor unions into spaces in which they gained the freedom to exercise more independent political leadership. They carried with them the basic labor ideology that power emanated from the bottom, not the top. Poor workers, though seemingly possessing little financial and political capital of their own, could change the conditions of their lives if they could simply organize their power collectively. Puerto Rican and black leaders who carried this ideology into social reform organizations in the city would catalyze one of the most vibrant political coalitions of people of color in the 1960s.

CHAPTER THREE

From Social Reform to Political Organizing

Building a New Consciousness of Resistance

When Manny Diaz began working as a teenage supervisor at the Union Settlement Association in East Harlem in the fall of 1953, he found himself at an important crossroads in his political life. A decade earlier, he had been manufacturing radios at Motorola Company and working as a shop steward for the United Electrical Workers. He and other factory workers had successfully pressured their boss to provide better ventilation inside the factory through a work slowdown. They also gained union representation by having a union leader negotiate on their behalf with their boss. Such experiences had taught Diaz that poor workers possessed an enormous power to demand better working conditions, if only they could organize themselves collectively. But he did not remain active in the labor movement for long. Despite labor unions' well-established structures of organizing workers, he found that they did not offer a free space in which Puerto Ricans could effectively express their grievances as racial minorities. After fighting in World War II, he continued his education upon his return home. With a bachelor's degree from City College of New York and a master's degree from Columbia University's School of Social Work, Diaz decided to pursue a career in social work.[1]

In the beginning, it was not clear whether East Harlem's white settlement house leaders and youth would be receptive to Diaz. Union Settlement Association's executive director, William Kirk, had hired him and two other people of color between 1952 and 1954 in order to racially integrate the settlement house. Agnes Louard, an African American woman, began working as the recreation and education director in 1952; Antonia Pantoja, a Puerto Rican woman, was hired to direct the settlement's adult programs in 1954.[2] Kirk hoped that the three leaders of color would help break the racial barrier of the settlement, which had mostly attended to

the needs of the neighborhood's predominant Italian and Jewish populations in the past. Diaz held special potential since he had the right academic credentials, as well as experience as a former member of a Puerto
Rican gang, the Dukes. Kirk had been making efforts to tackle the problem of juvenile delinquency in the neighborhood by organizing interracial
youth activities, but tensions between Italian and Puerto Rican gangs
had prevented Puerto Rican youth from participating in the settlement's
programs.[3]

Two weeks after Diaz was hired, however, it became clear that his presence in the organization would indeed change its racial dynamics and, as
a result, those of the rest of East Harlem. According to Diaz, three members of the Rebels, an Italian gang, had vowed to "get rid of the blacks and
spics before Christmas." Diaz recognized that this was "a power struggle
as to who was this new guy who's taking over our program." After Diaz issued a two-week suspension to gang members for bringing weapons into
the settlement, one of the Rebel leaders, dressed in a "zoot suit, and [with]
a long chain below his knee," came up to him and said, "Don't you live at
1062 Colgate Avenue? Don't you have a wife named Alice? Don't you have
a daughter named Lisa?" Familiar with such intimidation tactics, Diaz responded, "Motherfucker! You'd better pray that my wife and my daughter don't fall down a flight of stairs or get run over by a taxicab . . . but
if anything should happen to them, I'm going after your throat. And it's
you and me." Surprised and perhaps pleased by Diaz's familiarity with his
street language, the Rebel member laughed and said, "Ok, I'll come back
in a couple of weeks." As Diaz explained years later, "That was the point
at which I earned my Master's in Social Work, because I dropped all my
school training, and I went to being a little gangster in the streets of East
Harlem."[4] That was also the point at which the settlement began to effectively bring the neighborhood's black and Puerto Rican residents into its
programs. Together with Louard and Pantoja, Diaz helped transform the
Union Settlement into a space of grassroots political organizing for blacks
and Puerto Ricans. According to Diaz, the settlement leaders' role in catalyzing the development of Puerto Rican political leadership was so important that "if anybody ever writes the history of the development of the
Puerto Rican community in New York City in accurate terms, the [Union]
Settlement . . . would have to play the central role, not in the leadership but
in the facilitation."[5]

This chapter analyzes how New York City's settlement houses and other
social reform organizations brought together Puerto Ricans, blacks, and

whites with various experiences of grassroots organizing in the 1950s through the mid-1960s. They became the first laboratories through which black and Puerto Rican civil rights leaders began to test their ideas about how to combat poverty and racial discrimination through a common political agenda.

As settlement house leaders and civil rights activists began to collaborate, black and Puerto Rican women and youth emerged as important political actors. Women of color in particular embraced a new ethos of "activist mothering." According to sociologist Nancy Naples, "activist mothering" embraces "political activism as a central component of mothering and community caretaking of those who are not part of one's defined household or family."[6] As the challenges of a deteriorating public school system and increasing rates of juvenile delinquency threatened the futures of Puerto Rican and black youth, their mothers seized every opportunity available to demand better life opportunities for them. The War on Poverty and the civil rights movement offered multiple spaces through which mothers of color could organize politically on behalf of their children. Mobilization for Youth, an antidelinquency program that served as a laboratory for future antipoverty programs, galvanized a group of mothers of color on the Lower East Side to demand better schools and housing for their children and families. The school boycott of 1964 emboldened students of color and their mothers to consider "black–Puerto Rican unity" a crucial political tool in the fight for quality public education. New Careers, an antipoverty program that allowed poor people to gain higher-paying jobs while receiving education and training, also offered mothers of color an ability to gain a foothold in the public school system as paraprofessionals.[7] Through these various spaces, Puerto Rican and black mothers fiercely advocated for the rights of their own children, but they also began embracing a broader commitment to build their local communities. Black and Puerto Rican youth also became politicized through education advocacy organizations like the Harlem Youth Opportunities Unlimited (HARYOU) and Aspira (after the Spanish word *aspirar*, "to aspire"). Tired of merely receiving social services from social workers, these youth embraced their racial and ethnic identities as a way of mobilizing themselves politically.

Puerto Ricans who participated in antidelinquency programs and school integration efforts embraced a new consciousness of political resistance. They began to see themselves as a group of culturally and politically marginalized people alongside African Americans. Certainly, Puerto

Ricans' consciousness as a politically distinct group did not entirely originate in the 1960s. They had nurtured a sense of coming from a particular island in the Caribbean since they migrated to the mainland in the late nineteenth century. When Puerto Rican migration accelerated in the postwar era, debates about the "Puerto Rican problem" had led some Puerto Rican leaders to avoid publicizing their identity as "Puerto Rican" too explicitly, lest too much public attention stigmatize them as a poor group of migrants. Even so, the postwar celebration of American cultural pluralism had encouraged Puerto Ricans to distinguish themselves as a separate cultural group. The term "Hispanic" had proved to be a safe and strategic term of self-identification during the 1950s, as it reflected their sensibilities as a Spanish-speaking people but also associated them with a group of Latin American and Caribbean immigrants who were considered to be "semi-white."

What was different in the 1960s, then, was that Puerto Rican activists began to identify more explicitly as "Puerto Rican" and as an "ethnic" group, and such an identity became the basis of their political collaboration with African Americans. It embodied their joint opposition to white supremacy. Adopting an ethnic identity as Puerto Ricans was "crucial for the Puerto Rican community because it coalesced us as a political group. We became a politically conscious group because we began to think about our ethnic identity," argued Hernan LaFontaine, a Puerto Rican educator. He had founded the Hispanic Association for Higher Education in 1956, but he changed the name to the Puerto Rican Educators' Association in 1964. "I consciously changed [the name] from Hispanic to Puerto Rican because this was the revolution of civil rights, a time when race and ethnicity defined who you were," he explained.[8]

Puerto Rican activists also began to increasingly self-identify as "minorities" in the 1960s. The term "minority" had been used in the 1930s and 1940s to refer to various groups of culturally distinct groups in America, including European immigrants. In New York City, Benjamin Franklin High School principal Leonardo Covello had referred to communities living in neighborhoods as varied as the "Little Italys," the "Jewish ghettoes," and the "Negro's Harlem" as "cultural minorities" who were forced to live in overpopulated slums and dilapidated housing and who developed a "feeling of inferiority or of 'not belonging'" in America as a result.[9] But in the 1950s and 1960s, New Yorkers began to use the term "minority" to refer specifically to those who were considered "nonwhite." As European immigrants and their descendants moved to wealthier suburbs, black and Puerto Rican migrants who were left to contend with the city's over-crowded housing and schools were more exclusively referred to as "minorities."[10] Puerto Ricans who were aware of the multiple meanings of "minority" thus used the term cautiously. Those who feared being stigmatized by the term disassociated themselves from it. But the majority of Puerto Rican activists saw tremendous value in attaching themselves to the national black civil rights movement by calling themselves "minorities" who, like African Americans, also suffered from racial discrimination.

Settlement Leaders as Catalysts of Grassroots Mobilization

White social reformers' practices of racial discrimination had not differed significantly from those of white labor leaders until the postwar era. Like labor leaders, settlement leaders had maintained a history of racial hierarchy and segregation. Even as they championed the needs of the "underprivileged" and the "poor" among European immigrants, they had excluded poor black migrants from their services. From their inception in the late nineteenth century through the mid-twentieth century, white settlement leaders had left the fate of poor African American city dwellers in the hands of black churches and missions. In the 1930s, there were a few settlement houses in New York City, Cleveland, and Pittsburgh that welcomed black youth into organized activities, but the majority of such programs were segregated.[11]

Manny Diaz's experiences in labor unions and social reform organizations, however, were emblematic of larger patterns that reflected differences between the two types of institutions. He found that settlement leaders were much more willing to adapt themselves to the demands of leaders of color in the postwar era because they had historically embraced the concept of "indigenous leadership." Since the late nineteenth century, settlement leaders had believed that the leadership of any given community should come from its "indigenous" residents—those who composed the majority population of the neighborhood. They claimed that, although "Anglo-Saxon" middle-class individuals might be more educated and familiar with the functioning of civic institutions, they should act only as catalysts and work toward the development of indigenous leaders among immigrants themselves—no matter how uneducated or poor they might be. Early in the twentieth century, the founder of the American settlement house movement, Jane Addams, argued that active citizen participation was a key component for the building of a "direct democracy." "Unless all men and all classes contribute to a good, we cannot even be sure that it is worth having," she claimed.[12] According to settlement leader Mary Simkhovitch from Greenwich Village, the ethos of settlement houses was "with, not for." She rejected a paternalistic, bureaucratic system of reform in favor of a system that involved the "mass democracy" of neighbors. "If social improvements are to be undertaken by one class on behalf of another, no permanent changes are likely to be effected," she claimed.[13] Reformers like Addams and Simkhovitch believed that indigenous leaders would learn to identify their own problems and collaborate with others in seeking solutions at a collective level. Rather than seeing immigrants as mere recipients of charity, Addams and Simkhovitch also saw them as equal partners who would soon assume their own rights and obligations as citizens and who would train others to practice "good citizenship." Settlement leaders' focus on cross-class cooperation between poor immigrants and middle-class reformers did not preclude the use of class confrontation when necessary. Although Addams had initially held ambivalent views about labor unions, she soon embraced them, viewing them as the best way through which immigrants could "secure a more orderly existence" in their work lives. She often acted as a mediator between strikers and company managers, and she helped secure protective labor legislation in Illinois.[14]

Certainly, Addams's ability to use a combination of conciliatory and confrontational tactics was not reflective of the settlement house leadership across all periods. During the 1920s, social workers' turn toward psychiatry led settlement leaders to attribute immigrants' poverty to an individual's deviance from an imagined norm, while ignoring the broader political economy that had shaped his poverty. When professionals with master's degrees in social work joined the leadership of settlement houses in significant numbers in the 1930s, they replaced the earlier group of settlement leaders who had lived in the neighborhoods that they served. Settlement leaders who identified more closely with their profession as "social workers" than their relationship with immigrants as "neighbors" became more distanced from the poor, whom they now referred to as "clients" and "patients."[15] Such trends meshed well with the national trend toward a consensus ideology in the Cold War era. In the context of the postwar economic boom and America's ideological conflict with the Soviet Union, many Americans came to believe that they lived in a classless society, so that the poor and the rich could solve class conflicts through conciliation and a commitment to serve the "common good." The burden of responsibility, however, was laid heavily on the poor, who were imagined as possessing psychological problems and in need of individual rehabilitation. According to sociologist Richard Cloward, settlement leaders' adoption of such a therapeutic framework made them ineffective advocates for the poor. The poor needed to gain a "heightened awareness of conflicting interests and the means to organize separately," he argued; conciliation would fail to change the broader political and economic structures that fundamentally shaped their poverty conditions.[16]

Cloward's critique certainly indicated the limitations of social reformers who adopted a therapeutic framework exclusively. New York City had its share of reformers with such a mind-set in the 1950s and 1960s. The East Harlem Youth Employment Services (EHYES) in particular had very little understanding of the broader socioeconomic and geopolitical forces that impacted Puerto Rican poverty. Beginning in 1961, the EHYES centered its activities on helping youth "rehabilitate" by teaching them proper methods of filling out an application form, with an emphasis on "grooming, health, and manners in public."[17] Using theories of youth psychology developed by Erik Erikson, the organization tried to "instill the real feelings of responsibility and self-worth" among youth since they believed that youth suffered from "occupational apathy."[18] By setting up a program based on the assumption that East Harlem youth did not have jobs because they did not have the right "attitude," they perpetuated the belief that unemployment was caused by workers' character flaws rather than instabilities of the labor economy.

Most ironically, EHYES revealed its ignorance of Puerto Ricans' political conditions by calling the program "Operation Bootstrap."[19] Despite Luis Muñoz Marín's claim that Operation Bootstrap allowed Puerto Ricans to "lift ourselves by our own bootstraps," the program had left the majority of Puerto Rico's rural population jobless. In fact, the program's failure to economically improve the lives of Puerto Ricans was the main reason why so many Puerto Ricans migrated to the mainland in the first place. Yet, by making Operation Bootstrap a symbol of "self-help" for youth of color in East Harlem, EHYES leaders reinforced the belief that Muñoz Marín had tried to inculcate among Puerto Ricans on the island a decade earlier: that workers could somehow lift themselves out of poverty while the state continued to support the interests of business.

For every social reform group that focused exclusively on individual rehabilitation, however, there were many others that combined it with increased state intervention and grassroots mobilization of leaders of color.

There were several factors that led social reformers in New York City to adopt the mobilization of black and Puerto Rican leaders as an essential component of their neighborhoods' vitality. The postwar celebration of American cultural pluralism led social reformers to view racially integrated neighborhoods as a sign of a healthy democracy. The growing characterization of juvenile delinquency as a "Negro" and "Puerto Rican problem" also demanded that social reformers hire black and Puerto Rican social workers to tackle this urban "epidemic." But, most important, the changing racial demographics of the city demanded that social reformers reverse their prior history of racial exclusion. As black and Puerto Rican migrants replaced white city residents in the 1940s and 1950s, settlement leaders recognized that their viability in the neighborhood depended on their ability to include the new residents of color in their programs.[20] Once settlement leaders adopted blacks and Puerto Ricans as their main constituents, they committed themselves to the development of black and Puerto Rican leadership as one of their main political goals. As it turned out, settlement leaders' traditional philosophy of "indigenous leadership" meshed well with the "participatory democracy" ethos of the New Left and the civil rights movement.

East Harlem was an ideal neighborhood for settlement leaders to develop a black and Puerto Rican leadership in the postwar era. The neighborhood had historically housed various immigrant groups. What had once been a wealthy neighborhood of descendants of Dutch immigrants had become a middle-class and working-class neighborhood of Jewish and Italian immigrants by the 1920s. With the influx of new migrants of color after World War II, there were approximately 80,000 Italian, 80,000 Puerto Rican, and 40,000 African American residents in the neighborhood.[21] With such a distribution of residents, East Harlem settlement leaders felt that they had a great chance to prove to East Harlem and the rest of the world that American racial democracy existed, and that it worked.

The Union Settlement Association and the James Weldon Johnson Community Center (JWJCC) stood out as two institutions that actively championed the mobilization of leaders of color in East Harlem in the 1950s. Leaders from the Union Settlement and JWJCC founded the East Harlem Project (EHP) in 1954 specifically to "catalyze local indigenous leadership" in the neighborhood. "We try not to do the neighborhood's job for it," argued Preston Wilcox, founder of EHP. Rather, "we serve as a catalyst, finding the natural leaders and guiding them in techniques that will help them solve their own problems," he claimed.[22] According to the executive director of JWJCC, Mildred Zucker, "developing leadership . . . and gearing our program towards the better integration of the different ethnic groups within the community" were crucial elements of creating a healthy neighborhood.[23] Placing a high premium on the development of a racially integrated, indigenous leadership, JWJCC leaders created a quota system by which Wilson Houses, a public housing project in East Harlem, would be "one third white, one third colored, and one third Puerto Rican."[24]

William Kirk's leadership reflected the combination of radical and liberal ideas that circulated among settlement leaders at this time. Arguably the most influential settlement leader in East Harlem in the 1950s, Kirk created an unusual balance between old and new, structure and spontaneity, conflict and compromise. Although trained as a Protestant minister, he quickly became more interested in community organizing than spiritual mentoring when he got involved with the Union Settlement in the 1930s. As a white leader, he was exceptional in his desire to empower black and Puerto Rican leadership in the neighborhood. As a settlement house leader, he sought to create changes in the socioeconomic conditions of East Harlem more than prescribe psychoanalytic solutions for the poor. His views on juvenile delinquency aligned closely with those of Saul Alinsky, a community organizer from Chicago. Along with Clifford Shaw and other Chicago-trained sociologists, Alinsky had developed an alternative model of dealing with juvenile delinquency in the 1930s. Rather than viewing it as a problem of psychologically "maladjusted" youth, Alinsky viewed it as reflective of disintegrated neighborhoods. By reestablishing traditional structures of local communities and developing their local autonomy, the youth would regain their foothold within their own environments. According to his co-worker and friend Eugene Sklar, Kirk's embrace of such viewpoints meant that he was often "off on the side" with the rest of the white settlement house leadership in the city. Sklar, who later served as executive director of the Union Settlement Association from 1980 to 1996, attributed Kirk's success as a leader to his willingness to "allow people in the neighborhood to achieve power." His leadership style was reflected in a "little rod iron" on his desk that said, "Come, let us reason together." Although Kirk stood out among settlement leaders in the 1950s, many of them followed his lead in the 1960s.[25]

The Metro North Citizens' Committee demonstrated a mix of reformist and radical ideas similar to those embodied by Kirk. Metro North was an East Harlem neighborhood of seven blocks located north of the Metropolitan Hospital, starting at 99th Street and east of Second Avenue. As more and more public housing projects were built in the neighborhood in the 1950s, and as landlords let buildings rapidly deteriorate, tenants began to organize themselves spontaneously to demand better housing conditions. Pura Rodriguez, a Puerto Rican mother of seven children and resident of the Teper buildings on 100th Street, began organizing tenants in her building in 1961. Soon after, Mildred Ryan, another Puerto Rican woman who had lived all her life in Metro North, also became involved. Although Ryan had "apathetically accepted East Harlem's decay for herself and her four children," she found inspiration through tenants like Rodriguez. Addie Lewis, an African American migrant from Savannah, Georgia, also joined the group. When they officially formed the Metro North Citizens' Committee in 1963, they agreed to share the office, meeting space, and other institutional resources of the East Harlem Protestant Parish. Parish leaders had been working with East Harlemites struggling with slum housing and drug addiction problems since 1947, and they were eager to support the efforts being spearheaded by Metro North tenants.[26]

Metro North certainly adopted a conciliatory method to solve tensions between landlords and tenants. Its members believed that landlords who failed to make repairs in East Harlem's deteriorating buildings were not villains, but victims within a larger bureaucracy of urban renewal. "Some of us think that it is wrong to have landlords at our meeting, that oil and water do not mix," stated Metro North leaders at a meeting in 1964. But they insisted in the landlords' participation in their meetings because "we are using the Democratic way of life, listening to both sides . . . trying to get both sides to an agreement of cooperation in a peaceful manner . . . in order to better this neighborhood." Metro North leaders opposed the Spiegal Act of 1962, which stipulated that state funds, in the form of housing allowances for welfare recipients, be withheld from landlords who flagrantly violated housing codes. Norman Eddy believed that this legislation "crippled" landlords so that they could not make repairs on buildings even if they wanted to, making the situation worse for their tenants.[27] Eddy's fear that the Spiegal Act would "cripple" landlords was misplaced, as landlords who felt financially handicapped by the law simply ended up refusing to rent to welfare recipients.[28] Landlords were not victimized by urban renewal policies in the same way that tenants were, as they often had the upper hand in avoiding the most detrimental impacts of the laws.

Notwithstanding Metro North leaders' emphasis on neighborly cooperation, they were not completely naive about the power structures that fundamentally governed the lives of East Harlem's residents. They understood that the neighborhood's housing conditions had been jeopardized by banks and loan companies that closed off credit to East Harlem's landlords and by City Hall officials who designated East Harlem as a dumping site for public housing. But Metro North leaders did not hesitate to make demands on city officials who had the power to turn things around. They organized rent strikes and demonstrations to bring public attention to their predicament and forced city authorities to act. In the winter of 1963–64, a street funeral for "dead buildings" organized by Metro North members forced the city to take the Teper buildings on 100th Street into receivership. That same year, they were able to move tenants from twenty-one uninhabitable buildings to new locations; demolish nine buildings; force into receivership four buildings when the landlords refused to make repairs; and improve the conditions of ninety-three buildings.[29] This was no small feat, considering the fact that the activities of the better-known rent strike organizer Jesse Gray remained within the realms of publicity events. Gray garnered media attention by organizing events such as the protest against the eviction of a woman confined to a wheelchair. But the Wagner administration often responded to his actions through symbolic gestures, jailing a few landlords in a piecemeal fashion while leaving the overall unequal relationship between tenants and landlords intact.[30] Metro North leaders' negotiations with East Harlem councilman Carlos Ríos and Mayor Robert Wagner in 1964 did lead the city's Rent and Rehabilitation Administration to hire staff members from the neighborhood to conduct surveys of housing conditions and consider their input for housing policies in Metro North. By 1965, Metro North's collaboration with the Kate Maremont Foundation, the Union Settlement Association, St. Lucy's Roman Catholic Church, the Federal Housing and Urban Development Department, and architect William Conklin from Conklin & Rossant led to the construction of Metro North Plaza in 1965. Conklin's design included spot demolition, vest-pocket parks (small urban parks), and no street closures. The inclusion of East Harlem residents in the design process resulted in a plan that improved the housing stock yet preserved the built infrastructure of the tenement streetscape. The final version of the plaza consisted of a reduced version of the original design, but it still represented an alternative to mass demolitions.[31]

Such an accomplishment resulted from leaders who had absorbed parts of the consensus ideology of the postwar era, as well as the ethos of social action of the 1960s. To Metro North leader Mildred Ryan, the organization's success was a by-product of a "minor revolution" that was happening in East Harlem and all over the world. "The minority groups are just tired and they are reaching up and they are talking and they are fighting. They are doing something about themselves," she proudly declared.[32]

Black and Puerto Rican Social Workers:
A New Political Leadership

In the 1950s, activists in East Harlem did not know whether blacks and Puerto Ricans would create a common political agenda. In the fall of 1954, Ella Baker, president of the local branch of the NAACP, launched Parents in Action against Educational Discrimination, a grassroots coalition that aimed to integrate schools in New York City. Empowered by the court decision of *Brown v. Board of Education* in the same year, Baker called on both black and Puerto Rican parents to demand school integration and greater parental participation in the public education system. Even as Baker tried to organize both groups of parents, however, she held doubts about the feasibility of such a coalition. A year before she launched Parents in Action, Baker asked in an NAACP bulletin, "Puerto Ricans—are they and members of other minority groups discriminated against too? What effect is the recent large influx of Puerto Ricans having on the problems faced by the Negro?"[33]

Social workers and educators from JWJCC, the Union Settlement, and the Commission on Intergroup Relations (COIR) became especially puzzled when they launched a voluntary busing program for East Harlem children to schools in Yorkville in 1960 and realized that few Puerto Rican parents were willing to send their children to Yorkville schools, which were mostly white. Although the sending schools from East Harlem were predominantly Puerto Rican, the majority of the children who were bused were black. From P.S. 109, which was 32 percent black and 65 percent Puerto Rican, forty black children and sixteen Puerto Rican children were bused to P.S. 183. From P.S. 121, which was 27 percent black and 71 percent Puerto Rican, eighteen black children and six Puerto Rican children were bused.[34]

Disappointed by Puerto Rican parents' lack of response to busing programs, black social workers blamed Puerto Ricans' "submissive" culture for their lack of enthusiasm. Preston Wilcox, a black social worker and founder of the EHP, noted that "the cultural attitudes of the Puerto Rican and Negro segments toward authority are in direct contradiction to each other. Puerto Ricans tended to be submissive toward authority and thus easily came under the domination of a single leader who did little to de-

FIGURE 3.1 Mothers' meeting organized by the Union Settlement Association, undated. (Union Settlement Association Records, Rare Book & Manuscript Library, Columbia University in the City of New York)

velop their potential. The Negro segment tended to be aggressive toward authority." Patricia Cayo Sexton, a white sociologist who wrote about East Harlem and saw herself as a member of the community, echoed Wilcox's assessment. She claimed that "Puerto Ricans are 'more American than Americans,' and that anything in the United States goes with them; they do not complain."[35]

Many Puerto Ricans themselves interpreted their lack of community involvement as reflective of a "submissive culture." Marta Valle, a young Puerto Rican social worker who began to work with Wilcox at the EHP in 1959, tried to create a parent group among Puerto Rican women, but with little success. After visiting sixteen homes for a Puerto Rican leadership recruitment program, only two Puerto Rican women showed up at the Mothers' Club meeting. Disappointed by the low turnout, Valle concluded that most Puerto Rican mothers had not come, because "Puerto Ricans culturally have a non-questioning attitude toward the school." According to another Puerto Rican education leader, "social protest is just not the Puerto Ricans' style of life. They are far more used to going in with hat in hand and saying please. This is their feudal heritage." To many of these

Puerto Rican observers, Puerto Ricans' "style of life," "attitude," or "heritage" taught them that it is better to respect authority than challenge it.[36]

These were gross generalizations about Puerto Rican and black culture, characteristics that would constantly shift according to the historical circumstances in which certain ideas and actions would surface within each of these communities. Puerto Ricans, who had a rich history of political resistance, simply demonstrated a different set of political priorities from those of black civil rights activists when they hesitated to send their children on busing programs. Black New Yorkers, far from being "naturally aggressive," had undergone their own period of political silencing as their political protest had become severely constrained under McCarthy witch hunts. They had been able to organize successful boycotts and pickets to push for greater inclusion in hiring policies, housing, and education in the 1930s and 1940s. In the 1950s, however, they had been forced to stop engaging in such actions since the "color-blind" philosophy of the Cold War era dictated that workers should be hired based on merit exclusively, regardless of their past experiences with racial discrimination.[37] Black activists themselves did not have a consensus on the desirability of school integration; most black nationalists fiercely opposed it from the outset, and the majority of civil rights activists also rejected it in the late 1960s. But there was no Puerto Rican organization in 1960 that could offer an alternative to busing programs, nor was there any Puerto Rican leader who could effectively defend his compatriots from being caricatured as naturally "passive."

A new generation of black and Puerto Rican leaders learned to contextualize differences in their political priorities as they created independent spaces of political organizing. A group of upwardly mobile and professionally trained social workers, psychologists, and civil rights activists of color acknowledged cultural differences between the two groups but did not consider them as barriers to their collaborative political work. Puerto Rican social workers like Antonia Pantoja, Manny Diaz, Julio Morales, Ted Velez, Maria Canino, Yolanda Sanchez, and Josephine Nieves met black social workers and psychologists like Kenneth B. Clark, Cyril Tyson, Preston Wilcox, and Olivia Frost through settlement houses or the Columbia School of Social Work. Born in the 1910s and 1920s, these black professionals represented a segment of the upwardly mobile group of blacks who sought to combine scientific expertise with political mobilization in order to change the fundamental structures of power in the city. They did not earn salaries equivalent to their white counterparts, but they had greater access to higher education, professional training, and social networks than their parents did. A slightly younger generation of Puerto Rican social workers born in the 1920s through the 1940s formed a similar group of upwardly mobile Puerto Rican professionals. "We formed the Puerto Rican middle class who had grown up in poverty," explained social worker Julio Morales.[38] As authorities within juvenile delinquency debates, black and Puerto Rican social workers gained access to expanding political networks through antipoverty and civil rights initiatives. This new class of black and Puerto Rican professionals opened up a new space for political self-expression.

Black and Puerto Rican social workers were able to use the field of social work as a platform for political organizing because the field itself was in flux. Social workers had incorporated Freudian ego psychology into their practices in the 1920s. This knowledge base had given social workers a scientific means to understand human behavior and a sense of "objectivity" while intervening in the lives of the poor. The fields of psychology and psychiatry, however, went through drastic changes during World War II. The high rate of psychological malfunctioning among soldiers during the war led the federal government to invest heavily in the use of psychotherapy in the military. Military medical practitioners found that a combination of individual psychotherapy, combined with rest, sleep, and food and the maintenance of established social relationships brought remarkable results to soldiers suffering from "combat exhaustion." The success of mental health treatment in the military led the federal government to recommend its use in civilian communities as well.[39] As psychiatrists began to view mental health as a web of environmental conditions and individual malfunctions, they envisioned psychotherapy as a unit within a broader therapy program that could transform not only individuals but entire communities. Social psychologists rose in prominence at the same time. Kenneth Clark brought national attention to the field of social psychology by using psychological studies of black and white children to influence the court's ruling in *Brown v. Board of Education*. His research showed that if one's environment could shape one's mental makeup, then school desegregation could relieve black children from their "feelings of inferiority."[40] Following his example, a new generation of black and Puerto Rican social workers began to use social psychology to tackle juvenile delinquency and economic disparities in New York City.

Antonia Pantoja's early professional and political career exemplifies how social work facilitated the development of a new Puerto Rican leadership. Through a master's degree in social work from Columbia University and two years of social work experience at Union Settlement, Pantoja gained the credentials to join COIR as chief of the Community Relations Department in 1956. The mentorship she received from COIR's African American director, Frank Horne, helped her contextualize her own personal experiences as a dark Puerto Rican woman within the larger history of racism in the United States. She learned about the "history of racism against blacks, Jews and Native Americans" and the institutions that were developed in order to resist racial discrimination, such as the NAACP, the Urban League, the American Jewish Committee, and the Anti-Defamation League. "Even though it may sound incredible," she revealed in her memoir, "it was in those planning meetings [at COIR] that I fully realized and understood that I was a black woman."[41]

Possessing a common sensibility with African Americans as a "black woman," Pantoja became a fierce fighter for Puerto Rican political empowerment. She had helped form the Hispanic Young Adult Association (HYAA) through the support of the Union Settlement in 1954, but HYAA had remained a service- and recreation-oriented institution. When HYAA began to focus its activities on youth organizing, however, participants began engaging in discussions related to the history of Puerto Rico, Puerto Rican children's lack of education, and the discrimination they faced from the larger society. As group members became more conscious of the racial discrimination they faced as "Puerto Rican," they decided to change the name from HYAA to the Puerto Rican Association for Community Affairs (PRACA), demonstrating their stance of resistance against their racialization. In 1957, Pantoja renamed the organization once more, to the Puerto Rican Forum, focusing on the development of Puerto Rican leadership as its main goal. She had learned about Frank Horne's leadership in The Forum, a group of young black professionals from the South dedicated to creating public policies against racism. She sought to develop a similar Puerto Rican group to identify the nature of Puerto Ricans' particular oppression, establish lines of cooperation with other struggling groups, and organize institutions that would help them fight against racism. She set the Puerto Rican Forum's goal as "identifying problems and creating solutions for and by Puerto Ricans."[42] Soon after, in 1961, Pantoja founded Aspira, an education advocacy organization that fostered Puerto Rican youth's political mobilization. Aspira provided a structured space for Puerto Rican high school students to pursue a quality education and address together issues that affected their lives.[43]

FIGURE 3.2 Hispanic Young Adults Association (HYAA) meeting, c. 1954. Antonia Pantoja sits on the far right. Manny Diaz stands on the far left. (Antonia Pantoja Papers, Centro de Estudios Puertorriqueños, Hunter College, CUNY)

Just as Pantoja modeled her political career after Horne's example, Manny Diaz's career as a social worker and political activist was heavily influenced by his black mentor, Kenneth Clark. Clark possessed a broad perspective on issues related to youth of color in New York City. Although he was primarily committed to advocating on behalf of black youth, he also recognized that Puerto Ricans were essential in determining the political destinies of African Americans. His personal upbringing likely influenced such a view. Born in the Panama Canal Zone and raised by Jamaican parents, Clark grew up in a world inhabited by people of African descent spread all across the Caribbean islands. The Panama Canal Zone had brought many workers from the West Indies to the region in the years between 1880 and 1914, and his father was one of them. His father was a supervisor for the United Fruit Company and later chief timekeeper for the Panama Agencies Company and the Grace Steamship Company. By the time his family immigrated to New York City, he was fluent in both Spanish and English. As a bilingual, Clark was known by his Irish and

African American friends as "Spanie."[44] It is likely that his exposure to the world of Afro-descendants beyond the United States led him to adopt a broad view of the political relationship between blacks and Puerto Ricans. Rather than placing the two groups in a hierarchy, he saw them as inter-dependent. At Northside Center for Child Development, a child guidance clinic that he operated with his wife, Mamie Phipps Clark, Clark integrated Puerto Rican children and caseworkers with their black and white counterparts as early as 1949. Under his leadership, psychiatrists at the Northside Center came to believe that it was important to understand how "minority groups" from a "whole range of social and cultural variables" responded to therapy and educational remedial programs.[45] In 1967, soon after he founded the Metropolitan Applied Research Corporation (MARC), a research group designed to advocate for the urban poor, Clark recruited Puerto Rican leaders into the organization. While Puerto Rican leaders applauded him for his willingness to involve himself with the Puerto Rican community, Clark claimed instead that he was being "selfish" for wanting to bring more Puerto Ricans into his organization. He believed that bringing Puerto Rican perspectives to the table would only enhance MARC's effectiveness as a research institution dedicated to serving the needs of the urban poor.[46]

Clark's belief in the interdependence of Puerto Ricans and African Americans significantly influenced Diaz, one of his students. Diaz had already been involved with civil rights work as a member of the NAACP chapter at City College of New York in the 1940s. When he began taking courses from Clark at City College, he realized that he too could take part in the monumental intellectual and social movement that was taking place in the nation. Clark had just become the first tenured black professor at City College, and he was gathering the psychological research that would later provide the scientific knowledge behind the Brown v. Board of Education case. As Diaz later remembered, "Over time, Ken Clark had confidence in me and included me in some of his activities, including getting together with four to five students and Thurgood Marshall when they were preparing the brief that resulted in the elimination of 'separate but equal.'" Through Clark's mentorship, he enrolled in Columbia University's School of Social Work. While he was a student, he met Malcolm X. "I was awestricken, I really was. [I felt] admiration, reverence, all of these things. I was surprised he would even talk to me." At Malcolm X's invitation, Diaz shared a cup of coffee and his own life story. "He was asking me about the Puerto Ricans in New York, and what were our problems, and how do we feel about racism and so forth . . . so we kind of hit it off. I felt more relaxed and more able to share on a friendship basis, not just an awesome figure that happened to walk through my life."[47] Kenneth Clark and Malcolm X left a deep imprint on the formation of ideas and life goals for young Diaz. He learned that Puerto Ricans' and African Americans' political destinies were linked.

Puerto Rican and black social workers who became politically active in the 1950s and 1960s occupied shifting class positions within their communities. Although the majority of them had grown up in poverty, their professional degrees granted them a middle-class status—a privilege that some valued more than others. As a result of their education and professional training, they were given more prominent leadership positions by their white superiors than those given to labor leaders like Frank Perez and Florence Rice from the International Ladies Garment Workers' Union. Although they shared the structuralist viewpoint of most labor leaders of color—they believed that the labor economy fundamentally limited blacks' and Puerto Ricans' ability to gain upward mobility—their familiarity with the therapeutic framework gave them a common language of communication with social reformers and city officials that labor leaders did not have.

Some Puerto Rican activists believed that Puerto Rican social workers' familiarity with the perspectives of white social reformers made them thoroughly middle class. Antonia Pantoja had a particular reputation among her co-ethnics as a middle-class leader. Humberto Cintrón, who worked as a youth counselor at a boys' athletic club in the late 1950s, believed that Aspira, the education advocacy organization that Pantoja founded, worked exclusively with young people who "were going to college" and "were going to succeed already," leaving out "the kids in the streets who didn't have . . . any sense of guidance" and those who "weren't directed in the right ways." Cintrón had focused his community work on steering the latter group of Puerto Rican youth away from gangs through sports—organizing basketball, softball, and football teams for every block in the area where he worked—but did not see Aspira making any efforts to reach out to them.[48]

Certainly, Cintrón's charges against Aspira are somewhat overstated. In the 1950s and 1960s, the majority of Puerto Rican students were advised by their guidance counselors to attend vocational high schools and take up low-paying jobs as secretaries or auto repair mechanics. Aspira reached out to many of these youth and advised them to attend college instead. Irma Olmedo, who served as an Aspira faculty adviser at Central Commercial High School in the 1960s, found that most Puerto Rican students did not even consider applying to college until they joined Aspira high school clubs.[49]

That said, it is likely that Aspira brought together a group of Puerto Rican advisers who had a mixture of working-class and middle-class sensibilities. It is also likely that Aspira, like many other Puerto Rican organizations, experienced a political radicalization, so that its initial middle-class orientation was replaced by a more communitarian outlook by the late 1960s. A 1963 fund-raising letter from Aspira's Board of Directors chairman Francisco Trilla indicates that the organization aimed to encourage youth along a mainstream educational path, viewing individual upward mobility as its main goal. The organization sought to guide Puerto Ricans to "aspire to . . . a first class education" and adopt an "adequate self-image" in their preparation to enter a "complex urban society."[50] A 1969 report, however, reveals that Aspira leaders adopted a much more community-based vision for Puerto Rican youth. "Although we live in an individualistic age," the report stated, "young Puerto Ricans who are guided by Aspira . . . do not study to become wise for their own pride; they do not strive to gain only for themselves. Their gains are for the community; their knowledge will become the means of change for their families and friends." The report rejected an individualistic pathway of upward mobility. It noted that the "upwardly mobile individual struggles upward at the cost of increased anxiety, increased neuroticism, and of lowered self-esteem" since "each move forward seems like a betrayal of family and friends." The cure for this type of anxiety was a "mobility that is for the service of the group rather than simply for the individual."[51] Aspirantes were encouraged to continue supporting the organization after entering college by serving as high school tutors and counselors. Puerto Ricans who aspired to attain a middle-class status could not effectively fight against their racial marginalization on an individual basis unless they engaged in this fight collectively—often with those who were poorer and less educated than they were. Otherwise, the few well-to-do Puerto Ricans would perpetually be stereotyped as the "special" Puerto Rican who defied cultural expectations.

The variability of Puerto Rican social workers' class politics was a source of frustration for some New Yorkers who wanted to draw clear lines between "middle-class" reformers and "working-class" radicals. But to many social workers themselves, the ambiguity of their class politics indicated the malleability of their professional field. According to Julio Morales, many considered Puerto Rican social workers to be "clinicians," but they thought of themselves as "organizers."[52] While their professional degrees gave them access to white reformers who viewed poor people of color through a therapeutic lens, they could use their professional networks to mobilize poor people of color and create a new political leadership of their own.

Building a New Consciousness of Resistance:
The March on Washington and the School Boycott

Manny Diaz took advantage of his profession's flexibility when he joined Mobilization for Youth (MFY) in 1962. Although MFY started out as a settlement house program designed to treat juvenile delinquents through individual counseling, Diaz's collaboration with social workers and labor activists helped transform it into a space of political organizing for Puerto Ricans. The idea for a juvenile delinquency program on the Lower East Side started with a group of leaders at Henry Street Settlement in 1957. According to Henry Street leaders' first proposal, MFY would "bring treatment . . . to the individual youngster who is infected with the social disease of delinquency."[53] Leaders from the National Institute of Mental Health and the Ford Foundation, however, tended to locate the causes of juvenile delinquency in the institutional environment more than the individual poor. Since they had connections to the President's Committee on Juvenile Delinquency and controlled much of the funding that would back MFY, they were able to intercept Henry Street leaders' therapeutic approach. Under their direction, sociologists Richard Cloward and Lloyd Ohlin and others from Columbia University's Research Division in the School of Social Work joined the team and led MFY to take on a more political role. Cloward and Ohlin believed that juvenile delinquency was the result of a "discrepancy between aspiration and opportunity" instead of "psychological and cultural pathologies" and thus called for a "reorganization of slum communities." They wanted to involve parents, school principals, and city officials in a larger social movement meant to change the educational and economic structures of the city so that poor youth would have a better chance at becoming successful adults.[54] A restructuring of the city's civic institutions would result in school authorities being more responsive to the educational needs of black and Puerto Rican students; housing officials providing more adequate housing and less relocation for the city's poor residents; and a labor economy that would provide better-paying jobs for its unskilled labor force. These structural changes would redirect juvenile delinquents' attention away from drugs and crime and facilitate their integration into mainstream American life. Despite the differences of opinion, this group of sociologists, social workers, and public policymakers with wide-ranging views on juvenile delinquency began to work together. Joining other programs from the President's Committee in cities like Philadelphia, Minneapolis, Boston, New Haven, and Cleveland, MFY was launched with a budget of $14 million for a three-year-long experiment beginning in 1962. Although not officially publicized as "poverty" programs, these juvenile delinquency programs became important precursors to the War on Poverty.[55]

Initially, despite MFY leaders' focus on political restructuring, it was not clear that MFY would have any relationship with the broader black freedom struggle sweeping the nation. President's Committee Executive Director David Hackett and Attorney General Robert F. Kennedy had originally selected the Lower East Side as the first testing laboratory for an antipoverty program because it was seen as a neighborhood of European immigrants. According to Herbert Krosney, author of *Beyond Welfare: Poverty in the Supercity* (1966), "The fact that there were whites in the neighborhood made good propaganda and a good public image." Federal policymakers believed it would be easier to sell an antipoverty program in a "white" neighborhood.[56] Clearly, they did not know about Puerto Ricans' particularly ambiguous racial position within this neighborhood that was known to be "semi-white." Puerto Ricans composed 26 percent of the population on the Lower East Side, whereas Jews composed 27 percent and Italians 11 percent. They also did not expect that the majority of the MFY clientele would be composed of those considered to be "nonwhite"— Puerto Ricans at 74 percent and African Americans at 20 percent.[57]

MFY leaders also did not initially know if their clients themselves were interested in engaging in political work. During the first two years of the program, MFY staff workers initiated various employment training, social action, and community development projects to foster leadership among black and Puerto Rican youth, but none of them had sustaining power. Community development programs fizzled out as soon as staff workers left the organization, and the youth left the jobs as soon as they had satisfied their immediate financial needs.[58] MFY staff also ran into additional problems with Puerto Rican youth by assuming that they shared black youth's politics. The Young Adult Action Group, led by three white staff workers and one black worker, managed to sponsor a food drive for Mississippi and a demonstration for passage of civil rights and youth-employment legislation. But the group lost many of its Puerto Rican members once it began to

FIGURE 3.3 Manny Diaz giving a tour to Attorney General Robert F. Kennedy on the Lower East Side, c. 1963 (Courtesy of Andrea Diaz)

emphasize civil rights issues.[59] Lacking a coherent political agenda, MFY looked more like a social services agency than a political group.

Then, in the summer of 1963, Puerto Ricans learned that they could gain significant political advantage by joining African Americans' fight against racial discrimination. Cloward hired Manny Diaz as MFY's director of Community Affairs and Special Projects after meeting him at the Columbia University School of Social Work. Soon after joining the MFY, Diaz received an invitation from Bayard Rustin to bring Puerto Ricans to the March on Washington for Jobs and Freedom. Through his contacts with Puerto Ricans involved in settlement houses and the MFY, as well as his friend Gilberto Gerena Valentín's contacts with Puerto Rican labor leaders and hometown groups, Diaz and Gerena were able to bring more than 2,000 Puerto Ricans to join the march at the nation's capital on August 28, 1963.[60]

Many Puerto Rican leaders believed that this event demonstrated Puerto Ricans' common fate with African Americans as a "minority" group. Celia Vice, president of Puerto Rican Organizations of Brooklyn, claimed that "the problems of colored people are equal to those of Puerto Ricans—for being minorities—and that, by supporting them, Puerto Ricans are helping themselves." Assemblyman Frank Torres echoed Vice's declaration. "The interests of colored people are our interests. Our march received great applauses . . . because they saw in us an example of brotherhood toward all human beings without any racial discrimination." Rather than seeing the marchers' fight against racial discrimination as a foreign idea, these Puerto Rican leaders believed that it represented their own racial struggle.[61]

Manny Diaz took it one step further. He saw the march as emblematic of Puerto Ricans' common struggle with blacks against class exploitation as well. "At the heart of the problem raised by the movement for integration is the question of whether we are a group prepared and ready to identify with the majority group, like middle-class Puerto Ricans do, or with the minority group with special problems," stated Diaz. To Diaz, issues of race and class exploitation were inextricably linked. The civil rights movement represented much more than one racial group's efforts to advance its interests in society. It was a broader social critique that most Puerto Rican workers could identify with. "I work with working-class Puerto Ricans who are ready to march shoulder to shoulder with Negroes and to deal with the same problems of unemployment, lack of opportunities, and discrimination in housing," Diaz concluded. Such an interpretation was not surprising for someone who had worked as a labor organizer in the Electrical Workers' Union in the early 1940s and who saw the importance of labor unions in bringing Puerto Ricans to the march.[62]

At this critical juncture, there were a few Puerto Ricans who did not believe that they could gain anything from participating in the march. Monserrate Flores from Organizaciones Unidas del Bronx argued that going to the march would not be worth the effort because "we don't have as many problems as do Negroes." Others were subtler in distancing themselves from African Americans. They stated that their participation in the march represented their support for an African American movement, not a self-identification with them. Members of Movimiento Pro Independencia, a Puerto Rican nationalist organization, stated that they would go to Washington "to support American Negroes' fight for the recognition of their civil rights."[63]

Despite the voices of such critics, it became clear that the march had had a deep impact upon Puerto Rican participants when they returned home. As one of the directors of MFY, Daniel Kronenfeld, recounted, "As [Puerto Ricans] began to see how the Negro had organized on the East Side and more broadly in the community," they began to "listen to the Negroes because of this collective involvement" and to think that "it was important for Puerto Ricans to do likewise." Between the winter of 1963 and the summer of 1964, a group of thirty to forty Puerto Rican families met regularly to discuss welfare rights, rent strikes, and paraprofessionals' power. The leadership of the group shifted from the original MFY community organizing staff to a number of "articulate Puerto Rican women."[64] The issues that Puerto Rican women raised through MFY at this time—welfare, housing, and jobs—had concerned them long before the summer of 1963. Yet their participation in the march proved to them that social movements of marginalized communities could create political change.

By the end of 1963, a social revolution began to take place on the Lower East Side. Emboldened by the national civil rights movement and the rent strikes being organized by Jesse Gray and activists from the Congress of Racial Equality (CORE) in Harlem, scores of tenant groups emerged in the neighborhood. The New York University CORE chapter convinced ninety-four Puerto Rican and black tenants to withhold rent based on Multiple Dwellings Law violations. This pressure on landlords forced some of them to give up their tenements. The rapid radicalization of tenants led MFY to create its own Legal Services Unit and the Tenement Housing Program. While Legal Services gave free legal advice for tenants undergoing unfair evictions from public housing, the Housing Program collected records of housing violations and enabled them to prosecute the worst landlords. MFY staff and clients alike began to see that public protest and effective use of the law could bring some relief to poor tenants on the Lower East Side.[65]

While the March on Washington catalyzed the political mobilization of Puerto Ricans in the city of New York, the citywide school boycott of 1964 intensified their political relationship with African Americans. Having worked with Diaz and Gerena in organizing the March on Washington, Rustin invited the two leaders to mobilize the Puerto Rican community in a local protest against the city's Board of Education. This action reinforced Puerto Ricans' reputation as a minority group because it was a highly publicized and contentious event that faced opposition even from the most progressive New Yorkers. School integration itself was not an ideal that all black freedom fighters embraced. The NAACP, the Urban League of Greater New York, and a number of grassroots leaders believed that school integration would allow African Americans to achieve greater racial equality, but many black nationalists, including Malcolm X, opposed the effort.[66] Even among those who favored school integration as a political goal, some felt that a boycott was too forceful a method. Brooklyn minister Milton Galamison, Bayard Rustin, the Harlem Parents Committee, and a number of other parent groups believed that only a protracted boycott would create the kind of pressure on the Board of Education that would push it to create a timetable for school integration. But many disagreed. The Urban League did not participate in the boycott because it did not want to be known as a "protest group." Roy Wilkins feared that it could make black children look more delinquent. Even Kenneth Clark, who so deeply believed in racial integration, opposed the school boycott. He believed that schools in black neighborhoods could be improved on their own, and that integration could occur more gradually as black children's academic performance improved.[67]

Despite the stigma attached to engaging in such an act of civil disobedience, Diaz and Gerena decided to participate in the school boycott. Rustin's astute negotiating skills facilitated Puerto Rican leaders' ease in forging this coalition with African American leaders. Although organizing a direct action primarily aimed at advancing the interests of black students, Rustin opened up the boycott to include Puerto Ricans and their particular concerns. He allowed Diaz and Gerena to carefully choose a platform of negotiation with him before entering this coalition. Diaz and Gerena claimed that Puerto Ricans, as the more recent migrant group and as the smaller minority group in the city, possessed much less political clout than blacks. By 1960, blacks composed 14 percent of the city's population; Puerto Ricans made up a little over half of that amount, at 7.9 percent.[68] To assure that this black–Puerto Rican coalition would not repeat the unequal structure of power between whites and people of color and that the Puerto Rican perspective would be adequately heard within the civil rights leadership, Gerena and Diaz demanded that representatives from the two groups have equal voting power within the committee. Gerena claimed, "There are two armies to do battle—one is the black army, one is the Puerto Rican army. . . . Each army should be able to veto any activity of the other army. The two of us should have the same power as the twelve of [you]." To the surprise of Gerena and Diaz, Rustin agreed. "You call the shots, all right, you call the shots. Come on in," he told them. To Diaz, Rustin's decision to grant them such power meant that he was an astute negotiator. "Bayard didn't give a shit as to how we got it, he just wanted us involved. That was the beauty of Bayard—he knew how to negotiate."[69]

Having established a sense of equal footing with black leaders, Diaz and Gerena helped bring together a large number of Puerto Rican parents and students to participate in the citywide school boycott of February 3, 1964. With this direct action, Diaz and Gerena convinced El Diario to use its pages to publicize the boycott. The newspaper ran several articles related to the boycott in the days preceding it. It featured copies of the pamphlets used to recruit parent participation, which read, "Out with Segregated Schools! Out with Inferior Schools! Boycott: Do Not Send Your Children to Schools, Monday, February 3rd. Children Will Attend Freedom Schools."[70] To the surprise of many, the boycott was successful in garnering participation from a large section of the Puerto Rican and black communities in the city. According to the New York Times, more than 464,361 students stayed out of the city's public schools that morning. More than three-fourths of the students from the heavily black-populated neighborhoods of Central Harlem and Washington Heights and the Puerto Rican–dominant neighborhoods of the Lower East Side and East Harlem did not go to school. Many civil rights leaders proudly claimed that this was a day of victory. According to head organizer Bayard Rustin, "More significant than the statistics of [the] protest . . . was the fact that the Negro and Puerto Rican communities had joined together to work for common objectives."[71] By keeping their children from going to school that day, many Puerto Rican parents publicly expressed their support and their own investment in the civil rights cause.

Fighting alongside Blacks, but Not as "Black"

As Puerto Rican civil rights leaders and parents forged a highly publicized coalition with African American leaders, they expressed varying levels of comfort in being so closely associated with the largest and best-known racial minority group in the country. Diaz revealed in a recent interview that some Puerto Ricans told him after the boycott that "he was too close to blacks."[72] They feared that their close relationship with African Americans would lead to their own racialization as "black." In order to avoid such a fate, some Puerto Ricans dichotomized Puerto Ricans as an *ethnic/cultural* group, and African Americans as a *racial* group. While associating "ethnic" with a group of people who simply had a distinct culture and history of their own, they assumed that "racial" referred to particular groups whose marginalization was somehow permanent or natural.

Director of the Office of the Commonwealth Joseph Monserrat expressed such a view. Monserrat was not opposed to the idea of working closely with black leaders entirely. He was a firm supporter of the school boycott, and he believed that Puerto Ricans' participation in such demonstrations would bring a better system of education for them. Yet he insisted on creating a strict distinction between Puerto Ricans as "ethnic" and African Americans as "racial." At the Conference on Integration in New York City Public Schools at Columbia University's Teachers College in 1963, Monserrat argued that, "in discussing the issues of integration in New York City schools, Negroes and Puerto Ricans are referred to constantly almost as if they were one and the same. They are not. Unlike the Negro, we Puerto Ricans are not a race. We are, at most, an ethnic group." Expecting an audience that might wonder at the difference between a "racial" and an "ethnic" group, especially given the significant portion of Puerto Ricans who were dark-skinned and treated as "black" in New York, Monserrat presented a history of Puerto Rican slavery that was drastically different from that of North America. "Puerto Rico was the only area in the Caribbean where the Negro slave did not rebel against his master, for right from the beginning there was a strong movement to free the . . . Negro." Laying aside the contradictions of his statement—a slave society without slave rebellions, a system of subjugation that immediately freed the subject—Monserrat performed intellectual acrobatics in order to portray Puerto Ricans as race-less. To him, African descendants in Puerto Rico had experienced slavery but did not carry its sting. Whatever racial discrimination they had faced was minimal in significance because they were exceptionally successful in combatting it. In another publication put out by the New York City Board of Education, Monserrat portrayed Puerto Ricans as free from any history of oppression. He asserted that "the Puerto Rican, by experience, conditioning, and history is not a member of a minority group. . . . In Puerto Rico, the Puerto Rican in a racial sense has— and has had—all his rights for almost four centuries. . . . The Puerto Rican has possessed what the Negro now is fighting to attain."[73]

Monserrat was clearly drawing on a growing literature of comparative slavery studies between North America and Latin America/Caribbean, a field that exaggerated differences between the two systems in order to support nation-building projects on both sides. As historian Micol Seigel argued, "The contrast between racial harmony in Brazil and purity in the United States helped explain and defend exceptionalisms on both sides."[74] Monserrat hoped to create a notion of Puerto Ricans as an exceptional group of African descendants. Although they shared a history of slavery with African Americans, Puerto Ricans did not bear its marks. Similarly, although they might be segregated into an inferior education alongside African Americans in the twentieth century, they were not racialized by the process. By characterizing African Americans as the exclusive group of people who bore the negative impact of racism and Puerto Ricans as those who were immune from it, Monserrat was helping to make "race" all over again. By the late 1950s, studies commissioned by UNESCO had already undermined the idea of a "racial democracy" in Brazil and other Latin American countries, showing how racism worked even in a society that was more racially fluid than that of the United States.[75] Yet Monserrat still hoped to draw on the myth of Latin American "racial democracy" to differentiate Puerto Ricans from African Americans.

Such a tactic of self-elevation did not go unnoticed by African American New Yorkers. Responding to Monserrat's claim that the Puerto Rican was "not a member of a minority group" and that he "possessed what the Negro now is fighting to attain," a woman named Leila Cromer wrote an editorial in the *Amsterdam News*. "This is not true, the Puerto Rican did not have complete freedom in his homeland for almost four centuries," Cromer asserted. Writing that Puerto Ricans for four centuries "were filled with the same things that the Negroes' centuries were filled with," she argued that "the Puerto Rican, whether he wants to believe it or not, is a member of a minority group in America, as is the Negro." Cromer resented the fact that Monserrat's assertions were not based on an objective analysis of Puerto Rico's history but represented an attempt to instill the notion that Puerto Ricans are "better than the Negro."[76]

Not all efforts to distinguish Puerto Ricans from African Americans stemmed from a desire for self-elevation, however. Some Puerto Ricans believed that they needed to simply maintain their cultural distinctiveness while forging political coalitions with blacks. During the week preceding the boycott, Puerto Rican leaders formed the Puerto Rican Parent-Teacher Association and the National Association for Puerto Rican Civil Rights (NAPRCR) specifically to ensure that Puerto Rican leaders would speak for themselves. "It should be made clear that in supporting Dr. Galamison's boycott we are not giving him nor his group nor any other non–Puerto Rican association, the right to speak in the name of our community," stated members of the Puerto Rican Parent-Teacher Association in an *El Diario* editorial. "We will speak for ourselves," they insisted. According to *El Diario* journalist Luisa Quintero, the NAPRCR was also formed to create a "pressure group" similar to those of "other nationalities, such as those that the Negro race has with the NAACP."[77] Many Puerto Ricans who participated in the boycott also used a different language from that of black civil rights leaders to explain their motivations and goals. According to Quintero, they preferred to use the word "liberty" rather than "integration" as a goal because they believed that "there was something much more profound than placing a white child next to a Negro child." To them, racial integration was not a panacea for all the problems affecting Puerto Rican children's education.[78]

Puerto Ricans' determination to establish separate Puerto Rican organizations may also have been a response to African American leaders' tendency to stress black–Puerto Rican "sameness" in order to highlight their political unity. When referring to a speech made by Yolanda Sanchez at the Puerto Rican Association for Community Affairs Conference in the weeks following the school boycott, an *Amsterdam News* journalist noted that "what she said sounded like it came from the mouths of Negro parents in Harlem, South Bronx, and Bedford-Stuyvesant." Sanchez had simply made references to the importance of quality education for a better future, yet the writer was eager to note Sanchez's similarity to black parents. The *Amsterdam News*' reportage of the Puerto Rican march for better schools, organized a month after the February boycott, also ignored the reasons why Puerto Rican leaders organized a separate march in the first place. "There is no split in our civil rights forces. We of the National Association for Puerto Rican Civil Rights fully support Rev. Galamison," stated Irma Vidal Santaella of NAPRCR, according to the newspaper article. Without explaining why some even thought Puerto Ricans opposed Galamison, Santaella was simply quoted as saying, "United we stand. Divided we fall. We refuse to be divided." *Amsterdam News* journalists seemed to be so concerned about creating an image of political unity between blacks and Puerto Ricans that they refused to acknowledge any difference of opinion between the two groups.[79]

Most Puerto Rican leaders, however, hoped to build political unity with black leaders while maintaining their own cultural distinctiveness. They believed it was possible to create a unified coalition that still acknowledged differences of opinion among its many parts. Manny Diaz and his colleague Roland Cintrón put forth such a proposal in a meeting with members of the city's Board of Education in January 1964. They echoed Monserrat's argument that Puerto Ricans had a distinct history and culture. Emphasizing the fact that there were "special and unique dimensions to the solution of problems which affect the Puerto Rican in his pursuit of full education," Diaz and Cintrón argued that the Puerto Rican should no longer be viewed as "a buried statistical appendage to the Negro." As representatives of a Spanish-speaking group, they felt that the teaching of the Spanish language should be an important pedagogical tool "to improve the self-image of the Puerto Rican child." They also felt that an improvement of local schools would be preferable to busing children to schools located in white neighborhoods because Puerto Ricans were already "wholly integrated racially." Voluntary busing programs were "hardening" the segregation of poor quality schools, and their voluntary nature rendered them ineffective in changing the school system overall. In addition, they called for a reorganization of vocational high schools, better teachers, and greater involvement of Puerto Rican parents in the school system as part of an overall effort to provide quality education. While stating the particular interests of Puerto Rican educators, however, Diaz and Cintrón did not draw hard lines between their goals and those of black educators. They acknowledged that some "Puerto Ricans are identified as Negro through their dark skins" and that "segregation of Puerto Ricans exists"—even though some of their compatriots "question[ed]" this premise. Thus, they believed in the need for "integrated education" *and* "quality education." Racial integration was not their only educational goal, but neither was it irrelevant to their goals. While cultural and racial differences existed between Puerto Ricans and African Americans, they did not need to be overstated.[80]

In the preamble of the NAPRCR, Gilberto Gerena Valentín eloquently stated the tenuous balance that Puerto Rican civil rights leaders sought to strike as partners of black civil rights leaders. While fighting alongside blacks, they would not be mistaken as "black." This was not a tactic of cultural self-elevation but of cultural integrity:

We, the Puerto Rican people, in our way of life, do not practice separation of race either by law, by custom, by tradition or by desire. Notwithstanding this and suspectedly because of this, in the nomenclature of race relations on the Continent, we are designated neither White nor Negro, but a special group denominated Puerto Ricans. This objectivity, aggravated by our distinctiveness of culture has made us the victims of the same type of discrimination and social persecution that is visited upon the Negro group of this Country. The result has been to make us more conscious of the justice and righteousness of the cause of the Negro in America today. We, therefore, feel impelled to identify ourselves with the Negro's struggle and lend him our support, while at the same time conserving our own cultural integrity and our own way of life. We, therefore, launch ourselves into the arena of today's struggles for a full and complete education alongside the Negro with the full knowledge that, by so doing, we are advancing our own cause.[81]

Diaz's and Gerena's hard work in delineating Puerto Ricans' specific stance toward the black civil rights leadership paid off. Although they could not influence the rhetoric of all blacks in the city, they could shape the practices of those that they worked with closely. While preparing for the school boycott with Rustin and Galamison, Diaz and Gerena were able to include the teaching of Puerto Rican history in the freedom schools that replaced the regular classrooms. Along with lessons on Harriet Tubman, Sojourner Truth, and Frederick Douglass, New York children who attended freedom schools on February 3 were able to learn about Ramón Emeterio Betances, Eugenia María de Hostos, and the work of many others who fought for Puerto Rican independence. The teaching guide put together by the Harlem Parents Committee paid special attention to the similarities between Puerto Rican and African American history and literature—the Spanish Abolitionist Society's newspaper El Abolicionista was compared to Frederick Douglass's "North Star," and the poetry of Luis Palés Matos was compared to that of Langston Hughes. Puerto Rican culture, however, was presented as having merits of its own, with its "own heroes," who provided modern-day Puerto Ricans with the ability to "develop our own courage for our own battles in this present day."[82] The teaching of Puerto Rican history at these freedom schools indicated that if leaders of color took the time to listen to each other, they could create a political movement that respected each other's distinct histories and cultures.

The Politicization of Puerto Rican Mothers and Youth

Direct action catalyzed by school integration and antidelinquency programs had a tremendous impact in bringing youth and women into the center of Puerto Rican political leadership. Previous generations of Puerto

Rican leaders in New York City had been dominated by men. From labor leaders like Bernardo Vega, Jesus Colón, Gilberto Gerena Valentín, and Frank Perez to electoral leaders like Carlos Tapia, Oscar García Rivera, Carlos Ríos, Antonio Méndez, and Felipe Torres, Puerto Rican men had controlled the city's Puerto Rican politics in the first half of the twentieth century. Lola Rodríguez de Tío and Luisa Capetillo had organized groups of women tobacco workers and feminists in the early part of the century, but they were the exception to the rule.[83] More Puerto Rican women, such as Antonia Pantoja, Marta Valle, and Yolanda Sanchez, began to engage in the political process through the field of social work in the 1950s. But MFY and the school boycott led massive numbers of Puerto Rican women, many of whom had previously seen themselves as apolitical, to begin seeing their power as political actors. Mothers from the Lower East Side had already started to hold regular meetings following the March on Washington, but they felt even more emboldened by the school boycott. In late February 1964, they began to make specific demands to school principals and administrators after the boycott. Mothers from the Council of Puerto Rican Organizations and Puertorriqueños Unidos demanded that the assistant superintendent of schools on the Lower East Side resign. Mobilization for Mothers also demanded that PTA meetings be held in English and new textbooks be purchased and that teachers and school administrators learn to be more sensitive to the needs of Spanish-speaking people.[84] Instead of seeing themselves merely as recipients of social services, these Puerto Rican women began to assert their own voices within their neighborhood's political structures.

The Puerto Rican Association for Community Affairs (PRACA) and Aspira also became important spaces in which Puerto Rican youth began developing a new political consciousness of resistance. PRACA was a youth organization developed by the Hispanic Young Adults Association (HYAA) in 1957. As students involved with PRACA began to take more pride in their ethnic identity as "Puerto Rican," they also began to consider it an important tool in unifying Puerto Ricans into a cohesive political group. A speech by Julio Morales during a 1963 Puerto Rican Youth Conference titled "A Question of Identity" illustrates this transformation. Prior to his involvement with PRACA, he confessed that he "had accepted the stereotyped ideas that non–Puerto Rican New Yorkers had of us. . . . When I saw Puerto Ricans yelling in the subways or drunks in the streets . . . I felt ashamed and humiliated . . . and I had seen myself as an exception." At a time when Puerto Ricans were described by city newspapers as "the Puerto

Rican problem," Morales had disassociated himself from them. After meeting Puerto Rican doctors, lawyers, and teachers at PRACA conferences, however, Morales realized that, by rejecting his Puerto Rican roots, he had "rejected [him]self." Morales began to encourage his fellow Puerto Rican youth to nurture their Puerto Rican identity instead. "Let us keep our language and our traditions, let us keep our heritage alive—let us not lose our identity," exhorted Morales.[85] With such an ethnic orientation, Morales became a fierce advocate of Puerto Ricans' education and tenant rights throughout the 1960s.

Founded in 1961, Aspira helped spread a similar kind of cultural self-determination among Puerto Rican youth. The president of Aspira, Antonia Pantoja, shaped much of the pedagogy and politics embedded in its programs. She envisioned a youth leadership training program in which Puerto Rican youth would be exposed to a variety of models of social action, such as those developed by black and Jewish leaders from the NAACP, Harlem Youth Opportunities Unlimited (HARYOU), and Hillel. She particularly relied on HARYOU as a model for Aspira programming. HARYOU leaders used an ethos of "culture building" rather than "problem solving" to train black youth leaders. Tired of white social workers' tendency to view black youth as "problems" to be solved, HARYOU leaders Kenneth Clark, Kenneth Marshall, Cyril Tyson, and James Jones developed a program in which Harlem youth would create a "community of excellence" through their own strengths and cultural assets. Instead of seeking individual assimilation into the broader society, black youth would invest in building their own communities. Pantoja applied this "culture-building" pedagogy to galvanize Puerto Rican youth leadership as well. She helped Aspira leaders rediscover Puerto Rican history by naming Aspira clubs after famous figures and places on the island. One club, for example, named itself "Areyto," a native Borinquen Indian word that referred to the ceremony in which tribe leaders imparted knowledge of their ancestors to the youth.[86] Through such practices, Puerto Rican youth created a new identity and vision for themselves. The similarities between Aspira and HARYOU youth programs brought Pantoja criticism from her compatriots. Many argued that Aspira segregated Puerto Rican youth and suggested that their children did not need a distinctly "Puerto Rican" organization in order to adjust to the city. Despite such criticism, however, Aspira clubs mushroomed rapidly throughout the city. By 1964, they had spread to more than thirteen high schools.[87]

With the school boycott, Aspira critics realized that they could not turn back the tide of the Puerto Rican civil rights revolution. At the Sixth Annual Puerto Rican Youth Conference organized by PRACA in February 1964, more than 300 Puerto Rican high school and college students gathered to map out their vision for the future of their communities. Impressed with the organizational capacities of black civil rights leaders demonstrated at the school boycott, Puerto Rican youth came to believe that creating a robust Puerto Rican civil rights agenda should be an important part of developing Puerto Ricans' own political leadership in the city. "We of this generation will not repeat the mistakes of our parents," stated Benjamin Franklin High School student Efrain Velez. "We know the rights that Negroes are demanding should have been theirs from birth." For the skeptics who were "reluctant to jump into New York City's civil rights fight," Velez argued that Puerto Ricans' investment in the civil rights movement should be based on a "selfish point of view." "A chain is as strong as its weakest link. If Negroes go down in defeat, we Puerto Ricans will be next," he asserted. Puerto Rican youth began to see that if they could follow the black model and organize themselves into a coherent political unit, they could change their communities and the city's racial politics. Seeking to become "united . . . like the Negroes," Puerto Rican youth began taking bolder steps in imagining their role in the creation of a new political landscape in New York.[88]

Conclusion

Puerto Rican and black migrants in New York started out working with white social reformers in the 1950s as clients of social services. They were seen as "juvenile delinquents" and individuals with moral and psychological problems who simply needed to be fixed. Puerto Rican and black clients, however, used institutional spaces provided by white social workers to pursue their own political goals. Capturing settlement leaders' historic ethos of "indigenous leadership," leaders of color called for greater Puerto Rican and black leadership in East Harlem. While being trained in social work at the moment of the field's intellectual shift from psychoanalytic methods to social action, black and Puerto Rican social workers used their professional networks to strategize the reorganization of their communities.

Puerto Rican mothers and youth who became acquainted with U.S. racial politics through juvenile delinquency and school integration debates experienced a profound political transformation. While still harboring reservations about embracing a black protest model too closely, they saw that constructing a Puerto Rican ethnic identity similar to African Americans' racial identity could give them an effective political tool to fight against racial subjugation. No longer did parents of color simply sit back as their children were tossed from one "special school" to another narcotics program. They questioned school principals and administrators, demanding that they rehabilitate their schools before asking students of color to change their individual habits. By organizing marches and school boycotts, they began to see that a black–Puerto Rican coalition could create an alternative model of democracy in New York City.

CHAPTER FOUR

If You Have a Black Numero Uno, Let's Have a Puerto Rican Numero Dos

Building Puerto Rican and Black Political Power through the War on Poverty

When Gloria Quiñones finished her undergraduate studies at Fordham University in 1965, she was simply looking for a job. The daughter of a garment worker, Quiñones had had a few experiences with community work as an Aspira member and as a participant in a voter registration drive with Mobilization for Youth, but she was otherwise unaccustomed to the work of community organizing. Little did she know that her first job would change her life. As a twenty-one-year-old, she applied to work as a "community stimulator" in the Massive Economic Neighborhood Development (MEND) in East Harlem. New York City's Council against Poverty had recently designated MEND as the main organization that would coordinate antipoverty programs in East Harlem. According to MEND executive director Humberto Cintrón, Quiñones got the job despite her young age because she said the magic words he was looking for: "I want to help my people." That was the spirit he was looking for, and she had it.[1]

Working as a director of a MEND subcommunity proved to be a transformative experience for Quiñones. "It made a total difference in my choices," claimed Quiñones, recollecting her experiences decades later. Not only did she earn a good salary—$9,600 a year as a starting salary— but she was able to lead a whole "army" of leaders committed to rebuilding El Barrio. Together with ten other "community stimulators" and her assistant, Willie Soto, Quiñones led the Aguilar subcommunity, which encompassed the area between 106th Street and 116th Street and Third Avenue and Park Avenue. She and other Aguilar residents learned how to use the legal system to secure their rights as tenants. "We learned how to call HPD [Housing Preservation and Development] to get code enforcement, to get the apartment repairs. We learned about rent strikes, gave tenants advice on that, pending the arrival of legal services. . . . It was a matter of people learning their rights," she recounted. Quiñones found it exhilarating to participate in the War on Poverty. "I loved the idea of maximum feasible participation of the poor. When I went out there, I was like a firebrand, we're going to rule this area!" Leading a neighborhood that was predominantly Puerto Rican but also home to African Americans, Quiñones was certainly conscious of tensions that existed between political leaders of the two groups. On the ground, however, she believed that antipoverty organizations created more solidarity than divisions between African Americans and Puerto Ricans. "Internally, in our own subcommunity, there was a lot of solidarity. We spent a lot of time together, went to each other's houses. We could talk about the differences and the clashes. It was fabulous," she affirmed.[2]

Executive Director Humberto Cintrón believed that MEND's success stemmed from its leaders' commitment to creating a racially representative leadership. While fostering solidarity among Puerto Ricans and African Americans in East Harlem, MEND leaders did not ignore the importance of creating a leadership that would represent each of the two groups. When Cintrón applied to become MEND's executive director, he suggested that he should co-direct it with Berlin Kelly, a black consultant. "We knew that the blacks would be happy because Butch [Berlin] was there, and the Puerto Ricans would be happy because I was there," noted Cintrón. Cintrón and Kelly believed that their ability to collaborate with each other at the leadership level while simultaneously developing race-specific constituencies would encourage the rest of East Harlem to engage in cross-racial work. "We dispelled that whole myth that people couldn't work together and that each other had his own turf," asserted Cintrón. "If you have similar goals, and you know what it is you want, then you talk to the other person about your passion, and you find out that you have more in common than you have that separates you." To Cintrón and other MEND leaders, developing race-specific leadership and fostering cross-racial organizing went hand in hand.[3]

Building off of the momentum created by the March on Washington and the 1964 school boycott, Puerto Rican leaders who became involved in antipoverty programs solidified their political alliance and self-identification with African American leaders. As they expanded their earlier neighborhood-based work to citywide programs funded by the federal, state, and municipal governments, their resolve to fight for racial equity together deepened. This chapter expands the War on Poverty literature by focusing on the multiracial collaborations that undergirded antipoverty operations in New York City. War on Poverty studies of black/Latino interactions have thus far focused on the federal program's impact in fostering race essentialism and conflict.[4] According to historian Brian Behnken, "Blacks and Chicanos did appreciate each other's cultural nationalism," but "separatism frustrated attempts at unity because, quite simply, separation *separated* blacks and Chicanos."[5] The operation of the War on Poverty in New York City reveals a very different story. Not only did black and Puerto Rican leaders appreciate each other's nationalism, but they also actively facilitated it. Black New Yorkers used the War on Poverty to mobilize their own communities *and* to facilitate the mobilization of Puerto Ricans. As the numerically larger and better-known minority group, African Americans knew that they had certain advantages over Puerto Ricans, such as more established political networks. They thus shared their resources with Puerto Ricans and encouraged the development of Puerto Ricans' political independence. Puerto Ricans, though still wrestling with questions about their racial and ethnic identities, eagerly followed the black model of fighting against poverty and racial inequity through antipoverty infrastructures. Ultimately, the implementation of Black Power ideals in antipoverty programs liberated the political imaginations of not only African Americans—as documented by historians like Rhonda Williams, Annelise Orleck, and Felicia Kornbluh—but also other people of color.[6] Black and Puerto Rican nationalism developed as two intertwined and mutually dependent political movements.

Puerto Ricans' and African Americans' collaborations in War on Poverty programs were not based solely on a mutual desire to gain federal monies. Puerto Ricans did not, as commonly imagined, adopt black political tactics as "outsiders" only after they became attached to material rewards. They shared a long history of collaboration with African Americans, which dated back to the independence movements of Puerto Rico and Cuba in the late nineteenth century and intensified through the Harlem Renaissance in the 1920s and 1930s and the settlement house and parent networks forged in the 1950s and early 1960s.[7] By the time President Johnson announced the Great Society programs in 1964, Puerto Ricans and African Americans had already developed a common political identity as minorities committed to fighting against racial injustice. Puerto Rican activists also did not stop working closely with African American activists when the War on Poverty coalition crumbled. Having experienced similar frustrations with the limitations and inefficacy of antipoverty programs together, the two groups forged the community control movement to pursue their political goals more independently from white antipoverty leaders. Calling for race-specific, locally grounded leadership, Puerto Rican and black community control leaders inspired their constituents to use their own local resources and their sense of cultural pride to rebuild their schools and neighborhoods. In the late 1960s, black and Puerto Rican nationalism did feed political patronage systems that increasingly pitted the two groups against each other, but its earliest manifestations in the period from 1964 to 1968 came in the form of much more decentralized and cross-racial political mobilizations.

The next two chapters chronicle the development of antipoverty and community control programs in two neighborhoods in New York City from the mid-1960s through the early 1970s. The stories that took place in East Harlem and the South Bronx are highlighted in these chapters because they demonstrated the highest level of engagement between African Americans and Puerto Ricans, who dominated the local population in both places.[8] In 1960, East Harlem was approximately 39 percent Puerto Rican and 32 percent black and the South Bronx was 39 percent Puerto Rican and 16 percent black.[9] By 1970, the numbers had grown to 44 percent Puerto Rican and 34 percent black in East Harlem, and 51 percent Puerto Rican and 29 percent black in the South Bronx. Since New York City as a whole was 11 percent Puerto Rican and 21 percent black in 1970, these two neighborhoods had the highest concentrations of the two minority groups in the city, giving them higher chances to control local resources.[10]

Beyond "Messenger Boys and Girls":
Establishing Representative Antipoverty Leadership

The federal mandate of the War on Poverty was simple and clear: first, to reduce poverty, and second, to do so by increasing poor people's participation in American democracy. Leading a country that had just arisen as a global superpower in the Cold War era, President Johnson promised to prove the strength of both American capitalism and American democracy through the War on Poverty. There were a number of economic policies that Johnson inherited from the Kennedy administration that continued to disadvantage poor American workers. Wage-price guideposts continued to stifle labor unions, the liberalization of depreciation allowances privileged rich investors, and the relocation of U.S. factories to overseas plants daily increased unemployment rates.[11] Yet Johnson promised that poor Americans would still rise out of poverty by providing them with resources that would help them self-rehabilitate. "Our fight against poverty will be an investment in the most valuable of our resources—the skills and strengths of our people," claimed Johnson in a speech in 1964. "We are not content to accept the endless growth of relief rolls or welfare rolls. We want to offer the forgotten fifth of our people opportunity, not doles," Johnson declared.[12] "Opportunity" would mainly be given to the poor through the Community Action Program (CAP). Of all the antipoverty programs, CAP held the most promise to restructure the lives of poor Americans because it called for including their voices in the formulation of federal, state, and local programs designed for them.[13] According to the Economic Opportunity Act of 1964, CAPs would be "developed, conducted, and administered with the maximum feasible participation of residents of the area and members of the groups involved."[14] The Johnson administration envisioned that a vital part of poor people's self-rehabilitation would involve their self-organization into established antipoverty organizations. It was an ideal program for federal policymakers who sought to establish their legitimacy on both economic and moral grounds. It also reflected the consensus ideology that dominated white liberalism in the postwar era, which posited that government structures were open, democratic, and responsive to all citizens, regardless of their class positions.[15]

The implementation of CAPs at the local level, however, immediately brought out class conflicts. The *Community Action Program Guide* issued by the Office of Economic Opportunity (OEO) in February 1965 mandated that the board representation for community action agencies (CAAs) would be equally divided among three groups of people: public and private institutions dealing with the poor; community elements such as churches, unions, and civil rights groups; and poor people themselves. Just how these three groups would collaborate and negotiate their various interests together, however, was never seriously discussed nor planned. Richard Boone, one of the designers of CAP, later admitted that federal antipoverty planners naively expected that a creative synthesis would spring up, according to which the poor would stage protests, institutional leaders would respond positively to them, and the protesting poor would happily accept the necessity of compromise.[16]

By assuming that a consensus would organically build between the poor and city officials, federal policymakers designed a program that was doomed to turmoil. City officials resisted ceding power to a new group of political actors. In December 1964, Mayor Robert F. Wagner submitted a grant proposal to lead antipoverty funds through his own administration's Antipoverty Operation Board. This board was composed entirely of city officials, without any inclusion of poor people. The secrecy of his actions, which quickly became publicized, stirred protest among activists. At a meeting with the Board of Trustees of the James Weldon Johnson Community Center in April 1965, executive director Mildred Zucker expressed her suspicion that city officials sought to steal antipoverty funds away from poor people. Local leaders from East Harlem had organized themselves into an antipoverty organization, but they had not received any responses from letters they had written to city officials, nor had they seen any proposals for Community Progress Centers (CPCs). "It was the feeling of all those concerned that the city's attitude was completely contrary to the very intent of the Anti Poverty Act," Zucker asserted, and "the very secrecy was an indication to the community of the way in which the City was by-passing them." By November 1965, even mainstream newspapers like the *New York Times* reported the sense of outrage that poor New Yorkers felt toward city officials. "The whole point of involving the poor people in the antipoverty programs would be lost if they were relegated to being messenger boys and girls," noted the reporter.[17]

When the OEO denied Mayor Wagner's proposal based on its exclusion of poor participants, he changed the makeup of the Council against Poverty slightly. He added five prominent citizens to the group of eleven city officials already on the council. The new arrangement, however, continued to invite attacks from political activists in the city. Antonia Pantoja complained that there was only one Puerto Rican on the council—Herman Badillo, then commissioner of the Department of Relocation. Congressman Adam Clayton Powell Jr. used his contacts to effectively block Wagner's plans. He asked the controller general of the United States to deny Wagner the antipoverty funds, claiming that Wagner's proposal fundamentally violated the intent of the Economic Opportunity Act.[18] Wagner likely realized at this point that he had to respond to these accusations or risk losing his credibility in the city, especially among black and Puerto Rican constituencies—a huge loss since the black and Puerto Rican vote had been crucial to his reelection in 1961, when he had tried to change his image as a handpicked Democratic "machine" politician by running for the first time without its support. Since then, black and Puerto Rican voters had become increasingly influential in determining election results.[19] Robert F. Kennedy in his senatorial campaign and Johnson in his presidential campaign in 1964 had both received the highest margin of victory in the city's black and Puerto Rican neighborhoods. Wagner himself acknowledged in November 1964 that "the ethnic groups in the United States played a role of paramount importance in . . . achieving great Democratic victories in the Northeast, Midwest and Southwest."[20] Sensing pressure from an important part of his constituency, Wagner expanded the Council against Poverty to sixty-two members. City officials, however, remained in control of antipoverty operations. They still determined the flow of antipoverty funds distributed to the various CAAs that sprang up in New York neighborhoods.[21]

City officials drew further criticism from New York City activists by demonstrating their lack of knowledge about how to facilitate poor people's political organization. The Council against Poverty, despite its proclaimed position of leadership in the city, did not know how to develop representative leadership among the poor. It never provided guidelines on how to conduct elections designed to select antipoverty representatives for each CPC. Dan Carpenter, a settlement house leader from the Lower West Side, argued that his neighborhood's Community Committee, which was responsible for electing CPC representatives, was "window-dressing." Although an election had been called, it was only "superficially democratic" since many parent groups had not been invited and the election was carried out in a single evening. While federal antipoverty leaders boasted that CPCs fostered "maximum feasible participation" of the poor, Carpenter saw "two or three people controlling things" in his neighborhood.[22] As in many other cities across the country, CPC elections in New York City embarrassed War on Poverty policymakers. The Council against Poverty spent close to $121,000 on staging elections across eleven community centers in the city, but few of those elections actually resulted in a leadership of poor people.[23] Many of the CPCs across the country experienced similar failures. CPC election voter turnout ranged from 4.2 percent in Cleveland to 0.7 percent in Los Angeles. By March 1966, OEO director Sargent Shriver halted CPC elections, claiming that "we don't believe we receive our money's worth in these elections."[24] The lack of coordination between city officials and poor citizens made the CPC elections a joke.

Members of the Council against Poverty further revealed their lack of knowledge about the poor by using OEO's strict definitions of "the poor" to select CPC membership. In the Hunts Point CPC, poor nonprofessionals who lived in public housing signed up to join the CPC, composing close to two-thirds of the elected committee. The Council against Poverty, however, required the Hunts Point CPC to have additional membership among the poor because these individuals, whose yearly incomes exceeded the

$3,000 per year poverty line, were not poor enough to qualify as "poor" according to OEO guidelines.[25] These were the upwardly mobile poor who were ready to take up the responsibility of being community leaders, but their relatively high incomes meant that they did not satisfy the OEO's strict guidelines.

Federal antipoverty lawmakers did not understand the mechanics of stimulating grassroots leadership, nor did they grasp the true nature of class conflict in urban politics. If the workings of democracy actually depended upon the leadership of top officials, the War on Poverty was surely bound to become a big fiasco. New York City's grassroots leaders, however, seized upon this opportunity to make the program work for their own benefit. They turned federal lawmakers' *idea* of "maximum feasible participation" of the poor into real *action*.

The Nuts and Bolts of Creating a
Puerto Rican Antipoverty Program

Soon after President Johnson announced his ambitious War on Poverty agenda, a group of grassroots leaders in New York City gathered to strategize how to formulate a Puerto Rican antipoverty agenda within this federal structure. In the fall of 1964, leaders from the Puerto Rican Forum, including Manny Diaz, Gilberto Gerena Valentín, and Antonia Pantoja, met with leading academic and civic figures in the city, such as Frank Riessman, Richard Cloward, Cyril Tyson, Kenneth Clark, and Henry Cohen.[26] Galvanized by the March on Washington and the 1964 citywide school boycott, Puerto Rican activists were eager to seize this opportunity to further develop Puerto Ricans' political networks in the city. They faced several challenges, however, in making a case for a Puerto Rican antipoverty program. In particular, they had a difficult time coming up with how to convince national and local government leaders that they deserved antipoverty funds, when the program was publicly known as a "black" program.

The official language in the Economic Opportunity Act of 1964 was racially neutral. It emphasized that CAPs simply aimed to foster the "maximum feasible participation of the poor." Few Americans, however, could deny the influence of civil rights campaigns on the Democratic Party's formulation of antipoverty policies. The War on Poverty was announced on the heels of the March on Washington in August 1963 and the bombing of the Sixteenth Street Baptist Church in Birmingham the following month. OEO director Sargent Shriver publicly admitted at the time that the Economic Opportunity Act was regarded as "but the logical counterpart of the Civil Rights Act which had just been passed in June." A former official of the Council of Economic Advisors, Daniel Capron, revealed a decade later that CAP's racially neutral language was a political tactic designed to temper opposition from white Southern Democrats. "We knew that it would be death . . . to bill any kind of program as a help-the-black program, but that doesn't mean that we didn't realize that this program was very important in terms of the black vote."[27] While publicly announcing the program as a racially neutral program, federal policymakers were thus clearly targeting a black constituency in their formulation of the War on Poverty.

Puerto Rican leaders, as representatives of a numerically smaller and racially ambiguous minority group, knew that they would have a difficult time positioning themselves as rightful recipients of antipoverty funds. The entire nation was trying to solve black-white tensions—what did federal antipoverty designers know about Puerto Ricans? According to social work scholar Fred Barbaro, the average American knew nothing about Puerto Rico besides that "Puerto Rico is a vacation paradise that is somehow related politically to this country."[28] Making a case for the 1.5 million Puerto Ricans who were mostly concentrated in New York City was much harder than making a case for 22 million African Americans spread all over the country.

Puerto Ricans' racially ambiguous reputation did not help matters. At a time when oppression was primarily viewed as "racial," Puerto Rican leaders faced difficulty presenting themselves as worthy of special federal aid. Puerto Ricans were treated as a "nonwhite" group by white New Yorkers in daily life, but they were often referred to as "white" in official documents. In a 1965 conference presentation, for example, the regional director of the U.S. Department of Labor, Herbert Bienstock, placed Puerto Ricans under the "white" category when measuring racial gaps in New York City's poverty rates. His breakdown of the city's poverty rates was divided between "whites"—who were either "Puerto Rican" or "non–Puerto Rican"—and "nonwhites."[29]

Their racial ambiguity certainly made the logistics of applying for antipoverty funds difficult. According to the guidelines set by federal policymakers, CAA funds were distributed to neighborhood representatives so that poor residents would organize and mobilize local resources from their own neighborhood to solve their problems. African Americans, who were segregated in particular neighborhoods, could thus access such funds by applying as members of a neighborhood, such as Central Harlem or

Bedford-Stuyvesant. Puerto Ricans, who were scattered in seventeen different neighborhoods in the city, could not. As a result of their racially ambiguous identity and their frequent relocations caused by urban renewal projects, Puerto Ricans had not formed an ethnic enclave anywhere. They shared the three neighborhoods where they were most heavily concentrated—East Harlem, the Lower East Side, and the South Bronx—with Jewish, Irish, Italian, and black residents. When applying for CAA funding, they had to somehow make an appeal for Puerto Ricans in particular without making their ethnic interests too explicit. The scattered nature of Puerto Rican residence in the city, which indicated their advantage over blacks in crossing racial segregation lines in housing, presented a liability here.[30]

Besides the complications of applying for antipoverty funds as a racially ambiguous group, Puerto Ricans also faced the difficult task of creating contacts with national antipoverty officials. African American national leaders, such as NAACP executive director Roy Wilkins and Congressman Adam Clayton Powell Jr., had direct access to President Johnson and leaders from the OEO. Powell was credited as the architect of the Economic Opportunity Act. According to Ohio's Republican congressman, William Ayers, "Without Adam, there would have been no War on Poverty." During his conflict with Mayor Wagner over the handling of antipoverty programs in New York City, Powell was able to use his influence not only to temporarily block antipoverty funds from reaching Wagner's office, but also to install his ally, Arthur Logan, as head of the city's Council against Poverty. Black activists in New York City knew that they could expect Powell to wield his influence on behalf of poor African Americans.[31] Puerto Ricans had no equivalent national spokesperson. When White House aide Lee C. White recommended that President Johnson support Puerto Ricans' quest for voting rights, given U.S. "plans for petrochemical developments in Puerto Rico," Johnson replied hastily, "They might want to talk to Sen. Kennedy."[32]

President Johnson and his White House aides did not include Puerto Ricans in their initial formulation of antipoverty or civil rights programs because they did not see Spanish-speaking voters as vital to the Democratic Party's survival, nor did they understand the nature of their racial oppression. They understood that Spanish-speaking Americans' high rates of poverty and lack of political representation indicated that they faced particular problems but did not necessarily know the root causes of those problems. According to White House aide David S. North, "Spanish-speaking Americans" such as Puerto Ricans and Mexican Americans suffered an entirely different form of discrimination from that experienced by African Americans, as it was "non-statutory" and it stemmed primarily from their "language and cultural differences."[33] Furthermore, Johnson's aides were already experiencing political fatigue from the black civil rights movement by the mid-1960s, which made them hesitant to adopt another and separate civil rights agenda. After repeated demands from Puerto Rican and Mexican American activists, Special Assistant to the President Joseph Califano agreed to meet with Puerto Rican and Mexican American leaders in September 1966 to discuss the unique problems facing "Spanish surname communities." But Califano specified in an internal memo to the president that he and his colleagues did not "want to go through all the complications and expenses of a big planning session as [they] did with the Negro Civil Rights Conference" but wanted "small day-long meetings" instead.[34]

Washington officials were hesitant to create a separate civil rights agenda for Spanish-speaking Americans, but they were willing to include them in War on Poverty programs by lumping them with African Americans as "minorities." For example, in a 1965 press release, the President's Committee on Equal Employment Opportunity prepared an announcement regarding a task force representative of major national corporations who would expose "young Negros" to new economic opportunities made available for them. The announcement, however, was changed at the last minute to include "young minority group members—Mexican American, Negro, Puerto Ricans, American Indians, etc."—simply by crossing out the word "Negro" and replacing it with these groups. Washington officials' lack of interest in knowing the particular experience of each group was evident in the rest of the announcement: there were references to the disparities that existed between "white" and "nonwhite" teenage unemployment rates, but there was no clarification as to whether Puerto Ricans and Mexican Americans were included within the "nonwhite" category.[35] Still, Puerto Rican activists operating within such a national political framework likely concluded that embracing their designation as "minority" would at least get a foot in the door of federal antipoverty programs.

More difficult than convincing federal officials of Puerto Ricans' legitimacy as recipients of antipoverty funds, however, was getting the support of Puerto Rican constituents themselves. When Manny Diaz first began to publicize antipoverty programs, he encountered opposition on the ground. Some Puerto Ricans denied the fact that Puerto Ricans needed an antipoverty program. A Puerto Rican man in Brooklyn told him, "I don't know what you are talking about. We are not poor. We are mentally poor. Poverty is in the mind. We are not black—we are Puerto Rican."[36] In reality, Puerto Ricans were poorer than blacks. Puerto Ricans on average earned less than African Americans for the same occupational groups. In 1960, black male operatives (semiskilled industrial workers) earned $6,187, while Puerto Rican male operatives earned $5,148; black female clerical workers earned $4,867, while Puerto Rican female clerical workers earned $4,563.[37] Puerto Ricans' association of "blackness" with poverty, however, was not made based on an objective analysis of salary averages or unemployment patterns. Poverty was often seen as an indication of an individual's proclivity to a weak morality and poor work ethic—traits that had been considered biologically determined in the past but which reflected "cultural personalities" in the postwar era.[38] What Diaz found was a fear among Puerto Ricans that they might become, like African Americans, a people considered to be "naturally" poor and dependent on government aid.

In a proposal for bilingual social service agencies, leaders from the Puerto Rican Social Services (PRSS) revealed their assumptions about blacks' "proclivity" to ask for government help. Writing a proposal for a bilingual staff, PRSS leaders claimed that Puerto Ricans have a "Latin American personality structure referred to as 'dignidad de la persona,'" which made their "attitude . . . in approaching an institution for help . . . fraught with the danger of loss of dignity and status." "In contrast," they argued that "the American disabled or disabled of other ethnic minorities . . . have a long history of fighting for, of knowing about, and of using the give-and-take of impersonal relationships with staff personnel of large organizations."[39] PRSS leaders did not clarify who these "disabled American minorities" were, but they were likely comparing Puerto Ricans to African Americans. While they themselves were applying for government aid, PRSS leaders stereotyped African Americans as being "used to" asking for help, while Puerto Rican supplicants were overwhelmed by a "loss of dignity."

This was a gross mischaracterization of African Americans and Puerto Ricans. If some people felt qualms about receiving government aid and others did not, such variances existed across both groups. According to a 1965 news bulletin put out by the president of the Harlem Council for Economic Development, James Lawson, not enough blacks were using antipoverty programs to find relief from personal economic hardship. Although there were scores of "hungry people in Harlem," people burdened with excessive medical expense, and young people whose criminal records rendered them unemployable, poor Harlemites were not asking for help because they were "too proud to accept welfare." Instead of trying to "fool their neighbors that they are in good shape," Lawson encouraged blacks to "admit they are poor and seek help."[40] Far from being a "Latin American personality trait," the fear of being stigmatized as "dependent" affected poor people across racial groups. Puerto Ricans' belief that "black poverty" and "black dependence" were "natural" reflected the racial stereotypes that helped them cope with their own poverty conditions. Puerto Rican activists interested in getting their constituents to sign up for antipoverty programs thus faced the difficult task of convincing them that such an activity would not racially stigmatize them but would instead help them find solutions to their problems. Otherwise, Puerto Ricans could follow the path of poor Polish Americans and Italian Americans in New York City, who often did not participate in antipoverty programs because they did not want their neighborhoods to be associated with "black programs."[41]

When Puerto Rican leaders met with the city's leading academic and civic figures in the fall of 1964, they first tackled the logistical challenge of developing a Puerto Rican antipoverty program given their geographic distribution in the city. Mobilization for Youth creator Richard Cloward suggested that the best way to devise an independent Puerto Rican antipoverty structure would be to create a "holding company." He suggested that a core group of Puerto Ricans apply for federal antipoverty funding through a holding company, which would then develop contracts with different groups of Puerto Rican organizations scattered throughout the city. The holding company would offer a salary for the director and would pay for rent and telephone services, but the rest would be left up to each organization in East Harlem, the South Bronx, Williamsburg, the Lower East Side, and other neighborhoods. Diaz, Gerena, and Pantoja all agreed. Under the leadership of Pantoja, the Puerto Rican Forum submitted a proposal and received $49,000 from the city's administration.[42]

There were a number of existing Puerto Rican organizations that were eager to tap into antipoverty funds to expand their programs, such as the Council of Hometown Clubs, the Congress of Puerto Rican Municipalities, the Puerto Rican Parade, the Bronx Council of Organizations, and Ateneo Puertorriqueño. They had the most extensive connections with ordinary Puerto Rican migrants since their function was primarily social—members of hometown clubs, for example, came together mostly to dance, eat, converse, and find a family atmosphere. But hometown club leaders could use their social networks for political purposes if they had access to additional resources, such as a paid community worker to coordinate meetings and direct action initiatives.[43] When the Puerto Rican Forum received antipoverty funding, such grassroots Puerto Rican leaders signed up to receive training on community development and youth leadership. After six months of training, they officially formed the first Puerto Rican antipoverty organization, the Puerto Rican Community Development Project (PRCDP). In its first year of operation, the PRCDP worked successfully. As Diaz later explained, "That was the first time these organizations were able to breathe. It was starters. It worked beautifully."[44]

A year after the PRCDP was formed, Puerto Rican leaders were able to secure federal antipoverty funds through direct OEO contacts. Having met OEO director Sargent Shriver while working at the Mobilization for Youth, Diaz was able to get an appointment with him in Washington, D.C. He took along with him four of his good friends: lawyer Joe Erazo, Rev. Ruben Dario Colón, businessman Luis Hernandez, and labor organizer Gilberto Gerena Valentín. When PRCDP leaders made the case for Puerto Rican antipoverty programs, Shriver responded positively, demanding an immediate proposal: "Get thee a hotel, get thee a secretary, and get thee a proposal on my desk by 9 A.M. tomorrow morning."[45] After staying up all night, PRCDP leaders submitted a proposal to Shriver the following morning and received a grant of $3.5 million. This was an incredible feat—it was ten times less than the $40 million that black antipoverty groups in New York City had received, but $3.5 million was more than they had ever expected.[46] By accessing federal support, the PRCDP became one of the hundreds of CAAs that began challenging local politics across the country.

Wrestling with the Meanings of Race and Class

By leading antipoverty programs, Puerto Rican leaders began to present themselves more distinctly as representatives of a working-class community and a racialized ethnic group. Drawing from the lessons they had learned in the March on Washington and the school boycott, they continued to speak more openly about Puerto Ricans' position of racial subjugation. Puerto Rican Forum leaders who wrote the first proposal for the PRCDP revealed that their determination to break Puerto Ricans' "poverty cycle problem" stemmed largely from their realization that "the story of the Puerto Ricans will not be the same as the story of the groups of immigrants who came before." Although Puerto Ricans did not want to "accept the concept that race is a barrier to economic achievement," they came to the "sobering and disillusioning realization" that "Puerto Ricans are *not* 'making it' once they learn English."[47] This last statement represented a significant break from the past since so many Puerto Ricans and other New Yorkers had previously distinguished Puerto Ricans from African Americans by arguing that their problems stemmed largely from their language difficulties. PRCDP leaders concluded instead that their main barrier to economic achievement had been racial.

PRCDP leaders believed that forging a stronger ethnic identity as "Puerto Rican" would give them the tools to fight against their racial subjugation. According to PRCDP consultant Dr. Frank Bonilla, Puerto Ricans' desire to create a "culturally based program of action against poverty" came from a renewed hunger for an ethnic identification. Bonilla conjectured that Puerto Ricans' prior self-identification as *hispano* could have reflected their "insecurity and self-hatred" or simply their understanding that their island was too "remote and inconsequential" to be recognized by mainlanders. Regardless, Bonilla claimed that Puerto Rican migrants were now embracing their identity as "Puerto Rican" instead, since "the ethnic identification had begun to provide modest premium in opportunities for jobs, prestige, and power at the middle levels of the city's organizational life." Ethnically based organizations were becoming so widespread within the Puerto Rican community that he was convinced that "the only way to motivate and prepare young Puerto Ricans to effectively contribute services and provide leadership for their own group is by affirming and strengthening their ethnic identification."[48]

PRCDP leaders used the term "ethnic" not so much in contrast to African Americans' "racial" identity—as some Puerto Rican leaders had done in the past—but as an equivalent of it. "The political success and moral impact of Negro protest will accentuate the tendency to structure all efforts for reform and change along ethnic lines," they claimed. They still compared Puerto Ricans to Jewish immigrants, who also had to carefully negotiate their displays of ethnicity in the past. But they understood that black political protest would ultimately define the meanings attached to ethnicity in this era.[49]

Puerto Rican leaders' leaning toward a black protest model paralleled their closer identification with their working-class constituents. As they saw the importance of confronting their ethnic identities, they also came to believe that their legitimacy as leaders rested on their ability to politically empower a broad working-class constituency. PRCDP leaders deemed it crucial that a broad section of poor Puerto Ricans organize themselves politically. They placed a heavy emphasis on power being handled *by* the people and *for* the people. Internal divisions that developed within the PRCDP reveal its leaders' search for what this working-class leadership should look like. In March 1965, a split occurred within the PRCDP. Twenty-one members of the board resigned. Pantoja led the group that resigned; Gerena and Diaz led the opposing group. According to Hector Velez, he left PRCDP with Pantoja because Gerena's group was "made up of so-called 'leaders' who are more interested in their own welfare and their own political futures, demagogues who use our people to bolster their own ego." Ironically, the charge from Gerena's group against Pantoja was the same. Gerena criticized Pantoja and Puerto Rican Forum leaders for "using the name of Puerto Rican leadership and the Puerto Rican people to present a program to the Federal government," when in fact they were "creating an agency just for the inner group." According to Diaz, Pantoja demonstrated her elitism when she proposed to compose the PRCDP Board of Directors with fifteen members of the Puerto Rican Forum, which was mostly made up of social workers, and ten members from Congreso del Pueblos, whose members did not necessarily carry educational credentials. This effectively concentrated power in the hands of Puerto Rican professionals. Diaz called this a battle between the "*perfumados*" (perfumed ones) and the "community."[50]

It is difficult to know whether either side empowered their working-class constituents any better than the other. As is often the case, it is harder to trace the voices of Congreso members than those of their leaders. Diaz claimed that Pantoja's group represented the "professionals" since they were made up of social workers and that Gerena's group embodied the "labor" leadership. But the division was not so clear, as Gerena's group included social workers like Diaz himself. Individuals such as Maria Canino, Josephine Nieves, Yolanda Sanchez, and Antonia Pantoja composed the educated Puerto Rican middle class, but they did not view themselves as that different from the general Puerto Rican population, as many of them had grown up in poverty themselves.[51] Regardless of the slight variations that may have existed between those who had educational pedigrees and those who had labor-organizing experience, the striking fact was that Puerto Rican antipoverty leaders rooted their politics in the interests of a broad, working-class constituency in the mid-1960s. Although they clearly held a position of class privilege compared to most Puerto Ricans, they determined their political agenda based on the needs of their less fortunate compatriots.

Black–Puerto Rican Antipoverty Coalitions

Alongside the PRCDP, Puerto Rican antipoverty leaders engaged in multiple cross-racial efforts with white and black antipoverty leaders throughout the city of New York. Those originating from East Harlem resulted in the most fruitful collaborations between African Americans and Puerto Ricans in the city. One of the advantages of the East Harlemites was that black and Puerto Rican antipoverty leaders had established networks of political organizing before the federal program started. White settlement house leaders William Kirk and Mildred Zucker had been working closely with black social workers like Preston Wilcox through the East Harlem Project in the 1950s, long before the Johnson administration had intervened in any of East Harlem's local affairs. Kirk and Zucker knew Puerto Rican youth organizers like Robert de León through juvenile delinquency programs developed in the 1950s. This meant that their relationships were not so easily shaken up by racial conflicts when their community involvement became attached to material rewards. Their debates about political legitimacy were cushioned by the goodwill and organizational structures that they had already built.

Although white settlement leaders Kirk and Zucker had been the official leaders of East Harlem's community progress center (CPC), they effectively handed the leadership over to Preston Wilcox. Born in Youngstown, Ohio, in 1923, Wilcox was a community activist and scholar known mostly for his commitment to black empowerment. After working with Malcolm X and earning a master's degree in social work at Columbia University, he became a national leader in the field of black education and community development. Through his involvement with local struggles in New York City, he founded the National Association of Afro-American Educators and remained active in the National Council of Black Studies and the Congressional Black Caucus.[52] Wilcox's Afro-centric advocacy, however, did not clash with his commitment to develop leadership among all poor people, including Puerto Ricans. As he laid out his plan for the development of leadership among the poor through antipoverty structures, Wilcox articulated his deep belief in poor people's abilities to govern their lives. Poor people, "when treated with respect, listened to and allowed to make mistakes, to experience learning, to participate in decisions that affect their lives . . . will respond even beyond their own expectations," claimed Wilcox.[53] According to his friend Charles Wilson, the beauty of Wilcox was that he was an enormously trusting person. "He was trying to make the world better, and he thought that that's what they [whites] wanted."[54] Although some viewed him as naive for maintaining close relationships with white social workers, Wilcox believed that he needed the help of white professionals in his work. As a result of the many years he invested in working with them, he gained the opportunity to lead the entire antipoverty experiment in East Harlem.

Wilcox developed a brilliant strategy to allow every social group to have a stake in the development of the East Harlem CPC. The official name of the antipoverty organization was Massive Economic Neighborhood Development (MEND). He dealt with tensions between professionals and nonprofessionals by requiring that every leader reside in East Harlem. Most white professionals working in East Harlem lived outside the neighborhood, but those who did live in East Harlem were considered legitimate "locals" who could take leadership roles in MEND. He carefully delineated the roles that these professionals could take within the organization. "Benevolent do-gooders, rational professionals, anxious liberals, [and] tradition-laden conservatives" could no longer treat poor individuals as "consumers" of social services, Wilcox contended.[55] Professionals who had previously found ways of "maintaining control, puppeteering, tranquilizing, and insisting that the poor engage in public striptease in order to receive services" could no longer deal with the poor with such condescension. Passing out leaflets and serving coffee would no longer be tolerated as "meaningful participation for the poor." While admonishing professionals against paternalism, Wilcox validated their role as important to the poor: "This does not mean that the location of the poor on policymaking bodies is sufficient. The poor cannot alter their plight without the aid of others." Wilcox stressed that professionals should act as "advocates" of the poor. The litmus test for professionals would be the results of their services to the poor. Professional skills "which will not result in an improved ability of the recipients of such services to face new challenges at a higher level" would be considered obsolete, but those that resulted in poor people's increased capacity to advocate for themselves would be continuously valued and utilized.[56] Such were the foundations of what became a productive collaborative relationship between professionals and poor people involved in MEND.

Wilcox balanced the distribution of power among blacks, Puerto Ricans, and whites on the Board of Directors of MEND as well. Board members were 23 percent black, 23 percent Puerto Rican, 23 percent Italian, and 31 percent other. This distribution did not exactly reflect East Harlem's population, which was approximately 32 percent black, 39 percent Puerto Rican, and 29 percent white in 1960, but MEND leaders were satisfied with it. Board members included individuals ranging from Italian district leader John Merli, to black welfare recipient Ruth Atkins, to Puerto Rican social worker Ted Velez. Also included were community leaders from churches, public housing programs, and education programs.[57]

Wilcox gave autonomy to each ethnic group to develop its own leadership within MEND by decentralizing East Harlem into ten subcommunities. Each subcommunity employed a director, an assistant director, ten "community stimulators," and two consultants. Some of these subcommunities had a dominant Italian, black, or Puerto Rican population, while others had a mixture of two or three of these. Community stimulators for each subcommunity were assigned to the areas where they could represent each community ethnically. The Aguilar subcommunity, for example, encompassing the area from 106th Street to 116th Street, between Third Avenue and Park Avenue, included a mixture of blacks and Puerto Ricans. Since Puerto Ricans composed the majority of the Aguilar population, however, its director, Gloria Quiñones, was Puerto Rican. The Mount Morris Park subcommunity, which extended from 116th Street to 132nd Street, between Fifth Avenue and Park Avenue, was a predominantly black neighborhood. As a result, Sara Frierson, an African American, became the director for this area. Community stimulators were charged with the task of identifying the problems and needs of residents within their given subcommunity and developing solutions to these problems. MEND leaders officially represented these subcommunities before city and federal antipoverty officials and distributed funds to each of these subcommunities, but subcommunity leaders designed their own goals and strategies. Such a structure allowed residents who did not have prior political connections or educational pedigrees to still have the autonomy to design their own programs.[58]

As black and Puerto Rican leaders established a space where members of both groups felt equally validated, East Harlem residents used their resources creatively to build their community. Organized under the leadership of Juanita Davis, a group of twenty-one individuals from the Mother's Club of James Weldon Johnson Community Center ranging from the ages of eighteen to fifty put together theatrical productions that reflected the lived experiences of East Harlemites. The local theater group called itself the Theater Arts Center (TAC) and aimed to develop "street theatre." Understanding that "theatre is both a means and an end in education, an

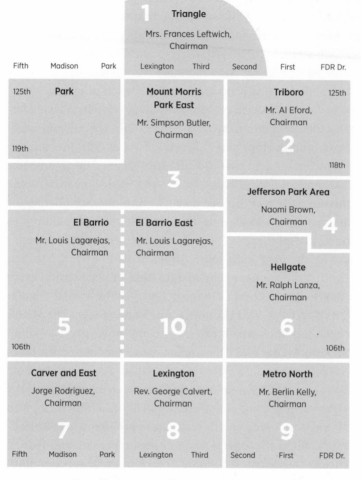

FIGURE 4.1 Map of MEND ten subcommunities, 1964 (JWJCCR, Schomburg Center for Research in Black Culture)

important form of recreation, and a social force to be reckoned with," TAC sought to create "a mirror for people who have no image for themselves, or at best, a distorted one."[59] Theater group members included mothers and professional actors, but the majority of them were youth from the mental health clinic. TAC leaders hoped that they could channel the psychological troubles of youth into creative artistic productions that would empower them and the communities around them. By "seeking to absorb rather than reject many of these troubled and troublesome youngsters," group worker Angel Martinez and volunteer Enrique Vargas dedicated themselves to helping youth write and produce plays.[60]

TAC functioned as a vehicle of black and Puerto Rican cultural production. Its theatrical productions included plays that East Harlemites themselves wrote, such as "Junkie's Paradise" and "Medea in Africa," as well as the staging of more famous plays, such as Langston Hughes's *Simply Heavenly* and *The Life of Malcolm X*. In plays such as "Medea in Africa," TAC members used fictionalized accounts of events such as the Portuguese invasion of Angola in the nineteenth century to give blacks and Puerto Ricans a way of expressing their contemporary struggles with whites in New York City. Some of the plays were performed in English; others were done in Spanish. TAC director Nils Cruz had some difficulty with the limited reading capacities of some students and the problem of "working with accents," but he recognized that youth participants nevertheless thrived in their ability to dance, act, and perform. These productions became instantly popular within their most immediate surroundings: they were performed at public housing projects like DeWitt Clinton Houses, high schools such as P.S. 104, P.S. 82, and Benjamin Franklin High School, and universities like Colgate and Bucknell.[61] The productions cultivated black and Puerto Rican youth's artistic expressions and gave community residents a sense of possessing a common history. Black and Puerto Rican youth participants also learned to engage in cross-racial work while developing their distinctive forms of cultural nationalism.

The East Harlem Tenants Council (EHTC) developed a more distinct commitment to Puerto Rican nationalism than MEND or TAC. But this ethnic particularity did not keep the organization from working with a multiracial group of Puerto Rican and black tenants. EHTC's founder, Ted Velez, was familiar with the needs of Puerto Rican tenants in the city. His own family had suffered a great deal under tightfisted landlords. His grandmother had been struck on the head by a falling decayed ceiling. Instead of fixing the ceiling, her landlord made her sign a statement absolving him from any blame, even though she did not know a word of English. As a young man trained in social work, Velez might have used the traditional form of individual casework to deal with tenants like his grandmother, but two events radically shifted his life trajectory.[62] He married the daughter of Stanley Faulkner, the Jewish defense attorney of the Fair Play for Cuba Committee, and he met Jesse Gray, an African American tenant organizer based in Harlem. Faulkner and Gray were political activists who were challenging political authorities at the local and international levels. Through his relationship with his father-in-law, Velez began to demonstrate in Washington, D.C., against the House Un-American Activities Committee investigations of students who were taking trips to Cuba and supporting Fidel Castro.[63] Jesse Gray, who had been mobilizing tenants through the Harlem Tenants Council since 1954, inspired Velez to organize his own tenants' council in East Harlem in 1962. Through Gray's example, Velez learned to use section 755 of the New York Real Property Actions and Proceedings Law, which sanctioned rent strikes under severe conditions of disrepair. He also learned to confront police authorities through Gray's example. When Francisco Rodriguez, who had been voted "Boy of the Year" by the Boys Club, was shot in the back of the head and killed by an off-duty policeman on February 18, 1964, Velez led a group of people from EHTC to picket the 23rd Police Precinct in East Harlem to protest Rodriguez's slaying. Others from the Union Settlement Association, the East Harlem Protestant Parish, and St. Edward the Martyr Church joined EHTC to form the Committee for Police-Community Relations. By the time antipoverty funds became available in the fall of 1964, Velez was ready to expand a vibrant grassroots organization he had been building for several years with his Puerto Rican compatriots.[64]

Velez developed an antipoverty program that simultaneously advocated on behalf of black and Puerto Rican tenants while developing an organizational base for Puerto Ricans in particular. In a 1964 EHTC report of operations and proposals, Velez argued that one of the values of organizing tenants was that tenant discussions "strengthen[ed] the lines of communications between Negro and Puerto Rican families." At the same time, however, he envisioned that EHTC would be a "voluntary organization of Puerto Rican citizens . . . formed to meet some of the basic needs of the Puerto Rican population in East Harlem." EHTC would be an organization built by Puerto Ricans and for Puerto Ricans. He used family networks created by the Puerto Rican cultural practice of *compadrasgo* (godparenting) as a method of expanding tenant networks.[65]

Like Velez, Evelina Antonetty developed an antipoverty program primarily dedicated to helping Puerto Rican parents and tenants in the South Bronx. But its advocacy also included African Americans. By the time President Johnson announced the federal program, Antonetty had been working as a community organizer for several decades. Born in Salinas, Puerto Rico, Antonetty migrated to the mainland at the age of ten and settled in El Barrio in 1932. Although her mother had been active as a union leader in Puerto Rico, her family had not raised her with any particular political ideology. When she met her husband, Binaldo Montenegro, however, he introduced her to a circle of socialists, and soon Antonetty was working for Italian congressman Vito Marcantonio and labor organizer Jesus Colón.[66] As a young teenager, Antonetty had already expressed her desire to serve poor people by distributing food to them from the Welfare Department during the Great Depression. With the help of her cousin, who drove trolleys in the city, Antonetty took the papers of several poor families to the Welfare Department, gave excuses as to why they could not come, and later distributed the food to the families, telling them, "Don't be embarrassed to take it. This is just to get your feet on the ground." In 1946, under the guidance of Marcantonio and Colón, she became a labor organizer in District 65, Retail, Wholesale and Distributive Workers' Union. By the mid-1950s, she had brought more than 4,000 Spanish-speaking workers into the union and helped them organize a Spanish Affairs Committee within the union. As discussions related to juvenile delinquency and urban renewal increasingly galvanized poor residents of the South Bronx, Antonetty founded the United Friends and Neighbors of the Bronx in 1965 to help parents and tenants in need.[67]

Given Antonetty's long history of community organizing from the 1930s through the 1950s, it is probable that, with or without the War on Poverty, she would have become a force to be reckoned with. Federal funding, however, became vital to her ability to expand her leadership and mobilize larger numbers of poor people. In 1966, she developed the Teenage Housing Leadership Program through a grant of $26,000 from the OEO, the Urban Coalition, and the Department of Health, Education, and Welfare. Despite city officials' attempts to keep all antipoverty programs under their control, grassroots leaders like Antonetty were able to bypass municipal control and tap into federal funds directly through the OEO. Federal dollars became helpful, as she was able to employ youth to survey housing conditions of poor people and report them to the city's Housing Authority. As the situation in New York City's public schools worsened in the 1960s, she focused her activities on organizing parents. As a mother of three children, she had previously served as the president of the Parents' Association of P.S. 25. Through the help of her friend Ellen Lurie, a Jewish American who had been organizing parents in East Harlem since the 1950s, Antonetty developed a robust program of parent training that came to be known as the United Bronx Parents. She designed training sessions to help parents know how to approach principals and evaluate school curricula, teaching performance, administrative efficiency, and the school programs generally. Although the United Bronx Parents primarily organized Puerto Rican mothers, the group included a number of black mothers as well.[68]

The Origins of Puerto Rican Nationalism in the South Bronx

Antipoverty organizations in the South Bronx did not have the same level of coordination between black and Puerto Rican leaders as other neighborhoods in New York City. Leaders interested in developing black and Puerto Rican political power in this particular neighborhood did not see their political goals as necessarily synergistic. According to Evelina Antonetty, blacks and Puerto Ricans in the South Bronx were simply not as organized as those in Central Harlem, East Harlem, or Bedford-Stuyvesant because there had not been "time for the emergence . . . of significant indigenous community institutions," such as those of "large Negro churches or Puerto Rican clubs."[69] Indeed, the black and Puerto Rican community in the South Bronx was relatively new. Numbers surged significantly in the 1960s (39 percent Puerto Rican and 16 percent black), but in the 1950s, Puerto Ricans and blacks had only composed 13 percent and 5 percent of the neighborhood's population, respectively.[70] When the War on Poverty began, the two groups did not share any preexisting political networks, such as those created by settlement houses like the Union Settlement Association or the James Weldon Johnson Community Center in East Harlem. Such settlement houses had functioned as testing grounds through which black and Puerto Rican neighbors could address local problems on a more ad hoc basis, without the pressure of competing for large amounts of federal funds.

Given this type of political vacuum, the War on Poverty emerged in the South Bronx with an ethnically disproportionate leadership from the outset. While the Puerto Rican population in the South Bronx was larger than the black population, blacks dominated the leadership of the Community Progress Center (CPC) in the South Bronx. The same was the case for the surrounding neighborhoods in Mott Haven, Morrisania, Claremont, and Hunts Point.[71] It was not that Puerto Ricans lacked political leadership in the borough entirely. Herman Badillo had served as commissioner of the Department of Relocation since 1962 and as Bronx borough president since 1965. As a member of the Pondiac Club, a Democratic club in the Bronx, Eugene Rodríguez was elected state senator from the 29th District in 1966, covering the southern Bronx and northern Manhattan. Despite the presence of leaders such as Badillo and Rodríguez, however, Puerto Ricans in the Bronx did not benefit from the War on Poverty initially because these electoral leaders distanced themselves from the federal program. Badillo had always avoided being identified as an "ethnic" leader. According to one of his friends, during Badillo's first campaigns for political office, somebody in the audience had asked him if he was Puerto Rican or Italian. "He never really answered the question. He never has." At six-foot-one, he resented being called a "tall Puerto Rican." He insisted that Puerto Ricans were shorter than the average American due to a "poverty diet and lack of privilege" rather than their genetic makeup.[72] He disliked his reputation as an "exceptional Puerto Rican" and consistently revealed a certain unease in being associated too closely with his co-ethnics. When the War on Poverty programs began, he avoided getting enmeshed with a program that organized poor communities by ethnicity.

Notwithstanding Puerto Rican politicians' disinterest in antipoverty programs in the South Bronx, the first group of Puerto Rican antipoverty leaders in the neighborhood emerged through the active support of black antipoverty leaders. As Chapter 6 will reveal, Ramón Velez came to represent an especially exclusive and antiblack form of Puerto Rican nationalism in the late 1960s. But his political ascendance was only made possible through the initial backing of black leaders. Born in Hormigueros, Puerto Rico, in 1933, Velez moved to the New York metropolitan area in 1961. He first began organizing Puerto Rican migrant workers in Newark by forming the National Association of Puerto Rican Affairs. As a social worker and youth program fund-raiser working for the Office of the Commonwealth of Puerto Rico, he began to interact with Puerto Ricans in the Bronx in 1962. Seeing that many upwardly mobile Puerto Ricans were moving from East Harlem to the Bronx, he too moved there. Although the Bronx would suffer severe losses with the deindustrialization of the city in later years, it was still considered an industrial area that had employment opportunities in the early 1960s. The largest companies in Hunts Point, one of the neighborhoods of the South Bronx, included the American Bank Note Company, the National Gypsum Company, and several steel doorframe manufacturers and metal weaving companies. The large sewage treatment plant and the Terminal Produce Market employed about one-quarter of the Hunts Point working population.[73] At the South Bronx Neighborhood Orientation Center, Velez began working with Monserrate Flores and Mike Nuñez on housing, consumer fraud, and drug addiction problems. By 1966, he was elected to the board of the Hunts Point CPC, where he began to see that there was an enormous vacuum in the Puerto Rican antipoverty leadership.[74]

Ramón Velez took advantage of Mayor John Lindsay's reorganization of the War on Poverty structure to capture a new Puerto Rican political base in the South Bronx. When Lindsay took office in 1966, he promised to increase the efficiency of social service agencies and antipoverty programs in the city by bringing them under a "super agency," the Human Resources Administration (HRA). Mitchell Sviridoff, who was invited by Lindsay to study the operation of the city's social service programs, concluded that New York City was suffering from "scatteritis." Various groups of antipoverty programs had "mushroomed" and operated in the city "with little or no coordination, sometimes at cross purposes, often puzzling and frustrating the people whom they were designed to serve," Sviridoff noted. The "piecemeal expansion" of city programs had led to delays and confusion in their operation. With Sviridoff's recommendation, Lindsay changed the infrastructure of antipoverty programs, replacing the CPCs with community corporations (CCs), which would be supervised by the HRA. He promised that this reorganization would save the city $300 to $400 million.[75] Velez realized that he could claim a greater leadership position in the South Bronx through the new CCs.

In order to tap into the city's new antipoverty structure, however, Ramón Velez needed to coordinate his plans with black antipoverty leaders since they controlled the Hunts Point CPC and had ties with city officials. Initially, Hunts Point CPC president Helen Mitchell and her black colleagues were not interested in fostering the development of Puerto Rican leadership in their neighborhood. They changed their minds, however, when Cyril Tyson shared his vision of community development with them. As a board member of the Hunts Point CPC, deputy administrator for community relations at the HRA, and commissioner of the Manpower and Career Development Agency, Tyson had great influence with black antipoverty leaders and city officials. Unlike many of his black colleagues, Tyson argued that leaders from both black and Puerto Rican groups needed to lead Hunts Point antipoverty programs because both groups composed a significant portion of the neighborhood's population. According to City Planning Commission estimates in 1965, Hunts Point was 31 percent black and 47 percent Puerto Rican. "If you have a black *numero uno* [number one], let's have a Puerto Rican *numero dos* [number two]," pleaded Tyson. Through his close working relationships with Puerto Rican leaders Antonia Pantoja, Gilberto Gerena Valentín, and Manny Diaz since

FIGURE 4.2 Cyril Tyson
(Courtesy of Cyril Tyson)

the early 1960s, Tyson learned that "you can't move communities ahead if major segments are just simply being blocked out. . . . You can't have a community corporation so controlled by blacks that Puerto Ricans in that community have no way of participating."[76]

Tyson's views toward Puerto Rican leadership were influenced by his personal relationships. Born in 1927, he was the son of immigrants from Nevis, an island in the Anglophone Caribbean. He spent the first few years of his life in San Juan Hills, between 57th Street and 64th Street, and from 9th Avenue to 11th Avenue, which contained significant numbers of migrants from the South, West Indies, and Puerto Rico. He was surrounded by a multiethnic world of blacks who had come from across New York City and the Caribbean. His family and friends included Virgin Islanders who lived in Puerto Rico, as well as his own Puerto Rican wife, Sunchita Tyson. When asked to discuss his views on the relationship between blacks and Puerto Ricans, he asserted that "you can't answer that in terms of blacks as a monolith. Blacks from the Caribbean obviously knew about Puerto Ricans because they are Caribbean. There are many blacks who lived in Puerto Rico. You have all those mixtures." He did not believe that a strict line could be drawn between blacks and Puerto Ricans since their diaspora across the Caribbean and the United States bound them to a common world. He identified with both groups as "Caribbean." Furthermore, he believed that his decision to support Puerto Rican leadership in Hunts Point reflected his moral ethics. "I wasn't a black leader. I didn't belong to any political leader. . . . I took an ethical position."[77]

Many black Hunts Point board members initially rejected Tyson's suggestions. They wanted to keep the War on Poverty exclusively black because they saw it as a chance to seize black political power. Hunts Point board members challenged Tyson: "Wait a minute, some Puerto Ricans are getting jobs that we weren't able to get. How are we going to deal with that? Are they going to get equity before we get equity? We were slaves here!" Aside from access to jobs, many black leaders felt that being racially exclusive was part of the nature of dealing with politics in the United States. "That's not how white folks do it. When they are in control, they are in control," board members pointed out. This was their unique chance to practice a black nationalist politics. Tyson sympathized with black leaders in Hunts Point and understood why many of them handled antipoverty programs with territoriality. "It's very difficult when you have struggles of power to get people to see what the larger good may be," he recognized. If black leaders were to cede power to Puerto Ricans, he knew that many of them would feel that they were "losing at the moment." Nevertheless, he encouraged black leaders to "get everybody more empowered so they have the skills to do the job."[78]

Having won the moral argument, Tyson successfully convinced black Hunts Point CPC leaders to share political power with Puerto Ricans in the neighborhood. In 1967, Hunts Point director Helen Mitchell met with Mike Nuñez and gave him and other Puerto Rican leaders the chance to apply for the operation of a multi-service center. Under Section 703 of the Housing Act, Housing and Urban Development (HUD) made funds available to residents of a given neighborhood to coordinate public and private services all in one place. HUD grants would cover two-thirds of the cost of the building of the facility, and the city would finance the rest. A chief goal was to include local residents in operating and maintaining the programs.[79] With the backing of Tyson and Mitchell, Nuñez and Monserrate Flores began making plans for the Hunts Point multi-service center. They invited Ramón Velez to lead the effort, as they saw him as a "natural leader." In July 1967, the Hunts Point Multi-Service Center received an OEO grant to start inventorying its resources. By 1968, the center had a $2.9 million grant from the Department of Health, Education, and Welfare and a $91,500 grant from the Manpower and Career Development Agency. In less than a year, Velez developed manpower, health services, narcotics administration, welfare, education, child development, recreation, housing, and community action programs. Hunts Point residents suddenly gained access to jobs, education, and housing previously unavailable to them. Despite the initial racial imbalance of antipoverty operations in the South Bronx, black antipoverty leaders made a crucial contribution in helping Puerto Rican antipoverty leaders jumpstart their own operations.[80]

Racial and Class Fissures within Antipoverty Coalitions

A high level of cross-racial, cross-class collaborations took place in the first four years of antipoverty operations in the city, but problems appeared as early as 1966. As African Americans across the nation began to make calls for race-specific leadership through more confrontational methods, so too did Puerto Ricans. Disappointed by the Democratic Party's failure to listen to the demands of the Mississippi Freedom Democratic Party at the party's national convention in Atlantic City in 1964, leaders from the Student Nonviolent Coordinating Committee (SNCC) began moving away from the liberal framework of nonviolence and interracial organizing. In 1965, they publicly supported the use of arms by workers from the Lowndes County Freedom Organization in Alabama.[81] The following year, the Black Panther Party emerged in Oakland, California, focusing its vision on what poor African Americans could accomplish themselves through community programs rather than relying on the help of white liberal allies. Ted Velez from the East Harlem Tenants Council (EHTC) capitalized on this growing national sentiment to secure Puerto Rican political power in East Harlem. Although a former board member of MEND, he began to challenge its position of authority as the mediator between City Hall and antipoverty organizations in East Harlem. On November 2, 1966, Velez organized a group of sixty people, mostly young adolescents, to disrupt a MEND meeting. Through a hostile, public confrontation—clapping and stomping their feet in unison—Velez's group expressed its opposition to MEND. Velez claimed that EHTC should have the same representation before city officials as MEND, because EHTC represented "the poor" while MEND represented "established social work agencies." Shocked by Velez's claims, Mildred Zucker, one of the official representatives of the East Harlem CPC and MEND board member, questioned why EHTC, a "one-man organization" that had been established only in 1965, should have authority equal to that of MEND, which represented "much more established organizations." Zucker was technically correct, but what she missed was the fact that calls for Black Power had made ethnic identity as Puerto Rican a justification for political legitimacy, while making one's reputation as "white" and as "established" a liability.[82]

Ted Velez gained political power in East Harlem because his goals and tactics coincided with those of the broader Black Power movement. MEND exemplified the interracial, interclass, collaborative approach that had come from social reformers and civil rights leaders from the 1950s and early 1960s; EHTC manifested the more confrontational, race-specific and class-specific protest that paralleled the political ideals of the Black Power movement. Inspired by the Black Power movement, Velez called for a working-class, nationalist Puerto Rican leadership in East Harlem. He believed that Puerto Ricans should control antipoverty funds in the neighborhood because they composed the largest ethnic group, at 39 percent. He did not believe that white settlement house leaders should represent poor Puerto Ricans before city officials since their professional degrees no longer gave them legitimacy as leaders. Instead, he believed that Puerto Ricans themselves should take leadership positions and directly control the distribution of funds in their neighborhoods. According to Robert de León, a Puerto Rican leader from MEND, "Velez began to compete for funds and for dominance because his thing was, this is a Puerto Rican neighborhood, I have a Puerto Rican organization, so I should get all the money."[83]

By 1967, it no longer mattered that Ted Velez was not able to gain control over antipoverty funds through the local East Harlem political apparatus since he gained direct access to federal funds through Robert Kennedy. Just as Adam Clayton Powell Jr. had gained significant influence over antipoverty funds distribution in Central Harlem through his connections with President John F. Kennedy, so too did Velez seek control over East Harlem through his relationship with Senator Robert Kennedy. He convinced Kennedy that national and local leaders needed to pay attention to Puerto Ricans because they were the poorest group of New Yorkers. Kennedy responded sympathetically, attending conferences organized by the Puerto Rican Forum and informing the public about Puerto Ricans' pressing needs for poverty relief.[84] Most observers understood that Robert Kennedy and Velez had formed a tactical alliance based on each person's interest. According to Union Settlement Association executive director William Kirk, Kennedy was able to develop a "Puerto Rican apparatus in East Harlem" and Velez secured much-needed federal antipoverty funds. Even so, Kirk believed that Velez got the best of Kennedy. He asserted that Velez "excelled at manipulation" and that "he is now using Senator Kennedy rather than Kennedy using him."[85] In October 1967, Velez surprised many white settlement house leaders when EHTC received, along with MEND, 75 percent of the $2 million assigned to East Harlem's antipoverty organizations.[86] His rapid political rise in East Harlem was becoming unnerving to them.

Just as Ted Velez's political rise revealed racial cracks within the antipoverty leadership, the role of professionals within antipoverty organizations exposed growing class divides. Senate hearings on the War on Poverty held in May 1967 revealed some of these rifts. Some antipoverty leaders believed that the federal program was fulfilling its goal of fostering "participatory democracy." The executive director of Brownsville's CPC, Major Owens, stated that, as a result of antipoverty programs, "for the first time, poor communities are becoming aware of their rights, aware of avenues for change, and involving greater numbers of residents in socially meaningful programs." Owens was not naive about federal policymakers' original motivation in creating these programs. He recognized that a desire to "avoid riots" had been the primary impetus that pushed national leaders to pay attention to residents in impoverished cities, and that this narrow goal explained the minuscule amount of funding that had been apportioned for the programs. Even so, Owens believed that antipoverty programs had become "an investment in human beings" that held great potential to create real forms of participatory democracy. The chairman of the city's Council against Poverty, Arthur Logan, further stressed that CAPS allowed thousands of people who were considered "ignorant, apathetic, hard to reach, [and] alienated" to "participate in community meetings to plan and engage in attacks on the most complex domestic problems facing our country."[87]

Mayor Lindsay also boasted that the New Careers program, enacted by Congress through the Scheuer-Nelson Subprofessional Career Act of 1967, had resulted in real, tangible benefits for poor people. Poor people now had access to a number of career lines as paraprofessionals—as police aides, recreation aides, welfare aides, health aides, teachers' aides, and code enforcement inspectors. Rather than being selected based on traditional screening processes, such as intelligence measures, delinquency records, or school attainment, candidates were judged based on their performance in short-term, intensive training programs. By receiving additional training while working at the same time, paraprofessionals were given a path to advance their careers and attain higher salaries over time.

According to Frank Riessman, a New Careers program advocate, there was no better way for poor people to engage with their community while earning a livable income.[88]

Alice Kornegay, however, did not believe that antipoverty programs had such a democratizing impact. Although she shared Owens's position as a black antipoverty leader—she was the president of the Community Association of the East Harlem Triangle and board member of East Harlem's MEND—Kornegay was more critical of "professionals, some do-gooders and politicians" who made it difficult for the poor to participate "meaningfully in the war to help themselves." Far from viewing poor communities as "alienated" or "apathetic," she asserted that "block leaders and local leaders" had organized poor people *before* the War on Poverty began, yet their work had been undermined by "large bureaucratic organizations run by outsiders" who simply sought to "keep the poor in their place." Antipoverty officials were not the allies of poor people but paternalistic intruders who impeded their work. "The War on Poverty has often seemed like the War against the Poor," she concluded.[89] Owens's and Kornegay's differing viewpoints on the benefits of the War on Poverty reflected class differences that had been dormant during the first few years of antipoverty operations but that began to come to the surface with time. Whereas Kornegay had been a high school dropout and a former welfare client, Owens had been a librarian with a bachelor's degree from Morehouse College. Despite Owens's commitment to serve the poor, his education at one of the best private, all-male historically black colleges in the nation gave him a middle-class sensibility that aligned much more easily with that of white professionals than did Kornegay's.[90]

This is not to say that all poor people opposed professionals. Delores Ratcliffe, another welfare recipient from East Harlem who testified at the Senate hearings on the War on Poverty, disagreed with Kornegay's assertion that poor people should have greater control over antipoverty programs than professionals. Believing that the program had simply become a nepotistic "job placement program," she argued that "people from higher authority, not community representatives, but people who have training in community relations," should be in charge of job assignments. Kornegay believed in poor people's right and ability to govern their own programs, but Ratcliffe believed that professionals needed to restrain poor people's tendency toward corruption.[91]

The overall inefficiency of the antipoverty programs also made it difficult for leaders in general to continue asserting the legitimacy of these programs. The commissioner of the Manpower and Career Development Agency, Samuel Ganz, reported that out of 42,400 people who participated in job training programs provided by his organization in New York City between 1963 and 1967, only 20,000 had finished the training; out of that group, only 7,000 actually found jobs based on the training. When asked by Senator Robert Kennedy whether such figures were "satisfactory," the executive director of the New York State Department of Labor, Alfred Green, could not help but admit that that was a "minuscule number."[92] It was becoming increasingly clear that "rehabilitating" poor people through job training programs was not the best way to increase employment rates.

Antipoverty leaders across the city began to sense the increasing class and racial divides emerging within their organizations. Whereas the promise of "maximum feasible participation" of the poor had inspired professionals and nonprofessionals to work collaboratively in the early years of antipoverty operations, their failure to meet many of their goals fostered class conflict among them. Black and Puerto Rican antipoverty leaders, who believed that they could pursue black and Puerto Rican self-determination within the parameters set by white leaders, grew more skeptical of the sustainability of such a political path.

Conclusion

War on Poverty programs helped solidify Puerto Ricans' political alliance with African Americans. This alliance was based on a mutual willingness to confront their positions of racial and class subjugation. Although Puerto Rican leaders had equivocated between identifying themselves publicly as "Puerto Rican" or *hispano* in the past, antipoverty leaders embraced their ethnic identity as "Puerto Rican" more strongly. Puerto Rican leaders from previous generations had hoped that the acquisition of English would gradually grant Puerto Ricans economic mobility, but antipoverty leaders concluded that they would not progress unless they fought against the particular forms of racial discrimination they faced as "Puerto Rican." Puerto Rican antipoverty leaders also confronted their position as poor people, whose economic problems would not be solved without state intervention. Their confrontation with racial and class subjugation demonstrated their rejection of the European immigrant model as a path for the future. Individual hard work would not be enough; political protest and organization became essential components of their vision for progress. Adopting such a political perspective required that they shed whatever racist stereotypes they had held about African Americans as the exclusive group of minorities whose poverty and state dependence was somehow viewed as "natural."

Although some black and Puerto Rican antipoverty leaders would later use the War on Poverty structure to emulate white forms of political control, their initial efforts between 1964 and 1968 centered on creating more inclusive and cross-racial spaces of political mobilization. Their original premise was that whoever was poor and willing to confront his or her condition of poverty could become a leader in the movement. Black and Puerto Rican antipoverty leaders also constructed mutually supportive forms of black and Puerto Rican nationalism. Poor African Americans held greater visibility and legitimacy than poor Puerto Ricans as those considered to be the "rightful" recipients of antipoverty funds among national and municipal policymakers. But leaders from both groups took advantage of this federal program to mutually support each other's quest for political power. Wary of white reformists who might use this federal program to simply maintain the status of the poor as mere recipients of social services, leaders of color vigorously pursued the development of black and Puerto Rican political leadership by calling for racially representative antipoverty leadership. Far from tearing the two groups apart, black and Puerto Rican nationalist ideologies gave antipoverty leaders of color a common language of political protest. They used this common language as they built the community control movement as a response to the failures of the War on Poverty.

CHAPTER FIVE

From Racial Integration to Community Control

The Struggle for Quality Education

Soon after Evelina Antonetty founded the United Bronx Parents (UBP) in 1966, she realized that she could not change the city's public school system by simply "cooperating" with administrators from the Board of Education. More confrontational methods were necessary. When UBP activists demanded that a child molester be removed from his teaching position in one of the schools in the Bronx, the Board of Education simply transferred him from one school to another. Livid at such a feeble response, UBP activists found the molester's home address and demonstrated in front of his neighbor's house. They aimed to shame him in the midst of his own community. Disgraced, the molester resigned from his teaching position. Antonetty also began to challenge the systematic ways in which the city's Board of Education had relegated Puerto Rican children to an inferior education. With the prompting of Lorraine Hale, a black teacher and psychologist of mentally handicapped children at P.S. 25, Antonetty translated the IQ test into Spanish and demanded that the Spanish version of the test be given to Spanish-speaking children in the city.[1] The Board of Education had used the IQ test and reading tests to label a disproportionate number of black and Puerto Rican children as "mentally retarded" since the formation of 600 "special" schools in the late 1940s. Some educators had begun to challenge the validity of IQ tests as measurements of intelligence in the early 1960s. But psychologists' characterization of black and Puerto Rican children as "culturally maladjusted" and "emotionally troubled" led most white educators to continue believing that black and Puerto Rican students' low IQ scores reflected some type of inferiority, whether biological or cultural.[2] According to a 1969 report from the Bureau for Children with Retarded Mental Development, 5,578 (45 percent) of the students enrolled in "mentally retarded classes" in New York City were black and 3,706

(30 percent) were Puerto Rican. Together with Hale and other educators of color, Antonetty revealed how the IQ test tailored measurements of intelligence to fit the educational experiences of English-speaking, white middle-class children and thus failed to accurately measure intelligence levels of black and Puerto Rican children.[3]

Meanwhile, another group of parents in West and East Harlem also confronted white educators about their assumptions concerning the "unteachability" of students of color. Babette Edwards, a black parent, discovered that a principal in West Harlem had received a donation of violins but had sent them to another school. Together with other members of the Harlem Parents Committee, Edwards demanded that the principal get the violins back for the school. In a similar spirit, Hannah Brockington, a black parent from East Harlem, challenged teachers' tendencies to label black and Puerto Rican students as "unteachable" based on arbitrary judgments, such as claims that "they did not have fathers in the house," or "they didn't eat breakfast." Once a teacher labeled a student with such derogatory terms, these labels remained in the student's record permanently.[4]

Parents like Antonetty, Edwards, and Brockington challenged the basic premise of efforts to improve the education of students of color in the postwar era: the idea that they were "culturally deprived." With the growing application of social science research in the development of anti–juvenile delinquency programs in the early 1950s, social psychologists and anthropologists formulated a new term to refer to the predicament of poor students within the public school system. "Culturally deprived children" were described as those who did not have access to books, a motivation to pursue an education, or a healthy self-image as a result of their lower socioeconomic backgrounds. White and black researchers like Martin Deutsch, Allison Davis, and S. M. Miller had used a cultural approach to assess difficulties faced by students across racial backgrounds since the 1930s in order to avoid debates about innate racial differences.[5] But as the term "culturally deprived" became increasingly attached to postwar migrants living in urban centers in America—with recurrent references to children living in "slums" and within "female-headed households"—the term became synonymous with students of color.[6] Educators used the term to justify the benefits of school integration, arguing that minority children whose homes were ridden with a "culture of poverty" would gain a more positive self-image and a higher motivation to learn by immersing themselves in white, middle-class schools. The 1966 Coleman Report, for example, stated that "disadvantaged children" would gain "self-esteem" by associating with children from more fortunate families. Although many educators did not recognize it at the time, there was an implicit racism associated with this notion: the environment of "good" white schools would make up for whatever was lacking in "bad" black homes.[7] Black psychologist Kenneth Clark identified the racist connotations attached to the term "culturally deprived" early on: "To what extent are the contemporary social deprivation theories merely substituting notions of environmental immutability and fatalism for earlier notions of biologically determined educational unmodifiability?"[8]

Puerto Rican and black parents had protested the marginalization of their children in the city's public schools for more than a decade, but by the late 1960s, the Board of Education itself was forced to recognize how broken the school system had become. In 1966, black and Puerto Rican students made up the majority of the city's public school population at 50.2 percent, blacks making up 29.3 percent, and Puerto Ricans composing 20.9 percent.[9] Yet black and Puerto Rican students composed a meager 3.6 percent and 1.6 percent, respectively, of the academic high school graduates. Furthermore, only 1 percent of the city's school principals were black; there were no Puerto Rican principals at all.[10] Such numbers indicated to Frank Cordasco, a professor of education, the "total failure and bankruptcy of the social institution that is the school." At a Senate hearing in 1967, New York City's executive deputy superintendent of schools, Nathan Brown, admitted that he had "no defense" for such disproportions.[11]

Beginning in 1966, black and Puerto Rican parents built the community control movement. It was a multiracial movement that aimed to transform the public school system by restructuring power relationships among school professionals, parents, and students. Community control movements emerged in cities in the Northeast, Midwest, and West, such as Boston, New York, Philadelphia, Detroit, and Oakland, as well as in the South, for instance, in Hyde County in North Carolina. Community control activists demanded more equitable racial representation in other fields besides education, such as in the construction industry, in law enforcement, and in housing. But those centered on school struggles left the deepest imprints in the operation of social institutions.[12] Schools were the closest social institutions that could be molded by direct action, partially because school leaders had to remain accountable to the widely held belief that schools were the greatest social equalizers of American society. Although free public education was failing to provide upward mobility to America's poor, school leaders had to uphold this myth, at the very least, by meeting with parents and creating an image of "civic dialogue."[13]

At its core, the community control movement in New York City embodied black and Puerto Rican nationalist ideals. Similar to other black nationalist movements of the 1960s, it aimed to establish political self-determination for racialized minorities living within a multiracial and multiethnic society.[14] For the most part, it did not necessarily aim to establish a separate black or Puerto Rican nation. While some Puerto Rican leaders adopted the political independence of the island of Puerto Rico as one of their primary expressions of self-governance, most of them simply sought to have greater political influence on the mainland as a collective body within the framework set by the U.S. government.

Community control advocates' leaning toward self-governance largely reflected their response to the failures of postwar white liberalism. White liberals had tried to "help" racial and ethnic minorities through school integration, urban renewal, and the War on Poverty but had too often reinforced the racial status quo by restraining black and Puerto Rican leaders' efforts to make any meaningful change in the city's infrastructures. Growing increasingly skeptical of white liberals' intentions, community control leaders adopted black and Puerto Rican nationalism in order to achieve change more effectively. They valued poor people's knowledge above the expertise of white professionals. If postwar white liberalism was tied to the assumption that social science researchers and practitioners could use social engineering to lift the poor out of poverty, community control leaders argued that they could not use their professional degrees to wield power over poor people of color.[15] They argued that white teachers and psychologists needed to share their positions of authority with poor parents and community activists, who possessed a more intimate knowledge of children of color as the people who lived with them most intimately. They demanded that minority parents have greater control over school budgets, curriculum development, and personnel hiring and firing. Since many community control leaders emerged as leaders through War on Poverty programs—and, as a result, developed local identities as residents of particular neighborhoods—they also called for "local" empowerment. They claimed that local leaders should have more influence within programs administered in their neighborhoods since relationships growing out of face-to-face, daily interactions at the local level produced more creative solutions than those sprouting from absentee bureaucrats.

Along with local empowerment, community control advocates believed that they could establish greater black and Puerto Rican self-determination by fostering cultural and psychological independence. In order to institute a public school system that relied on the abilities of poor people of color more than white professionals' expertise, parents and educators needed to believe that a "black and Puerto Rican school" could indeed be as good as a "white school." They thus emphasized the importance of remaking their own conceptions of "black culture" and "Puerto Rican culture" in order to liberate their own minds from the trappings of internalized racism. They hired black and Puerto Rican teachers to teach black and Puerto Rican history, believing that having role models of color would lead students to gain a new sense of racial pride and individual self-esteem.

For Puerto Rican community control leaders, bilingual education became an essential feature of establishing a culturally nationalist pedagogy since Puerto Ricans' identity as Spanish speakers embodied a crucial part of their cultural identity. Younger activists born in the late 1940s and 1950s also began advocating for the political independence of the island of Puerto Rico. Although they were born on the mainland and had few family ties to the islanders, they linked themselves to the island's *independentistas* because they saw that the poverty of the Puerto Rican migrant population in New York City largely reflected the negative impact of U.S. colonialism on the island's economy and politics. While rooting themselves in the localism that older Puerto Rican community control activists had developed, young Puerto Rican activists reached beyond adults' focus on local communities to forge links with Puerto Ricans on the island and with anti-imperialists around the world.

Within the context of the community control movement in New York City, black and Puerto Rican nationalism emerged as two overlapping social movements. Far from "balkanizing" blacks and Puerto Ricans into isolated, alienated fringe groups, nationalist movements brought them closer together. The call for integration during the "classical phase" of the civil rights movement in the early 1960s had kept parents from the two groups separate. Puerto Rican parents had participated in the 1964 boycott, but they had generally hesitated to embrace the integrationist vision too strongly because they believed they were "already racially integrated" and saw the entire social experiment of racially mixing children as a "North American" concept. The call for community control of schools within their own neighborhoods, however, united the two groups because it shifted attention away from integration with whites toward a focus on building their own local resources. Rather than seeking progress through integration with middle-class whites, blacks and Puerto Ricans sought to create their own form of multiracial democracy by rooting their political vision in a working-class community.

The particularities of Puerto Rican nationalism—as embodied in the call for bilingual education and the island's political independence—did not create tensions with black nationalists since both groups possessed an international, multiracial vision of democracy. African American educators recognized that bilingual education would promote cultural pluralism in the city's school system broadly, creating an opening for the appreciation of black culture as well. Under the tenets of Third World solidarity, black nationalists also understood that the struggle to free Puerto Rico from its colonial status could catalyze Americans' commitment to decolonization movements all over the world. Far from alienating blacks into a beleaguered racial "other," black nationalism thus opened up a space for them to converse with Puerto Rican nationalists.[16] Together, this multiracial group of nationalists built a cultural pluralism that differed radically from that of white liberals. Whereas white liberals had celebrated cultural pluralism in order to buttress notions of American exceptionalism, the cultural pluralism of people of color exposed the cracks of American democracy.[17]

Looking at the community control movement through the lens of black and Puerto Rican New Yorkers allows us to see that it was much more cosmopolitan and culturally pluralistic than previously portrayed. Previous accounts of the community control movement in New York City were focused on the Ocean Hill–Brownsville conflict, and it was largely portrayed as a story of white-black polarization. Historian Jerald Podair argued that a "white middle-class culture" that was "integrationist, cosmopolitan and humanist" was replaced with a "black culture" that was deeply ambivalent about such values. Education scholar Daniel Perlstein acknowledged that New York City's school struggles involved a number of "immigrants who defied simple racial categories of black and white," but in his final analysis, the city's education history indicated essentially "black-white conflicts."[18] Scholars' tendency to leave Puerto Ricans out of this "black-white" narrative reflected their views on Puerto Ricans' racial status. They viewed Puerto Ricans as either "racially homogeneous" with blacks or completely racially separate from them.[19] Either way, Puerto Ricans were made invisible through these dichotomous logics: if they were the same as blacks, they did not warrant a separate analysis; if they were different from blacks, they were too numerically insignificant to compare to whites or blacks.

Rather than simplifying Puerto Rican nationalism to be identical to black nationalism or as completely separate from it, this chapter analyzes how it overlapped with the latter. Black and Puerto Rican nationalists developed distinct cultural identities of their own, but they also borrowed heavily from each other's ideas and resources. Their practices of self-governance were culturally specific yet universal in application. While some interpreted their cultural specificity to imply exclusion, many others recognized that it represented a broader stance of cultural pluralism for people of color across racial and ethnic boundaries.

Analyzing the community control movement through the lens of black and Puerto Rican coalitions also allows us to understand how organizations like the Young Lords Party (YLP, more commonly known as the Young Lords) left a deeper imprint in the city's infrastructures than previously assumed. The YLP has been known as a radical organization whose youthful idealism was short-circuited by autocratic leadership and ideological tensions surrounding its stance toward Marxist, Leninist, and Maoist philosophies.[20] The YLP, however, was not a fringe organization that emerged out of a political vacuum. Its young leaders worked alongside older black and Puerto Rican community control leaders. They were linked with organizations that identified themselves as both reformist and radical, and their call for black and Puerto Rican self-determination had a significant impact on the city's education system, health care system, and racial politics.

This chapter focuses on three movements that evolved among working-class blacks and Puerto Ricans in the late 1960s: community control, bilingual education, and youth movements. Although each of these movements had distinct goals, all three centered their activities on building black and Puerto Rican communities' cultural and political self-determination.

"50% Negro and 50% Puerto Rican": I.S. 201 and the Beginning of Community Control

Following the school boycott of 1964, it was clear that black and Puerto Rican parents were dissatisfied with the city's public education system. Beyond exposing the problem to both communities, however, there was little that was accomplished through the boycott. Compensatory education, which had been white liberals' preferred form of intervention, had produced few results. These programs included Ford Foundation–supported Great Cities School Improvement programs, Title I of the Elementary and

Secondary Education Act, Higher Horizons programs, and More Effective Schools programs. These programs aimed to provide extra help for "disadvantaged" students who were assumed to have learning deficiencies, but they did not consider how the entire school system itself needed to be reevaluated.[21] The meager efforts that had been directed toward school integration placed the burden of initiative on black and Puerto Rican parents, which meant that a very small number of them participated. Only 677 out of the 20,000 eligible junior high school students took advantage of the Open Enrollment program in 1960. By the end of the decade, the level of racial segregation among students had actually increased in public schools. Whereas 8 percent of New York City's public schools had black and Puerto Rican enrollments of over 85 percent in 1955, the proportion increased to 28 percent by 1968.[22]

The Board of Education remained stubbornly indifferent to the court order of *Brown v. Board of Education*. And, even more crucial, it failed to adjust the school system to the changes wrought by migration, white flight, and urban renewal. Puerto Rican and southern black migration had increased the number of students of color in schools. White flight severely shrank the city's white student population, as more than 2 million New Yorkers—the majority of whom were white—left the city for the suburbs between the 1940s and the 1960s.[23] Together, these two migrations dramatically changed the student population in schools, so that racial and ethnic minorities became numerical majorities in the schools. White teachers and school administrators who no longer identified with the city's student population watched the student dropout rate increase dramatically but did little to address what was wrong with the system. They let the physical condition of the schools deteriorate. In a Harlem school with a student body of 650, students had access to only one boys' bathroom and one girls' bathroom.[24] The majority of white teachers lived in the suburbs and resented having to work in the city. According to Charles Wilson, a black community control leader, white teachers were infamous for running out the school doors as soon as they heard the three o'clock bell, beating their own students in their hurry to leave the "ghetto" and go home.[25] Deborah Meier, a white teacher, recounted that many white teachers blamed the students' home environments for their low academic performance. They reasoned, "I've worked with other children, you know, the middle-income children, and they learned. Then it must be something wrong with these children. It can't be me. . . . So you think, 'well, it's the home . . . it must be the home. . . . We can't do anything about the home, so it's not our fault.'"[26] White teachers blamed their students' academic failings on their "bad" homes and their transience as migrants, but student transience was usually imposed on them by urban renewal. Urban renewal had relocated black and Puerto Rican families from borough to borough, exacerbating student turnover rates in schools. In a West Harlem school, the number for student turnover was higher than the total number of seats in the school in the mid-1960s.[27]

Facing a school system so deeply committed to maintaining the racial status quo, black and Puerto Rican parents struggled to find a common agenda that could effectively mobilize their communities. It was not until they faced a particularly humiliating experience in Harlem's I.S. 201 that they gained the impetus to create a new political vision for themselves. Due to overcrowding in Harlem schools, the Board of Education had agreed to build I.S. 201, a new school that would integrate black and white children and attract students by installing modern facilities, adult and teenage centers, and community relations school programs. The Board of Education, however, failed to deliver on all of these promises. Board officials claimed that the architecture of the school, which had no windows, provided an opportunity to bring technological innovation to the school in the form of an air conditioning system. The windowless building, however, was actually designed to avoid the cost of repairing broken windows. To black educator Kenneth B. Clark, the windowless building was a symbol of the "ghetto" experience, an image that reinforced the notion that "ghetto" children were perpetually confined in America's dark "ghettos."[28] While choosing a site on the boundary between Central Harlem and East Harlem—the corner of Madison Avenue and 127th Street—the board claimed that school integration would be possible because white families from Queens and the Bronx would voluntarily enroll their children in this school. To no one's surprise, no white student from the Bronx or Queens signed up to attend I.S. 201.

Most insulting, however, was the board's claim that I.S. 201 would be integrated because it would be half black and half Puerto Rican. Exploiting Puerto Ricans' ambiguous racial identity, District Superintendent of Schools Daniel Schreiber claimed in January 1966, "Yes, I.S. 201 will be integrated—50 percent Negro and 50 percent Puerto Rican." Schreiber intentionally gerrymandered a new feeder pattern of schools to achieve this racial composition by including P.S. 155 and P.S. 96 of East Harlem and excluding elementary schools in North Harlem.[29] At a time when black and Puerto Rican parents were fighting against segregation from white students and not from each other, such a statement was absurd. It had been more than a decade since the Board of Education itself had noted the increasing segregation of black and Puerto Rican students from white students, yet here they used Puerto Ricans as a white group in order to fake racial integration. Appalled by Schreiber's insincerity, Suki Ports, a Japanese American member of the Harlem Parents Committee (HPC), lamented, "This answer could only be construed as a cruel and vicious hoax for parents who had fought for integration since 1954."[30]

Disillusioned by the intransigence of white leaders, black integration advocates began to doubt the desirability of racial integration. The president of the HPC, Isaiah Robinson, wrote a letter to School Superintendent Bernard Donovan, stating, "We have knowledge that your office with deliberate calculation intends to use Puerto Rican students on a 50–50 basis to give the impression that I.S. 201 is racially integrated."[31] Robinson warned Donovan that "this tactic, sir, will attract the strongest, most militant protest from this organization . . . and will turn I.S. 201 into a battleground." Robinson, however, received no apology or retraction from Donovan. At a meeting with the HPC, Robinson later suggested, "almost as a joke, that since white children would not be sent into Harlem schools and black children were not being invited downtown in any meaningful numbers, *maybe the blacks had better accept segregation and run their own schools*."[32] It was a moment of disillusion for every parent on the HPC. The debacle of I.S. 201 became their last attempt at improving their children's education through school integration.

At the same time that black parents abandoned their hopes to integrate their children with whites, Puerto Rican parents also gave up hopes to be treated as white. Schreiber's manipulation of their ambiguous racial identity jolted them out of their ambivalence on the question of race. Although trying to straddle both the white and the black worlds, Puerto Ricans realized that their silence on their racial status made them into pawns in the system. The Board of Education treated them as "black," while referring to them as "white" when it was convenient to do so. Following the opening of I.S. 201, more than 150 Puerto Rican mothers and their supporters picketed in front of P.S. 96, expressing their resentment over the fact that their children were being bused north to I.S. 201 for the purpose of falsely "integrating" the school. Another group of Puerto Ricans provided a detailed account of the I.S. 201 story before the U.S. Civil Rights Commission hearings at the Salem Methodist Church.[33]

Parents in Harlem were incensed by the course of events surrounding

I.S. 201, but social worker Preston Wilcox took the opportunity to propose an alternative vision of educational reform. During a local school board meeting of District 4 in April 1966, Wilcox laid out his vision of a community-controlled school. He stated that the time had come for "a new approach to relations between the community and the public educational system." Although most Harlem parents felt that they had to resign themselves to accepting segregated black schools, he argued that "if one believes that a segregated white school can be a 'good' school, then one must believe that a segregated Negro and Puerto Rican school, like I.S. 201, can also be a 'good' school." Given the Board of Education's refusal to integrate black and white children, Wilcox argued that black and Puerto Rican parents had an opportunity to assume a leadership role in this school and establish a closer relationship between schools and the community. Calling for a "radical redistribution of power," he argued that community members should establish a school-community committee, and that this group of community leaders should select principals and teachers and build a community-centered school. As community leaders and teachers would together share the burden of responsibility in the schools, they would prove that "they do not have to be white to be a success." Black leaders who grew tired of integration plans and Puerto Rican leaders who saw no value in integration now found a common language of protest through Wilcox's vision of local power.[34]

Harlem parents presented Wilcox's new vision for a community-controlled school to the Board of Education, but this proposal escalated tensions between the two groups. While parents threatened to boycott I.S. 201 unless they were given the power to control it, the board claimed that this would violate state education laws. But the board's refusal to listen to the parents only served to embolden their desire to fight for their rights. When the rest of New York City public schools opened on September 12, 1966, Harlem parents successfully kept I.S. 201 closed. As negotiations with the Board of Education still did not move forward, HPC leaders Helen Testamark and Babette Edwards began to build a coalition of parents and boycott supporters. William Hall, a New York City–raised African American, watched Testamark's plea for "the people of good will in the community to come and help" on television. He immediately went to the parents' meeting that same evening. Hall, who had taken part in various civil rights protests organized by the Student Nonviolent Coordinating Committee (SNCC) in the South in the earlier part of that decade, was ready to bring his experiences from the South home.[35] Soon, other members of SNCC's

New York chapter, the Congress of Racial Equality (CORE), and the Organization of Afro-American Unity also joined the parents. Strengthened by a growing coalition, parents from I.S. 201 demanded the replacement of Stanley Lisser, a white principal chosen by the Board of Education, with a black principal. Members of the United Federation of Teachers (UFT) and the Council of Supervisory Associations (CSA) rejected the parents' demand. Stokely Carmichael's visit to I.S. 201 on September 21 solidified I.S. 201 as a battleground for Black Power in New York City. Babette Edwards, who invited him through her friend Ivanhoe Donaldson, claimed that Carmichael simply came to support the parents. His fame as the national spokesperson for the Black Power movement, however, stirred up fear among newspaper reporters, city officials, and law enforcement. City policemen encircled the I.S. 201 complex, creating a sense of siege and terror.[36] Suki Ports remembered the day: "The police helicopter was circling at the top of the building. . . . They had the entire school building protected by having the motorcycle cops, with the high leather jackets and hats. They had them in helmets, arms linked, and they surrounded the entire neighborhood. On all three surroundings, they had a sharp shooter on every other rooftop. For what? Stokely Carmichael and H. Rap Brown. We don't know what they feared, but there they were with their guns and ammunitions. We couldn't believe this display of armament. We were just fighting with words, but our words got them so nervous they didn't know what to do. It was an example of really no communication. It was the first reign of terror."[37]

Activists in Ocean Hill–Brownsville and the South Bronx who were engaged in similar battles with the Board of Education joined I.S. 201 leaders. Black leaders such as David Spencer, Babette Edwards, and Milton Galamison joined Puerto Rican leaders like Evelina Antonetty, Dolores Torres, and Vincent Negron to form the People's Board of Education in December 1966. White leaders such as Robert Nichol, Ellen Lurie, Rosalie Stutz, and John Powis also joined them. Together, they hoped to keep the Board of Education accountable for its failure to educate black and Puerto Rican children.[38] The Board of Education tried to appease the People's Board by authorizing the implementation of three experimental demonstration districts. In April 1967, the Board of Education chose I.S. 201 in Harlem, Ocean Hill–Brownsville in Brooklyn, and Two Bridges on the Lower East Side as laboratories to test the feasibility of including parents in the administration of schools. The demonstration districts were made up of a series of elementary and junior high schools within a given area.

The I.S. 201 complex, for example, was made up of seven schools: P.S. 133, P.S. 24, P.S. 39, P.S. 68, C.S. 30, C.S. 31, and I.S. 201.[39]

The demonstration districts represented a compromise between city authorities and parents of color—an alliance that blurred the different priorities guiding each group for the time being. Board officials called it an experiment in "decentralization," whereas black and Puerto Rican parents called it "community control."[40] "Decentralization" was Mayor Lindsay's strategy to gain additional funding from the state. By treating each of the five boroughs as separate entities, he could increase the amount allocated for the entire city. Following Lindsay's suggestion, board officials agreed to start an experiment with decentralization through demonstration districts. The board purported to become more responsive to its constituents by allowing local school boards of demonstration districts to make certain decisions in their local schools, but no real power was granted to them. Local school boards could change the schools' curriculum, but only within the framework set by the Board of Education. They could petition to increase minority faculty hiring, but hiring procedures remained firmly within the purview of the Board of Education.[41] Similar to antipoverty programs, demonstration districts included poor parents in the decision-making process but did not give them any real authority.

The Board of Education and parents of color also differed in their understanding of the ultimate goal of this experimentation. Black and Puerto Rican parents believed that the demonstration districts would be used as a template for broad, citywide reform of all public schools. Yet, the Board of Education's selection of the districts reflected its desire to limit the experiment as a project designed exclusively for racial and ethnic minorities. Parents from Manhattan's Upper West Side school district, which still had a 30 percent white student population, petitioned to become a demonstration district. But the Board of Education refused to include it in the experiment. In the words of Ford Foundation education expert Mario Fantini, this selectivity showed that the board viewed demonstration districts as "beleaguered outposts," not models of reform.[42]

The Board of Education's tentative attitude toward parents of color paralleled that of Mayor Lindsay. He partially supported efforts being made by I.S. 201 parents because he considered UFT another public employee union whose bureaucracy needed to be reformed. But he did not believe that school integration should be legally enforced. He agreed with the board's opinion that integration should happen only if and when white parents voluntarily chose to enroll their children in black schools. His at-

tempt to respond to the crisis in public schools through the Bundy Panel
also showed his lack of commitment to addressing the fundamental problems plaguing schools. He authorized Ford Foundation president Mc-
George Bundy and other members of his Bundy Panel to expose the bankruptcy of the school system and the need to break up UFT's monopoly
in their report. Yet Lindsay did little to create public support around the
Bundy Panel's recommendations, effectively destroying any possibility
that their suggestions could actually change the school system through
legislation.[43] He demonstrated his unwillingness to recognize the unequal
power relationship between the UFT and parents of color most clearly during the third teachers' strike in 1968. At a meeting at Brooklyn's East Midwood Jewish Center, he argued that both sides of the dispute were guilty
of "acts of vigilantism." At the conclusion of the strikes, his report stated
that both sides of the conflict showed "an appalling amount of racial prejudice."[44] A few hundred black and Puerto Rican parents with little official
authority confronted the power of a teachers' union that had more than
40,000 members and a Board of Education that controlled an annual budget of $50 billion—yet Lindsay judged the groups based on their expres-
sions of racial prejudice, as if all of them had an equal capacity to affect
public policy based on such prejudices.[45]

Creating the Building Blocs of a "Black and Puerto Rican Community"

The demonstration district of I.S. 201 emerged with severe constraints,
but its leaders took the opportunity to build a new model of education and
community building. The composition of the I.S. 201 governing board,
which was 73 percent black and 17 percent Puerto Rican, reflected the racial demographics of Harlem's student population, which was 83 percent
black and 16 percent Puerto Rican.[46] The governing board did not arrive at
this distribution of power without conflicts. Ted Velez had to complain to
the black-dominant leadership about the lack of Puerto Rican representation within the governing board's initial makeup. Once the complaint was
made, however, the governing board was more than willing to invite three
Puerto Rican leaders—Maria Canino, Sarah Scott, and Leila Ocasio—to
join the team.[47] Membership on the governing board also reflected the
strong working-class base of Harlem's families: 67 percent of the members were paraprofessionals or antipoverty workers who did not hold professional degrees. David Spencer had worked as an elevator operator before becoming the chairman of the governing board.[48] Many of the board

FIGURE 5.1 Charles Wilson, c. 1982 (Courtesy of Charles Wilson)

members also had prior experience in community organizing through War on Poverty programs. Spencer and Babette Edwards had both worked in the East Harlem Triangle subcommunity of Massive Economic Neighborhood Development (MEND). Their political organizing had predated the War on Poverty, but the federal program had helped them mobilize larger numbers of Harlemites into political action.

In the first year of I.S. 201's operation, unit administrator Charles Wilson made establishing a working relationship with the parents a priority. The son of immigrants from the British West Indies and Aruba, Wilson grew up familiar with the hard facts of life. His mother had died when he was only seven years old, and he had to work his way through school. While hauling garbage and pushing carts of clothes through the garment district at night, he managed to graduate from Brooklyn College and earn two master's degrees, in public administration and in educational psychology. When I.S. 201 parents recruited him to become the unit administrator in 1968, he decided to take the job because "I was touched by the parents' feelings." Many other black professionals hesitated to take the position because I.S. 201 was perceived to be a group of "militants," and if the experiment failed, careers could be jeopardized. Yet Wilson felt that he "had nothing to lose." He did not aspire to become part of the education "establishment" and simply saw I.S. 201 as a place where he could be "of service to black people."[49]

Wilson's black nationalist sentiments led him to identify strongly with the parents and to remain distant from the Board of Education. Memories of his father's political activism as a Garveyite in the early twentieth century had nurtured in him a deep hunger for black self-determination. He had never believed that integration offered the best solution to the problems of black children. In the early 1960s, Wilson had written articles in the *Liberator*, a black nationalist newsletter, in which he critiqued the "white liberal" and the "Negro bourgeoisie" for believing that they could desegregate America through a moral commitment based on Christianity. "The so-called Negro revolution was never about morality, it is about caste, power, and black people's attempts to secure an identity within the American community," Wilson wrote.[50] Distrustful of white liberals and black professionals alike, he made only minimal effort to secure support from the Board of Education or to abide by their rules when hiring his staff. He did not pressure the board to give his staff higher salaries, nor did he demand a higher salary for himself—even though his salary was $10,000 lower than Ocean Hill–Brownsville unit administrator Rhody McCoy.[51] He rarely met with School Superintendent Bernard Donovan, despite Donovan's repeated requests. He did not want to give Donovan the impression that he could be used as a pawn to "chastise" I.S. 201's governing board. He spent most of his days meeting with parents and community leaders instead. He insisted that he would remain accountable to the parents above everybody else because the parents had hired him, not the board.[52]

Wilson's approach resonated with some I.S. 201 leaders. Some I.S. 201 teachers also made parents' political goals a priority. They rejected the UFT's attempts to discredit the experiment and believed that they could share their knowledge and authority with parents. Some had belonged to the Teachers' Union, the left-wing predecessor of the UFT. Their communist ideologies, developed during the Depression of the 1930s, had taught them that black nationalism would be an essential element of a workers' revolution.[53] Others who had participated in Vista or Peace Corps programs in the early 1960s considered their teaching a "tour of social duty" and believed that their curriculum should reflect the community's needs. Many others had initially felt threatened by the presence of paraprofessionals—the majority of whom were poor people of color—and feared that they would replace regular teachers. But they quickly developed a sense of camaraderie with them, as paraprofessionals sought to unionize and attain job security through the same rules as those used by teachers.[54]

The majority of the teachers, however, were skeptical of the legitimacy of I.S. 201 leaders. They did not believe that the I.S. 201 governing board actually represented the "community" in the neighborhood. A number of them expressed their viewpoints in a 1968 article in *United Teacher*, a UFT publication. According to John Goldstein, a teacher at P.S. 68, a "smaller, militant group" of parents led by David Spencer and Babette Edwards took the leadership of I.S. 201, but they did not represent the majority of parents by any means. Another teacher asserted that I.S. 201 leaders were actually using education as a "means of getting jobs." Many teachers contested the I.S. 201 governing board's claims to represent the political leadership of the area. Jean Lloyd, a teacher from P.S. 68, claimed that "the real organizations of the neighborhood" were not represented on the board because MEND, an "East Harlem" group, dominated the board instead of "HARYOU Community Corporation," which represented the actual "territory" of I.S. 201. In her opinion, Harlem Youth Opportunities Unlimited represented the "real" leadership of I.S. 201 because the schools were located in Central Harlem, not East Harlem. Terry Leonard from P.S. 39, on the other hand, claimed that "the real parents are not represented" on the governing board because her school was "65% Spanish-speaking," yet the board had only two "Spanish-speaking members."[55]

Teachers like Lloyd and Leonard claimed to know what I.S. 201's "real" community should look like based on narrow understandings of the neighborhood's racial and ethnic boundaries. The I.S. 201 complex was formed out of an area that was much broader than simply the "territory" of Central Harlem or the Spanish-speaking population. The complex was located on the boundary between Central Harlem and East Harlem at 127th Street and Madison Avenue, and I.S. 201's leadership reflected the political influence of MEND, which was officially known as an "East Harlem" anti-poverty group but whose subcommunities included areas that overlapped with Central Harlem. The I.S. 201 student population also reflected the racial and ethnic mixture of the area, which was both black and Puerto Rican. Some schools in the complex, such as P.S. 39, had large Puerto Rican populations at 45 percent, but others, like P.S. 68, had smaller ones at 1.5 percent.[56] Thus, any narrow understanding of who made up the "real" community at I.S. 201 did not reflect the actual heterogeneity of the population.

Real and imagined barriers could have kept black and Puerto Rican communities from collaborating with each other at I.S. 201. A presentation given by a group of I.S. 201 guidance counselors, psychologists, and teachers to the New York State Commission on Education in 1971 reveals some of the assumptions presenters held regarding Puerto Rican attitudes toward black protest. A team of guidance counselors from the I.S. 201 complex wrote a fictitious story of a Puerto Rican family named the "Lopez Family" in order to demonstrate how community leaders had been able to improve the education of Puerto Rican children through a community-focused approach. According to this text, Mrs. Lopez initially does not send her son Juan to school because "she has heard of 'Black militants' and feels that Black teachers and Black children may pick on Juan without provocation." It is not until a bilingual teacher brings Juan and Mrs. Lopez to school that Mrs. Lopez realizes that "Black children were not actually pitted against Puerto Rican children, and Juan could safely attend school." Although a fictitious account, it demonstrated I.S. 201 educators' perception of reality: Puerto Rican families most likely refused to send their children to I.S. 201 due to their fear of black radical activists.[57]

Fear of "Black militants," however, was not a particularly Puerto Rican response to the Black Power movement. According to Hannah Brockington, a black parent and member of the I.S. 201 governing board, black parents were as afraid of black radical groups as anybody else. Ironically, when black parents organized the boycott of I.S. 201 in the fall of 1966, some children did not go to school because "when the parents saw the Black Panthers, the parents grabbed their kids and ran like hell." Members of the New York chapter of the Black Panthers had come to I.S. 201 to support black parents, but the parents did not recognize them as allies because they had come to know the Black Panthers through mainstream media, which portrayed them as "violent" and "revolutionary." Brockington was saddened by the fact that some black parents did not understand "who is for you and who is against you," but their reaction revealed the reality that black parents involved in I.S. 201 were not a monolithic group of "radical" individuals.[58] If I.S. 201 leaders had to convince Puerto Rican parents that Black Power was a worthy cause to pursue, so too did they have to persuade black parents. Puerto Ricans' perceived fear of "black militants" therefore did not indicate racial tensions between blacks and Puerto Ricans but an ideological tension between a new group of black radicals and a general population that did not understand them.

Black and Puerto Rican professionals at I.S. 201 certainly felt conscious of how their skin color could determine perceptions of their legitimacy. Unit administrator Charles Wilson believed that Puerto Ricans doubted his leadership capacities because he was dark skinned. "[Puerto Ricans] were not always sure about leadership by black people. Because of *limpieza de sangre* [purity of blood], they saw this darkness. You couldn't be smart."[59] Drawing on his knowledge of Spanish constructions of race and his own color consciousness as a second-generation West Indian immigrant, Wilson believed that some Puerto Ricans assumed he was incompetent simply due to his skin color. He did not attribute colorism (discrimination based on skin color) simply to Puerto Ricans—he believed that black parents had also demonstrated colorism by selecting Rhody McCoy, a light-skinned African American, as the unit administrator of the Ocean Hill–Brownsville district. Nevertheless, he felt especially judged by Puerto Ricans' color prejudices.

Light-skinned Puerto Rican professionals also felt conscious of how their skin color would be read by black participants of I.S. 201. Hernan LaFontaine, who became assistant principal of C.S. 30, recalled having a difficult time earning the trust of certain blacks because he looked "white." He overheard many of them asking, "Who the hell is that? Who is that white honkie?" When others clarified that he was Puerto Rican, their response was no more accepting. Instead of calling him a "honkie," they called him a "spic." LaFontaine understood that he was caught in a racially charged environment that increasingly reduced people to the color of their skin and associated "blackness" with legitimacy and everything else with fraudulence. LaFontaine remembered waking up everyday shaking in fear during his first days of work at I.S. 201. According to Babette Edwards, however, I.S. 201 leaders' suspicions of LaFontaine actually had nothing to do with his skin color. "No one was against him because he looked white. People were against LaFontaine, if anything, because he came from the Board of Ed[ucation]."[60] LaFontaine was one of the few Puerto Ricans whose credentials fulfilled civil service requirements enforced by the board and who were hired at I.S. 201 by the board instead of by the parents. While it is difficult to ascertain the actual reasons behind black leaders' suspicions of him, LaFontaine's memories of being called a "honkie" and "spic" indicate the extent to which race became the primary marker of self-understanding for I.S. 201 professionals during the years of the schools' operation.

Emerging racial and ethnic self-identities, however, did not keep blacks and Puerto Ricans from working together. As the heat of confrontation cooled, people's loyalties and motivations became evident. After two years of working at I.S. 201, LaFontaine felt accepted by blacks at the school, "because they saw me work[;] I was there at six in the morning, trying to get coverage for absentee teachers. . . . I really broke my back, working for two years, and they knew it. Nobody could deny that."[61] Black and Puerto Rican professionals held prejudices against one another, but those involved in building I.S. 201 were able to collaborate because they had one goal in mind: to give a quality education to poor children.

If black and Puerto Rican professionals' color consciousness presented a challenge that needed to be overcome, black and Puerto Rican parents did not pay much attention to it. Unlike professionals, parents of color embraced each other's support more eagerly because they sensed the urgency of their children's needs more intensely. They also had little to lose by finding allies among other ethnic groups. "When people are suffering the same thing, they don't have the time to look at what your skin is," recounted Hannah Brockington. According to her, black and Puerto Rican parents did not have problems working with each other because poor people knew they needed each other. "If the man don't give heat in my apartment, you don't have it either. We have to join together as tenants to get the heat. This is the same thing in the schools. Wherever I'm suffering, you're suffering. I don't have time to find out if you're Puerto Rican or what."[62]

Babette Edwards also sensed that she shared a history of oppression with Puerto Rican parents. "We [blacks and Puerto Ricans] acted as one because our children were suffering the same oppressors. We had the same issues, the same concerns. That's why we got together."[63] While living in the same public housing projects and watching their children struggle in school together, black and Puerto Rican parents knew about each other's cultural differences but rooted their relationships in their common experiences as poor people.

Black and Puerto Rican parents found ways to overcome real and perceived cultural barriers. Preston Wilcox had mischaracterized Puerto Ricans and blacks in the early 1960s by seeing the former as culturally "submissive" and the latter as "aggressive."[64] Black parents at I.S. 201, however, did not let simplistic notions of cultural difference get in the way of their collaboration. Rather than assume that Puerto Rican culture was inherently different from black culture, they began to use Puerto Rican school aides as translators to help them overcome language barriers between the two groups. "The parents were more apt to talk to school aides than anybody else because they spoke their language," Brockington recounted. Although Puerto Rican parents initially hesitated to collaborate with black parents, they began to do so when Puerto Rican school aides served as translators between the two groups. Babette Edwards also claimed that training black parents to become better advocates of their children was not that different from training Puerto Rican parents. The difference between confrontational and nonconfrontational parents was not culture but knowledge. "That went on not only for Latino parents, but also for black parents. They thought that teacher and principal knew best. But once you show them stats, of where their schools were in the line up of New York City schools, then it opened their eyes. Once it became evident, that would radicalize them."[65]

The 1968 teachers' strikes that erupted from the conflict between Ocean Hill–Brownsville district's parents and teachers further solidified blacks and Puerto Ricans' shared identity as oppressed minorities. The strike represented the culmination of the conflict that had developed between Ocean Hill–Brownsville's white teachers and the neighborhood's pre- dominantly black and Puerto Rican parents. The neighborhood had ex- perienced a large outmigration of Jewish families in the early 1960s. The Board of Education had allowed the parents to institute some changes in the schools' curriculum by designating Ocean Hill–Brownsville one of the three demonstration districts of the city. But the experiment had only ex- acerbated tensions between parents and teachers, as parents felt that they did not have enough influence over personnel, curriculum, and financing, whereas teachers felt that parents had too much power. The strike, which was triggered by the demonstration district governing board's transfer of nineteen white teachers and administrators from J.H.S. 271, polarized ra- cial tensions between white and black New Yorkers.[66]

But it also affected the city's Puerto Rican leadership. It caused even the most conservative sectors of the Puerto Rican leadership to identify more closely with black activists than with established white authorities. Journalists from El Diario had reported on the formation of black–Puerto Rican coalitions throughout the 1960s by dichotomizing Puerto Ricans as an "ethnic" and African Americans as a "racial" group (see Chapter 3). Even with the I.S. 201 boycott of 1966, an El Diario editorial had denigrated black parents' demands for black teachers as illegitimate since it was based on a "racial standpoint," while validating Puerto Rican parents' de- mands for Spanish-speaking teachers as "practical." By November 1968, however, El Diario editorials began supporting Ocean Hill–Brownsville's parents and condemning the UFT unequivocally. The citywide teachers' strikes had been dragging on for more than five months, forcing students to miss a total of thirty-six days of school. Referring to UFT's third strike, the editorialist argued that whatever complaints UFT could have against the Board of Education or the district governing board, "this does not give the Union the moral right to victimize the children and parents of New

York."[67] Puerto Rican Community Development Project executive director Amalia Betanzos, who perennially depicted blacks as "violent" and Puerto Ricans as "peaceful," also expressed her support for black community control leaders. Together with many Puerto Rican leaders, Betanzos signed a statement that read: "The UFT has taken a position that directly ignores its professional obligations and priorities concerning the public schools system. . . . The union is acting like an incompetent teacher who punishes the entire class for the alleged transgression of one student."[68] Puerto Rican leaders who had formerly kept black civil rights leaders at arm's length began identifying with them more closely due to the extreme actions taken by white teachers.

As increasing numbers of Puerto Ricans identified with the community control movement, the network of black and Puerto Rican parent organizations expanded. The United Bronx Parents (UBP), which had been organizing parents since 1966, broadened its program beyond the Bronx in 1968. UBP executive director Evelina Antonetty now began to forge coalitions across the city and the country, sharing parent-training materials with black and Puerto Rican parents in East Harlem, Mexican parents in California, Native American parents on reservations, and even middle-class parents in New York.[69] Julio Morales, who had previously worked as a tenant organizer in MEND's Metro North subcommunity, followed in Antonetty's footsteps. He founded the East Harlem Coalition for Community Control (EHCCC) in 1968 to organize parents as well. Funded by the Community Development Agency with a grant of $18,000, parents from EHCCC attended lectures by community control advocates like Rhody McCoy and Antonetty while receiving a stipend of $90 a week. They learned about their basic rights as parents, such as the right to talk to administrators and teachers, to investigate issues such as lunches, drugs, suspensions, and safety, to know the reading scores of their children's schools, and to form Spanish-speaking chapters of parent associations.[70]

The experience was life transforming for some parents. After working with the EHCCC for a year, Darie Castro wrote a letter to Morales in 1969: "I never knew that we as parents could have a say in the schools. Not only that, I didn't know that we as citizens are entitled to get assistance from all sources." Castro's increased awareness of her civic rights produced a higher sense of inner confidence as well. "Through this program I was able to learn more about my community, to be able to talk out, and not be afraid, that when one believes in something no one can change their ideas," she wrote. Marie Lane, mother of eight children, also experienced a

FIGURE 5.2 United Bronx Parents' meeting, 1970s (United Bronx Parents Records, Centro de Estudios Puertorriqueños, Hunter College, CUNY)

dramatic shift in her attitude toward education. While the teachers' strike had left her feeling "confused and disgusted," her participation in EHCCC helped her support teachers and principals "because in our hearts we felt this was the right thing to do." Emboldened by her experience, Lane, a high school dropout, decided to go back to school "so that I can be better equipped to help my children."[71] Getting involved in parent activism was not simply an act of political will; it gave black and Puerto Rican parents a renewed sense of confidence and self-efficacy as individuals.

Bilingual Education as a Practice of Cultural Self-Determination

A crucial part of the community control movement involved improving Puerto Rican youth's education through bilingual education. Puerto Rican parents confronted the fact that they had become the newest victims of a long history of language discrimination, in which America was mythologized as a monolingual nation. Certainly, bilingual education advocates of the 1960s did not invent the idea of bilingual education. As historian Carlos Blanton has shown, bilingual education was a "thoroughly American education" in the mid-nineteenth century.[72] Before the rise of Progressivism and World War I–era xenophobia, American educators had felt perfectly comfortable teaching English in conjunction with many European languages, such as German, Czech, and Spanish. A tendency toward parochialism combined with an appreciation for cultural pluralism had led both government officials and immigrants to agree that teaching children how to speak English at the same time that they retained their home language was good pedagogical practice. It was only when locally controlled education systems were nationally centralized under Progressives' drive toward increased efficiency that the first English-only law was enacted, in 1918.[73]

Since the time of the U.S. invasion of Puerto Rico in 1898, Puerto Ricans had fought against North Americans' impulse to impose English as the official language of instruction in the island's schools. It was only in 1945 that Puerto Rico's commissioner of education, Rafael Pico, was able to establish that Puerto Rican children would be educationally best served through the use of Spanish as the official language of instruction, with the teaching of English as a separate subject.[74] When Puerto Ricans migrated to the mainland, however, many of them encouraged their children to acquire English fluency quickly, even if it came at the cost of their Spanish fluency. They believed that language assimilation would bring them economic mobility.

During the community control movement, however, Puerto Rican parents began to reconsider the impact of language assimilation. Alma Bagu, a Puerto Rican mother who got involved in the Ocean Hill–Brownsville demonstration district, realized that her children's language assimilation did not necessarily guarantee them academic success: "When I had my own children, I wanted them to speak only English in order to avoid the same problems I had [when I was a child]. Because I wanted my children to be accepted by the *Americanos*, I closed the door on my own heritage. I finished the job on my children that my teachers started on me. The irony of the whole thing was that my children weren't accepted anyway."[75]

Bagu's frustration with Puerto Ricans' marginalization in the broader society reflected the sentiments guiding the majority of bilingual education advocates. Bilingual education advocates had conflicting opinions on what bilingual education was and what its goals were, but there was a consensus that it could help repair Puerto Rican children's damaged self-images. Testimonies presented at the 1967 U.S. Senate hearings on bilingual education demonstrate this dominant opinion. Through the support of the National Education Association and Senator Ralph Yarborough of Texas, Mexican American leaders had introduced Bill S. 428, a law that would institute bilingual education as a federally funded program for Spanish-speaking students at the elementary and secondary school levels.[76] Puerto Rican leaders, as representatives of the second-largest Spanish-speaking group in the United States, joined Mexican American leaders in expressing the basis of their support for such a bill. The director of the Migration Division of the Commonwealth of Puerto Rico, Joseph Monserrat, recounted his own past as a Puerto Rican migrant whose assimilation into American society had come at a psychological cost. "I do not think we have ever measured the psychic cost of the melting pot," he stated. The pressure to "speak English without a Spanish accent," "buy a Brooks Bros. suit," and get "short cuts" on his hair had all caused a certain loss of himself. Bilingual education was one way to help Puerto Ricans repair this "psychic" loss, Monserrat claimed. Bronx borough president Herman Badillo also believed that bilingual education could help Puerto Ricans regain an appreciation for their culture. The "key provision" of bilingual education, Badillo stated, should be "programs designed to impart to Spanish-speaking students a knowledge of and pride in their ancestral culture and language" so that Puerto Rican children could step outside the "Puerto Rican ghetto" and learn that "Puerto Ricans can perform." In a city where "we have ridiculous arguments . . . about whether a Puerto Rican can get to be a bricklayer," Puerto Rican children could learn that "in Puerto Rico we build 20-story buildings, not only with Puerto Rican bricklayers but with Puerto Rican architects," Badillo stated.[77] Puerto Ricans from most sectors of society—ranging from poor parents in Brooklyn to elected officials and prominent civic leaders—believed that Puerto Rican children suffered from low self-esteem and that bilingual education could help correct the problem.

Those who believed in this premise also believed that the job could be done best by Puerto Rican teachers. Leaders ranging from Aspira's executive director Frank Negron to president of the Puerto Rican Educators' Association Hernan LaFontaine and deputy commissioner of Manpower Operations Louis Cardona stated that Puerto Rican teachers with the appropriate licenses should teach bilingual education classes. "Puerto Rican teachers, who know and understand the Puerto Rican heritage, are best qualified to impart to our children the knowledge of and pride in their culture and language," stated Cardona. Bilingual education was not simply a program to teach children the Spanish language or the English language; it was a program designed to instill ethnic pride through role models who shared students' ethnicity. "I don't think you can serve a people if you are not identified with them in a significant way," Cardona asserted.[78] Although Puerto Rican leaders would later become more critical of Puerto Rican teachers' elitism and lack of identification with Puerto Rican students, during these initial conversations, they believed that Puerto Rican teachers and students mostly shared a similar experience of marginalization. What else could explain the fact that less than 1 percent of New York City public school teachers were Puerto Rican?[79]

Differences of opinion, however, existed between those who viewed bilingual education as a tool of assimilation and those who viewed it as a vehicle to further cultural pluralism. The majority of white elected officials saw bilingual education as a better method of teaching English to Puerto Rican students. Congressman Jacob H. Gilbert, Congressman William F. Ryan, and Senator Ralph Yarborough all claimed that their ultimate goal was Puerto Ricans' integration into the English-speaking, mainstream society. Solving "language problems" was one way of breaking the "cycle of low education, inadequate jobs, and poverty" among Puerto Ricans, stated Congressman Ryan. The education coordinator of the Migration Division of the Commonwealth of Puerto Rico, Carmen Dinos, however, had a different vision. She believed that bilingual education would actually be "most advantageous" to students who were fluent in English but not Spanish. These were the students who needed help the most since their barrier to success was not their inability to communicate with the majority society but the "psychic damage" they suffered from feeling "ashamed of the language of their parents."[80] Dinos's suggestion was later echoed by educator Eduardo Seda, who argued that bilingual education was a tool to "liberate" Puerto Ricans from the "colonization of the mind."[81]

Congressman Ryan's and Congressman Dinos's differing viewpoints on the goals of bilingual education reflected the two main frameworks through which bilingual education would be debated in subsequent years. Ryan's viewpoint reflected the transitional bilingual education (TBE) model, which viewed instruction in Spanish as a pedagogy to be transitioned out of. Dinos's viewpoint reflected the developmental bilingual education (DBE) model or maintenance bilingual education (MBE) model, in which students would develop or maintain an ability to speak Spanish. Although most Americans associated bilingual education with the transitional model, most of the original Puerto Rican advocates of bilingual education saw it as a program for English-speaking children, including black Americans and white Americans. Their main goal was not the reduction of poverty through assimilation into the English-speaking society but the maintenance of cultural pluralism through a permanent practice of bilingualism.[82]

Puerto Rican leaders' focus on cultural pluralism provided the basis for black community control leaders' support of the first bilingual education programs in New York City. Puerto Rican parents from the Bilingual Advisory Committee of Spanish-speaking Parents at P.S. 155 proposed the creation of a bilingual education program to the governing board of the Ocean Hill–Brownsville demonstration district. The governing board, which was 73 percent black and 16 percent Puerto Rican, welcomed their suggestions. It created the first bilingual program in the city in 1968 in P.S. 155. Puerto Rican students composed only 25 percent of the school's student body, but the governing board founded the program in the hope that Puerto Rican *and* African American students would take advantage of the program.[83] Black educators who were turning away from the ideal of racial integration understood the politics of cultural self-determination that led Puerto Rican parents to desire a pedagogy more centered on their own culture. Students at P.S. 155 took a series of classes, some in English, others in Spanish, and some combining both. The developmental and transitional model of bilingual education was implemented so that some students developed an ability to speak Spanish; others maintained the Spanish they already spoke. The bilingual program in Spanish was accompanied by Swahili lessons, which were designed to stimulate student interest in African cultures. The program brought remarkable academic results. School attendance was far better in the bilingual sub-school classes than in the rest of the monolingual classes held at P.S. 155. The overall environment of the school improved as students began to create a community of their own. Although frequent evictions in the neighborhood had made most of the student population at P.S. 155 a "floating school population," student uprooting decreased significantly after 1968 as parents made efforts to stay in the area.[84]

The success of the bilingual education program at P.S. 155 quickly convinced Puerto Rican professionals of its pedagogical benefits. Initially, they had opposed bilingual education. Puerto Rican teachers and administrators who belonged to the Puerto Rican Educators' Association had voted against bilingual education in 1967.[85] Luis Fuentes, who was invited to become the administrator of the first bilingual education program in the city in 1968, recounted that he did not want to participate in such a program at first. While receiving his education and working as a principal in Georgia in the 1950s, Fuentes had passed as "white." For a man who had experienced the benefits of white assimilation and a middle-class status, it was hard to imagine why bilingual education was necessary, much less beneficial. "At the beginning, I lent myself to it [bilingual education] reluctantly," Fuentes later remembered. But as he began to work with parents who "knew a lot more about what was happening than I did," he changed his mind. After watching children in bilingual education programs for six months, Fuentes became an ardent supporter of it. Bilingual education "brought them out; it made them bloom. For the first time they were talking in a language they knew and were accustomed to." In the process of reevaluating his pedagogy, Fuentes also began to embrace his own ethnic identity as Puerto Rican. "All of a sudden I became aware of the fact that I was more Anglo than Puerto Rican, in thinking anyway." Rather than seeing himself as "Anglo," Fuentes began to see himself as a "Puerto Rican" man.[86] By 1970, the Puerto Rican Educators' Association also embraced bilingual education. Its president, Awilda Orta, claimed that "all over the United States the trend is towards seeking and developing a positive self-image. . . . Our struggle is to develop a pride in our culture and instill [in] our children our *Puertorriqueñismo*."[87]

Based on the lessons they learned from the bilingual education program at P.S. 155, Puerto Rican educators moved on to build P.S. 25, the first bilingual school in the Northeast. UBP leaders had been pressuring the Board of Education for such a school for a number of years. Federal funds for bilingual education became available with the passage of the Bilingual Education Act of 1968. This law, which was incorporated as Title VII of the Elementary and Secondary Education Act, provided $7.5 million for the establishment of bilingual education programs in small demonstration projects throughout the country.[88] New York City received only $500,000 from these federal funds, but this was enough to start an experiment. District 7 superintendent Bernard Friedman approved the experiment as an annex and recommended that it be housed at P.S. 25, an old school that had been closed due to teacher shortages. UBP leaders hired Hernan La-Fontaine as the school principal based on his experience at I.S. 201. La-Fontaine convinced the city's Board of Examiners to conduct the teachers' licensing examination in Puerto Rico and recruited fifteen of the islanders who passed to join P.S. 25. Five Puerto Rican teachers from the city joined the team as well. To LaFontaine, the whole experience made him feel like "I went to heaven."[89] For the first time in the city's history, Puerto Ricans founded their own school, where they taught students on their own terms. P.S. 25 administrators recruited a student body that was 15 percent black—a high number for a voluntary registration system. Black student enrollment in this experimental school demonstrated yet again that a significant portion of black parents and students supported bilingual education.[90] Much like P.S. 155 in Ocean Hill–Brownsville, P.S. 25 in the South Bronx produced high student enthusiasm. LaFontaine did not see bilingual education "as some sort of panacea" for all the educational problems that the Puerto Rican child faced, but he recognized that it produced significant improvements: attendance was good, disciplinary problems were minimal, and students came to school because "they feel a special effort is being made to help them."[91] Recognizing that P.S. 25 generated an "extremely favorable reception by parents and other members of the community," Superintendent Friedman officially recognized the annex as a separate school in 1969.[92]

Many black New Yorkers supported bilingual education in its early days of implementation. Some viewed it as a deeply political process whereby Puerto Ricans could help blacks build cultural self-determination as a fellow minority group. Others saw it simply as a way of improving communications between blacks and Puerto Ricans. Andrew Donaldson, elected superintendent of School Board District 9 in the South Bronx by a predominantly black and Puerto Rican school board in 1971, supported bilingual education because it was an important issue for his Puerto Rican constituents. His district's student population was 46 percent black and 43 percent Puerto Rican.[93] He viewed bilingual education, African American history, and school budget issues alike within the framework of community control. Likewise, the superintendent of Donaldson's neighboring District 12, Edyth Gaines, an African American, welcomed the initiative of UBP to create a bilingual subdistrict in 1970. The subdistrict would be composed of four schools, J.H.S. 98, P.S. 50, P.S. 61, and P.S. 66, and it would be run by a bilingual administration. The implementation of such a program would be logistically challenging, but Gaines gladly welcomed the challenge because her constituents supported the program.[94] In an article in *Community News Service*, a Harlem-based newspaper organized by black and Puerto Rican journalists, an African American parent, Lucile Williams, expressed her own investment in bilingual education. "My children are learning a second language and will be able to communicate with the other children much better. If we're going to live together, then we may as well learn to communicate with one another," she explained.[95]

Bilingual education was only one out of the many methods through which community control leaders sought to build black and Puerto Rican practices of cultural self-determination. White New Yorkers had responded to calls for Black Power in schools as an inherently "separatist" pedagogy. Publisher and editor Jason Epstein, for example, believed that teaching Swahili and Yoruba to black children was unwise because "culturally the majority [of Negroes] remains quintessentially American."[96] What community control advocates sought to prove, however, was that one could be "black" and "American." One could speak Spanish and English. Their vision of cultural nationalism called for the reform of American educational institutions rather than the establishment of a separate nation. I.S. 201 leaders, for example, hoped to surround the streets of Harlem with black and Puerto Rican cultural markers by renaming existing public schools in the neighborhood. In 1970, I.S. 201 governing board chairman David Spencer proposed renaming C.S. 30 and C.S. 31 the Rafael Hernández Community School and the Langston Hughes Community School, respectively. Spencer believed that Hernández's composition of "Lamento Borinqueño," a song that expressed a "deeply felt patriotic outcry against the misery of colonialism," made him into a "national Puerto Rican hero" worthy of memorialization. Likewise, Spencer believed that Hughes's poetry, which "captured the heart and soul of Black people," "mirrored the existence" of black students in C.S. 31. By renaming schools after famous black and Puerto Rican cultural figures, Spencer hoped that black and Puerto Rican nationalist ideologies would become engraved on the very physical landscape of New York City. Having such cultural markers on the streets could inspire youth to learn more about their culture, and it could create a sense of belonging and ownership for Harlem's residents.[97] Leaders like Spencer saw black and Puerto Rican nationalism as mutually reinforcing tools of educational reform and civic engagement.

Activists' investment in black and Puerto Rican nationalism also led them to promote the recruitment of professionals of color for public schools. They believed that children of color could only recover their damaged self-images through the presence of role models who shared their racial and ethnic backgrounds. They also hoped to address the gross racial disparities that existed in the employment patterns of public schools. Information collected by parents from UBP revealed shocking statistics. In

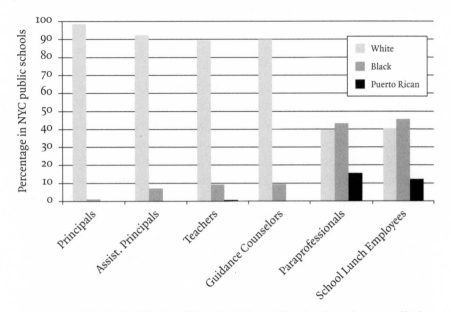

FIGURE 5.3 Ethnic distribution of New York City public school employees, 1968–69 (IRF, New York City Municipal Archives)

1968–69, at a time when black and Puerto Rican students composed well over half of the city's public school population, only 1 percent of the principals were black, and there were no Puerto Rican principals at all. Blacks fared better in positions of teaching and counseling, as they composed 9.2 percent of teachers and 9.5 percent of guidance counselors. Puerto Ricans, however, were still grossly underrepresented in those fields—they composed only 0.64 percent and 0.2 percent of teachers and guidance counselors, respectively. The majority of blacks and Puerto Ricans employed by the school system were found on the bottom rungs, as paraprofessionals and school lunch employees. Puerto Rican leaders of District 7 in the South Bronx had fought hard to get blacks and Puerto Ricans employed by schools as paraprofessionals, such as teachers' aides. They decided, however, not to stop there.[98]

In 1970, the New York Association of Black School Supervisors and Administrators and the Puerto Rican Educators' Association filed a suit against the Board of Examiners. With the support of lawyers from the NAACP Legal Defense and Education Fund, this group of educators charged that the licensing system used to select school principals in the city "discriminated against members of minority groups." They compared New York City patterns with those of cities with comparable racial demographic distributions to highlight New York's deplorable pattern of racial discrimination. While blacks and Puerto Ricans composed 16.7 percent of school principals in cities like Detroit and Philadelphia, they made up only 1.4 percent in New York City. By showing that whites were 1.5 times as likely to pass the examination as were blacks and Puerto Ricans, educators of color proved that the examination had a discriminatory effect. In July 1971, federal court judge Walter R. Mansfield ruled that the city's present system of selecting school supervisors was biased against blacks and Puerto Ricans. Judge Mansfield ordered school boards to select principals based on the list of all who passed the examinations rather than those who ranked at the top of a competitive list. On-the-job performance tests were also taken into account in the new selection process. These new guidelines produced significant changes in the pattern of employment in the school system. By the mid-1970s, 15 percent of school administrators were members of minority groups, bringing New York's numbers closer to those of comparable cities.[99]

The importance of black and Puerto Rican activists' self-identification along the lines of race and ethnicity becomes all the more apparent when compared to the fact that they did not use gender as a tool of political mobilization in the 1960s. Most parents involved in the community control movement were women. Women made up 73 percent of the governing boards at I.S. 201 and Ocean Hill–Brownsville. UBP's use of a language of domesticity in its literature reflected the heavy composition of mothers within the group. While explaining UBP's belief in using conflict as a political tactic, UBP leaders argued that "one cannot make an omelette without breaking eggs." That is, "One cannot resist and eliminate oppression . . . without struggling and using conflict tactics against those whose interests are in maintaining the status quo."[100] UBP's appreciation for the use of conflict to bring about change resembled other female styles of leadership that came out of the black freedom struggle. Ella Baker and Septima Clark had emphasized the need to have a more group-centered leadership rather than a hero-based one. They believed that the process of allowing various individuals to express their opinions fostered more democratic organizations and stronger styles of leadership. Likewise, Antonetty argued that "ego trips" were harmful to the building of "democratic participatory mechanisms for community people."[101]

Despite the dominance of women in the community control movement, however, they did not identify themselves publicly as "women" or as "mothers." They preferred to emphasize their identity as "black" and

"Puerto Rican." The fact that their identity centered on their race and ethnicity does not mean that gender was not a significant dimension of the movement. As geographer Laura Pulido argued, Chicana women who belonged to the Third World Left did not necessarily develop a women's program within their political framework, even though they experienced gender inequality.[102] It indicates, however, that their racial and ethnic identities as "black" and "Puerto Rican" resonated with their experiences the most and galvanized the greatest level of political action.

Forging Identities and Setting New Boundaries

Despite the great level of innovation that demonstration districts and bilingual education leaders brought into New York City public schools, their plans were short-circuited by New York state legislators. Following the enormous turmoil brought by the teachers' strikes, the New York State Legislature sought to create a decentralization plan that would silence the protests. The final Decentralization Act of 1969 created a system that decentralized decision making to thirty-one community school boards. The law gave some room for black and Puerto Rican leadership by allowing each borough president to select a member of the Interim Board of Education. Bronx borough president Herman Badillo selected Joseph Monserrat, and Manhattan borough president Percy Sutton chose Isaiah Robinson as new members of the board. But the new law did not significantly change the old distribution of power within the public education system. The Interim Board of Education retained a white majority—with Jewish leaders Seymour Lachman and Murry Bergtraum and Irish leader Mary Meade making up the rest of the board's membership. The authority of each community school board was still highly circumscribed by the mandates of the central Board of Education as well.[103]

There were two parts of the bill that enraged community control leaders and galvanized an enormous opposition to the bill. First, the bill gerrymandered certain districts so that the new boundaries would maximize racial integration of students. Second, the bill left the question of the three demonstration districts unanswered, giving freedom for the more powerful institutions—the Board of Education and the UFT—to effectively destroy them within this new decentralization plan.[104]

The voices of black and Puerto Rican New Yorkers who came to the decentralization public hearings and wrote letters to legislators in opposition to this bill demonstrate the transformation that had taken place within their political consciousness. The community control movement strengthened blacks' and Puerto Ricans' identity as a common class of racially marginalized people. Just when blacks and Puerto Ricans had given up on their hopes to assimilate and integrate with white Americans, legislators seemed to force an integration plan on them.[105] Black and Puerto Rican parents voiced clear and loud criticism of white liberals' attempt to break up their nascent political cohesion. Puerto Ricans, who had more or less followed black leadership within the demonstration districts of I.S. 201 and Ocean Hill–Brownsville, expressed much more self-interest in the maintenance of demonstration districts by 1969. Fearful that the Decentralization bill would destroy their newfound sense of community, fifty-five Puerto Rican parents from the Ocean Hill–Brownsville district wrote a letter to the Board of Education, proclaiming that "Ocean Hill–Brownsville is the only place in the city of New York [where] something meaningful has been done for Puerto Rican children and Puerto Rican teachers." Emphasizing their new spirit of militancy, the parents warned the board that "we are a peaceful people, but we are not going to play around with the education of our children."[106]

Puerto Rican leaders also expressed a desire to belong to a distinctly working-class community. Puerto Rican students, who composed the majority of East Harlem's students, had been split into two different school districts in the past: District 4, which they shared with black students from Central Harlem, and District 2, which they shared with white middle-class students from Yorkville–Lenox Hill. As the Board of Education drew new boundaries for school districts, Puerto Rican leaders from East Harlem and their advocates proposed that East Harlem students belong to a separate school district. They hoped that East Harlem's "economically disadvantaged" students could be "united into one family, . . . strengthened to speak with one voice, to get together to work for a common purpose."[107] Robert Nichol, a white minister and member of the EHCCC, argued that East Harlem students from District 2 got an unfair deal under present district boundaries because they shared schools with white middle-class children in Yorkville but were segregated into inferior classes within those schools. Their achievement scores, which were consistently lower than those of Yorkville students, clearly indicated that they were receiving an inferior education. Placing Puerto Rican students in Yorkville schools gave the semblance of integration, but Nichol contended that "integration in any true sense has never existed in old District 2. Rather, what has oper-

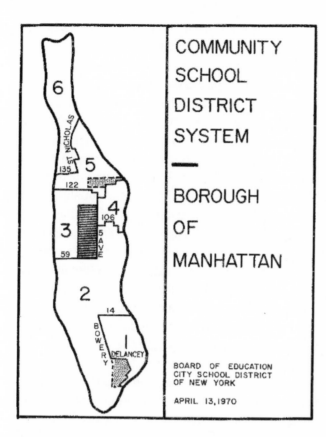

FIGURE 5.4
A map reflecting the
Board of Education's
deliberations on the 1970
redistricting plans. Re-
sponding to East Harlem
parents' demands, the
Board brought the south-
ern boundary of District
4 down to 96th Street
(not reflected in the map),
making the district pre-
dominantly Puerto Rican
(IRF, New York City
Municipal Archives)

ated is a relationship of domination and often outright discrimination between Yorkville and East Harlem."[108]

East Harlem leaders' strategy to concentrate East Harlem students into one school district partially relied on their access to Title I funds, which were distributed to school districts with high percentages of students from low-income families and low academic performance. As Humberto Cintrón argued, by being mixed with high-performing white middle-class students, Puerto Rican students attending Yorkville schools had access to fewer federal funds than if they were concentrated in a separate East Harlem district.[109] But the desire to concentrate poor students into one school district reflected more than a mere strategy to have greater access to federal funds. It reflected Puerto Rican leaders' internal rejection of white middle-class ideals. If they had believed in the past that absorbing white middle-class culture was the best means of attaining social mobility, participating in the community control movement through I.S. 201 now convinced them that they could pursue an alternative path of progress by embracing their identity as working-class individuals.

Within this broad coalition of community control leaders, there was a dissenting minority. Not all working-class people of color wanted their children to be concentrated in areas that would be marked as "economically disadvantaged." Out of the 138 speakers who testified at the decentralization and demonstration district public hearings held in December 1969, 18 opposed the maintenance of demonstration districts. A parent from the Lower East Side claimed that her "community" was made up of "junkies, pushers, addicts, small thieves, [and] hippies." Why should her children attend schools in an area where they were "doomed to meet only junkies and thieves?" Why could they not attend schools along 59th Street, where they would hear about "physicists, chemists, biologists, economists" and where they would meet "white middle-class" children? Critics of demonstration districts claimed that upward mobility came from exposure to white middle-class Americans, not a political coalition of poor leaders of color. Others were also skeptical of the legitimacy of community control leaders. Beatrice Chu, a Chinese parent from the Lower East Side's Two Bridges demonstration district, argued that the district had received a tremendous amount of funding—more than $40,000 from the Ford Foundation—but "there has been no accounting." Another group of parents from the Lower East Side further noted that Two Bridges was dominated by "militants," who were invested in keeping the area "poor" because they were antipoverty workers being paid to work in the area. For these parents, minority antipoverty leaders were no more credible than white middle-class professionals.[110]

Lower East Side parents' criticism of Two Bridges reveals the instability that afflicted this demonstration district from the outset. Unlike I.S. 201 or Ocean Hill–Brownsville, Two Bridges had not been formed by a broad-based coalition of parents and antipoverty leaders of color. I.S. 201 and Ocean Hill–Brownsville had become demonstration districts due to parent pressure, but Two Bridges had been designated a demonstration district as a result of a top-down decision made by Board of Education officials. Board officials thought Two Bridges would add a useful component to the demonstration district experiment due to the "racial and ethnic heterogeneity" of the district's student population, which was 40 percent Puerto Rican, 35 percent Chinese, 13 percent black, and 12 percent "other/white."[111] Having been selected by the board, the leadership of Two Bridges reflected its influence: many of the governing board members were middle-class professionals, and six out of the eight school principals were white. Although 90 percent of governing board members were parents of color, these parents did not have any political cohesion as racial minorities or working-class individuals. From its inception, Two Bridges was a community fabricated by the Board of Education. Its original lack of internal cohesion thus made it highly vulnerable to the manipulation of antipoverty leaders. Although I.S. 201 and Ocean Hill–Brownsville would also be taken over by corrupt antipoverty leaders by the mid-1970s, Two Bridges parents' early criticism of antipoverty leaders indicates that they never shared a working-class identity with them.

Despite the presence of internal divisions within the community control movement, nobody could deny that the movement had created a new political force in the education field by the early 1970s. The movement coalesced a remarkable group of progressive educators and parents, and their vision of education reform for children of color carried a strong appeal to many who had grown tired of racial integration and its false promises. Despite their many opponents, community control leaders made some gains. They were able to keep the demonstration districts of I.S. 201 and Ocean Hill–Brownsville operating until 1971, when I.S. 201 was absorbed into District 5 and Ocean Hill–Brownsville was absorbed into District 23.[112] The Board of Education also redistricted Districts 2 and 4 so that the latter would have a dominant Puerto Rican working-class population, as demanded by East Harlem leaders. By 1972, Luis Fuentes became the first Puerto Rican superintendent in the city's history. By the following year, the school board of District 4 was composed entirely of people of color: six Puerto Ricans and three African Americans.[113] Although community control leaders did not dramatically improve the quality of education offered to students of color, at the very least, they helped establish greater black and Puerto Rican representation within the public school system's administrative leadership.

Youth Movements: From the "Community" to the National and the Global

Many young African Americans and Puerto Ricans became politicized within the antipoverty and the community control movements. Although they distinguished themselves from the older generation of activists of color who came of age in the 1950s and early 1960s, many young activists who formed organizations like the Young Lords Party (YLP), the Puerto

Rican Student Union (PRSU), and El Comité took their first steps of political action within political structures set up by their elders. A number of young activists who later joined the YLP began organizing as teenagers in East Harlem by founding an antipoverty organization, the Real Great Society (RGS). Its main leadership was made up of youth of color: the founders were former gang leaders of the Lower East Side Dragons and the Assassins. According to former RGS member Miguel "Mickey" Melendez, RGS attracted a strong youth membership because "it recognized the emerging Puerto Rican nationalism and militancy being expressed by the young people." But many of their political actions were made possible through resources and connections established by their elders. Following the East New York and East Harlem riots of 1966 and 1967, they accessed municipal funds that became available through Mayor Lindsay's Urban Task Force and private foundations like the Vincent Astor Foundation. Melendez developed tutoring and mentoring programs for El Barrio's youth through the help of Arnaldo (Arnie) Segarra from the East Harlem Tenants Council and Humberto Cintrón from MEND.[114] In 1968, RGS sent a group of black and Latino youth to attend a youth conference in Denver, Colorado, organized by Crusade for Justice. It was there that RGS members Iris Morales and Denis Oliver got to meet José "Cha Cha" Jiménez and other members of the Chicago Young Lords for the first time.[115] They began developing an identity as members of a new generation of radical activists. They adopted a global understanding of U.S. imperialism and white supremacy from the perspective of their own experiences growing up in poor neighborhoods as well as the liberation struggles taking place in Latin America, the Caribbean, Africa, and Asia. Their ability to come together, however, was in many ways made possible through the organizing networks created by their elders.

RGS was only one out of many organizations through which adults paved the way for young activists' politicization. Many of the students who organized the takeover of City University of New York (CUNY) in 1969 learned about the importance of black and Puerto Rican self-determination through the parents who organized the community control movement in K-12 public schools. For example, Eduardo "Pancho" Cruz, one of the leaders of the CUNY student strike, first learned to confront school authorities during the 1968 UFT teachers' strike when he was a high school student. Many of the student activists had participated in SEEK (Search for Education, Elevation and Knowledge), a remedial program established by CUNY administrators in order to recruit black and Puerto Rican college students.

After facing multiple instances of racial discrimination in the SEEK program, Puerto Rican students formed Puerto Ricans Involved in Student Action (PRISA). Some of them also belonged to Onyx, the black counterpart to PRISA. When leaders from the two groups decided to organize a takeover of CUNY campuses to demand a better education for themselves, they followed the example set by their elders from the community control movement. They demanded the establishment of Black and Puerto Rican Studies, classes in black and Puerto Rican history coupled with Spanish classes, and control over hiring and firing of SEEK staff. As a result of their protest, the open admissions policy implemented throughout CUNY campuses resulted in a significant increase in black and Puerto Rican student enrollment. Even as students took the principles of community control to the higher education system in the city, many of them credited the elders in their communities for their success. According to PRISA leader Fernando "Tony" González, student organizers were allowed to take over CUNY campuses for two weeks without police intervention because "we had so much community support." Hundreds of parents from the Lower East Side, the South Bronx, and Harlem came to hold the gates of the campuses and to feed the student strikers. Leaders ranging from Gilberto Gerena Valentín to Evelina Antonetty also extended their support to the students.[116]

Many of the Young Lords' political actions reflected the lessons they learned from community control leaders as well. In 1969, they adopted their first political action, the "garbage offensive," by asking the "people" of East Harlem what they wanted. Some of the YLP members initially felt disappointed that their first "revolutionary" action amounted to an activity as mundane as grabbing brooms and sweeping dirty streets. But they boldly took brooms from the Sanitation Department and swept the streets of East Harlem because they knew that the wishes of "the people" would lead the revolution. This was an idea they learned from books written by Karl Marx, Mao Zedong, Frantz Fanon, Che Guevara, and others, but it was also an idea lived out by the elders involved in the community control movement.[117]

Furthermore, YLP actively collaborated with community control leaders from UBP during their takeover of the Lincoln Hospital in 1970. A mix of older and younger activists formed the Think Lincoln Committee. The group was made up of members from the YLP, the Black Panther Party, the Health Revolutionary Unity Movement, the UBP, and the Doctors' Collective. They collaboratively gathered information about health care services offered at Lincoln Hospital. They discovered that patients in the South Bronx had to wait for eighteen hours at the emergency room, that they felt abused by non–Spanish-speaking doctors, that gynecologists sterilized black and Puerto Rican women without their consent, and that there was no drug detoxification program at the hospital, even though one out of every five residents of Mott Haven suffered from substance abuse. They initiated a drug detoxification program that combined traditional psychotherapy with political education. Drug addicts built their lives back up not only through medical intervention but also through political work. According to Stephen Levin, a Jewish psychiatry resident who participated in the Lincoln Hospital takeover, participants in this detoxification program were "bright young people, whose lives had been smashed by drugs and other miseries in the ghetto," but who "came to an understanding of what had happened in their lives . . . and got through what it took to change . . . on the basis of a new life and a new political perspective." The detoxification program at Lincoln Hospital was so successful that it was implemented in several different hospitals in the city, and it was recognized by the United Nations for its innovative work in substance recovery. Think Lincoln Committee's ability to accomplish such work was made possible through the initiative of young people, but it was also facilitated by networks of people of color forged by the UBP in earlier years.[118]

While rooting themselves in local communities, young activists of color used their self-consciousness as "young" to revitalize what they saw as the calcification of political activism among their elders. In the 1970s, antipoverty and community control leaders alike succumbed to a politics of territoriality and patronage that bore little resemblance to the mass participation that had originally built their movements. When black and Puerto Rican antipoverty leaders began to increasingly compete with one another in their pursuit of racial and ethnic representation, the Young Lords reminded them of their original agenda of cross-racial collaboration. Hunts Point Multi-Service Center leaders Monserrate Flores and Ramón Velez were engaged in a bitter battle with black antipoverty leaders over the nomination of the main administrator of Lincoln Hospital in 1970. They threatened to lead a picket line at the hospital if the hospital's Community Advisory Board would not make Dr. Antero Lacot, a doctor from Puerto Rico, the next appointee. Under the leadership of the Young Lords and the Black Panthers, however, Flores and Velez met with black leaders from the community corporations of the Bronx and developed a common working plan for both groups.[119]

When MEND became embroiled in charges of bribery and embezzlement, Puerto Rican students liberated a college preparatory program from its inept leadership. Much like Monserrate Flores and Ramón Velez, executive director of MEND William del Toro adopted an increasingly territorial attitude while accruing massive amounts of antipoverty funds and creating patronage circles in East Harlem. In 1970, Puerto Rican students learned that MEND had received a grant designed to offer remedial education services for high school dropouts through a program called the Experimental Bilingual Institute (EBI) yet had failed to actually deliver any services. Students immediately demanded that a new EBI director be hired. Due to the students' pressure, del Toro was forced to let them select the new director. They chose Gloria Quiñones, who had worked with MEND since its formation in 1964. Quiñones quickly learned that there were major discrepancies between MEND budget proposals and the actual provision of services. MEND had received funding for a library, but there was no library. It had funding to pay its staff members, but the staff worked as volunteers. When Quiñones realized that MEND was cheating the students, she liberated EBI from MEND and established it as a separate institution. With the help of students Miguel Rivera and Hector Lucca and faculty Herb Hyman, Agustín Rivera, and Steve Sherman, Quiñones delivered all the services that had been promised to the students—a library, teachers, counselors, and supplementary funding for postsecondary education. Recounting her experiences, Quiñones claimed that she would not have gotten involved with EBI had it not been for the persuasion of the students. "The students brought me. They wanted their organization. I was just there to help make it happen," she stated.[120]

Moreover, young activists of color advanced the political ideologies of their elders by probing more introspectively into Puerto Ricans' own internalized racism. Puerto Rican antipoverty and community control leaders had developed a common identification with blacks as "minorities" who experienced similar forms of racial marginalization by white New Yorkers. Yet most of them had not thought of themselves as "black," nor had they spoken publicly about how they themselves held racist notions against African Americans. The Young Lords, however, confronted these issues as part of the "internal revolution" they hoped to experience in their own minds. According to YLP member Pablo "Yoruba" Guzmán, "Once we started talking about pelo malo [bad hair] and pelo bueno [good hair], that really got us into a serious discussion. How can we still talk about that shit if we're still carrying that baggage?"[121] Richie Perez argued that they could no longer point their fingers only at whites since "we were talking about internal issues that people didn't want to talk about. We talked about anti-black prejudice inside the Latino community."[122]

By unearthing Puerto Ricans' own prejudices, many young Puerto Rican activists began to embrace their own identities as "black" and "Afro-Caribbean." PRSU leaders forged stronger ties with African Americans by calling themselves an "Afro-Antillean" people. "Our music, our slang, our customs all derive from an Afro-Antillean culture that has been developed over the centuries," claimed PRSU leaders in a 1969 proposal. They still emphasized their parallel identity with African Americans as an "exploited minority"—a terminology their elders used more frequently. But they acknowledged that their shared culture with blacks extended beyond their experiences as "minorities" in the United States; they also shared an "African root" with them. Felipe Luciano embodied the Afro-Boricua identity forged by members of the Young Lords. During a SEEK rally at CUNY, Luciano enthralled a group of students by reciting a poem entitled "Jíbaro, My Pretty Nigger." By using the terms jíbaro and "nigger," Luciano linked Puerto Rico's most popular imagery of the "authentic" Puerto Rican (typically imagined as "white") with the imagery of the "authentic" black person from the United States. Luciano, along with many other Young Lords members, grew an Afro and joined blacks in forging a new black aesthetic.[123]

The Young Lords' open acknowledgment of internal racism made their organization more inclusive of dark-skinned individuals, which included both Puerto Ricans and African Americans. Prior to joining the Young Lords, Gabriel Torres-Rivera's social world was mostly made up of blacks because he felt most accepted by them. While serving as a translator for his dark-skinned Puerto Rican mother at welfare offices and hospitals, Torres saw that whites and Puerto Ricans alike did not treat her well. "I just know that black people treated her nice," explained Torres. Once he met Young Lords members during the takeover of the First Spanish Methodist Church of East Harlem, however, Torres made a connection with a group of Puerto Ricans that he found to be refreshingly more race-conscious. "I saw that these Puerto Ricans were culturally aware, and aware of racism, . . . so I went to join them," revealed Torres.[124]

African Americans of darker hues also found a home in the Young Lords. Although Torres generalized all "blacks" as more accepting of "dark" people, Cleo Silvers had found African Americans to be quite discriminatory against her dark skin. Silvers had grown up in Eastwick, a working-class suburb of Philadelphia. While attending Lincoln University in Pennsylvania, a historically black university, she felt that she "didn't fit in" with "middle-class African Americans [who] were more light-skinned." She found a mentor and a community, however, when she moved to New York City and joined Evelina Antonetty and the UBP family. Although she had initially connected with activists through the Black Panther Party, she joined the Young Lords when severe infiltration from COINTEL-PRO, the FBI counterintelligence program, threatened the existence of the New York chapter of the Black Panthers. Since the Young Lords and the Black Panthers had mutual collectives in the city's hospitals, it made no difference whether Silvers worked with one organization or another. Her African American background also did not keep her from participating in the Young Lords' efforts to support island-based Puerto Rican nationalists. With a working knowledge of the Spanish language and the history of Puerto Rico's political relationship with the United States, she traveled to the island during a celebration of El Grito de Lares, the 1868 nationalist revolt against Spanish rule. As an African American woman, she spoke specifically about the relationship between the struggle against slavery in Lares and the struggle in the United States. Silvers was only one out of many non–Puerto Ricans who belonged to the Young Lords. Although the group was known as a Puerto Rican nationalist group, 25 percent of its members were black; other members included Panamanians, Cubans, Dominicans, Mexicans, and Colombians.[125]

Young Puerto Rican activists' analysis of internal racism was accompanied by the broadening of their political imaginations from the "local" to the national and the global. They respected and validated their elders' work as mobilizers of local communities. Their commitment to foster social change by creating networks in local schools, public projects, and hospitals had built a significant reservoir of resources through which poor people could fight against unscrupulous teachers, landlords, and doctors. Yet for all the benefits of having a local "community," poor people of color still had little control over the political and economic structures that governed their lives. "The real power structure, where policy decisions are made for economic development, social legislation, foreign policy, etc.," lay outside of the influence of "community" leaders, claimed PRSU leaders. It was pointless, for example, to haggle with Manhattan's West Side antipoverty leaders or the city's Housing Authority over the need to build more low-income housing when their efforts could be instantly thwarted by the city's elite. The Lincoln Center for the Performing Arts was, after all, built through the overwhelming support of New York's elite, individuals with links to the military, major charitable foundations, Wall Street, and media empires, who were willing to invest $185 million to demolish large swaths of the city's old housing stock and build the new center. In order to change these "power structures," PRSU leaders argued that "we must take our fight beyond the community." Whereas activists who came of age in the 1950s and 1960s saw the "local" community as the primary ground through which they could build meaningful forms of democracy, those who came of age in the late 1960s and early 1970s began to see it as narrow and uncoupled from more foundational questions related to U.S. capitalism and imperialism.[126]

Forging national coalitions with other minority groups became one way through which young activists created a broader national agenda. The YLP linked up with radical youth organizations, such as the I Wor Kuen (a New York–based Chinese American organization), the Chicano Brown Berets, the American Indian Movement, and the Young Patriots (a group of poor whites with roots in the Appalachian Mountains).[127] Puerto Rican student organizations, such as PRSU, PRISA, and Aspira, established contacts with Chicano and black college student groups like Movimiento Estudiantil Chicano de Aztlán and the Black League of Afro-American Collegians. Through these national alliances, young students of color hoped to increase minority student enrollment in U.S. universities and colleges. They also hoped to change the foundational ways in which knowledge about race and ethnicity was produced in U.S. institutions of higher education.[128]

Linking local New York battles with anti-imperialist struggles in Puerto Rico and other parts of Latin America and the Caribbean allowed young activists to reach beyond the national to the global. El Comité, which grew out of a squatters' group in a storefront on 88th Street and Columbus Avenue in 1970, extended its organizing efforts to the struggle for Puerto Rico's independence two years later. They renamed themselves El Comité–MINP (Movimiento de Izquierda Nacional Puertorriqueño) and supported organizations like the Puerto Rico Solidarity Committee. Understandably, some of El Comité's members felt tensions as they overextended themselves by championing multiple causes. "Although I love Puerto Rico, we were a national minority," remembered El Comité member Julio Pabón. "When your kid got sick, you had to go to Lincoln Hospital and wait six or seven hours to see a doctor. So, then you leave there to go to a meeting to talk about issues in Puerto Rico or Angola?" he asked rhetorically.

Despite the immediacy of local battles, Sandra Trujillo stated that El Comité's commitment to support Puerto Rico's independence was based on the members' understanding that the island's status was important to all Americans committed to the notion of political self-determination. El Comité leaders also collaborated with Movimiento Pro Independencia (MPI), an older group of island-based Puerto Rican nationalists. MPI leaders had previously organized residents of the island exclusively. In the late 1960s, however, MPI leader Juan Mari Bras made the strategic decision to organize second-generation Puerto Ricans from the mainland, recognizing the interdependence of the island's political status and Puerto Rican migrants' lack of political power on the mainland.[129] He also linked up with SNCC leader Stokely Carmichael to forge a coalition of young radicals dedicated to supporting the national liberation of people across Asia, Africa, and Latin America.[130] This was the age of global revolutions, when the Cuban Revolution, the U.S. antiwar movement, and liberation movements stretching from Vietnam to Congo led activists across the globe to think of human liberation in cross-racial and transnational ways.

Conclusion

Community control leaders, as the next chapter will reveal, had only a short window of opportunity to implement their vision of a socially democratic and culturally pluralistic society. External repression led by UFT coupled with internal divisions crippled the community control movement, forcing its leaders to switch goals or simply pursue their goals on a smaller scale. Young radicals' political activities were particularly stifled by repressive actions taken by COINTEL-PRO.

That their experiment lasted only a few years should not diminish its historical significance. Black and Puerto Rican parents drew on their numerical strength as guardians of the majority of the city's public school students to reform a system that was breaking apart. They infused a new reformist impulse within schools by proving that cultural nationalism did not alienate students from the larger society but instead bolstered their civic engagement as American citizens. Community control leaders demonstrated that, in the context of a grassroots coalition, multiple forms of nationalisms could function symbiotically. By critiquing white teachers who had for too long abandoned their commitment to teach, parents of color also demonstrated that professional expertise should not be trusted as the only basis of knowledge. They showed that knowledge that grew experientially from those who felt the agony and desperation of poor youth of color was also important, as they alone could restore students' faith in their ability to learn. By rejecting the integration model in favor of the development of local schools, community control leaders created a useful alternative to the white middle-class ideal. Through the small successes of demonstration districts, poor students of color began to believe that they did not have to abandon their communities in order to find success. They could take part in a collective search for excellence by transforming the very foundations of an unequal system of education. Although community-based education lived on only within particular schools on a small scale after the 1970s, it provided a legitimate alternative for those seeking new solutions in public schools.

CHAPTER SIX

The Breaking of a Coalition

Institutionalizing Power and the Remaking of a Hispanic Identity

Community control leaders forged their movement based on the premise that black and Puerto Rican self-determination could remedy the fundamental inequalities shaping the education of their children. Inspired by the Black Power movement's tenacious critique of white supremacy as the central axis of oppression in America, community control leaders believed that a greater presence of black and Puerto Rican leaders within the public schools' administrative and teaching staff would allow their children to succeed academically. But as parents and teachers of color tried to implement their vision, significant class conflicts developed between the two groups. Black parents involved with I.S. 201 in East Harlem found it surprisingly difficult to work with black teachers in the schools. Black teachers displayed a sense of elitism toward parents, using their positions as "professionals" to dismiss suggestions coming from parents, who often did not have more than an elementary school education. "They [teachers] never, ever considered the possibility that they could just listen, talk about it, and take it easy," recounted Charles Wilson, I.S. 201 unit administrator. When teachers ran into conflicts with parents, they relied on Wilson or the principal to solve the problem for them. If a resolution was not reached quickly, they quit immediately. They did not acknowledge the political role that parents had played as those who had made I.S. 201 possible, nor did they trust them as capable leaders. "I became a total revisionist," claimed William Hall, an activist who worked closely with I.S. 201 parents. "We found out that many of these black teachers had as much contempt for black kids as others had." He had believed that offering a quality education involved "somehow having black teachers in front of black kids," but he later realized that "blackness" did not always engender a sense of responsibility for black children. With a few exceptions, parents did not find black teachers to be any more dedicated than white teachers at I.S. 201.[1]

Minor conflicts evolved into a significant class divide when the very existence of demonstration districts came under threat. The New York State Legislature imposed the Decentralization Act of 1969, which reduced the parents' broad vision of reform to a mere redistribution of power from the Board of Education's central office to thirty-one local school boards. The maintenance of demonstration districts was left undetermined, which meant that the United Federation of Teachers (UFT) could soon terminate their right to exist. Those who had personally invested in the community control experiment and become disillusioned with its failures fiercely debated what had gone wrong. Psychologist and educator Kenneth Clark blamed community control leaders for their self-corruption. Decentralization failed, he claimed in a 1972 *New York Times* article, because those involved "have forgotten what the purpose was." Leaders forgot that their original purpose was to improve "the quality of education" and instead engaged in a "struggle for power [and] control," Clark claimed. Instead of focusing on how to educate children, they used the schools to pursue a job placement program and create a platform for political patronage. His colleague Charles Wilson could not have disagreed more. Wilson, I.S. 201's former unit administrator, wrote in a private letter to Clark that he read Clark's remarks from the newspaper with "shock and dismay." To him, it was "not the people who lay waste the Dream" since "they never received it." Holders of the "status quo" had stolen their dream, and it was the "central system's corruption and incapacity" that constrained community control leaders' ability to implement their vision. No matter how much internal conflict existed, failure ultimately stemmed from external repression, not internal self-corruption, Wilson argued.[2]

Advocates of bilingual education also debated the reasons why bilingual education had failed to improve Puerto Rican students' academic performance beyond the first few years of its implementation. Puerto Rican parents had first envisioned it as a pedagogy that would help Spanish-speaking and English-speaking students *maintain* fluency in English and Spanish simultaneously, but the 1973 Aspira Consent Decree reduced it to an assimilationist program in which Spanish-speaking students would *transition out of* Spanish fluency. According to Pedro Pedraza, a Puerto Rican educator, lawyers from the Puerto Rican Legal Defense and Education Fund (PRLDEF) accepted the court's assimilationist model of bilingual education because "they wanted to win something. They were afraid they might lose everything." It was unclear, however, if Puerto Rican lawyers and teachers understood how much was lost in this political compromise. To many parents, Puerto Rican teachers seemed only too eager to accept this assimilationist program, so long as they could get jobs through it.[3]

This chapter analyzes the dissolution of black–Puerto Rican coalitions by focusing on the internal class divisions that tore the movements apart. Previous accounts of the freedom struggles of the 1960s have explained the decline of the movement by focusing on external repression and the rise of white backlash. President Richard Nixon used racially coded language, such as "law and order," to conflate the images of criminals and black civil rights activists. Increased funding in police departments and the criminalization of urban space indicated that the era of an activist federal government committed to social welfare was over; instead, an increasingly punitive and policing state began to manage social discontent and crime.[4] This narrative rings true for the demise of the black–Puerto Rican coalition in New York City as well. As recounted by previous historians, the community control movement in the city came to an end largely because UFT president Albert Shanker waged a battle against activists of color by portraying their movement's goals as violations of the "merit principle." His negotiations with members of the Board of Education and government officials led New York state legislators to dismantle the demonstration districts through the Decentralization Law of 1969.[5]

Such narratives of white backlash are important, but they do not explain how grassroots leaders of color themselves experienced the overall failure of their movement. Closer attention to class divisions within communities of color in the 1970s indicates that professionals and politicians of color played a vital role in dismantling the coalition that grassroots leaders had helped build. Black and Puerto Rican teachers, principals, lawyers, school board members, and politicians made up the rising class of middle-class minorities who tried to translate grassroots organizing into tangible forms of power in the form of electoral seats, school board seats, federal funding, and job security. They were "middle class" not only because of higher income levels or professional degrees, but also because of political orientation. They believed that they could achieve power more quickly and easily than could grassroots leaders by drawing resources top-down from established politicians, businessmen, and professionals rather than the bottom-up pressure of a mass, multiracial coalition. Their rise in power signified the success of the movement since they consolidated the hard work of grassroots organizers into institutionalized forms of power. Having Puerto Rican and black councilmen, congressmen, and school chancellors certainly allowed people of color to have greater access to government jobs and political power. Yet it also reflected the limitations of the movement as leaders became increasingly detached from the voices of their constituents. Middle-class blacks and Puerto Ricans reduced community control to a narrow calculation of measurable goals, such as test scores, jobs, and votes. They felt that institutionalizing some form of power was more important than actualizing their most radical dreams, whereas grassroots leaders felt that the drive toward institutionalization distracted movement leaders from their original goals.

It was this move toward the institutionalization of power—rather than a "natural" incompatibility between black and Puerto Rican cultures—that led Puerto Rican leaders to seek a power base separate from that of African Americans. In this chapter, I chronicle how a new middle-class Puerto Rican leadership transformed antipoverty and community control organizations into ethnic political patronage systems in the late 1960s and 1970s. Rather than drawing strength from a local grassroots multiracial coalition, they relied increasingly on establishing political visibility as "Hispanic" by focusing on bilingual education and bilingual ballots. Puerto Rican and African American leaders began to engage in a process that I call "bifurcated racialization," in which the cultures of subjugated groups were cast not only as fixed, but also as exaggerated opposites of others. While Puerto Rican elites prided themselves on their "patience" in contrast to blacks' "anger" and "violence," black nationalists promoted their "black" identity as the "most radical" form of political resistance to white racism. Although "Hispanicity" held multiple political meanings, Puerto Rican elites constructed it as mutually incompatible with "blackness."

I then discuss how this middle-class strategy dovetailed with white politicians' efforts to break up the black-Latino civil rights leadership. Mayor Ed Koch crystallized a politics of "ethnicity" in the 1980s, replacing the social movement that working-class African Americans and Puerto Ricans had built in the 1960s with a smaller middle-class ring of "ethnic" politicians and businessmen.[6] Koch used this ethnic framework to portray the city not as divided between whites and nonwhites, but as fragmented into numerous ethnic groups. Hispanicity became a crucial part of this ethnic strategy.

The War on Poverty in the Late 1960s:
From Participatory Democracy to Ethnic Fiefdoms

The political priorities of activists of color in the late 1960s and early 1970s were fundamentally shaped by the city's declining labor economy. White flight and deindustrialization had been draining the city of private jobs and tax revenues since the 1940s, but the financial losses wrought by these changes reached critical levels during this period. Between 1969 and 1977, New York City lost over 600,000 jobs, a 16 percent drop. The majority of job loss came from the manufacturing sectors, such as printing, apparel and textile, and foods and beverages. Citywide unemployment rose from 5 percent in 1970 to 12 percent in 1975. Black and Puerto Rican workers took the hardest hit with this job decline since two-thirds of them were employed in manufacturing jobs. While median income among white families in 1977 was $20,998, the equivalents for black and Puerto Rican families were $13,999 and $10,499, respectively.[7]

African Americans fared slightly better than Puerto Ricans by accessing jobs in the growing public sector. In 1971, blacks composed 28 percent, whereas Puerto Ricans made up 6 percent, of all city government jobs. But the growth of the welfare population in the city revealed the impact of New York's shrinking economy on poor blacks and Puerto Ricans alike. In 1960, 328,000 people depended on welfare in New York City; the number jumped to 1.25 million in 1972, making welfare recipients 16 percent of the city's population. The overwhelming majority of these welfare recipients were women of color: 40 percent were Puerto Rican, and 47 percent were black. Mayor Lindsay had been trying to rectify these desperate conditions of poverty through the War on Poverty, liberalizing welfare policies and funding the employment of poor people through federal antipoverty funds and loans borrowed from commercial banks. By 1972, however, Lindsay himself admitted that welfare was becoming an increasingly unpopular program that did not address even the minimum economic needs of poor New Yorkers. He declared that he wanted a "zero caseload growth" in welfare in the future.[8]

New York City's economic instabilities took a toll on poor people and political activists alike. Although antipoverty and community control leaders originally sought to fundamentally transform the city's structures of power, they found it hard to focus on anything else besides securing jobs for their poor constituents in the late 1960s and 1970s. The War on Poverty, which began as a movement toward participatory democracy, ossified into ethnic machines. During a 1967 meeting with Kenneth Clark and other leaders of the Metropolitan Applied Research Corporation (MARC), Julio Sabater bemoaned the growing tensions that had developed between Puerto Ricans and black nationalists in the Massive Economic Neighborhood Development (MEND), an antipoverty organization in East Harlem. "It has been like the attempt to mix oil and water. The Black nationalists have been saying that the Puerto Ricans must decide whether they are black or white," explained Sabater. Puerto Ricans refused to choose one or the other, however, because "they regard themselves as tolerant people."[9] Pitted against whites and blacks who were adopting increasingly polarizing racial language, Puerto Ricans maintained that "tolerance" marked their cultural distinctiveness.

Political tensions between blacks and Puerto Ricans, however, did not arise from a political vacuum. They emerged at a time when antipoverty leaders were accessing large amounts of antipoverty federal funding and adopting increasingly competitive and dictatorial strategies as a result. Puerto Rican antipoverty leaders competed not only with black antipoverty leaders, but also among themselves. In January 1969, the city's Community Development Agency released $950,000 of antipoverty funding to MEND, a sum far heftier than the $300,000 and $310,000 awarded to the East Harlem Tenants Council and the East Harlem Community Corporation, respectively.[10] A few months later, members of MEND's board of directors sent a petition to the city's Council against Poverty, calling for help regarding the "dictatorial mismanagement and the selfish tyranny of one or two persons" who had taken over MEND's leadership. Board members claimed that the chairman of the board unilaterally overrode the promotion of personnel as recommended by MEND's executive director without any consultation with staff members or other board members, causing "the destruction of personnel morale." By 1974, MEND became widely known as a Puerto Rican political machine, whose leaders used tactics no less corrupt than those of leaders of Tammany Hall. MEND's executive director, William Del Toro, was convicted of offering a bribe of $15,000 to Pedro Morales, the deputy director of Harlem–East Harlem Model Cities office, in return for an approval of a $1 million lease on a building owned by Acme Hamilton Manufacturing. Although Del Toro spent nine months in jail, once released, he continued to control the allocation of antipoverty funding through his position in MEND and his brother Angelo Del Toro's position as assemblyman in the 72nd District of Manhattan.[11] Although many Puerto Rican residents of East Harlem disapproved of his methods,

Del Toro continued to maintain his presence among politicians as the savviest political representative of Puerto Ricans in East Harlem.

In the South Bronx, the competition for antipoverty funding became more racially divisive than in East Harlem due to the neighborhood's lack of political organization. Whereas Central Harlem had been established as a "black" neighborhood since the early twentieth century, with East Harlem as a "Puerto Rican" neighborhood since the 1940s, the population of the South Bronx was still in flux through much of the 1950s. The majority of its residents of color did not arrive there until the mid-1950s and 1960s. Operating within such a political vacuum, antipoverty leader Ramón Velez effectively capitalized on black–Puerto Rican tensions to solidify the whole neighborhood as a Puerto Rican stronghold. Part of his hostility toward blacks stemmed from a legitimate grievance against City Hall officials' tendency to favor black over Puerto Rican antipoverty leaders until the late 1960s. In January 1968, the Hunts Point Community Corporation elections resulted in Puerto Ricans becoming the majority of its board members. Through Velez's skillful coordination of mass voter registration drives, Puerto Ricans won twenty-one of the twenty-four seats on the Hunts Point board; blacks won one seat and whites won two. Black leaders from Hunts Point contested the election results. Even though they had been willing to share antipoverty leadership with Puerto Ricans to a certain extent, they did not expect Puerto Rican leaders to overturn the antipoverty leadership in the neighborhood entirely. They charged the Velez group with engaging in illegal assistance to voters, and they pleaded with the city's Council against Poverty to intervene. The Council against Poverty responded favorably to black leaders, ordering the appointment of thirteen blacks to the Hunts Point Community Corporation in order to "bring about ethnic balance." Puerto Ricans felt betrayed by both white members of the Council against Poverty and the black leaders from Hunts Point. More than 150 angry Puerto Ricans staged a protest in front of City Hall, using a flower-decked coffin with the sign, "Poverty Council Buries Puerto Rican Civil Rights." Even Herman Badillo, who typically did not like to associate himself with antipoverty issues, came to the protest at City Hall.[12]

Ramón Velez's grievances also stemmed from the fact that, until 1969, black antipoverty leaders received a disproportionate amount of antipoverty funds compared to Puerto Ricans. According to a 1968 City Council report, black-dominant neighborhoods such as Central Harlem and Bedford-Stuyvesant received a greater share of antipoverty allocations than Puerto Rican–heavy neighborhoods like East Harlem, the South

Bronx, and Williamsburg. According to the City Council's calculations of antipoverty funds allocations in 1968–69, Bedford-Stuyvesant should have received $3,445,200 in 1968–69, but it actually received $5,104,600 (48 percent over); Central Harlem should have received $2,328,700, but it received $5,720,300 (146 percent over). Meanwhile, East Harlem received only $2,095,400 out of the allocated $2,233,000 (6 percent under), the South Bronx received $1,005,300 out of $1,371,700 (27 percent under), and Williamsburg received $1,393,600 out of $2,009,700 (31 percent under). Puerto Rican leaders felt that this disproportionality was unjust since Puerto Ricans were on average poorer than African Americans.[13]

While Puerto Rican antipoverty leaders held minor grievances against black antipoverty leaders, Ramón Velez exaggerated these grievances to mount a vicious battle that pitted Puerto Ricans against whites and blacks alike. Drawing on his military service to plan his strategies, he referred to his programs as "guerrilla squads" and devised ways to plant "spies in enemy camps." He demonized Father Louis Gigante, an Italian priest who was fluent in Spanish and who had worked with Puerto Rican teenagers in Hunts Point, simply because he was not a Puerto Rican. He treated black leaders with similar contempt. Calling black leaders "niggers," he spoke without restraint about his desire to wrest power away from them. Just as blacks "had" Harlem and Brooklyn, so would Puerto Ricans "have" the South Bronx, he claimed.[14]

Some believed that Velez had simply created an effective patronage system for Puerto Ricans. "He took the mechanism, and did in fact what America is all about," claimed Cyril Tyson, a black antipoverty leader who had supported Velez's earlier political career. "He used the power of his budget to get the people he wanted, put them in the right place, and interlocked them" so that they would not be able to challenge him. Others, however, believed that Velez used unnecessarily antagonistic tactics. Leroi Archible, a black antipoverty leader from Morrisania in the Bronx, vowed to never work with Velez after attending one of his meetings. Velez had begun the meeting by saying, "I'm locking everybody in and everybody's down with me. Everybody who wants to get down can get out of here now." Archible could not bring himself to support a person who would demand total allegiance, especially when he was famous for being "anti-black."[15]

As manipulative as Velez was, black leaders in the Bronx fanned his flames by maligning calls for Puerto Rican political self-determination as "racist." In response to Puerto Rican antipoverty leaders' desire to have more Puerto Rican representation on the Council against Poverty, members from the Citywide Council of Black Organizations against Poverty argued in 1969 that these "Puerto Rican 'poverty-crats' . . . are unscrupulous misleaders, racially prejudiced against black people and unfit to direct or administer any public agency." The Council against Poverty was racially unrepresentative—only eight out of the fifty-one council members were Puerto Rican—but black leaders called Puerto Ricans' demand for more equitable representation a form of "racism."[16] In 1972, the United Bronx-wide Black Leadership Coalition also argued that Puerto Ricans' desire to have a Puerto Rican director for the Overall Economic Development Planning Committee in the South Bronx was "racist," even though the area was 65 percent Puerto Rican.[17]

Some black leaders went so far as delegitimizing Puerto Ricans' access to poverty funds by mischaracterizing them as "immigrants." "We cannot allow another immigrant group to come to this country and rise on the backs of blacks, as the European has done. We will not be the Puerto Ricans' footstool," claimed Jerome Greene of the Morrisania Education Council. *Amsterdam News* columnist Marietta Tanner added that blacks deserved to have a greater share of antipoverty funding than Puerto Ricans due to their longer history of oppression in the United States. "When one brother has a four-hundred-year history of struggle in this country, and the other less than thirty years, well the blacks may rise up and claim their birthright, for they have suffered the most unfair imbalance of all," claimed Tanner.[18] While Tanner's general claim that African Americans' history of oppression was longer than that of Puerto Ricans was true, the specifics were certainly an exaggeration. Puerto Ricans' history of oppression under U.S. rule was much longer than thirty years—they had been subject to U.S. imperialism since 1898, and Puerto Rican migrants had been racially oppressed by whites on the mainland since then. The Puerto Rican experience in New York City was also entirely different from that of European immigrants. It was precisely Puerto Ricans' "non-whiteness" and colonial status that had attracted them to the black freedom struggle. Yet some black leaders misrepresented Puerto Ricans' colonial history to portray them as "unworthy" recipients of state aid.

Puerto Rican leaders insisted that black political self-determination could coexist with Puerto Rican political self-determination. Luis Fuentes, principal of P.S. 155 in Ocean Hill–Brownsville, argued that Puerto Ricans' confrontation with certain black antipoverty leaders should not be considered an "attack on the whole black community." The executive director of the Puerto Rican Forum, Hector Vazquez, also claimed that Puerto Ricans' desire to not be lumped with African Americans as "black" was not a form of "racism." Puerto Ricans have "special needs, which cannot be lumped with those of others. For them, better education means bilingual education . . . [and] freedom means an opportunity for Puerto Ricans to sustain their own cultural heritage," Vazquez asserted in an *Amsterdam News* article. Since Puerto Ricans had distinct needs and since these goals were not "antithetical to Black aims," Vazquez believed that the bond between blacks and Puerto Ricans could be strengthened if blacks would "recognize" and "accept" Puerto Ricans' distinctiveness.[19] But most black leaders interpreted Puerto Ricans' refusal to adopt a "black" identity—especially among dark-skinned Puerto Ricans—as a manifestation of racism and self-denial.

Minority leaders' conflicts over Puerto Ricans' refusal to assume a "black" identity stemmed partially from their different interpretations of the meanings of "blackness." African Americans who joined the Black Power movement associated "blackness" with a radical political stance that carried subversive class connotations. Since middle-class African Americans had tried to elevate themselves above their poorer compatriots through colorism in the past—calling themselves "colored" and set apart from "Negroes" or "blacks"—African American activists believed that calling themselves "black" signified their most radical rejection of both white racism and class elitism.[20] Espousing "blackness" as the most authentic self-identity for African Americans, they believed that Puerto Ricans who looked "black" should embrace it too. Since the Black Power movement evolved on U.S. soil, however, Puerto Ricans associated "blackness" with a North American formulation of race. Although they self-identified with the political aspirations of African Americans, they considered it their highest priority to retain their cultural distinction as coming from the Spanish Caribbean. As colonized subjects, they had an aversion to being absorbed into North American culture, be that white or black. African Americans' self-identification as "black" and Puerto Ricans' as "Puerto Rican" thus did not reflect the radicalism of the former or the delusion of the latter, but each group's expression of its own cultural integrity.

Eventually, Ramón Velez's and William Del Toro's aggressive efforts to secure antipoverty funds for their own turf resulted in Puerto Rican neighborhoods accessing higher amounts of antipoverty funds than black neighborhoods in 1969. Velez and Del Toro took advantage of funding for multi-service centers made available through Housing and Urban Development (HUD). Between April and August 1969, HUD granted $1 million to the Brownsville Multi-Service Center, $4.2 million to Central Harlem and East Harlem Multi-Service Centers, and $4 million to Hunts Point Multi-Service Center alone.[21] Velez had at first been able to tap into multi-service funding through contacts provided by black antipoverty leaders in the South Bronx, but in less than a year he outstripped them as the leading recipient of antipoverty funding in the neighborhood. With so much money in their hands, Hunts Point Multi-Service Center leaders firmly established themselves as a force to be reckoned with in the South Bronx. Their success, however, came at a great cost. Many residents of the South Bronx appreciated the new jobs that Velez offered through the multi-service centers but wondered if they were worth the animosity he had created between blacks and Puerto Ricans in the process.

A Turn to the Right: Suspicions and Splinters
between Parents and Professionals of Color

Nationalism fostered conflict between black and Puerto Rican antipoverty leaders beginning in 1968, but it did not create rifts within the community control movement until the early 1970s. It was only when demonstration district leaders were forced to work within the constraints of the Decentralization Law of 1969 that they began abandoning their commitment to institute black and Puerto Rican self-determination in the city's schools. The new law established a decentralized system, whereby thirty-one community school boards (CSBs) would be in charge of administering the city's public schools. Each CSB had a certain amount of independence from the central leadership—for example, CSB leaders had the power to select district superintendents and principals, allocate funding under $250,000, and revise procedures such as suspension policies. But each CSB leadership still remained under the ultimate supervision of the central Board of Education.[22]

Some community control leaders tried to resist the decentralization plan by boycotting the CSB elections in 1969. In a *New York Post* newspaper article, Rev. Milton Galamison called on "black people" to boycott the elections since CSBs represented "the same vested interests" that had held the school system "in bondage" in the past.[23] Isaiah Robinson later tried to contest election results, claiming that "Black and Spanish communities across the city viewed the decentralization law . . . [as] a 'hoax' and urged non-participation." He claimed that most parents had chosen not to participate in what they saw as a competition to simply gain control of vast sums of money and find a path to political prestige. Based on their observation in forty-five different elementary schools in the South Bronx, Hunts Point, Morrisania, and East Tremont, Evelina Antonetty and Ramón Velez also tried to contest election results, claiming that the elections disenfranchised Spanish-speaking parents. Only eighteen out of the 130 Board of Election officials in the schools spoke Spanish; parents were told to "wait until you speak English"; and Spanish-speaking parents felt intimidated even at P.S. 25, a bilingual school. Elections brought out an extremely low voter turnout of 6 percent.[24]

The Board of Education ignored such contestations, however, as election results had firmly reestablished UFT control over administrative leadership in schools citywide. Members who ran on a UFT slate had won nineteen out of the thirty-one districts. School board elections also resulted in a clear reconstitution of the racial and gender status quo in the schools' administrative leadership. Twenty-five of the CSBs were dominated by a white, male, professionally trained membership. At a time when black and Puerto Rican students made up more than 60 percent of the student population, only 15 percent of the elected CSB members were black and only 10 percent were Puerto Rican. The only exceptions to this pattern occurred in the six districts in which leaders of color had been most active—Districts 4 and 5 in Harlem, Districts 7 and 9 in the South Bronx, and Districts 15 and 23 in Ocean Hill–Brownsville. In these districts, many community control leaders had accepted their defeat and chosen to work within the limited parameters set by the Board of Education. Sara Frierson and Helen Testamark from East Harlem, for example, had urged parents of color to cast their votes and present themselves as an important constituency on the District 4 school board. District 4 elections thus resulted in a membership composed of four Puerto Ricans, two blacks, and three whites.[25]

With the establishment of CSBs' new leadership, the Board of Education claimed that the I.S. 201 and Ocean Hill–Brownsville demonstration districts could remain as two special units, even as they were absorbed by CSB 4 and CSB 23, respectively. Community control leaders from these districts did not believe that they would be given any real authority from the new CSB leadership, but they tried to hold on to their experiments as long as possible.[26] A combination of external repression and internal divisions, however, led community control leaders to realize that they no longer had the capacity to effectively advocate on behalf of poor black and Puerto Rican students within this new political structure. Events that took place at I.S. 201 between 1969 and 1971 reveal how community control leaders came to this conclusion.

Despite their great hopes, black parents involved with I.S. 201 became increasingly impatient with black administrators' inability to effect academic change quickly. Four years after I.S. 201 leaders brought in a new group of teachers and principals, I.S. 201 still ranked second from the bottom among all intermediate schools in Manhattan in 1971. Parents blamed their children's academic failures on the principals and unit administrators. They felt that principals did not exercise their power to enforce teacher competence. According to Hannah Brockington, a black parent, I.S. 201 principal Ronald Evans "wasn't putting a tight range on his teachers. He wasn't doing nothing. He was just getting paid. He was writing books." To Brockington, Evans's decision to continue writing his doctoral dissertation while holding a job as school principal signaled a lack of devotion to the immediate needs of the children at I.S. 201. Parents were equally disappointed with the performance of unit administrators. Unit administrators were in charge of coordinating efforts between professionals and community leaders, but they failed to establish a working relationship between the two groups. "We call upon the unit administrator to assert his leadership and not continue to reward ineptness by his refusal to correct what he knows needs correcting," claimed I.S. 201 parents in a 1971 press release. Unit administrator Merle Stewart, who replaced Charles Wilson in 1969, defended himself by arguing that he could have "no authority over . . . anarchy in the schools." Parents, however, believed that Stewart could have controlled the chaos. His failure to do so necessitated that he "step aside for someone who is capable of resolving the educational crisis in this district."[27]

Black parents began to increasingly develop class tensions with black professionals, viewing them as elitists whose goals clashed with their own. In a 1969 *Foresight* article titled the "Black Professional—Judas in the Living Room," Babette Edwards, a black parent, argued that "professionalism" produced a spirit of "disdain among Black professionals for lay Blacks." While the "lay Black community" sought to create "relevancy, accountability, and collective achievement," black professionals wanted "individual position, security and safety." Lay blacks used "direct confrontation" to achieve their goals, but black professionals chose to "wheel-and-deal and use individual contacts usually with whites" to secure their interests. Most important, lay blacks felt "responsible" to the "Black community," whereas black professionals displayed their loyalty to the "White community."[28]

Echoing Brockington's and Edwards's complaints, Evelina Antonetty also expressed grievances against Puerto Rican teachers. "We as padres puertorriqueños are always made to feel stupid and powerless even by our 'professional whores,'" claimed Antonetty in a 1975 United Bronx Parents publication. With the flow of bilingual education funding coming from the Department of Health, Education and Welfare, Antonetty felt that Puerto Rican professionals had become preoccupied with pursuing job security while not maintaining enough communication with Puerto Rican parents. Dismissing Puerto Rican parents as "uneducated" or "crude," Puerto Rican teachers did not have the basic self-awareness to recognize that, "whether you are a professional or not, you will just be a Puerto Rican," claimed Antonetty.[29]

Parents of color identified class elitism as the main source of conflict between themselves and teachers, but teachers believed that parents had unrealistic expectations about what professionals could accomplish. Parents expected teachers to reverse the years of bad education that the children had received purely through the power of their charisma and devotion to the students. Teachers, however, could not come close to accomplishing such a task if they were not given a larger infrastructure to support their work in the classrooms. In a letter addressed to Ronald Evans, a group of black and white teachers at I.S. 201 claimed that they were not the "traitors," but the "victims of betrayal." They claimed that in order to succeed as teachers, they needed to have "Guidance Programs" that could help them handle students with discipline problems. They needed teachers' aides who could help them with "children needing extra hours in remedial reading." They needed funds to develop new courses that would be more relevant to the students' interests. But none of these resources were available to them. Instead, the "I don't give a damn" attitude of administrators toward teachers left them feeling burned out, which was driving them away in droves.[30]

Parents of color blamed administrators of color for the failure of schools, but the latter did not actually possess any real authority within demonstration districts. Despite the Board of Education's claim that community leaders would be "included" in the process of hiring personnel in the demonstration districts, the Board of Education by no means granted community leaders the authority to handle such matters. Unit administrator Merle Stewart claimed in a letter to Chancellor Harvey Scribner that the I.S. complex office was "stymied in its attempt to do an effective job" because "at no time ha[d] it been possible to obtain an adequate Complex Office staff." Oftentimes the Board of Education promised unit administrators funding for a certain initiative and unit administrators hired staff to execute the program, but then the new staff did not receive their paychecks from the Board of Education. For example, the supervisor of continuing education had authorized $45,000 to start an After School Community Center and Adult Education Program at I.S. 201 in 1970, but Stewart had to pester Chancellor Scribner repeatedly for the transfer of funds for these programs. On another occasion, District 5 staff sent the paraprofessional payroll to 110 Livingston Street (the central Board of Education office) rather than to I.S. 201, thereby delaying the paychecks for I.S. 201 parapro-fessionals for a week.[31]

Board officials constantly undermined community leadership at I.S. 201. Events that took place at C.S. 39 illustrate how outside repression ef-fectively undermined internal leaders' ability to exercise authority. In April 1969, parents from C.S. 39—one of the elementary schools included in the I.S. 201 complex—requested that their children be removed from the classrooms of seven teachers. The reasons behind this request were never stated, but members of the I.S. 201 governing board agreed to transfer these teachers out of C.S. 39. The teachers, however, refused to be trans-ferred and asked leaders from UFT and the central Board of Education to reinstate them at the school. Without any warning or attempt at media-tion, school superintendent Bernard E. Donovan walked into C.S. 39 dur-ing school hours, ordered school principal Sylvester King to reassign the seven teachers to the children, and threatened that C.S. 39 would be re-moved from the I.S. 201 complex if King did not comply with his order. Under such a "show down" of power, I.S. 201 leaders chose to resist out-side forces by boycotting the operation of C.S. 39. The boycott, which lasted nine days, disrupted the education of children once again. Only 200 out of the 600 children from C.S. 39 went to schools in the alternative loca-tions, and C.S. 39 principal Sylvester King resigned. Despite their attempt at resisting outside intrusion, I.S. 201 leaders were ultimately forced to ac-cept orders from the Board of Education. Authorities from various sectors of the city—policemen, UFT personnel, Mayor Lindsay's staff, and central Board of Education staff—all came to C.S. 39 on April 30 to ensure that the children would be placed back in the classrooms of the seven teachers.[32]

I.S. 201 leaders reached the sober conclusion that there was little they could accomplish given the constant intrusion and opposition they faced from the Board of Education. "The degeneration of the School System has reached a new low," claimed David Spencer, chairman of the I.S. 201 gov-erning board. "Children are moved like checkers, parents intimidated, the community locked out, and the police used to suppress legitimate black and Puerto Rican efforts to protect their children and improve their schools." As Preston Wilcox, the original author of the community control concept in East Harlem, sadly accepted, "There was never any plan to permit Blacks to control the education of their own children. The schools were never run by the community. In fact, the central Board exercised more control locally than it did before."[33]

The failure of internal leadership thus stemmed largely from external sabotage, but community control leaders grew most exhausted from battling against internal leaders who had broken the movement's cohesion. When Babette Edwards and Hannah Brockington resigned from the I.S. 201 governing board in February 1971, they directed the harshest criticism not at the Board of Education but at black professionals. "We are still fighting the same fight," Edwards claimed in her letter of resignation. "Only, conditions are worse because the cripplers in the past (largely white) have now been joined by destructive opportunistic education pimps (largely black), who prey on the Harlem community, sucking its life blood, the community's future, which is embodied in their children." It was precisely black professionals' position as members of an oppressed racial minority that made Edwards that much more upset over their alignment with the status quo. When Edwards saw that black professionals had a "perverted allegiance to 110 Livingston Street" and that they "identified with the master more than the master identified with himself," she concluded that community control was an impossible dream to achieve.[34]

A palpable sense of disillusionment set in as many community control leaders realized that "blackness" no longer signified a commitment to racial equality in schools. In a desperate plea for black solidarity, an anonymous writer wrote in a 1971 article in the Forum, "There must be a difference in Black!" Writing in the African American Teachers Association's publication, the author bemoaned the fact that "some Black educators continue to function as tools of the establishment." The writer pleaded with black teachers to remember their "common heritage, and therefore a common identity" with black children. But as the author's plea implied, it was hard to envision black teachers being committed to the broader goals of community control at this time. The radical vision that had brought parents and teachers, blacks and Puerto Ricans, grassroots activists and politicians together under the "People Power" coalition was breaking apart.[35] Soon after Edwards and Brockington resigned, the chairman of the governing board, David Spencer, followed suit. Four months later, in June

1971, I.S. 201 as a demonstration district was officially dissolved. The experiment was over.[36]

Internal class conflicts within the community control movement thus helped break the coalition apart. Being disappointed at those in whom they had placed their greatest hopes, parents of color began to lose their morale and the mutual trust that had nurtured their hopes in the first place. Having a unified identity as a "black and Puerto Rican community" had given them the strength to challenge white authorities in the beginning, but fissures within this community now cast doubt over the very essence of their hopes. Did a "black and Puerto Rican community" even exist? As unit administrator Merle Stewart watched the I.S. 201 experiment crumble before his eyes, he stated that "personal agendas, egos, self-hatred, negativism, and individual aggrandizement" had destroyed their future, and that they could not rebuild it unless "each individual adult personality" would once again show forth a "willingness to work for the communal good."[37] In the final days of I.S. 201, community leaders did not blame "white racism" alone for their failures. They claimed that the cynicism and elitism that festered within their own communities helped break their experiment.

The Rise of Political Patronage and Bilingual Education as a Hispanic Program

With the dissolution of demonstration districts, a new era of political conservatism was set in place in the city's education system. UFT leaders co-opted members of the community control movement by organizing paraprofessionals as regular UFT union members. Paraprofessionals had originally been paid by the Board of Education through funds provided by antipoverty community corporations and Title I of the Elementary and Secondary Education Act. Community control leaders had first hired them within demonstration districts as a way of bringing poor people of color onto the teaching and administrative staffs in public schools. Due to paraprofessionals' close relationship with community control activists, members of the UFT and the Board of Education had viewed them as a possible threat to regular teachers' job security. As a result, the Board of Education at times had not paid them regularly, but paraprofessionals had no recourse to express their grievances.[38] In 1971, the UFT capitalized on paraprofessionals' grievances as workers and established itself as the exclusive bargaining representative of paraprofessionals, promising them college training accompanied by paid stipends. As paraprofessionals gained a clear path through which they could become regular teachers and maintain job security, they no longer had an inimical relationship with the UFT, but now they grew more distant from parents and activists. As paraprofessionals began to take more time away from teaching in order to advance their own careers, parents felt that they became more detached from their students. "If a Paraprofessional is released [from teaching] four afternoons a week, how does that Paraprofessional get to serve that child that it's released from?" asked Sister Gwen Cottman, rhetorically, in an article in the *Forum*.[39]

UFT leaders were not the only ones who steered black and Puerto Rican paraprofessionals' attention toward individual career advancement. The majority of black and Puerto Rican activists who became involved with the community school boards (CSBs) adopted the hiring of minority staff as their primary goal as well. Some were former community control leaders who felt forced to narrow their goals in such a way and others were outsiders who intentionally sought to build political patronage systems out of CSBs, but both groups came to regard the employment of minorities as their only feasible and desirable goal in the 1970s. Leaders from CSB 4 in East Harlem and CSB 12 in the Bronx took advantage of the transition between the old system and the new decentralized system to hire a number of principals of color since the "interim acting principals" category had more lax certification requirements. They believed that such an effort constituted an important step toward restructuring the racial hierarchy of the schools' administrative leadership.[40] But minority CSB leaders' narrow focus on hiring minority staff made public schools a target of political patronage systems. CSB 4, which was made up entirely of minorities in 1973 (six Puerto Ricans and three blacks), became known as another wing of William Del Toro's and Robert Anazagasti's political machines in East Harlem. Parents and public officials accused CSB 4 members of creating a "self-serving poverty bureaucracy" by contracting District 4 lunch services out to Anazagasti's East Harlem Community Corporation. The most extreme case of political manipulation came from Assemblyman Samuel Wright, who transformed the community control experiment in Ocean Hill–Brownsville into the base of his political patronage. After removing community control advocates from the CSB 23 ballot based on technicalities, he took control over the district. He used Board of Education money to finance his political activities and to grant leases for buildings owned by officials of his political club. Wright's corruption was extreme, but many other districts were also plagued by scandals involving the selling and buying of school principalships and contract kickbacks.[41]

The remarkable academic performance of students from District 4 during Anthony Alvarado's tenure as district superintendent in 1973–83 stands out as one of the rare examples of children's academic performance improving under CSB leadership. During that time period, District 4 rose from thirty-second to fifteenth place among the city's school districts, even surpassing the academic achievements of more affluent districts. The district became known as the "miracle in East Harlem."[42] Part of the success stemmed from Alvarado's pragmatic flexibility in dealing with various political and educational factions. He rose from the ranks at the height of the community control movement, but he was much less committed to its ideologies. He felt no compunction about negotiating with Del Toro and Anazagasti while meeting the educational needs of the students. He hired a number of principals he considered to be incompetent in exchange for the hiring of teachers of his choice. While making District 4 a bilingual school district, he also adopted other forms of educational reform, such as using arts as a new mode of learning.[43] The success of District 4 was, however, a far cry from the original vision of community control advocates. Guided by a wholly different set of ideals focused on individual competition rather than community empowerment, District 4 molded students to pursue a middle-class career more than a life of political activism. Alvarado himself conceded that, the more he reflected on his tenure, "the less I am impressed with the results."[44]

Without the support of a broader social movement, bilingual education advocates also adjusted the parameters of bilingual education into a more assimilationist model. Much of this shift resulted from pressures coming from the UFT. UFT leaders saw bilingual education advocates' insistence on hiring Puerto Rican teachers as a sign of racial exclusivity. Puerto Rican parents had demanded the hiring of Puerto Rican teachers because they believed that only fellow Puerto Ricans could instill pride about Puerto Rican culture in Puerto Rican children. The hiring of Puerto Rican teachers threatened white teachers' sense of control over the schools' teaching staff, however, and the UFT set in motion an all-out attack on bilingual education. UFT president Albert Shanker ran several advertisements in the *New York Times* between 1972 and 1974, propagating the notion that bilingual education essentially created a "separate, segregated school system." He portrayed the needs of black and Puerto Rican children as mutually exclusive, arguing that the establishment of a bilingual program in a school in the Bronx eliminated a reading program for "black children." He claimed that bilingual education created an unnecessary system of segregation by taking "non-Hispanic teachers who speak both English and Spanish" away from Puerto Rican children, giving them instead "teachers who are not fluent in either language." The number of bilingual teachers who were not Hispanic in the school system was minuscule, yet Shanker contended that there was a vast pool of such talented teachers who were being dismissed by an unreasonable "ethnic quota" system.[45] UFT members also distributed flyers that portrayed bilingual education as antithetical to merit principles: "Should Puerto Rican children be taught by teachers who are not required to meet the same high standards . . . as other teachers?" By creating a separate hiring system for bilingual teachers, the Board of Education had created a system in which bilingualism stood as a substitute for "competence in mathematics, social studies, science or any other subject," Shanker claimed.[46]

The battle between UFT members and bilingual education advocates over bilingual education involved, at its core, a heated debate about the role of cultural nationalism in the education system of the city. But it eventually came to be known as a mere competition for jobs from both sides. UFT members complained that bilingual education advocates made the program into a "job control program."[47] Meanwhile, they proposed a new policy through which they would have priority over Spanish-speaking teachers in securing bilingual teaching jobs. They suggested that ancillary certificates for bilingual teaching should be granted on the basis of license and seniority rather than ethnicity, effectively privileging white teachers over Puerto Rican ones. Puerto Rican parents and teachers argued that this policy would have a discriminatory effect against Puerto Ricans, even though it was racially neutral in theory.[48]

The UFT campaign effectively destroyed bilingual education's public reputation. As black leaders watched white and Puerto Rican teachers fight with each other for bilingual teaching jobs, they too began to see it simply as a political game. Iona Edwards, a black member of CSB 7 in the South Bronx, condemned Puerto Rican leaders for using bilingual programs for a "political cause" and for "crippling all our children" as a result.[49] "I [had] supported the emergence of black studies and bilingual education because I thought it would give black children another language," claimed I.S. 201 unit administrator Charles Wilson. As black children were no longer invited into bilingual schools, however, Wilson dismissed it as a program that had "no clout" and "no muscle."[50] With negative publicity surrounding the program, Congress dispensed federal funds allocated for bilingual education with extreme caution. The Bilingual Education Act of

1968 had reserved $135 million for bilingual teacher training in the years 1969 through 1973 nationwide, but Congress dispensed only $10 million in fiscal year 1969.[51]

Troubled by such political opposition, Puerto Rican lawyers and other professionals came to the conclusion that litigation would provide their last chance to institute bilingual education programs on a citywide level.[52] Puerto Rican lawyers César A. Perales, Jorge Batista, and Victor Marrero founded the Puerto Rican Legal Defense and Education Fund (PRLDEF) in 1972.[53] In *Aspira of New York, Inc. v. Board of Education* (1972), PRLDEF attorneys sued the Board of Education for preventing 800,000 Puerto Rican children of limited English proficiency from fully participating in the city's public schools. Using arguments similar to those of NAACP attorneys in *Brown v. Board of Education*, PRLDEF attorneys argued that Puerto Rican children's lack of English proficiency led them to have unequal educational experiences, which violated "a right of equal educational opportunity" protected by the equal protection clause of the Fourteenth Amendment.[54] Building off of the progress that civil rights attorneys had made toward desegregation in the previous twenty years, Puerto Rican attorneys hoped to guarantee educational rights for Puerto Rican children as well.

Puerto Rican attorneys, however, had little chance of winning a bilingual education program at a time when angry white ethnics maligned racial and ethnic minorities' demands for civil rights as "segregationist." In the same year that the Aspira Consent Decree would be signed, the U.S. Supreme Court ruled in *Milliken v. Bradley* (1974) that white families in the suburbs would be exempt from desegregation efforts unless deliberate intent of discrimination could be proven. Judges who ruled in the conflict between Aspira and the New York City Board of Education were thus heavily influenced by the white backlash discourse, which portrayed white parents as victims of overzealous upper-class liberals and "militant" black radicals. When PRLDEF attorneys presented a culturally pluralist program to the judges, the judges forced them to downsize their vision to an assimilationist English-as-a-Second-Language program. According to the final agreement signed by New York City's Board of Education and Aspira in 1974, only Spanish-speaking children who could not speak English would be offered bilingual education, and then only until they could phase out of Spanish usage.[55] When Aspira leaders tried to push back and demand a broader program that would include English-speaking Puerto Rican high school dropouts—whose academic troubles extended beyond language difficulties—the courts refused them, arguing that they would not deal with all "disturbed, deprived, culturally ghettoized" children because "our jurisdiction does not extend . . . to all the world's ills."[56] The court refused to see problems affecting Puerto Rican students through any lens other than the single issue of language barriers.

Final negotiations preceding the signing of the Aspira Consent Decree revealed significant disagreements between Puerto Rican professionals and parents. According to Pedro Pedraza, a Puerto Rican educator, PRLDEF lawyers and Aspira leaders wanted to accept the Consent Decree as dictated by U.S. District Judge Irving Frankel because it represented a legal victory. Although it did not represent the ideal victory they had hoped for, a victory was important for lawyers, who needed to establish their positions as capable legal advocates of a minority group. They considered it no small feat to have any program designed for Spanish-speaking children as a legal mandate.[57] Parents, however, felt that PRLDEF lawyers and Aspira leaders had made a rather weak political compromise for the sake of their legal careers. The Consent Decree compartmentalized Puerto Rican students' underachievement into a single issue, treating bilingual education as a panacea for the multiple barriers that the students faced. All of the other conditions that perpetuated Puerto Rican students' underachievement—high dropout rates, lack of guidance services, parental involvement, and Puerto Rican representation in teaching and administrative positions—remained intact. The more than 60 percent of the Puerto Rican student population who were fluent in English were left with no educational program to address their problems in schools.[58] During the school year of 1975–76 in which the Consent Decree was implemented, only 51,590 of the 310,548 (17 percent) Spanish-surnamed students in the city's schools received bilingual education. Only 728 Hispanic bilingual teachers were hired to teach this group of students, which represented less than 1 percent of the total teaching staff of the city's school system.[59] Despite UFT members' fears about bilingual education, the program ended up making little difference in the educational experience of Puerto Rican students and the city's school system overall.

The Aspira Consent Decree thus represented both the victories and the limitations of the Puerto Rican community control movement. Although it institutionalized the goals of poor Puerto Rican parents in the form of a legal mandate, it reduced their broad vision of cultural pluralism into an assimilationist program that benefited a small class of Puerto Rican lawyers and teachers and only a small section of the Puerto Rican student population. Bilingual education was born out of a radical experiment in which Puerto Rican, white, and black American students would maintain fluency in Spanish and English. Their bilingualism was intended not only to facilitate Puerto Ricans' integration into the broader American society but also to instill the value of language pluralism in all Americans. The Aspira Consent Decree, however, isolated Spanish-speaking students as the exclusive recipients of bilingual education, making it an exclusively Hispanic program.

The formulation of bilingual education as an exclusively Hispanic program resulted mostly from the court's decision, but it also reflected the political aspirations of Puerto Rican professionals who had long sought to establish a civil rights agenda separately from African Americans. In a 1968 national conference titled Hemos Trabajado Bien (We Have Worked Well), Aspira leaders brought together Puerto Rican educators from various cities in the Northeast with Mexican American educators from other parts of the country. While highlighting the vital role that the "Black Revolution" had played in the political awakening of Puerto Ricans, Puerto Rican conference participants revealed their fears about being absorbed into a black identity. Frank Bonilla, a professor from the Massachusetts Institute of Technology, believed that Puerto Ricans should join African Americans in a broader struggle against racial inequality, but he also thought "it would be suicidal for Puerto Ricans to be engulfed in a more aggressive group, the Negroes, [who have] a more specific, firm philosophy." Cooperation between the two groups, he stated, should only be sought "so far as they advance Puerto Rican aims." Puerto Rican educators' desire for a separate civil rights agenda thus stemmed partially from their belief in the principle of self-determination, which Puerto Ricans shared with African American educators. This principle taught them that they should create their own movement, not only apart from white liberals, but also apart from black civil rights leaders.[60]

But the desire for separation also stemmed from older cultural stereotypes about blacks. Aspira executive director Antonia Pantoja contended that "the problem[s] of the Puerto Rican had to be separated from those of the Negro" because "their cultures and histories were different." Pantoja used traditional cultural tropes to distinguish Puerto Ricans from blacks: "Negroes . . . have built up a greater anger against the white power structure and they are impatient with us, because we do not feel as angry." Angel Martínez, a community organizer at the Aspira Bronx Center, expressed his contempt toward "black violence" more bluntly. What could Puerto Ricans possibly learn from black Americans' "Burn, baby, burn revolution?" he asked rhetorically.[61] The polarization of blacks as "aggressive" and Puerto Ricans as "submissive" had been the very myth that Puerto Rican and black parents had been debunking by forming coalitions throughout the 1960s. Puerto Rican youth were adopting political tactics no less "militant" than those used by black activists at this time, as evidenced by the Young Lords' burning of garbage on Third Street and stealing of mobile X-ray trucks. Some Puerto Rican activists from the United Bronx Parents even characterized their entire group as "militant" in comparison to the more "passive, timid" Dominican immigrants who were hesitant to mobilize themselves politically. Having lived most of their lives in New York City, many second-generation Puerto Rican migrants saw themselves as urban and politically conscious, while the more recently arrived Dominican immigrants seemed uneducated and apolitical in their eyes.[62] This was a crude generalization of Dominicans, but it nevertheless indicated the extent to which many Puerto Ricans no longer self-identified as a "patient" people.

Yet Puerto Rican professionals revived the old myth of Puerto Rican "docility" in order to justify their desire for a separate political base from blacks. Having benefited from accessing African Americans' broader political networks, Puerto Rican professionals nevertheless sought to distance themselves from blacks when the urban riots of the late 1960s led the larger public to reduce black protest to a mere manifestation of "black violence." It was this middle-class leadership that conceptualized bilingual education as the base of a Puerto Rican–specific civil rights agenda and paved the way for its construction as an exclusively Hispanic program through the Aspira Consent Decree of 1974. Ignoring Puerto Ricans' marginalization as class and racial subjects, middle-class Puerto Rican leaders constructed the group's self-identity as a linguistic minority exclusively.

Electoral Politics and the Illusion of Power

With the decline of the community control movement, electoral politics came to dominate political activity among people of color in the 1970s and 1980s. Minority politicians, although often hailed as symbols of the accomplishments of the black and Puerto Rican freedom struggles of the 1960s, did not capitalize on these gains through their positions of power. The grassroots coalitions that had made their political ascendance possible were breaking apart as they were elected into office. Lacking a coherent political ideology that could unite a broad coalition of poor people of color, minority politicians held uneasy relationships with their poor constituents and the broader political establishment. It was from this weakened position of political power that Puerto Rican politicians tried to assert their legitimacy as representatives of a new "Hispanic" voting bloc. They increasingly used a politics of ethnic territoriality to carve out a political base apart from black politicians. This is not to say that "Hispanicity" was always mutually exclusive from "blackness" in the 1970s and onward. Puerto Rican labor activists, educators, artists, students, and many other grassroots activists continued to build a cross-racial movement toward racial justice while building Puerto Rican and Hispanic-specific institutions. Their political deployment of "Hispanicity" was malleable enough to include a stance of solidarity and even self-identification with "blackness." Minority politicians who used "Hispanicity" in a more racially exclusive manner, however, became the most visible leaders of Puerto Ricans in New York City.

Puerto Rican electoral representation certainly increased in the 1970s and onward. The number of elected officials of Puerto Rican descent in the city increased from four in 1970 to twelve in 1978.[63] Part of this political ascendance reflected demographic shifts in the city. As a result of white flight, blacks and Puerto Ricans together came to compose 32 percent of the city's population by 1970, which increased their chances of winning a number of new districts.[64] Puerto Rican voters were also expected to become more significant electoral constituents because the courts removed legal barriers to their vote. Section 4(e) of the Voting Rights Act, amended in 1966, exempted Puerto Ricans from the English literacy test and allowed them to register to vote based on a proof of completion of a sixth grade education from Puerto Rico. Additionally, through *Torres v. Sachs* (1974), language minorities gained the right to have access to bilingual ballots in order to make their vote effective.[65] Such federal provisions allowed Puerto Rican politicians to rely on a growing Puerto Rican voting electorate. Congressman Herman Badillo, who represented the 21st Congressional District in the South Bronx from 1970 to 1978, was able to pass on his seat to a continuous string of Puerto Rican politicians from his tenure all the way up to the present.[66]

Puerto Ricans' increased electoral power, however, did not translate into actual benefits to the majority of working-class Puerto Ricans. Despite their ability to increase Puerto Ricans' visibility, Puerto Rican electoral leaders did not realize the full potential of their power. Upwardly mobile jobs remained out of the reach of most working-class Puerto Ricans.[67]

Unemployment rates actually increased among Puerto Ricans on the mainland, jumping from 12.6 percent in 1972 to 14.3 percent in 1985. The average annual income of Puerto Rican families on the mainland declined from 59 percent of the U.S. average in 1974 to 33 percent by the late 1980s. By then, sociologists began stressing the importance of discussing the Puerto Rican "underclass," given that Puerto Rican families in the United States were twice as likely as black families to be on welfare.[68]

The rise and fall of Herman Badillo's political career demonstrates the reasons why Puerto Rican electoral leaders did not effectively represent their Puerto Rican constituents in the 1970s. As the nation's first Puerto Rican congressman, Badillo was known among his compatriots as an "ethnic trailblazer," the Puerto Rican equivalent of a political giant like Adam Clayton Powell Jr. for African Americans.[69] If anybody could capture Puerto Rican political strength, many believed it would be Badillo. He had secured the highest positions of power as a Puerto Rican in the 1960s. He was the commissioner of the Department of Relocation in 1962, Bronx borough president in 1965, and U.S. congressman in 1970. Even as he was recognized as a prototypical "Puerto Rican" politician, however, Badillo tried to maintain a broad, interracial constituency. He tried to establish himself as a representative of Puerto Rican, white, and black New Yorkers. While securing endorsements from prominent black politicians like Manhattan borough president Percy Sutton and state assemblyman Charles Rangel during his congressional campaign, he also had his campaign manager, Walter Diamond, give away Brillo pads with the slogan "Brillo for Badillo," hoping to lead Italians to think he was Italian.[70]

Badillo, however, found it difficult to remain a racial chameleon during a time of racial and class polarization. From the beginning of his political career, Badillo had never established a close relationship with his poor constituents of color, the majority of whom had become politicized through the War on Poverty and the community control movement. Badillo had preferred to stay away from antipoverty programs because he did not want to get embroiled with challenging black antipoverty leaders, nor did he want to be involved with petty scandals. In later years, he lambasted the entire War on Poverty program for accomplishing nothing but the "maximum feasible stealing from the poor by the poor." He preferred to associate himself with already established white authorities, such as President Kennedy, Mayors Wagner and Lindsay, and Governor Rockefeller through electoral campaigns.[71] His prominence as the most powerful Puerto Rican politician earned him enough minority votes to win the 21st Congressional

District seat—most of his votes came from the minority-dominant neigh-borhoods of Central Harlem–East Harlem (the 72nd Assembly District) and Mott Haven–South Bronx (the 73rd Assembly District)—but his lack of connection with grassroots organizers of color made it difficult for him to serve his poor constituents of color effectively.[72]

The congressional district he represented reached acute levels of pov-erty and abandonment in the 1970s. Almost half of all families living on Charlotte Street in the South Bronx were on welfare. Fires tripled in the neighborhoods of Hunts Point and Morrisania, from 11,185 in 1960 to 33,465 in 1974. In 1975, there was an outbreak of forty fires in the Bronx in a three-hour period, leading FBI director Clarence Kelley to acknowledge that the majority of the fires in the Bronx resulted from arson. Catholic priests in the Bronx made a compelling argument that government poli-cies had actually made arson a lucrative practice for landlords in the city: landlords knew that they could count on fire insurance and government-backed renovation monies available for already-vacant buildings.[73] City officials even promoted abandonment by withdrawing social services from the South Bronx. Through a program known as "planned shrink-age," Housing Commissioner Roger Starr tried to cause the disappearance of the "worst parts" of the South Bronx by purposely closing subway sta-tions, police stations, firehouses, hospitals, and schools. Grassroots or-ganizer Gennie Brooks tried to pressure Badillo, Planning Commissioner John Zucotti, bankers, realtors, the fire and police departments, and insur-ance companies to create a workable solution to combat arson, but with-out much success.

Badillo tried to address the multiple problems plaguing poor residents in the South Bronx by rebuilding houses through federal funds. He asked President Jimmy Carter for $1.5 billion for the development of 26,000 new dwellings on Charlotte Street. Badillo persuaded President Carter to visit Charlotte Street in 1977, but the visit seemed to accomplish little besides putting the South Bronx in the national spotlight as an example of a New York "ghetto." President Carter was dissuaded from investing in Charlotte Street after meeting with Mayor Ed Koch the following year. Koch had won the mayoral campaign of 1977 with a platform of financial austerity and op-position to antipoverty leaders, whom he referred to as "poverty pimps." He convinced Carter that even a moderate reformist like Badillo was un-trustworthy when it came to antipoverty measures. Carter's aides also ad-vised him that less government intervention would be more effective at alleviating poverty in large cities. As a result, Badillo was forced to reduce his housing rehabilitation plans to the renovation of eighty-one homes on Charlotte Street, which he financed through the support of Governor Mario Cuomo four years later.[74]

The Charlotte Street redevelopment debacle signified only the beginning of a long era of government retrenchment, which had been triggered by the fiscal crisis of 1975. The liberal coalition that had made possible the administrations of Mayors Wagner and Lindsay crumbled, giving way to the ascent of conservative fiscal policies in New York City. Following the fiscal crisis, Mayor Abraham Beame introduced an austere city budget through a series of layoffs and cutbacks. During the first three years of the crisis, he laid off 25,000 of the city's 300,000 employees. Former mayors had taken pride in the city's liberal policies that favored the needs of the working class, but Beame placed the city' finances under the control of corporations like Chase Manhattan Bank and Merrill Lynch.[75] He assumed that officers of such corporations could rescue the city from the "irresponsible" programs that had drained the city's coffers in "wasteful" welfare programs and public housing. The financial crisis had resulted from a combination of geopolitical conflicts in the Middle East, rising municipal costs, and a declining tax base caused by job loss and white flight, but poor New Yorkers proved to be handy scapegoats in this time of financial chaos. Mayor Koch cemented Beame's policies of fiscal austerity in the 1980s by continuing to favor the development of business districts over the construction of public housing or the provision of welfare and Medicaid to the city's poor residents.[76]

Mayor Koch also forged a political realignment by capitalizing on multiple fissures within the black–Puerto Rican coalition. Although these fissures emerged as early as the late 1960s, they became crystallized during the Koch administration in the late 1970s and 1980s. His 1985 mayoral victory demonstrates how this shift occurred. Mayor Koch masterfully broke up the black–Puerto Rican coalition by taking advantage of various groups' fractures along the lines of class, ethnicity, and borough. Many saw his rhetoric as bordering on race-baiting, but he won a significant portion of the black and Latino vote: he received 37 percent of the black vote and 70 percent of the Latino vote. A large percentage of those votes came from middle-class blacks and Latinos, who were increasingly moving out of poor neighborhoods and becoming homeowners. His neoliberal economic policies and "tough" stance on poverty, welfare, and crime appealed to their class sensibilities.[77]

Furthermore, Koch capitalized on emerging ethnic divisions within the black–Puerto Rican coalition. Although West Indian immigrants and their descendants had maintained a common political identity with African Americans as "Negro" and "black" throughout the 1960s, slight tensions developed between the two groups as African American antipoverty and community control leaders began dominating the Brooklyn black leadership in the late 1960s. Congressman Major Owens, State Assemblyman Albert Vann, State Assemblyman Roger Green, and State Senator Velmanette Montgomery formed the leadership that came to be known as the new "Black insurgents." When Koch made appeals to West Indian cultural brokers from Brooklyn, his courting led to the formation of "Caribbeans for Koch," which effectively allowed him to carry the central Brooklyn electoral district in the 1985 election. According to Dr. Lamuel Stanislaus, founder of Caribbeans for Koch, it was Koch's courting more than any of his policies that persuaded him to support the mayor.[78]

Koch reaped the most benefit, however, from capitalizing on emerging ethnic tensions between blacks and Puerto Ricans. At the beginning of his administration, in 1978, he had rhetorically antagonized black and Puerto Rican New Yorkers through his "tough on crime" stance and promise to stamp out "poverty pimps." In reality, however, he absorbed black and Puerto Rican antipoverty leaders into his own political machine. He dismantled the Puerto Rican Community Development Project (PRCDP) during Ramón Velez's tenure as executive director, but he allowed Velez to maintain his leadership in the Bronx through the Hunts Point Multi-Service Center. During his 1985 mayoral campaign, he successfully gained the endorsement of Velez, as well as other Puerto Rican city council members. He also boasted that he had placed more blacks in high-level positions in city government than had previous mayors. While incorporating a few Puerto Rican and black leaders into his administration, however, Koch also used a subtle rhetoric of antiblack racism to appeal to white and Latino New Yorkers' prejudices. When addressing a group of Italians in the Bronx, he urged them to vote for him and stay in the neighborhood because their houses were not "burned out and deserted" like those of others, and "we need people like you in this city."[79] At a news conference in August 1985, he promised to help poor "Hispanics" because they were "the worst off and most deserving of government help."[80]

Koch's portrayal of Hispanics as the "most deserving" of state aid was clearly intended to compare them to blacks, who, by implication, were "less deserving." Grassroots black and Puerto Rican organizers urged their communities not to fall for Koch's divisive tactics. "We see Koch using every means he can to divide Blacks and Hispanics," noted Barbara Omolade, a member of Black Single Mothers. Fighting against such tactics, she urged "Blacks and Hispanics" to form a "rainbow coalition with a majority of people of color" and focus on the "real enemies of our city: the landlords, the bankers, the racist cops . . . the mayor and his supporters." The executive director of the Institute for Puerto Rican Policy, Angelo Falcón, urged people of color to remember the long history of New York politicians who tried to "play the one group against the other" and think more strategically about how to forge coalitions instead of falling into notions of "natural" differences.[81] Latinos, however, turned out overwhelmingly in favor of Koch's candidacy. Koch won the 1985 election, with 70 percent of the Latino vote.

Koch's appeal to the Latino vote was effective in part because his divisive tactics dovetailed with territorial practices that were becoming increasingly widespread among black and Latino politicians in the 1970s. Black Democrats in Manhattan led by Raymond Jones made deals with Puerto Rican politicians in the Bronx, promising to support Puerto Rican candidates in the Bronx in exchange for Puerto Ricans' support of black politicians in Manhattan. Jones had used a combination of "confrontation and accommodation" tactics with the Irish and Italian leaders of Tammany Hall to carve out a black political base within the Democratic Party in the city since the 1950s. Jones's uncanny ability to mentor black candidates of high caliber and to coalesce broad sections of the black electorate earned him the title of "Harlem Fox."[82] As a moderate politician who still sought to work within the establishment of the Democratic Party, however, Jones made certain compromises with white leaders of the party. He promised to block the rise of black politicians in the Bronx and Brooklyn so long as the Democratic Party would support black politicians in Manhattan. According to Cyril Tyson, a black antipoverty leader, "Ray Jones was used to prevent blacks from making moves in the Bronx" in order to allow Bronx County Democratic Party leader Charles Buckley to "hang on longer."[83] As Puerto Ricans began making inroads into Bronx politics in the 1970s, this exchange turned into acquiescence for Latino leadership in the Bronx. Dennis Coleman, who was elected state senator in 1965 and became one of the first black politicians to upset the white-dominant Bronx Democratic structure, claimed that "the leadership in Harlem always just abdicated to Latinos in the Bronx . . . and ignored the black population in the Bronx." It was not that Coleman did not want to support Latino leadership. He, in fact, had worked closely with Badillo when Badillo was Bronx borough president and he was a state senator in the 1960s.[84] It was politicians' willingness to carve out their territories along ethnic lines behind closed doors that left many others feeling resentful toward the few who benefited from such machinations.

It thus became evident that Koch could reap the most political dividends by capitalizing on multiple ethnic divisions. As sociologist Philip Kasinitz has argued, Koch portrayed the city not as divided between whites and nonwhites but as fragmented into a "myriad of ethnic, class, and neighborhood interest groups vying for power and patronage."[85] African Americans, West Indians, Puerto Ricans, and Jews were all "ethnic" groups who simply competed for some form of political power but whose ultimate political goal was to bring different groups of people into the social order, not to transform it. Within this framework, Puerto Ricans, who were cast as the "better" ethnic minority group in comparison to blacks, became known as the "Hispanic" voting bloc.

Koch was not the first New Yorker to use Hispanic ethnicity to foster divisions between blacks and Puerto Ricans. White and Puerto Rican New Yorkers had used ethnic politics in a similar way in the 1950s. Black and Puerto Rican leaders from the antipoverty and community control movements had replaced it with a "minority politics" in which the two groups saw blacks' and Puerto Ricans' identities as overlapping and malleable. But in the late 1960s, those who felt threatened by the rise of the Black Power movement revived the notion that Puerto Ricans' "ethnicity" differed radically from African Americans' "race" in order to malign the latter group.

Sociologists Nathan Glazer and Daniel Patrick Moynihan were proponents of such a view. As white liberals who had served as antipoverty consultants under the Kennedy and Johnson administrations, they had grown disillusioned with the failure of federal programs to address racial grievances. After watching black discontent evolve into the Black Power movement and urban riots, they joined many neoconservatives in blaming the problems of the late 1960s on poor African Americans rather than the lack of government action. They called the evolution of the "Black, Brown, Yellow and Red" movements an "ominous" and "monstrous" development. While praising the government for making discrimination in public accommodation "just about disappear" in the South, they argued that blacks themselves were to be blamed for whatever marginalization they still experienced, since many of them chose not to register to vote.[86]

In their rampage against poor African Americans, it became convenient for Glazer and Moynihan to advance their argument by contrasting Puerto Ricans as the more "moderate" minority group against the more "militant" group of blacks. Writing in 1970, the two authors argued that "Puerto Ricans still see themselves in the immigrant-ethnic model" and thus interpret "their poor economic and political position as reflecting recency of arrival" rather than circumstances that "demand revolutionary change." They explained differences between black "militants" and Puerto Rican "reformists" through cultural explanations, arguing that "Puerto Ricans do not express as much resentment and anger" as blacks. Using Aspira as a representative Puerto Rican organization, they argued that the average Puerto Rican adopted a "moderate tone of politics" that emphasized "personal mobility" and a "resistance to full identification with militant blacks." In their final remark, they completely erased the history of Puerto Rican anticolonialism by claiming that the "few" Puerto Ricans who thought of themselves as "colonized" had adopted such a view because they had come under the inordinate influence of "radical white college youth."[87] Glazer and Moynihan's superficial and inaccurate statements about Puerto Rican politics indicated that they knew little about the subject matter. But the oversimplification of Puerto Ricans as the "ethnic" and more "moderate" minority group helped them advance their larger argument about the "irrationality" of black militancy.

Middle-class Puerto Ricans joined white neoconservatives in mischaracterizing Puerto Ricans as "immigrants." Congressman Badillo featured his personal story of success in Cecyle Neidle's 1973 compilation of biographies titled Great Immigrants, linking his Horatio Alger story of self-improvement with those of Jewish labor leader David Dubinsky and the Irish founder of Nation, Edwin Godkin. Writing at the height of the black and Puerto Rican nationalist movements, he distanced himself from the black and Puerto Rican constituents who had elected him to Congress, claiming that he sought to represent the voices of the "Irish, Italians, Greeks, Blacks, and Puerto Ricans" without distinguishing one group from another.[88] Badillo's political ascendance had been made possible only by Puerto Ricans' politicization as a "nonwhite" minority group, yet he insisted on blurring the lines between Puerto Rican and European immigrants. Despite the overwhelmingly high rates of unemployment and welfare dependence among Puerto Ricans in the 1970s, the commissioner of the Youth Services Agency, Amalia Betanzos, also portrayed Puerto Ricans as successful immigrants. She claimed in 1974 that Puerto Ricans, "like so many immigrants before [them,] . . . are being assimilated into the life of the city and America, in general, faster than any other group."[89] Betanzos boasted that the class of "Puerto Rican professionals" was growing, with Puerto Rican "policemen and welfare workers, teachers and social workers . . . independent businessmen, doctors and lawyers, psychologists and counselors" increasingly populating the city of New York. Her reference to the growing class of "Puerto Rican professionals" was not entirely untrue—after all, they were the ones dominating Puerto Rican public discourse in the 1970s. But they formed an extremely small portion of the Puerto Rican population in New York City. As of 1963, only 1 percent of academic diplomas granted in the city's public schools went to Puerto Rican high school students; out of that minuscule group, only 14 percent of them entered college.[90] Focusing on the personal experiences of this tiny fraction of Puerto Rican professionals, however, allowed Betanzos to construct the image of Puerto Ricans as "immigrants" whose poverty was temporary. For those who had been skeptical of Puerto Ricans' coalition with blacks from the beginning, holding onto an "immigrant" framework seemed a strategic way to repair Puerto Ricans' growing reputation as "militant radicals."[91]

Having embraced an "immigrant" and "Hispanic ethnic" model, Puerto Rican politicians saw the rise of their electoral presence in the city throughout the 1970s and 1980s, but their politics became increasingly divorced from the interests of their working-class constituents. Badillo was replaced in Congress in 1978 by Robert García, who attracted national attention for his co-sponsorship of the Kemp-García Bill. The resulting act, passed in 1981, created urban enterprise zones in inner cities that were designed to boost economic development through generous tax incentives to private corporations rather than direct government intervention. García claimed at the time that deregulation of business through tax exemptions would "aid the unemployed and the minority populations."[92] By pursuing a "growth politics" based on economic development projects that carried high visibility, however, García paved the way for the gentrification of the city. Private corporations did not employ poor people of color as much as they drove them out of their neighborhoods.[93] Presidents Nixon and Reagan eroded the political gains made by the grassroots activists of the 1960s by abolishing many of the federally funded antipoverty programs, but minority politicians like García reinforced such efforts by pursuing neoliberal economic policies on their own initiative.[94]

Practices of Cultural Self-Determination within a Neoliberal Order

The shift toward a more Hispanic-specific political agenda did not always entail a shift toward antiblack or neoliberal policies. Puerto Rican labor leaders also established a separate labor organization for themselves at this time. In 1969, a group of 150 Puerto Rican labor leaders came together through the leadership of Harry Van Arsdale, president of the New York City Central Labor Council, to form the Hispanic Labor Committee (HLC). Puerto Rican leaders formed HLC in part because they sought to forge coalitions with other Latino unionists. According to HLC executive director Eddie Gonzalez, Puerto Rican leaders made efforts to work closely with Hondurans, Colombians, Ecuadorians, and other immigrants from Latin America because "many of their concerns are not so different from that of other ethnic Latino and immigrant groups."[95] HLC's desire for a separate labor base, however, did not signify feelings of hostility toward black labor leaders. It still worked closely with black labor leaders who created their own labor organizations, such as the Coalition of Black Trade Unionists.[96] But the overall turn toward race- and ethnic-specific organizations in the late 1960s and early 1970s signaled the new perception of people of color that they could empower themselves most effectively through separate organizations.

Puerto Rican educators also continued to formulate community-based educational practices while pursuing a Puerto Rican/Hispanic program. Antonia Pantoja and Víctor Alicea founded Boricua College in 1973, an institution of higher education committed to research and teaching about Puerto Ricans and for Puerto Ricans. One of its first research projects involved analyzing factors contributing to Puerto Rican high school students' high dropout rates. Pantoja stated that "it was our philosophy and commitment that the study could only be valid if the people who were to be studied actually participated in the design and implementation of the study." Funded by the U.S. Office of Education and supported by Native American and black community-based colleges, Boricua College represented Puerto Rican educators' commitment to institutionalize practices of cultural self-determination even within the constraints of 1970s neoliberalism.[97]

The battle to save Hostos Community College in 1975–76 also brought together a remarkable group of grassroots activists and politicians of color to support the survival of an institution of higher education specifically dedicated to Latino college students. Hostos had been founded in the fall

of 1970 in response to the expanding enrollment of minority students that came with the implementation of open admission at the City University of New York. The naming of the college after Eugenio María de Hostos signified the college's particular commitment to Latino students. Hostos was a renowned leader of the independence movements in Cuba and Puerto Rico, as well as of the establishment of the public education system in the Dominican Republic. The college's location at an important South Bronx crossroads at 475 Grand Concourse represented its commitment to the local community in which it resided. As a fiscal austerity measure, however, Mayor Beame threatened to close Hostos in 1975. An extraordinary coalition came together to save the college, which included politicians, college professors, single mothers, Vietnam veterans, ex-prisoners, former gang members, and South Bronx activists. While activists used direct action aimed at garnering media attention (for example, dragging chairs to the Grand Concourse and seizing the Board of Higher Education buildings in Manhattan), the Black and Puerto Rican Caucus leveraged its power to ultimately force Governor Hugh Carey to provide funding for Hostos. The victory of this coalition came with a price—Hostos continued to operate without its Nursing Department, and faculty numbers shrunk from 170 to 100—but the Hostos coalition still allowed the community college to weather the worst political backlash and financial crisis it has encountered.[98]

The vision of community control for Puerto Rican high school students also survived on a small scale through El Puente Academy for Peace and Justice. Former Young Lords member Luis Garden Acosta founded it in 1982 at a time when the streets of north Brooklyn had become "killing fields," with, on average, one Latino/a youth being killed each week as a result of gang violence. Rejecting a "service-provider ideology," cofounders Melissa Rivera and Pedro Pedraza claimed that El Puente educators emphasized "a practice of self-determination and community development." They established "reciprocal relationships" between students and teaching staff and fostered a curriculum based in Latino/a cultures and histories. Despite the Latino-centric framework of El Puente, its student body was made up of Latino/a students (87 percent) and black students (11 percent).[99]

The struggle for Puerto Rico's political independence also continued to bring together multiracial groups of activists. The Puerto Rican Solidarity Committee (PRSC), formed in 1975, was led by older veterans of the southern black freedom movement and the Old Left, such as Ella Baker and Annie Stein, as well as younger radicals who were leading the Black (Amiri Baraka and Frances Beal), Native American (Clyde Bellecourt), Chicano (Corky Gonzalez), Asian American (Yuri Kochiyama), and Puerto Rican (José Velázquez) nationalist movements. PRSC leaders sought to support the independence of Puerto Rico in its broader fight against "imperialism, capitalism, and racism." They brought an international perspective to their understanding of human oppression and recognized that Puerto Rico's colonial relationship to the United States highlighted the contradictions of U.S. democracy. Blacks continued to emphasize cultural specificity within PRSC through the formation of the Black Committee within the organization. It was charged with the task of "building support of Black people for Puerto Rican independence."[100] To James Early, a black member of PRSC, participating in the movement for Puerto Rican independence "opened up . . . a sense of humanity bigger than Black or white without [him] having to give up [his] primary Black identity."[101]

Working within the neoliberal agenda set by Presidents Nixon, Ford, and Carter, political activists had a difficult time changing much of America's political and social orders through their efforts. Reformists who sought to include people of color within established social institutions saw the rewards of their labor more tangibly than radicals who sought to fundamentally restructure power relationships. In 1978, PRSC members became involved with Vieques fishermen's struggles for economic survival when intensified U.S. Navy bombings on the island began destroying its marine life. They framed their battle as one of human rights and social justice rather than anticolonialism in order to bring a broad constituency of people regardless of their views on Puerto Rico's colonial status. Even with such a softened political rhetoric, however, the Vieques coalition failed to stop the U.S. Navy from continuing its practices in the 1970s and 1980s, fulfilling its goal only in 2003.[102]

Those who sought to continue expressing their ideal of Puerto Rican cultural self-determination left the most visible marks through the arts. Following the masterful accomplishment of Piri Thomas in *Down These Mean Streets* (1967), many Puerto Ricans began to write about the lives of Puerto Rican youth who had grown up under poverty and racism. Pedro Pietri's *Puerto Rican Obituary* (1973), Miguel Piñero's *Short Eyes* (1974), and Miguel Algarín's *Nuyorican Poetry* (1975) set the tone of a new literary form of Puerto Rican protest. Defying the modernist convention of making "art for art's sake," these Puerto Rican artists produced artistic expressions of their lived experiences as both "black" and "Puerto Rican" in order to give voice to their struggles for dignity and group survival. Since artists allowed the meanings of their work to be interpreted by their audiences rather than through explicitly political messages, they continued to forge black–Puerto Rican collaborations with much more ease than did political activists. Algarín and Piñero worked closely with Amiri Baraka and other black artists from the Black Arts Repertory Theater School, creating a Black and Puerto Rican poetics simultaneously. They founded the Nuyorican Poets Café in 1974, creating a space for artistic production and performance that would continue to attract young poets of color for decades to come.[103]

Nuyorican youth who shared lived experiences with black youth in public housing and schools in the 1970s also created hip-hop as an enduring, cross-racial artistic expression. By MCing, rapping, DJing, break dancing, and making graffiti, Nuyoricans like Q-Unique (Anthony Quiles), DJ Tony Touch, and D-Stroy created a form of music that represented the experience of black and Puerto Rican youth who had grown up in ghettos, victimized by police brutality and urban poverty. Following the long lineage of Caribbean and African American musical traditions such as jazz, funk, samba, mambo, and bomba, hip-hop demonstrated the influence of Kongo qualities of sound throughout the Americas. Despite the public construction of hip-hop as an exclusively "black" cultural production, the original founders of hip-hop imagined their artistic production as an expression of both "blackness" and "Latinidad."[104]

Conclusion

Black and Puerto Rican nationalism had inspired activists from both groups to create an alternative system of self-governance based on the principles of cultural pluralism and participatory democracy in the late 1960s. In the 1970s and 1980s, however, white leaders like Albert Shanker and Ed Koch successfully delegitimized the political goals of activists of color by characterizing calls for cultural pluralism as a form of "reverse racism" and reducing the notion of social welfare to "wasteful spending." In the context of such a politically hostile environment, class and ethnic tensions emerged within the black–Puerto Rican coalition. While defending themselves against their political opponents' multiple attacks and interferences, activists of color found that they themselves could no longer hold onto a coherent, common political vision. Stripped of their ability to continue forging a movement of their own, black and Puerto Rican grassroots activists relinquished their most radical dreams. Meanwhile, a new middle-class Puerto Rican leadership became the official representatives of the Puerto Rican community, even as they aligned themselves to a Hispanic ethnic strategy controlled by white leaders.

Although "Hispanicity" held multiple political meanings, it became most politically useful as a cultural signifier that portrayed Spanish-speaking people as cultural opposites of African Americans. Lacking a political ideology that could unite people of color under a common agenda, this new Puerto Rican middle-class leadership reverted back to dichotomizing Puerto Ricans as an immigrant, ethnic group, and blacks as a racial group—despite the history of cross-racial collaboration that had proved such facile differentiations to be false. "Blackness" and "Puerto Rican-ness," which had once inspired leaders of color to create an alternative to the white middle-class ideal, no longer held such a liberatory potential. Instead, they became mere vehicles of inclusion for leaders of color who adopted an increasingly middle-class orientation—a leaning much more focused on seeking escape from poverty rather than its eradication.

Epilogue

Black-Latino politics has become an increasingly salient topic since 2003 when Latinos surpassed African Americans as the largest minority group in the United States, and since Obama's presidency sparked all sorts of hopeful and catastrophic predictions about an America that will soon become a "majority-minority" nation. According to the 2010 U.S. Census, Latinos reached 16 percent of the nation's population at 50.5 million, while blacks composed 13 percent at 38.9 million.[1] Those numbers, along with a growing Asian American population, led demographers to predict that racial and ethnic minorities will become the majority of the U.S. population by the middle of the twenty-first century. Whether this shift in racial demographics will translate into significant changes in the political and socioeconomic structures in the United States or simply the absorption of people of color into the cultural and political patterns set up by white Americans in the past depends on the meanings that "blackness" and "Latinidad" carry in the twenty-first century.

More than ever before, the black-Latino conflict narrative dominates public conversations about blacks and Latinos today. As sociologist John Márquez notes, tales of minorities fighting and killing each other dovetail with the dominant racial fatigue among Americans.[2] Whites and nonwhites alike seem to have grown so tired of blaming whites for the perpetual racial problems plaguing America that blaming blacks and Latinos for their self-oppression creates a more "interesting" or, at least, a new conversation about race in popular media. Pitting Latinos against blacks by mischaracterizing all Latinos as "immigrants" and blacks as "natives" is a particularly appealing trope. Whether the debate is centered on the lack of jobs in the U.S. economy or affirmative action specifically designed for minorities, blacks are imagined as "natives" who deserve good jobs, whereas Latinos are continually imagined as undeserving "immigrants."[3] Despite having in common positions of economic marginality, blacks and Latinos are presumably constrained by a racial pecking order that pits one group against the other.

On the cultural front, however, Latinos' "immigrant" status places them above African Americans as the more "assimilable" type of American. Sociologists like George Yancey argue that, based on marriage, residential patterns, and attitudes about the salience of race, Latinos and Asian Americans are becoming more like "whites" and will therefore become functionally "white." Even though these "nonblack" minorities wear their ethnicity "thinly," they are for all practical purposes living and "thinking like whites in that they are dismissing the importance of race in the United States," claims Yancey. Sociologist Orlando Patterson even makes the bold claim that, "for nonblacks, assimilation is alive and well in America." In sharp contrast to Latinos, Patterson argues that blacks have remained as the perpetual "underclass," a special class of people whose experiences of racial subjugation, in both the past and the present, are of an entirely different kind from those faced by other racial and ethnic minorities.[4] Although Yancey and Patterson account for Latino and Asian assimilability using different measures, they view the two groups predominantly through an "immigrant" framework. The presumed novelty of their presence in the United States makes their position of cultural marginality appear dynamic and malleable, whereas African Americans' historic marginality seems entrenched and fixed.

Within these debates, the political fates of African Americans and Latinos are seen as diverging, as if the rise of one group must come at the expense of the other. If African Americans are to succeed through special claims to a "minority" status, they need to secure their position as the more "legitimate" victims of racial subjugation. Latinos are imagined as the perpetual "foreigners" who will never be considered "native" enough to deserve the benefits of full citizenship.[5] On the other hand, if Latinos are to succeed by incorporating themselves into the mainstream through assimilation, they must prove their "work ethics" and "high motivation" in contrast to African Americans' perpetual "inability" to absorb such American values. Whether claiming fitness for citizenship based on the experience of historic wrongs or on present performance, Latinos and African Americans are viewed as competing in a zero-sum game.

These narratives, however, obscure Latinos' shared past and present with African Americans. Although immigrants from Latin America do make up the majority of immigrants in the United States—they composed 53.6 percent of the immigrant population in 2007—to label all Latinos as "immigrants" is a gross mischaracterization. The two largest Latino groups are dominated by native-born U.S. citizens rather than the foreign-born—in 2000, 58 percent of Mexican Americans and 60 percent of Puerto Ricans were native born. Up to 7.8 percent of the foreign-born U.S. population was also composed of blacks, with the majority coming from Jamaica, Haiti, Trinidad and Tobago, Nigeria, Ethiopia, and Ghana.[6] Thus, significant portions of the black and Latino communities have had to fight for their rights in the United States as noncitizen immigrants *and* as legal citizens.

A recent conversation among black and Puerto Rican activists demonstrates the common challenges that many black and Latino workers continue to face in the United States today. In 2010, Noel Sanchez, a Puerto Rican construction worker, stated his deep ambivalence about the growing Central American immigrant population in New York City to other black and Puerto Rican members of Fight Back. James Haughton, the son of a Jamaican immigrant, had founded Fight Back as an unemployment center in Harlem in 1964 and had operated it continuously as an organizing center for construction workers of color since then. Sanchez had held only the lowest-paying jobs in the construction industry. Whereas white construction workers had gotten the "general contractor" jobs—including sweeping, cleaning, and other jobs involving light manual labor—Sanchez had only had "demo" work, which involves higher occupational hazard risks, such as working with asbestos and other harmful products. He complained that he had even lost access to "demo" work recently, however, because construction companies in the city had begun hiring Ecuadorian workers for such jobs at lower salaries. Sanchez pointed to the company's irresponsibility in exploiting Ecuadorian workers, arguing that "they [Ecuadorians] shouldn't be treated this way." Still, he revealed his nativist sentiments against Ecuadorians, claiming that the jobs should have been given to "real citizens" like himself and other black and Puerto Rican workers. "We lived here, we was born here, educated here, why we cannot get work? Wouldn't you get angry?" he asked. Feeling trapped by his own need to make ends meet and his sympathy toward poor immigrants, he lamented, "Now you gotta fight because you gotta fight for your family. How can you distinguish between hating and not hating?"[7] The fear of job insecurity is real and often stokes ethnic tensions among poor workers, but Sanchez's account demonstrates that this fear cuts across the black-Latino divide and permeates relationships within the Latino community.

More important, Sanchez's account reflects the failure of the labor movement to help workers of color fight against the interests of corporate America. Caught in a neoliberal economic order where the drive toward the maximization of profits cuts above all ideologies of justice, Sanchez found himself unable to challenge the forces that have created a racially segmented construction labor economy. Breaking through the racial barrier between the white-dominant "general contractor" jobs and the minority-dominant "demo" work was not even within the realm of possibilities for Sanchez. Instead, he focused narrowly on the competition he faced with Ecuadorian immigrants as a Puerto Rican construction worker. Sanchez's narrow vision is a product of building trade unions and private corporations' long history of intransigence toward demands for racial equality. Despite the few gains that black and Puerto Rican activists made in education and electoral politics through the War on Poverty and the community control movement in the 1960s and 1970s, they were unable to affect the entrenched power of labor and private corporations. With the exception of the Retail, Wholesale and Department Store Union and Local 1199, which later joined the Services Employees International Union, labor unions in New York City resisted efforts made by black and Puerto Rican labor activists to eliminate racial discrimination in the workplace.[8] Meanwhile, private companies relocated their factories to the South and abroad, leaving most of the black and Puerto Rican labor force without a means of economic survival. Economists and government officials claimed that "market forces" would create a "natural" balance between capital and labor, but surplus labor became an unwieldy, intractable problem for the whole city.

Black workers made more gains within the municipal sector in comparison to Latinos, but not enough to improve their overall economic position. The Equal Employment Opportunity Act of 1971, which prohibited discrimination in local government, contributed to black employment, leaving black workers with as much as 35 percent of all New York City municipal jobs in 1990. In comparison, Latino workers held only a third as many municipal jobs as black workers. Social work became a predominantly black niche, with black social workers making up 63 percent of the workforce in the Department of Social Services in 1990.[9] Yet the rise of this small black and Latino middle class made little difference for the millions of black and Latino welfare recipients whose access to a social safety net was constantly under threat. In 2010, the poverty rate among white New Yorkers was 13 percent, whereas the black and Latino rate far exceeded that of whites, at 24 percent and 29 percent, respectively.[10]

Today, activists interested in forging a more racially democratic society face barriers far higher than those faced by activists in the 1960s and 1970s. Since post-1965 immigration law changes and civil wars in Latin America and the Caribbean have brought increasingly diverse populations of Latino immigrants to the United States, activists have had a difficult time forging political unity among Latinos with vastly different histories. In 2010, Latinos reached levels of close to a third of New York City's population, but they were a fragmented population that was 30.8 percent Puerto Rican, 25.3 percent Dominican, 14.3 percent Mexican, 8.8 percent Ecuadorian, and 4.2 percent Colombian.[11] The newer Latino immigrants, who had not experienced the civil rights movement, the War on Poverty, or the national mobilization of the Vietnam War, do not have the same understanding of the politics of race and ethnicity as do Puerto Rican activists who came of age during the 1960s. They often oppose bilingual education and do not see the importance of forging political coalitions with African Americans.[12] Ethnic fragmentation, which was accentuated in the city during Mayor Koch's administration, has increased Latinos' political weakness in the twenty-first century.

The black and Puerto Rican grassroots base that had led the freedom movements of the 1960s and 1970s has also suffered severe economic and psychological setbacks. The explosive growth of underground economies and the high levels of incarceration of young men of color since the 1970s has created two generations of black men, in particular, who are poorly educated and denied access to resources that might lift them and their families out of poverty. From 1980 to 2008, the U.S. incarceration rate has grown from 139 per 100,000 to 509 per 100,000—a five-fold increase. Black men today experience the highest imprisonment rate of all groups: the black incarceration rate is 6.5 times that of white males and 2.5 times that of Latino males. As a result, an unprecedented number of men of color are incarcerated today in America: 11.7 percent of black men and 4 percent of Latino men between the ages of twenty-five and twenty-nine are in prison.[13] Lorraine Montenegro, Evelina Antonetty's daughter and the current executive director of the United Bronx Parents (UBP), believes that substance abuse and incarceration have incapacitated communities of color to the point that systemic transformation is nearly impossible. Although Montenegro was one of the first organizers from the 1960s era to pay significant attention to substance abuse in the South Bronx (she started a substance abuse treatment program when she saw parents at UBP training sessions falling asleep), she sees little hope that people of color in the South Bronx will find relief from the debilitating effects of drugs, HIV infection, and incarceration anytime soon. "I think it's a losing battle. . . . My thing is to make sure that UBP is here and the door is always open for people to come in. But systemically?"[14] Montenegro finds little reason to be optimistic.

Despite these challenges, the political ideas advocated by black and Puerto Rican activists of the 1960s continue to energize and unite sections of the black and Latino population today. Black and Puerto Rican parents and social workers formed the foundational grassroots leadership of the antipoverty and community control movements in the 1960s by organizing citywide school boycotts, parent groups, and community-based antipoverty centers. They first rejected the expertise of white professionals who sought to treat people of color solely as recipients of social services and later refused the leadership of professionals of color who gave priority to their job security above true educational reform for students of color. They boldly confronted the entrenched powers of the city's Board of Education and teachers' union because they believed that they, as representatives of the "people," had the capacity to create a better, fairer system of education for their children. The "culture of poverty" literature had exaggerated cultural differences between blacks and Puerto Ricans by typifying blacks as "aggressive" and Puerto Ricans as "submissive." But grassroots activists' ability to work together and create sustainable cross-racial coalitions shattered notions of cultural incompatibilities between the two groups. Their vision of black and Puerto Rican nationalism animated the political aspirations of broad sectors of American society, bringing together cross-racial, cross-class coalitions of people committed to antiracism. Although class and ethnic tensions persisted throughout the building of their movement, such tensions did not impede activists' ability to create a unifying, common political agenda. In the process, black and Puerto Rican activists forged notions of "blackness" and "Puerto Rican-ness" that increasingly intersected alongside a common working-class politics.

In a similar fashion, the struggle to protect the Puerto Rican island of Vieques from the massive environmental destruction caused by U.S. Navy bombings brought together an international protest movement in the early 2000s. According to Vicente "Panama" Alba, a former member of the Young Lords, the movement was aided by a large coalition of New Yorkers, but it was led by the example and priorities set by the Vieques fishermen. The fishermen initiated the protests by sailing eighteen-foot fishing boats into the firing range and thereby blockading U.S. warships. Although those who joined the protests had varying ideological leanings regarding the island's political status, they decided to frame the struggle broadly as a human rights issue so as to follow the fishermen's wishes. "People like Néstor Guishard de Jesús, home grown from the neighborhood of Vieques . . . has given his life to that struggle . . . [and] represents . . . the grassroots approach to the struggle," claimed Alba. In addition to having a grassroots leadership, the Vieques movement also drew strong support from a network of people of color. When Alba helped organize the David Sanes Brigade (named for David Sanes Rodríguez, whose death in 1999 became a rallying point for the Vieques protests), it included strong contingencies of Puerto Ricans, Dominicans, African Americans, and Asians. Black leaders such as Jesse Jackson and Al Sharpton maintained contacts with Puerto Rican activists engaged in police brutality and racial profiling cases throughout the 1980s and 1990s. With the Vieques struggle, they found value in extending their political sensibility as "people of color" within domestic politics to an international fight for human rights.[15]

Just as the War on Poverty and the community control movements were culturally and politically flexible enough to accommodate the interests of both blacks and Puerto Ricans, so too did the Vieques protests provide room for multiple constituencies to express their various political visions as well. For example, in Chicago, Congressman Luis Gutiérrez gathered a strong contingent of Mexican Americans to join Puerto Ricans marching on behalf of Vieques in 2001. Mexican American marchers, who deeply sympathized with the Viequenses but also faced their own challenges under intense anti-immigrant attacks, spontaneously chanted, "¡Amnistía, Si se puede!" and "¡Boricua, mexicano, luchando mano a mano!" ("Amnesty, yes we can!" and "Puerto Ricans, Mexicans, struggling hand in hand!")[16] Whether calling for the rights of Vieques fishermen to preserve their own land or the rights of undocumented Mexican immigrants to keep their jobs and family ties in the United States, these marchers expressed a Latino sensibility that was both ethnic-specific and coalitional.

The struggle of undocumented immigrants in the second decade of the twenty-first century has similarly galvanized a multiracial group of grassroots activists across the nation. Rather than seeing immigration narrowly as a "Latino" issue, black leaders such as Jesse Jackson, Congressman John Lewis, and Al Sharpton framed it broadly as a social democratic reform issue relevant to all Americans invested in protecting basic civil rights. Leaders like Congressman Gutiérrez have been crucial in consistently linking the immigration struggle to the history of the civil rights movement.

Just as African American leaders used their positions of privilege as those possessing more extensive political networks to help Puerto Ricans develop their own antipoverty programs in the mid-1960s, so too has Gutiérrez urged Puerto Ricans and African Americans to use their privilege as legal citizens to advocate on behalf of undocumented immigrants. The civil rights movement accelerated, claimed Gutiérrez to an audience in Cleveland in 2010, "when the best and most comfortable African Americans were willing to risk their comfort."[17] Other labor and civil rights leaders who had connections with the Puerto Rican movement of the 1960s and 1970s have also become vocal advocates for immigrants. Lawyers from the Puerto Rican Legal Defense and Education Fund (recently renamed Latino Justice), Puerto Rican labor leader Hector Figueroa from Local 23BJ of the Services Employees International Union, and former Young Lords member Sonia Ivany have pushed for progressive immigration reform.[18] The bonds that tie these activists to undocumented immigrants today include their working-class identities, as well as their racial and ethnic identities as "black" and "Puerto Rican." "Blackness" and "Puerto Ricanness," which carried a commitment to antiracism and anticolonialism in the 1960s, carry the potential to reenergize struggles for racial democracy and international justice today.

The struggle for racial justice and political liberation is being waged by a new generation of activists. The legacies left by activists of the 1960s may still hold radical potential for them. While 1960s activists demanded government resources to accomplish their political goals, they never relied on the "expertise" of government officials or their bureaucrats. They held firmly to their racial and ethnic identities, but they did not attach fixed cultural meanings to such identities. Their identities were flexible enough to galvanize political action among various sectors of the American citizenry. Such political wisdom may yet provide a departure point for new radical dreams of liberation in the twenty-first century.

Notes

L6P   Local 6 Hotel, Motel and Club Employees' Union Papers, Tamiment Library & Robert F. Wagner Labor Archives, New York University, New York, N.Y.

LBJPP   Lyndon B. Johnson Presidential Papers, Lyndon B. Johnson Library, Austin, Tex.

NBF   Nathan Brown Files, Municipal Archives, New York, N.Y.

NHHCER   National Hospital and Health Care Employees Records, Kheel Center, Cornell University, Ithaca, N.Y.

NLCR   Negro Labor Committee Records, Government Documents and Microform Collections, Harvard University, Cambridge, Mass.

NYCHAC   New York City Housing Authority Collection, LaGuardia and Wagner Archives, LaGuardia Community College, New York, N.Y.

NYT   *New York Times*

OFP   Olivia Frost Papers, Schomburg Center for Research in Black Culture, New York, N.Y.

PRLDEFR   Puerto Rican Legal Defense and Education Fund Records, Center for Puerto Rican Studies, Hunter College, New York, N.Y.

PWP   Preston Wilcox Papers, Schomburg Center for Research in Black Culture, New York, N.Y.

RFKP   Robert F. Kennedy Papers, John F. Kennedy Library, Boston, Mass.

RPP   Richard Parrish Papers, Schomburg Center for Research in Black Culture, New York, N.Y.

RWMP   Robert F. Wagner Mayoral Papers, Municipal Archives, New York, N.Y.

SDHR   State Division of Human Rights, New York State Archives, Albany, N.Y.

SLF   Seymour Lachman Files, Municipal Archives, New York, N.Y.

UBPR   United Bronx Parents Records, Center for Puerto Rican Studies, Hunter College, New York, N.Y.

UFTR   United Federation of Teachers Records, Tamiment Library & Robert F. Wagner Labor Archives, New York University, New York, N.Y.

USAR   Union Settlement Association Records, Rare Book and Manuscript Library, Columbia University, New York, N.Y.

INTRODUCTION

1. Martin Luther King, Jr., "The Power of Nonviolence," in King, *A Testament of Hope*, 14.

2. Evelina Antonetty's statement, undated (c. mid-1970s), box 2, folder 5, UBPR.

3. O'Connor, *Poverty Knowledge*, 45–53.

4. U.S. Department of Labor, *Negro Family*; Oscar Lewis, *La Vida*.

5. Minutes of meeting, People's Board of Education, 1967, box 9, ElLP; Evelina Antonetty, *Foresight* 1, no. 4 (August 1969), box 24, folder 1, PWP; "Evaluation of the Bronx Chapter of the Coalition in Defense of Puerto Rican and Hispanic Rights," box 8, folder 6, UBPR.

6. Andrés Torres, *Between Melting Pot and Mosaic*, 65.

7. Theoharis and Woodard, *Freedom North*; MacLean, *Freedom Is Not Enough*; Kurashige, *Shifting Grounds of Race*; Hoffnung-Garskof, *A Tale of Two Cities*; Kusmer and Trotter, *African American Urban History*; Bernstein, *Bridges of Reform*; Brilliant, *The Color of America Has Changed*; Carroll, "Grassroots Feminism."

8. Sánchez Korrol, *From Colonia to Community*; Felix M. Padilla, *Latino Ethnic Consciousness*; Whalen, *From Puerto Rico to Philadelphia*; Lorrin Thomas, *Puerto Rican Citizen*; Rúa, *A Grounded Identidad*.

9. Brubaker and Cooper, "Beyond Identity," 21–23. Due to the highly contested use of the terms "racial" and "ethnic," I use both terms to refer to the historical process through which Puerto Ricans shaped their representation in this book. Although some may consider the two terms synonymous, I use both terms in order to give voice to those who differentiated the connotations attached to each term.

10. Fredrickson, *Racism: A Short History*, 154; David Theo Goldberg, "The Semantics of Race," 564; Murji and Solomos, *Racialization*; Alvarez and Widener, "A History of Black and Brown."

11. Fernandez, "Between Social Service Reform and Revolutionary Politics"; Pulido, *Black, Brown, Yellow, and Left*; Ogbar, "Rainbow Radicalism"; Araiza, "In Common Struggle against a Common Oppression."

12. Bauman, *Race and the War on Poverty*; Foley, *Quest for Equality*; Brilliant, *The Color of America Has Changed*; Behnken, *Fighting Their Own Battles*; Clayson, "The War on Poverty."

13. Martínez and Vásquez, *Viva la raza*, 3; Iris Morales, "¡Palante, Siempre Palante! The Young Lords."

14. Kasinitz, *Caribbean New York*; Torres-Saillant, "Divisible Blackness."

15. Higginbotham, "African-American Women's History," 253.

16. Brilliant, *The Color of America Has Changed*, chap. 8.

17. Puerto Rican racialization has mostly been theorized under the category of "Hispanic/Latino" racialization studies because Puerto Ricans have been lumped with Mexican Americans under this broader umbrella since the 1970s. See Oboler, *Ethnic Labels, Latino Lives*; Flores, "Pan-Latino/Trans-Latino"; Klor de Alva, "The Invention of Ethnic Origins"; Gracia and De Greiff, *Hispanics/Latinos in the United States*; Cobas, Duany, and Feagin, *How the United States Racializes Latinos*.

18. Holt, *The Problem of Race in the Twenty-first Century*, 17; Cornell and Hartmann, "Conceptual Confusions and Divides," 30–36.

19. Virginia Dominguez as quoted in Alcoff, "Is Latina/o Identity a Racial Identity," 37.

20. Hattam, "Ethnicity: An American Genealogy."

21. David Theo Goldberg, "The Semantics of Race," 544.

22. Barrett and Roediger, "Inbetween Peoples"; Jacobson, *Whiteness of a Different Color*; Guglielmo, "Fighting for Caucasian Rights."

23. Lorrin Thomas, *Puerto Rican Citizen*, 78; Elena Padilla, *Up from Puerto Rico*, 53.

24. Brubaker and Cooper, "Beyond Identity," 40.

25. Guridy, *Forging Diaspora*, 9.

26. Laó-Montes and Dávila, *Mambo Montage*; Flores, *From Bomba to Hip Hop*.

27. According to Gilbert Osofsky, there were 54,754 "foreign Negroes" in New York

City in 1930. Since there were 327,706 "Negroes" in the city at the time, the black immigrant population numbered 17 percent of the total. Osofsky, *Harlem*, 128–31; Waters, *Black Identities*, 33.

28. Hoffnung-Garskof, "The Migrations of Arturo Schomburg," 40.

29. Matos Rodríguez, "Their Islands and Our People"; Okihiro, "Colonial Vision, Racial Visibility."

30. Guridy, *Forging Diaspora*, 2; Brock and Castañeda Fuertes, *Between Race and Empire*; Andrews, *Afro-Latin America*; Dzidzienyo and Oboler, *Neither Enemies nor Friends*; Jiménez Román and Flores, *The Afro-Latin@ Reader*, 1–7; Laó-Montes, "Afro-Latinidades"; James, *Holding Aloft*.

31. Gleason, *Speaking of Diversity*, 155–72.

32. Bernstein, *Bridges of Reform*; Records of the Union Settlement Association and James Weldon Johnson Community Center.

33. NAACP Bulletin, 1953, box 4, folder 2, EBP; Preston Wilcox, "Relocation and the Social Worker," 1963, box 11, folder 14, JWJCCR.

34. Robeson Taj P. Frazier, "Thunder in the East."

35. W. E. B. Du Bois as quoted in Grosfoguel, *Colonial Subjects*, 152.

36. Alamo, "Dispatches from a Colonial Outpost."

37. Blauner, *Still the Big News*, 44–71.

38. Rainwater, *Moynihan Report and the Politics of Controversy*, 76; Oscar Lewis, *La Vida*, xlviii, xlv.

39. Elena Padilla, *Up from Puerto Rico*, 53.

40. Katz, *The Undeserving Poor*, 86.

41. Julio Morales, *Puerto Rican Poverty and Migration*, 54.

42. Klor de Alva, "The Invention of Ethnic Origins," 66; Fanon, *Black Skin, White Masks*, 80–81.

43. Velázquez, "Another West Side Story"; Lorrin Thomas, *Puerto Rican Citizen*, 226.

44. Gilroy, *Black Atlantic*, 4; Rodríguez-Morazzani, "Beyond the Rainbow," 164; Alcoff, "Is Latina/o Identity a Racial Identity," 40; Márquez, "One Boricua's Baldwin," 462.

45. Sugrue and Skrentny, "The White Ethnic Strategy," 187; Brilliant, *The Color of America Has Changed*, 6; Mollenkopf, *A Phoenix in the Ashes*, 4–5.

46. Kasinitz, *Caribbean New York*, 236.

47. Giménez, "U.S. Ethnic Politics," 8–13; Moore and Pinderhughes, *In the Barrios*.

48. Dr. Ramiro Ramírez Fernandez de Castro, "'Reelected' Bosses of Local 6 Humiliate Puerto Rican Leader," July 1977, L6P; George Santiago, "Union Power and Affiliation within a Local Trade Union," 1987, IBEWA.

49. Martin, "Cornell University's Puerto Rican Labor Leadership Project," 15.

50. Jiménez Román, "*Un hombre (negro) del pueblo*," 21; Arlene Torres, "La Gran Familia Puertorriqueña," 285; Márquez, "Raza, racism, e historia," 18; Ayala and Bernabe, *Puerto Rico in the American Century*, 118–25.

51. Godreau, "Changing Space, Making Race," 284; Arlene Torres, "La Gran Familia Puertorriqueña," 289, 297.

52. Ševčenko, "Making Loisaida," 302.

53. Bennett, *Colonial Blackness*; Vinson and Restall, *Black Mexico*.

54. Freeman, *Working-Class New York*; Biondi, *To Stand and Fight*.

55. Morris and Braine, "Social Movements and Oppositional Consciousness," 27.

56. New York City Planning Commission, *Plan for New York City, 1969*. These demographics are based on my best estimate of the racial and ethnic distribution provided by the graphs of this report.

57. Chavez, *Out of the Barrio*, 150.

58. Center for Latin American, Caribbean, and Latino Studies, "The Latino Population of New York City."

59. Cruz, "Interminority Relations in Urban Settings"; Whalen, *From Puerto Rico to Philadelphia*; Pérez, *The Near Northwest Side Story*; Whalen and Vázquez-Hernández, *The Puerto Rican Diaspora*; Rúa, *A Grounded Identidad*; Fernandez, *Brown in the Windy City*.

60. Alcoff, "Is Latina/o Identity a Racial Identity?" 39.

CHAPTER ONE

1. *Armando Boullon v. Frank De Bello, Owner of Barbershop at 113 Flatbush Avenue, Brooklyn, N.Y.*, Case No. CP-5107-58, box 21, series 10409-83, Discrimination Case Files, SDHR.

2. Gleason, *Speaking of Diversity*, 155–72; Handlin, *The Newcomers*.

3. Harrington, *The Other America*; U.S. Department of Labor, *Negro Family*; Oscar Lewis, *La Vida*.

4. Matos Rodríguez, "Their Islands and Our People," 38.

5. Santiago-Valles, "On the Historical Links," 112.

6. Whitelaw Reid as quoted in Okihiro, "Colonial Vision, Racial Visibility," 27.

7. Matos Rodríguez, "Their Islands and Our People," 41.

8. Rodríguez-Domínguez, "The Racialization of Mexican Americans and Puerto Ricans," 90.

9. McKay, *Harlem*, 136.

10. Laó-Montes, "Introduction," 19.

11. Sánchez Korrol, *From Colonia to Community*, 59, 151.

12. McKay, *Harlem*, 136–37.

13. Vega and Iglesias, *Memoirs of Bernardo Vega*, 143.

14. Glasser, *My Music Is My Flag*, 76.

15. Vega and Iglesias, *Memoirs of Bernardo Vega*, 35.

16. Ibid., 174–75.

17. Lorrin Thomas, *Puerto Rican Citizen*, 29–30, 84, 116–24; Vega and Iglesias, *Memoirs of Bernardo Vega*, 35, 174–75.

18. Plunz, *A History of Housing*, 274; Bellush, "Housing: The Scattered-Site Controversy," 108; Andrés Torres, *Between Melting Pot and Mosaic*, 65.

19. U.S. Census Bureau, *U.S. Censuses of Population and Housing, 1960*.

20. Pantoja, *Memoir of a Visionary*, 53–55.

21. Interview with Robert de León; interview with William Hall. As an African American who was born and raised in New York City, Hall also recounted being shocked the first time he realized he had to sit in the back of the bus while visiting his family in North Carolina.

22. Jiménez Román, "Un hombre (negro) del pueblo, 10–11.

23. Oboler and Dzidzienyo, "Flows and Counterflows," 11; Duany, "Neither White nor Black," 176.

24. Kinsbruner, Not of Pure Blood, 31.

25. Jiménez Román, "Un hombre (negro) del pueblo," 21–22.

26. Seigel, "Beyond Compare."

27. Interview with Manny Diaz.

28. Interview with Frank Torres.

29. Interview with Felipe Luciano.

30. Gleason, Speaking of Diversity, 166; Guterl, The Color of Race, 84.

31. O'Connor, Poverty Knowledge, 45–53.

32. Trotter, "The Great Migration," 86; Gleason, Speaking of Diversity, 100.

33. Gleason, Speaking of Diversity, 155–72.

34. Ibid., 93; Sollors, "The Multiculturalism Debate"; Montagu, "What Every Child and Adult Should Know about 'Race,'" 262–64.

35. Wirth, "The Problem of Minority Groups," 347.

36. Ibid., 350, 370; Gleason, Speaking of Diversity, 165.

37. O'Connor, Poverty Knowledge, 81–85; E. Franklin Frazier, "Problems and Needs of Negro Children," 269–77.

38. Savage, Broadcasting Freedom, 22.

39. Lumet, Twelve Angry Men.

40. Later interpreters assumed that the boy was Puerto Rican, given that the original playwright, Reginald Rose, lived in New York City and that public debates surrounding "slums" centered on Puerto Ricans and African Americans. The script itself did not have any specific references to his racial or ethnic background.

41. Handlin, The Newcomers, 2, 118–19.

42. Glazer and Moynihan, Beyond the Melting Pot, 37–44.

43. Ibid., xii.

44. William J. Collins, "Race, Roosevelt, and Wartime Production," 272.

45. Biondi, To Stand and Fight, 9, 269; Freeman, Working-Class New York, 70.

46. Cohen, A Consumer's Republic, 122; Robert M. Collins, "Growth Liberalism in the Sixties," 19.

47. Handlin, The Newcomers, 110, 49; Glazer and Moynihan, Beyond the Melting Pot, xx, 52.

48. Pérez, The Near Northwest Side Story, 10, 37–38; Ayala and Bernabe, Puerto Rico in the American Century, 100–101.

49. Luis Muñoz Marín as quoted in Galvin, Organized Labor Movement in Puerto Rico, 90.

50. Maldonado, Luis Muñoz Marín, 245–49.

51. Briggs, Reproducing Empire, 83–85.

52. Maldonado, Luis Muñoz Marín, 279, 282; Ayala and Bernabe, Puerto Rico in the American Century, 189; Centro de Estudios Puertorriqueños, History Task Force, Labor Migration, 128–38.

53. Galvin, Organized Labor Movement in Puerto Rico, 146, 151–61; Maldonado, Teodoro Moscoso, 137–38, 142.

54. Galvin, Organized Labor Movement in Puerto Rico, 94.

55. NYT, July 2, 1955; Galvin, *Organized Labor Movement in Puerto Rico*, 98.

56. Baver, *The Political Economy of Colonialism*, 27; Centro de Estudios Puertorriqueños, History Task Force, *Labor Migration*, 120; Lapp, "Managing Migration," 160; Ayala and Bernabe, *Puerto Rico in the American Century*, 194.

57. Ayala and Bernabe, *Puerto Rico in the American Century*, 194; Centro de Estudios Puertorriqueños, History Task Force, *Labor Migration*, 123; José Vázquez Calzada as quoted in Whalen, *From Puerto Rico to Philadelphia*, 2.

58. Whalen, "Colonialism, Citizenship," 2–3.

59. Mass, "Puerto Rico: A Case Study," 73.

60. Ibid., 77, 71.

61. Briggs, *Reproducing Empire*, 93.

62. Ayala and Bernabe, *Puerto Rico in the American Century*, 181.

63. Senior, *Strangers—Then Neighbors*, 51–56.

64. Grosfoguel, *Colonial Subjects*, 46.

65. Ayala and Bernabe, *Puerto Rico in the American Century*, 181; Centro de Estudios Puertorriqueños, History Task Force, *Labor Migration*, 127.

66. Whalen and Vázquez-Hernández, *The Puerto Rican Diaspora*, 3; Sánchez Korrol, *From Colonia to Community*, 213.

67. *Time*, August 11, 1947, as quoted in Meléndez Vélez, "The Puerto Rican Journey Revisited," 197.

68. Meléndez Vélez, "The Puerto Rican Journey Revisited," 207; Mele, *Selling the Lower East Side*, 129.

69. NYT, August 4, 1947.

70. Harrington, *The Other America*, 6–7, 68, 77, 141–45.

71. Ibid., 6–7, 68.

72. McNickle, *To Be Mayor of New York*, 130.

73. O'Connor, *Poverty Knowledge*, 100–101.

74. Harrington, *The Other America*, 176.

75. U.S. Department of Labor, *Negro Family*; Oscar Lewis, *La Vida*.

76. Oscar Lewis as quoted in O'Connor, *Poverty Knowledge*, 119.

77. Freeman, *Working-Class New York*, 143.

78. Whalen, *From Puerto Rico to Philadelphia*; Sugrue, *The Origins of the Urban Crisis*; Hirsch, *Making the Second Ghetto*.

79. Sánchez, "Housing Puerto Ricans," 174; Waldinger, *Still the Promised City*, 107.

80. New York City Commission on Human Rights, *Ethnic Survey*.

81. Rodríguez, "Economic Factors Affecting Puerto Ricans," 205.

82. Bell, *Coming of Post-industrial Society*, 17.

83. Glazer and Moynihan, *Beyond the Melting Pot*, 118–22.

84. Zipp, *Manhattan Projects*, 22–23.

85. Bellush and Hausknecht, "Urban Renewal: An Historical Overview," 10–13; Zipp, *Manhattan Projects*.

86. Jones, *South Bronx Rising*, 121.

87. Zipp, *Manhattan Projects*, 211–12.

88. Schneider, *Vampires*, 42–44.

89. Bellush and Hausknecht, "Relocation and Managed Mobility," 371.

90. Sexton, *Spanish Harlem*, 35; Zipp, *Manhattan Projects*, 261; Gonzalez, *The Bronx*, 124.

91. Zipp, *Manhattan Projects*, 266–68.

92. New York City Planning Commission, *Plan for New York City*, 1969, vol. 4; Zipp, *Manhattan Projects*, 306.

93. Bernard Roshco, "The Integration Problem and Public Housing," *New Leader*, July 4–11, 1960, box 60E7, folder 10, NYCHAC; New York City Housing Authority, "Racial Distribution in Operation Projects at Initial Occupancy and on December 31, 1971," box 92E1, folder 12, NYCHAC.

94. Williams, *The Politics of Public Housing*, 37–38.

95. Pritchett, *Brownsville, Brooklyn*, 66, 114–16.

96. Biondi, *To Stand and Fight*, 233–40; Pritchett, *Brownsville, Brooklyn*, 116–17.

97. NYT, October 3, 1949.

98. Letter from Robert Moses to Thomas Shanahan, President of Federation Bank & Trust Co., May 8, 1953, box 68C3, folder 7, NYCHAC.

99. Sánchez, "Housing Puerto Ricans," 408.

100. Jones, *South Bronx Rising*, 112.

101. Schneider, *Vampires*, 71, 89.

102. "Night Cloaks Crime in City's Toughest Block," NYT, July 25, 1960.

103. Letter from East Harlem Protestant Parish and Union Settlement Association to the NYT, July 28, 1960, box 36, folder 12, USAR.

104. Pérez, "From Assimilation to Annihilation."

105. Heather Lewis, "Protest, Place, and Pedagogy," 41–43.

106. Wakefield, *Island in the City*, 154.

107. Riessman, *The Culturally Deprived Child*, 53.

108. "Distribution of Pupil Population City-Wide," box 1, EdLP.

109. Sexton, *Spanish Harlem*, 11.

110. Interview with Suki Ports.

111. Nora Bowens, "Public Education: Its Successes, Its Failure, and Its Future," West Side Legislative Conference, April 20, 1963, box 17, folder 4, USAR.

112. Glazer as quoted in Daryl Michael Scott, *Contempt and Pity*, 144.

113. Riessman, *The Culturally Deprived Child*, 21–23.

114. Olivia Frost, "The Status of the Public School Education of Negro and Puerto Rican Children in New York City," October 1955, box 5, folder 3, OFP; Joseph Monserrat, "School Integration: A Puerto Rican View," Columbia University, May 1, 1963, in Board of Education of City of New York, *Puerto Rican Profiles: Resource Materials for Teachers* (New York: Board of Education, 1964–65), Puerto Rican folder, IBEWA.

115. Wakefield, *Island in the City*, 266.

116. Meyer, *Vito Marcantonio*, 150; Lorrin Thomas, *Puerto Rican Citizen*, 108–9, 123; Zipp, *Manhattan Projects*, 262.

117. Raymond M. Hilliard, Commissioner of Welfare, "The 'Puerto Rican Problem' of the City of New York Department of Welfare," September 6, 1949, box 68C5, folder 8, NYCHAC.

118. NYT, February 17, 1952.

119. Sánchez, "Housing Puerto Ricans," 407.

120. Lorrin Thomas, *Puerto Rican Citizen*, 154–55; Sánchez, "Housing Puerto Ricans," 303.

121. McKnickle, *To Be Mayor of New York*, 32–108.

122. Baver, "Puerto Rican Politics," 44.

123. Wakefield, *Island in the City*, 268.

124. Ruperto Ruiz, "Why the Mayor's Advisory Committee on Puerto Rican Affairs Should Be Abolished," box 68C5, folder 8, NYCHAC; "Ask Replacement of Mayor's Unity Committee," *Amsterdam News*, October 31, 1953.

125. Lapp, "Managing Migration," 136.

126. Ruiz, "Why the Mayor's Advisory Committee."

127. Benjamin, *Race Relations*, 35; Pantoja, *Memoir of a Visionary*, 84, 96–97.

128. Benjamin, *Race Relations*, 86.

129. New York City Commission on Human Rights, *Ethnic Survey*.

CHAPTER TWO

1. "Testimony of Herbert Hill, Special Consultant, House Committee on Education and Labor, before Subcommittee, House Committee on Education and Labor, August 17, 1962, New York City," collection 14, box 26, folder 8, ILGWUR.

2. *Justice*, September 1, 1962, collection 14, box 26, folder 8, ILGWUR.

3. Dubinsky and Raskin, *David Dubinsky*, 15.

4. Address by Charles Zimmerman before the Annual Conference of the National Urban League, September 9, 1959; Charles Zimmerman's statement of resignation from the Board of Trustees of the NAACP Legal Defense and Education Fund, October 11, 1962; and analysis of Herbert Hill's charges against the ILGWU by the Jewish Labor Committee; all in collection 14, box 26, folder 8, ILGWUR.

5. Andrés Torres, *Between Melting Pot and Mosaic*, 65; Waldinger, *Still the Promised City*, 148.

6. Freeman, *Working-Class New York*, 45.

7. Charles Zimmerman as quoted in the *Nation*, April 12, 1957.

8. Tom Brooks, "ILGWU Hand Picks Recruits for Famed 'Workers' West Point,'" in *Industrial Bulletin* 39, nos. 1–2 (January–February 1960), collection 5780/52, box 17, folder 1, ILGWUR.

9. Rice, "It Takes a While to Realize," 278–83; U.S. House of Representatives, *Hearings before the Ad Hoc Subcommittee*.

10. Interview with Florence Rice.

11. U.S. House of Representatives, *Hearings before the Ad Hoc Subcommittee*.

12. "El Diario Investigations," collection 14, box 26, folder 9, ILGWUR.

13. Franklin, *The Negro Labor Unionist*, 162; Freeman, *Working-Class New York*, 45.

14. Franklin, *The Negro Labor Unionist*, 202.

15. Ortiz, "En la aguja y el pedal," 63; Wrong, *The Negro in the Apparel Industry*, 53–54.

16. Due to the sensitive nature of this case, I have used pseudonyms to refer to the individuals involved. Case No. 2701–51, March 26, 1951, Discrimination Case Files, SDHR.

17. *Elsie Hunter v. International Ladies Garment Workers' Union*, Local 22, Case C-2992–52, April 25, 1952, Discrimination Case Files, SDHR.

18. Rice, "It Takes a While to Realize," 280; interview with Florence Rice.

19. Interview with Carmen Quiñones.

20. Interview with Ida Torres by Ismael García-Colón.

21. Ibid.

22. Feldstein, *Motherhood in Black and White*, 115–21; Orleck, *Storming Caesars Palace*, 82.

23. René Marqués as quoted in Acosta-Belén, "Ideology and Images of Women," 129, 131–33.

24. Richards, *Maida Springer*, 38; Kessler-Harris, "Organizing the Unorganizable," 7–8.

25. Richards, *Maida Springer*, 53.

26. James C. Scott, *Domination and the Arts of Resistance*, 2.

27. Kelley, *Race Rebels*, 8.

28. Sánchez, "Housing Puerto Ricans," 174; Waldinger, *Still the Promised City*, 107.

29. Ríos, "Gender, Industrialization, and Development," 136; Safa, *The Myth of the Male Breadwinner*, 65.

30. Boris, "Needlewomen under the New Deal," 36.

31. Freeman, *Working-Class New York*, 43.

32. Galvin, *Organized Labor Movement in Puerto Rico*, 154–61.

33. Interview with Joseph Monserrat.

34. Interview with Eddie Gonzalez.

35. Matthew Schoenwald, "Memo Regarding Incident Which Took Place in Q.T.," August 17, 1958, collection 22, box 8, folder 7, ILGWUR; letter from Martin Feldman (local manager of Local 132) to Rev. Clay Maxwell, October 15, 1958, collection 2, box 315, folder 3a–3b, ILGWUR; Lois Gray, "Puerto Rican Workers in New York (International Migration)," December 3–10, 1963, collection 14, box 30, folder 6, ILGWUR; Hill, "Guardians of the Sweatshops," 392.

36. T. R. Bassett, "Fired Puerto Ricans Seek Aid in Struggle at Plastics Ware Plant," *Daily Worker*, December 26, 1958, collection 3, box 22, folder 8, ILGWUR.

37. Letter from Maria Rodriguez to David Dubinsky, September 19, 1960, collection 2, box 321, folder 35a–b, ILGWUR.

38. Editorial, "The ILGWU and the Puerto Ricans," *El Diario*, June 21, 1957, collection 14, box 30, folder 6, ILGWUR.

39. Editorial, *La Prensa*, August 14, 1962, collection 14, box 26, folder 8, ILGWUR.

40. Sánchez Korrol, *From Colonia to Community*, 194.

41. Centro de Estudios Puertorriqueños, History Task Force, *Labor Migration*, 146.

42. Vega and Iglesias, *Memoirs of Bernardo Vega*, 22.

43. Charles Zimmerman as quoted in editorial, "The ILGWU and the Puerto Ricans," *El Diario*, June 21, 1957.

44. Gray, "Puerto Rican Workers in New York."

45. "Local 22 Educational and Recreational Activities," collection 14, box 21, folder 15, ILGWUR.

46. "Report of Manager Reiss on the Activities of Local 23," Executive Board/Members Meetings, May 11, 1954–December 17, 1957, collection 5780, box 59, folder 2, ILGWUR.

47. Charles Zimmerman's statement of resignation from the Board of Trustees of the NAACP Legal Defense and Education Fund, October 11, 1962, collection 14, box 26, folder 8, ILGWUR; Ortiz, "Historical Vignettes of Puerto Rican Women," 231.

48. Glazer and Moynihan, *Beyond the Melting Pot*, 144; Freeman, *Working-Class New York*, 45.

49. ILGWU leaders as quoted in Jonas, *Freedom's Sword*, 271.

50. Interview with Frank Perez.

51. H. W. Benson, "A New Advance in Union Democracy: When Organizers Organize," collection 5780/3, box 5, folder 3, ILGWUR.

52. Ibid.

53. Interview with Frank Perez.

54. Interview with Frank Perez; NYT, September 28, 1990.

55. Interview with Eddie Gonzalez; interview with Kathy Andrade.

56. Lois Gray, "Puerto Rican Workers in New York."

57. International Brotherhood of Electrical Workers, *Our Industry's Mosaic: A Portrait of Minority Participation in the Electrical Industry* (New York: Educational and Cultural Fund, Joint Industry Board of the Electrical Industry, 1993), IBEWA.

58. Foner, *Organized Labor and the Black Worker*, 359; Fink and Greenberg, *Upheaval in the Quiet Zone*.

59. Address by Dr. Martin Luther King to Prayer Pilgrimage, Sunday, July 22, 1962, collection 5510, box 47, folder 5, NHHCER.

60. NYT, March 2, 1964.

61. Sánchez Korrol, *From Colonia to Community*, 226.

62. NYT, April 14, 1958.

63. NYT, March 6, 1965.

64. Letter from A. Philip Randolph to David Dubinsky, September 1962, APRP.

65. Interview with James Haughton; interview with Florence Rice.

66. Korstad and Lichtenstein, "Opportunities Found and Lost," 787; Payne, *I've Got the Light of Freedom*, chap. 3.

67. Hill, "Black Workers, Organized Labor," 268–76; Foner, *Organized Labor and the Black Worker*, 334–39.

68. Daily Proceedings, International Ladies Garment Workers' Union 32nd Convention, May 19, 1965, Reel 14, NLCR.

69. Kasinitz, *Caribbean New York*, 211–17; Walter, *The Harlem Fox*, 1.

70. Sánchez, "Puerto Ricans and the Door of Participation," 126.

71. Haygood, *King of the Cats*, 239–44; Walter, *The Harlem Fox*, 124–31.

72. Haygood, *King of the Cats*, 278.

73. Ehrenreich, *The Altruistic Imagination*, 151.

74. Dudziak, "Desegregation as a Cold War Imperative," 79; Walter, *The Harlem Fox*, 137.

75. Hickey and Edwin, *Adam Clayton Powell*, 212–17; Haygood, *King of the Cats*, 289–90.

76. *Amsterdam News*, February 2, 1952; ibid., December 13, 1952.

77. *Amsterdam News*, September 25, 1954; ibid., October 9, 1954.

78. Edward Lewis, "The Urban League," 160–77; 45th Annual Report, 1955, box 2, folder 36, EdLP.

79. Jenkins, *Intergroup Empathy*, 54–63.

80. *Amsterdam News*, June 10, 1950.

81. Ibid., April 2, 1960.

82. NYT, March 28, 1960.

83. "A Reporter at Large," *New York*, November 10, 1951, box 18, folder 8, EHPPR.

84. NYT, July 24, 1960.

85. Opie, "Eating, Dancing, and Courting," 96–97; Naison, "It Takes a Village to Raise a Child," 9, 12, 14.

86. Piri Thomas, *Down These Mean Streets*, 153.

87. Letter from President of the Spanish-American Youth Bureau, Mr. Ruperto Ruiz, to Head Worker of the Union Settlement, Clyde E. Murray, December 21, 1943, box 4, folder 7, HANAR.

88. Sánchez, "Housing Puerto Ricans," 322.

89. Pantoja, *Memoir of a Visionary*, 69.

90. Interview with Hernan LaFontaine.

91. Mills, Senior, and Goldsen, *The Puerto Rican Journey*, 138.

92. Elena Padilla, *Up from Puerto Rico*, 36.

93. Colón, *A Puerto Rican in New York*, 194–95.

94. Ibid., 53; Vega and Iglesias, *Memoirs of Bernardo Vega*, 149.

95. Sánchez Korrol, *From Colonia to Community*, 76.

96. Laó-Montes, "Introduction," 5; Rodríguez-Morazzani, "Political Cultures of the Puerto Rican Left," 30.

97. McKay, *Harlem*, 132–37.

CHAPTER THREE

1. Interview with Manny Diaz.

2. Interview with Agnes Louard by Gene Sklar; Pantoja, *Memoir of a Visionary*, 92.

3. Interview with Manny Diaz by Gene Sklar; interview with Manny Diaz by Lillian Jiménez.

4. Manny Diaz, "Gangs—An East Side Story," box 3, folder 6, USAR.

5. Interview with Manny Diaz by Gene Sklar.

6. Naples, *Grassroots Warriors*, 11.

7. Pearl and Riessman, *New Careers for the Poor*; Orleck and Hazirjian, *The War on Poverty*, 12.

8. Interview with Hernan LaFontaine.

9. Leonardo Covello, "A Community Centered School and the Problem of Housing," box 12, folder 3, JWJCCR.

10. Preston Wilcox, "Relocation and the Social Worker," 1963, box 11, folder 14, JWJCCR.

11. Carlton-LaNey, *African American Leadership*; Lindenberg and Zittel, "The Settlement Scene Changes," 564–66.

12. Jane Addams as quoted in Katz, *The Undeserving Poor*, 98.

13. Mary Simkhovitch as quoted in Sicherman and Green, *Notable American Women*, 650; Simon, "Settlement Houses," 370–71.

14. Pastorello, "The Transfigured Few," 100–105.

15. Trolander, *Professionalism and Social Change*, 2; Lasch-Quinn, *Black Neighbors*, 153.

16. Richard Cloward as quoted in Trolander, *Professionalism and Social Change*, 184.

17. Robert A. Yangas, Director, "Operation Bootstrap," East Harlem Youth Employment Services, October 27, 1961, box 20, folder 11, USAR.

18. "East Harlem Youth Employment Services," January 1967, box 20, folder 11, USAR.

19. Yangas, "Operation Bootstrap."

20. Lasch-Quinn, *Black Neighbors*, 156.

21. Sexton, *Spanish Harlem*, 4–5; "New York City's Puerto Ricans: Asset or Liability?" box 10, folder 10, USAR.

22. Letter from Walter Lord, Chairman of the Board of Directors of USA, to Stephen R. Currier, President of the Taconic Foundation, November 8, 1963, box 11, folder 14, JWJCCR.

23. Executive Directors' Report, November 7, 1955, box 3, folder 6, JWJCCR.

24. Minutes of board meeting, 1951, box 3, folder 4, JWJCCR.

25. Interview with Eugene Sklar; O'Connor, *Poverty Knowledge*, 52.

26. George R. Metcalf, "Metro North Moves Mountains," 1966, reprinted from the *Reporter Magazine Company*, box 13, folder 20, JWJCCR.

27. Metro North Citizens' Committee, January 23, 1964, box 6, folder 1, USAR; Norm Eddy, East Harlem Council for Community Planning, Legislative Proposals in the Field of Housing and Neighborhood Development, December 15, 1966, box 11, folder 11, JWJCCR.

28. Hirsch, Hirsch, and Margolis, "The Effects of Habitability Laws upon Rent," 299–300.

29. Metcalf, "Metro North Moves Mountains."

30. Schwartz, "Tenant Power in the Liberal City," 176.

31. Metcalf, "Metro North Moves Mountains"; Zipp, *Manhattan Projects*, 339–41.

32. "Discussion: A City with Problems," *Jubilee: A Magazine of the Church and Her People* 14, no. 2 (June 1966), box 29, folder 8, EHPPR.

33. Ransby, *Ella Baker*, 153–54; Education Committee of the New York branch of the NAACP, flyer addressed to Negro and Puerto Rican parents, box 4, folder 20, EBP; NAACP Bulletin, 1953, box 4, folder 2, EBP.

34. East Harlem Project, "Unchaining Human Potential: A Survey of Manhattan Parents," box 17, folder 2, USAR.

35. Preston as quoted in Sexton, *Spanish Harlem*, 10.

36. Marta Valle, "East Harlem Project Final Evaluation, P.S. 121," 1959, box 17, folder 1, USAR; Rogers, *110 Livingston Street*, 125.

37. Biondi, *To Stand and Fight*, 260.

38. Interview with Julio Morales.

39. Berkman and Maramaldi, "Health, Mental Health, and Disabilities," 252; Grob, *From Asylum to Community*, 12–20.

40. Benjamin and Crouse, "American Psychological Association's Response," 235.

41. Benjamin, *Race Relations*, 141; Pantoja, *Memoir of a Visionary*, 84.

42. Pantoja, *Memoir of a Visionary*, 75–77, 84–87.

43. Letter from Francisco Trilla, Chairman of the Board of Directors of Aspira, to David Dubinsky, November 26, 1963, series 5780/52, box 41, folder 5, ILGWUR.

44. Waters, *Black Identities*, 22; Markowitz and Rosner, *Children, Race, and Power*, 24.

45. Northside Center for Child Development, Inc., Annual Report, 1953, box 90, folder 2, KCP; Paul K. Benedict, "Integration at Northside," box 90, folder 4, KCP.

46. Memorandum from George A. Dailey to Dr. Kenneth Clark, December 26, 1967, box 453, folder 8, KCP.

47. Interview with Manny Diaz; interview with Manny Diaz by Blanca Vazquez.

48. Interview with Humberto Cintrón.

49. Irma M. Olmedo, "The Aspira Experience: A Faculty Adviser Learns the Ropes," presented at the Puerto Rican Studies Association Conference, San Juan, Puerto Rico, October 2008.

50. Letter from Francisco Trilla to David Dubinsky.

51. "Aspira of America Development Program, 1969 to 1972," March 1969, collection 5780/52, box 41, folder 5, ILGWUR.

52. Interview with Julio Morales.

53. Helfgot, *Professional Reforming*, 19; Trolander, *Professionalism and Social Change*, 167–77.

54. Cloward and Ohlin, *Delinquency and Opportunity*, 108, 211.

55. Krosney, *Beyond Welfare*, 20; Trolander, *Professionalism and Social Change*, 167–77.

56. Krosney, *Beyond Welfare*, 19; Sugrue, *Sweet Land of Liberty*, 356.

57. Heifetz, "Introduction," 20; Hettie Jones, "Neighborhood Service Centers," 40.

58. Weissman, "Overview of Employment Opportunities," 27–28; Luther, "Negro Youth and Social Action," 151–53.

59. Luther, "Negro Youth and Social Action," 152.

60. Interview with Manny Diaz.

61. "Freedom and Jobs," El Diario, August 28, 1963; "200,000 Marchan en Washington," El Diario, August 29, 1963.

62. "Wagner asistirá a March W'shington," El Diario, August 22, 1963.

63. Ibid.; "MPI Participará en la Marcha a Washington," El Diario, May 26, 1963.

64. Kronenfeld, "A Case History of a Block Association," 35.

65. Schwartz, "Tenant Power in the Liberal City," 175.

66. Taylor, *Knocking at Our Own Door*, 119.

67. Ibid., 121–32; NYT, January 12, 1964; ibid., February 2, 1964.

68. Andrés Torres, *Between Melting Pot and Mosaic*, 65.

69. Interview with Manny Diaz.

70. "Ultiman Detalles Para el Boicot," El Diario, February 2, 1964.

71. NYT, February 4, 1964.

72. Interview with Manny Diaz.

73. Joseph Monserrat, "School Integration: A Puerto Rican View," address before the Conference on Integration in New York City Public Schools at Teachers College, Columbia University, May 1, 1963, in *Puerto Rican Profiles: Resource Materials for Teachers*, Board of Education of City of New York, Curriculum Bulletin No. 5, 1964–65 series (New York: Board of Education, 1964–65), in Puerto Rican folder, IBEWA; NYT, October 4, 1964; ibid., March 2, 1964.

74. Seigel, "Beyond Compare," 71.

75. Wade, *Race and Ethnicity in Latin America*, 51–57.

76. Editorial, *Amsterdam News*, November 21, 1964.

77. "Editorial: Puerto Rican Parent-Teacher Association," *El Diario*, January 28, 1964; Luisa A. Quintero, "Grupos de Derechos Civiles No Creen En Promesas; Afirman Irán Al Boicot," *El Diario*, January 31, 1964.

78. Luisa A. Quintero, "Puertorriqueños Piden la Igualdad Escolar," *El Diario*, February 3, 1964; Luisa A. Quintero, "Boricuas Irán A Boicot en Las Escuelas," *El Diario*, January 27, 1964; Nieto, *Puerto Rican Students in U.S. Schools*, 20.

79. *Amsterdam News*, February 22, 1964; ibid., February 28, 1964; ibid., March 14, 1964.

80. Manny Diaz and Roland Cintrón, "School Integration and Quality Education," January 13, 1964, microfilm 11, BRP.

81. "National Association for Puerto Rican Civil Rights: Draft Resolution on the Education of the Puerto Rican Child in New York City, February 6, 1964," microfilm 11, BRP; Sexton, *Spanish Harlem*, 48.

82. "Guide for Freedom School Leaders," microfilm 11, BRP.

83. Ortiz, "Historical Vignettes of Puerto Rican Women," 221.

84. Helfgot, *Professional Reforming*, 76; Mele, *Selling the Lower East Side*, 14.

85. Julio Morales, "A Question of Identity," address delivered at the Fifth Annual Puerto Rican Youth Conference, February 12, 1963, Columbia College, in Julio Morales's Personal Papers.

86. Quarterly Report for months of October, November, and December 1963, Aspira, series 5780/52, box 41, folder 5, ILGWUR.

87. Pantoja, *Memoir of a Visionary*, 86, 102; Krosney, *Beyond Welfare*, 50; Quarterly Report for months of January, February, and March 1965, Aspira, series 5780/52, box 41, folder 5, ILGWUR.

88. *Amsterdam News*, February 22, 1964.

CHAPTER FOUR

1. Interview with Gloria Quiñones; interview with Humberto Cintrón.

2. Interview with Gloria Quiñones.

3. Interview with Humberto Cintrón.

4. Bauman, *Race and the War on Poverty*; Behnken, *Fighting Their Own Battles*; Clayson, "The War on Poverty."

5. Behnken, *Fighting Their Own Battles*, 219.

6. Williams, *The Politics of Public Housing*; Orleck, *Storming Caesars Palace*; Kornbluh, *The Battle for Welfare Rights*.

7. Hoffnung-Garskof, "The Migrations of Arturo Schomburg"; Jiménez Román and Flores, *The Afro-Latin@ Reader*.

8. The geographic boundaries of the South Bronx have shifted over time. Although the South Bronx included the original neighborhoods of Mott Haven, Melrose, Morrisania-Claremont, and Hunts Point–Crotona Park to the east, it stretched to everything south of Fordham Road, from Highbridge and the lower Concourse to Tremont, University Heights, and lower Fordham in the 1970s. The defining features that determined the boundaries of the South Bronx seemed to be declining real estate investment, high crime rates, and an aging housing stock. See Gonzalez, *The Bronx*, 109.

9. New York City Planning Commission, *Plan for New York City,* 1969.

10. Andrés Torres, *Between Melting Pot and Mosaic,* 65.

11. Robert M. Collins, "Growth Liberalism in the Sixties," 17.

12. President Lyndon B. Johnson as quoted in James T. Patterson, *America's Struggle against Poverty,* 128.

13. There were many other pieces of legislation included in the War on Poverty, such as the Area Redevelopment bill, the Manpower Development and Training Act, Job Corps, and Title I of the Elementary and Secondary Education Act of 1965. Note that I use the terms community action programs (CAPs), community action agencies (CAAs), and Community Progress Centers (CPCs) interchangeably because antipoverty leaders used all three interchangeably as well. Matusow, *The Unraveling of America,* 100, 221, 244; James T. Patterson, *America's Struggle against Poverty,* 123.

14. Economic Opportunity Act of 1964 as quoted in Sugrue, *Sweet Land of Liberty,* 367.

15. Katznelson, *City Trenches,* 91.

16. Matusow, *The Unraveling of America,* 245–47.

17. Minutes of meeting of the Board of Trustees of the James Weldon Johnson Community Center, April 12, 1965, box 5, folder 1, JWJCCR; Cazenave, *Impossible Democracy,* 146–47; NYT, November 6, 1965.

18. "Ignoran a los Boricuas en Guerra Contra la Pobreza," El Diario, June 30, 1964; Cazenave, *Impossible Democracy,* 147.

19. McKnickle, *To Be Mayor of New York,* 154; interview with Frank Torres.

20. "Puertorriqueños y Negros Dan Margen de Victoria a Kennedy," El Diario, November 5, 1964; "Wagner Destaca Contribución de los Boricuas al Triunfo de Johnson," El Diario, November 16, 1964.

21. Sugrue, *Sweet Land of Liberty,* 371; letter from Arthur C. Logan, Chairman of the New York City Council against Poverty, to Antipoverty Leaders, July 12, 1965, box 13, folder 10, JWJCCR.

22. Saul Goldzweig, "Report on Settlement Experience with Establishment of CPC's as of November 24, 1965," United Neighborhood Houses of New York, box 4, folder 5, USAR.

23. Letter from Preston Wilcox to "Citizens of East Harlem, Re: 'Those People Are Messing with Us,'" March 10, 1966, box 4, folder 6, USAR.

24. Ibid.; Matusow, *The Unraveling of America,* 255.

25. Matusow, *The Unraveling of America,* 240.

26. Untitled document on Puerto Rican Community Leadership, box 24, folder 1, APP; interview with Manny Diaz.

27. Katz, *The Undeserving Poor,* 86.

28. Barbaro, "Ethnic Resentment," 83.

29. Herbert Bienstock, Regional Director, U.S. Department of Labor—Bureau of Labor Statistics, New York, N.Y., "The Facts of Poverty in New York City," March 11, 1965, box 87, folder "Poverty: NY," 1965, Legislative Subject File, RFKP.

30. Interview with Manny Diaz.

31. Haygood, *King of the Cats,* 314–19.

32. Letter from Lee C. White to President Johnson, April 8, 1965, box 21, EX ST 51-2 Puerto Rico, White House Central File Collection, LBJPP.

33. Memorandum from David S. North to Joseph Califano, November 11, 1966, box 327, LBJPP.

34. Memorandum from Joseph Califano to President Lyndon B. Johnson, September 22, 1966, box "Harry McPherson," folder "Mexican Americans," White House Aides Collection, LBJPP.

35. Press release from the President's Committee on Equal Employment Opportunity, April 29, 1965, box 33: Gen PU1/FG 415 Joint Economic Commission, Democratic National Committee Series Collection, LBJPP.

36. Interview with Manny Diaz.

37. Rodríguez, "Economic Factors," 205.

38. Katz, *The Undeserving Poor*, 10.

39. Puerto Rican Social Services, "Proposal for Establishment of Bilingual Municipal Information Centers," 1963, box 11, folder 133, roll 7, Subject Files, RWMP.

40. News Bulletin #4, Harlem Council for Economic Development, July 3, 1965, box 134, folder 1, KCP.

41. Barbaro, "Ethnic Resentment," 79.

42. Untitled document on Puerto Rican Community Leadership, box 24, folder 1, APP; interview with Manny Diaz.

43. "Hometown Clubs Attract Puerto Rican Immigrants," *CNS*, January 20, 1970. *Community News Service* had a seven-year run of daily community reports. It was established in 1969 as a Harlem-based newspaper and provided news about black and Hispanic communities in New York City. It sent reports to more than thirty subscribers, including the *New York Times*, the *Daily News*, the *Amsterdam News*, CBS-TV, CBS radio, WNBC-TV, and WLIB radio.

44. Interview with Manny Diaz; Pantoja, *Memoirs of a Visionary*, 111–19; Puerto Rican Forum, *The Puerto Rican Community Development Project*, 114.

45. Interview with Manny Diaz.

46. Conversation with Manny Diaz, José Morales, and José Morales Jr.

47. Puerto Rican Forum, *The Puerto Rican Community Development Project*, 9, 20.

48. Frank Bonilla, "Rationale for a Culturally Based Program of Action against Poverty among New York Puerto Ricans," undated, c. 1964, box 4, folder 1, APP.

49. Puerto Rican Forum, *The Puerto Rican Community Development Project*, 89, 82.

50. Untitled document on Puerto Rican Community Leadership, box 24, folder 1, APP; interview with Manny Diaz.

51. Interview with Julio Morales.

52. Herb Boyd, "Harlem Legend, Preston Wilcox Passes," Preston Wilcox Finding Aid, PWP.

53. MEND Board of Directors, "Application for Community Action Program," box 13, folder 14, JWJCCR.

54. Interview with Charles Wilson.

55. Preston Wilcox, "Some Ideas about the Involvement of the Poor," September 1965, box 11, folder 26, JWJCCR.

56. MEND Board of Directors, "Application to Community Action Program," box 13, folder 14, JWJCCR.

57. New York City Planning Commission, *Plan for New York City*, 1969, vol. 4; MEND

Board of Directors, "Application to Community Action Program," box 13, folder 14, JWJCCR.

58. Interview with Robert de León. The ten subcommunities in MEND included Triangle, Park, Mount Morris Park East, Triboro, El Barrio, El Barrio East, the Jefferson Park area, Hellgate, Carver and East, Lexington, and Metro North. See box 13, folder 13, JWJCCR.

59. Elise Bailen, "The Spanish-Speaking Drama Group," Advisory Committee Report, Theatre Arts Center, January 27, 1966, box 9, folder 15, JWJCCR.

60. "Appeal for Theatre Arts Center," undated, box 9, folder 15, JWJCCR.

61. Bailen, "The Spanish-Speaking Drama Group."

62. Ted Velez and Ramón Velez (whom I will refer to later) are not related.

63. Untitled document on Puerto Rican Community Leadership, box 24, folder 1, APP.

64. *Amsterdam News*, May 2, 1964; Schwartz, "Tenant Power in the Liberal City," 177.

65. Ted Velez, "Report of Operation and Proposals, East Harlem Tenants' Council," January–June 1964, box 30, folder 2, USAR.

66. Evelina Antonetty, "History of the United Bronx Parents," box 2, folder 14, UBPR; interview with Lorraine Montenegro.

67. Evelina Antonetty, "Preparation for School Decentralization: A Proposal to Organize and Train Parent and Community Leadership for Effective School Decentralization in the South Bronx," June 10, 1968, box 9, ELP; interview with Lorraine Montenegro.

68. Evelina Antonetty, "Preparation for School Decentralization: A Proposal to Organize and Train Parent and Community Leadership for Effective School Decentralization in the South Bronx," June 10, 1968, box 9, ELP; interview with Lorraine Montenegro.

69. Evelina Antonetty, "Educational Needs of the Puerto Rican Child in New York City with Special Emphasis on District 7," March 25, 1971, box 4, folder 4, UBPR.

70. New York City Planning Commission, *Plan for New York City*, 1969.

71. Jones, *South Bronx Rising*, 165.

72. Steiner, *The Islands*, 369; NYT, November 4, 1965.

73. New York City Planning Commission, *Plan for New York City*, 1969, vol. 2.

74. Velasquez, *The Ramón S. Vélez Story*, 11; interview with Humberto Cintrón; Jones, *South Bronx Rising*, 166.

75. U.S. Senate, *Hearings before the Subcommittee on Employment, Manpower, and Poverty*, box 36, Legislative Subject Files, RFKP; Cannato, *Ungovernable City*, 109; Jones, *South Bronx Rising*, 128.

76. Interview with Cyril Tyson.

77. Ibid.; interview with Cyril Tyson by Mark Naison.

78. Interview with Cyril Tyson.

79. "Progress Report to Hunts Point Panel," October 10, 1968, box 52, folder 949, microfilm 26, Subject Files, JLMP.

80. Jones, *South Bronx Rising*, 167, 183; NYT, January 9, 1968.

81. Austin, *Up against the Wall*, 13.

82. Letter from Mildred Zucker to Mr. Carl McCall, Chairman of the New York City Council Antipoverty Council, November 4, 1966, box 13, folder 32, JWJCCR; NYT, March 6, 1966.

83. Interview with Robert de León.

84. *Daily News*, February 29, 1968, box 2, folder 14, APP.

85. Letter from William Kirk to Clyde Murray, Social Welfare Consultant from Welfare Council of Metropolitan Chicago, June 22, 1966, box 30, folder 2, USAR.

86. Minutes of meeting of Board of Directors of JWJCC, October 26, 1967, box 5, folder 3, JWJCCR.

87. Statements of Major Owens and Dr. Arthur Logan, U.S. Senate, *Hearings before the Subcommittee on Employment, Manpower, and Poverty*, 1761–69.

88. Statement by Mayor John Lindsay, U.S. Senate, *Hearings before the Subcommittee on Employment, Manpower, and Poverty*, 1832; Frank Riessman, "The New Careers Concept," *American Child* (Winter 1967), box 52, RFKP; Pearl and Riessman, *New Careers for the Poor*, 14.

89. Statement of Alice Kornegay, U.S. Senate, *Hearings before the Subcommittee on Employment, Manpower, and Poverty*, 1807.

90. Memo from Gloria Edwards to Kenneth Clark on Committee on Antipoverty Action, May 20, 1965, box 133, folder 2, KCP; Pritchett, *Brownsville, Brooklyn*, 198.

91. Statement of Delores Ratcliffe, U.S. Senate, *Hearings before the Subcommittee on Employment, Manpower, and Poverty*, 1921.

92. Statements of Samuel Ganz and Alfred L. Green, ibid., 1821–27.

CHAPTER FIVE

1. Interview with Lorraine Montenegro; Hale, *Hale House*.

2. Riessman, *The Culturally Deprived Child*, 53.

3. Report to the Department of Health, Education, and Welfare by the New York City Board of Education, November 6, 1970, box 25, folder 2, SLF.

4. Phone interview with Babette Edwards; interview with Hannah Brockington.

5. Silver and Silver, *An Educational War on Poverty*, 125.

6. Riessman, *The Culturally Deprived Child*, 3–6.

7. Jeffrey, *Education for Children of the Poor*, 11; Fantini, Gittell, and Magat, *Community Control*, 33.

8. Clark, *Dark Ghetto*, 130.

9. *Amsterdam News*, May 13, 1967.

10. NYT, March 30, 1965; Harlem Parents Committee, "Memorial to the United States Commissioner of Education," October 19, 1965, box 48, folder 9, KCP; "Ethnic Distribution of New York City Public School Employees, 1968–69," box 17, folder 26, IRF.

11. Statement of Frank Cordasco; and statement of Nathan Brown; both in U.S. Senate, *Hearings before the Subcommittee on Bilingual Education*, 544, 531.

12. Goldberg and Griffey, *Black Power at Work*; Countryman, *Up South*; Cecelski, *Along Freedom Road*; Altshuler, *Community Control*; Levin and Pfautz, *Community Control of Schools*.

13. Preston Wilcox in Gittell, *Local Control in Education*, 4; Fantini, Gittell, and Magat, *Community Control*, 22.

14. Daryl Michael Scott, "How Black Nationalism Became Sui Generis," 6.

15. O'Connor, *Poverty Knowledge*.

16. Hoffnung-Garskof, *A Tale of Two Cities*.

17. Gloria Anzaldúa articulated a similar type of cultural pluralism, in *Borderlands*, 102–7.

18. Podair, *The Strike That Changed New York*, 5–7; Perlstein, *Justice, Justice*, 8.

19. Gittell, *Local Control in Education*, 136; Cannato, *Ungovernable City*, 298. Gittell portrays Puerto Ricans and blacks as essentially the same. She argues that the I.S. 201 struggle, which consisted primarily of black and Puerto Rican parents, was "racially homogeneous," whereas Two Bridges, which included blacks, Puerto Ricans, and Chinese parents, was "racially heterogeneous." In contrast, Cannato views blacks and Puerto Ricans as completely separate. He argues that the I.S. 201 leaders' black nationalism left "Puerto Ricans out in the cold."

20. Iris Morales, "¡Palante, Siempre Palante! The Young Lords," 220–21.

21. Fantini, "Community Participation," 326.

22. Cannato, *Ungovernable City*, 270; Fantini, Gittell, and Magat, *Community Control*, 7.

23. Perlstein, *Justice, Justice*, 8.

24. Wilson, "Lessons of the 201 Complex in Harlem."

25. Interview with Charles Wilson; interview with Babette Edwards.

26. A teacher as quoted in Perlstein, *Justice, Justice*, 27, 53–54.

27. Statement of Councilman Robert A. Low, U.S. Senate, *Hearings before the Subcommittee on Bilingual Education*, 532.

28. Clark, *Pathos of Power*, 9.

29. Ports, "Racism, Rejection, and Retardation," 76; "Sequence of Events Surrounding Community Involvement with Public School 201," box 9, EILP.

30. Interview with Suki Ports; Gertrude S. Goldberg, I.S. 201.

31. Isaiah Robinson as quoted in Cannato, *Ungovernable City*, 273.

32. Fantini, Gittell, and Magat, *Community Control*, 4.

33. Ports, "Racism, Rejection, and Retardation," 79.

34. Preston Wilcox, "The Controversy over I.S. 201," *Urban Review* (July 1966): 13, box 24, folder 1, PWP.

35. Interview with William Hall.

36. NYT, September 22, 1966; ibid., September 24, 1966; Gertrude S. Goldberg, I.S. 201; Fantini, Gittell, and Magat, *Community Control*, 9.

37. Interview with Suki Ports.

38. Minutes of meeting, People's Board of Education, 1967, box 9, EILP.

39. NYT, November 11, 1967; Gittell, *Local Control in Education*, 6. "P.S." stands for public school; "C.S." stands for community school; and "I.S." stands for intermediate school.

40. Cannato, *Ungovernable City*, 298.

41. Podair, *The Strike That Changed New York*, 77–79.

42. Fantini, Gittell, and Magat, *Community Control*, 143.

43. Cannato, *Ungovernable City*, 276–93.

44. Perlstein, *Justice, Justice*, 31; Podair, *The Strike That Changed New York*, 143.

45. Gittell, "Education: The Decentralization–Community Control Controversy," 140; Katz, "End Racism in Education," 348.

46. Gittell, *Demonstration for Social Change*, 12.

47. NYT, December 19, 1968.

48. Gittell, *Local Control in Education*, 15; interview with Hannah Brockington.

49. Interview with Charles Wilson; "Call Them Heroes" (New York: Silver Burdett, 1965), in Charles Wilson's Personal Papers, New York, N.Y.

50. C. E. Wilson, "Portrait of a Sick Society," *Liberator*, December 1963; C. E. Wilson, "What Ever Happened to the Negro's Friend?" *Liberator*, May 1964, in Charles Wilson's Personal Papers, New York, N.Y.; Smethurst, *The Black Arts Movement*, 127.

51. Gittell, *Local Control in Education*, 77–82.

52. Interview with Charles Wilson.

53. Perlstein, *Justice, Justice*, 48–54.

54. Gittell, *Local Control in Education*, 90–95.

55. Eugenia Kemble, "New York Experiments in School Decentralization," *United Teacher*, January 24, 1968, box 50, folder "Education," Research Division, Subject File, 1968 Presidential Campaign Papers, RFKP.

56. Preston Wilcox, "Proposal for an I.S. 201 Complex Community Education Center, February 28, 1968," box 24, folder 1, PWP.

57. "The Lopez Family of IS 201: The Guidance Teams Endeavors of the Past 3 Years at the IS 201 Educational Complex," Presentation to the New York State Commission on Education, February 19, 1971, box 25, folder 19, IRF.

58. Interview with Hannah Brockington.

59. Interview with Charles Wilson.

60. Interview with Hernan LaFontaine; interview with Babette Edwards.

61. Interview with Hernan LaFontaine.

62. Interview with Hannah Brockington.

63. Interview with Babette Edwards.

64. Preston Wilcox as quoted in Sexton, *Spanish Harlem*, 10.

65. Interview with Hannah Brockington; interview with Babette Edwards.

66. Podair, *The Strike That Changed New York*, 71–102. "J.H.S." stands for junior high school.

67. "Schools," *El Diario*, September 14, 1966; "Third Strike," *El Diario*, October 15, 1968.

68. "Suspenden Poda Presupuesto de Programa Boricua," *El Diario*, September 5, 1968; "Boricuas Atacan Maestros Por Huelga en Escuelas," ibid., October 18, 1968.

69. Evelina Antonetty, "History of the United Bronx Parents," box 2, folder 14, UBPR.

70. Interview with Julio Morales; NYT, August 30, 1969.

71. Letter from Darie Castro to Julio Morales, August 15, 1969; and letter from Marie Lane to Julio Morales, August 16, 1969; both in Julio Morales's Personal Papers.

72. Blanton, *Strange Career of Bilingual Education*, 151; Hacsi, *Children as Pawns*, 67.

73. Arsenian, *Bilingualism and Mental Development*, 12; Macnamara, *Bilingualism and Primary Education*, 17–30; Meyer, "Leonard Covello," 55–59.

74. Wakefield, *Island in the City*, 159–69.

75. Alma Bagu as quoted in Steiner, *The Islands*, 381.

76. Baez, "From Transformative School Goals," 76; Del Valle, *Language Rights*, 226.

77. Statement of Joseph Monserrat; and statement of Herman Badillo; both in U.S. Senate, *Hearings before the Subcommittee on Bilingual Education*, 74, 521.

78. Statement of Frank Negron; statement of Hernan LaFontaine; and statement of Louis Cardona; all in ibid., 563, 570, 582.

79. "Ethnic Distribution of New York City Public School Employees, 1968–69," box 17, folder 26, IRF.

80. Statement of Honorable Jacob H. Gilbert; statement of Honorable William F. Ryan; statement of Senator Ralph Yarborough; and statement of Carmen Dinos; all in U.S. Senate, *Hearings before the Subcommittee on Bilingual Education*, 505, 508, 515, 576.

81. Seda, "Bilingual Education in a Pluralistic Context," 21.

82. Baez, "From Transformative School Goals," 134.

83. Gittell, *Demonstration for Social Change*, 12; Rubinstein, "Visiting Ocean Hill–Brownsville," 240.

84. Rubinstein, "Visiting Ocean Hill–Brownsville," 242.

85. Interview with Luis Fuentes.

86. Jennings and Chapman, "Puerto Ricans and the Community Control Movement," 285; Rubinstein, "Visiting Ocean Hill–Brownsville," 240.

87. Gallardo, *Proceedings of the Conference on Education*, 65.

88. Baez, "From Transformative School Goals," 76; Del Valle, *Language Rights*, 226.

89. Letter from Bernard Friedman, District 7 Superintendent, to Bernard Donovan, Superintendent of Schools, November 27, 1967, box 5, folder 9, NBF; interview with Hernan LaFontaine.

90. "Supporting Statistics: Profile of the South Bronx and Its Schools," Appendix #1, box 4, folder 4, UBPR; interview with Hernan LaFontaine.

91. "An Interview with Hernan LaFontaine," *The Rican: Journal of Contemporary Puerto Rican Thought* 1, no. 4 (1974): 39.

92. Letter from Bernard Friedman to Miss Theresa Rakow, Elementary Division, 110 Livingston Street, February 5, 1969, box 5, folder 9, NBF.

93. Press release, "Community School Board 9 Elects Mr. Andrew George Donaldson," c. 1971, box 13, folder 21, IRF; NYT, February 1, 1971.

94. "Committee Set Up to Plan Bi-lingual District in Bronx," CNS, January 22, 1970.

95. Ibid.

96. Epstein, "The Politics of School Decentralization," 298.

97. Letter from David Spencer and Merle Stewart to Ben C. Quesada, Director, Education Facilities Planning Section, March 18, 1970, box 24, folder 12, IRF.

98. Letter from Carmen Martinez to Chancellor Harvey Scribner, December 23, 1970, box 13, folder 19, IRF; "Ethnic Distribution of New York City Public School Employees, 1968–69," box 17, folder 26, IRF.

99. *Amsterdam News*, July 4, 1970; ibid., August 7, 1971; Podair, *The Strike That Changed New York*, 151.

100. Gittell, *Local Control in Education*, 13; United Bronx Parents, undated and untitled, box 2, folder 14, UBPR.

101. Lawson and Payne, *Debating the Civil Rights Movement*, 160; Payne, *I've Got the Light of Freedom*, 90.

102. Pulido, *Black, Brown, Yellow, and Left*, 180–204.

103. Heather Lewis, "Protest, Place, and Pedagogy," 222–24.

104. Fantini, Gittell, and Magat, *Community Control*, 158–63.

105. Gittell, "Community Control of Education," 368.

106. "To the City of New York from Puerto Rican Parents of P.S. 155," December 1969, box 20, folder 8, IRF.

107. "Position Paper for an East Harlem School District," 1969, box 21, folder 21, IRF.

108. Robert Nichol, "Statement at Public Hearing for Manhattan Community School District Plan," April 8, 1970, box 21, folder 17, IRF.

109. Letter from Humberto Cintrón (Community Committee of Concerned Citizens of East Harlem) to Joseph Monserrat, October 8, 1969, box 21, folder 24, IRF; Jeffrey, *Education for Children of the Poor*, 132.

110. *Amsterdam News*, December 13, 1969; letter from Parents of Two Bridges to Honorable Joseph Monserrat and Other Members of the Board of Education, undated, box 22, folder 36, IRF; Fantini, Gittell, and Magat, *Community Control*, 147.

111. NYT, November 11, 1967; Gittell, *Local Control in Education*, 6, 14.

112. "IS 201 District to Be Dissolved," *News*, June 28, 1971, box 25, folder 18, IRF.

113. Heather Lewis, "Protest, Place, and Pedagogy," 243, 428.

114. Melendez, *We Took the Streets*, 73–75; Goldstein, *Poverty in Common*, 206–8.

115. Iris Morales, "¡Palante, Siempre Palante! The Young Lords," 211.

116. Jiménez, "Puerto Ricans and Educational Civil Rights."

117. Melendez, *We Took the Streets*, 97; Young Lords Party and Abramson, *Palante: Young Lords Party*, 75.

118. Interview with Stephen Levin; interview with Cleo Silvers; Melendez, *We Took the Streets*, 166–77.

119. "Lincoln Hospital Board Gives Terenzio Ultimatum," CNS, January 15, 1970; "South Bronx Community Backs Advisory Board in Lincoln Hospital Dispute with Terenzio," CNS, January 28, 1970.

120. Interview with Gloria Quiñones; NYT, April 7, 1973; ibid., December 1, 1973; ibid., June 13, 1974.

121. Iris Morales, *¡Palante, Siempre Palante! The Young Lords*.

122. Ibid.

123. PRSU, "A Proposal for a Policy and Perspective," box 10, folder 9, USAR; Melendez, *We Took the Streets*, 71.

124. Interview with Gabriel Torres-Rivera.

125. Interview with Cleo Silvers; Iris Morales, "¡Palante, Siempre Palante! The Young Lords," 215.

126. PRSU, "A Proposal for a Policy and Perspective," box 10, folder 9, p. 8, USAR; Zipp, *Manhattan Projects*, 173–74.

127. Fernandez, "Between Social Service Reform and Revolutionary Politics," 259–61.

128. Serrano, "Rifle, Cañón, y Escopeta," 126–27; Gutmann et al., *Perspectives on Las Américas*, 9.

129. Velázquez, "Another West Side Story"; Velázquez, "Coming Full Circle."

130. Lorrin Thomas, *Puerto Rican Citizen*, 226.

CHAPTER SIX

1. Interview with Charles Wilson; interview with William Hall.

2. NYT, May 8, 1972; letter from Charles Wilson to Kenneth Clark, May 17, 1972, box 370, folder 3, KCP.

3. Interview with Pedro Pedraza; Del Valle, "Bilingual Education."

4. Alexander, *The New Jim Crow*, 41; Thompson, "Why Mass Incarceration Matters"; Murch, *Living for the City*.

5. Podair, *The Strike That Changed New York*; Perlstein, *Justice, Justice*.

6. Sugrue and Skrentny, "The White Ethnic Strategy," 187; Mollenkopf, *A Phoenix in the Ashes*, 117, 191.

7. Freeman, *Working-Class New York*, 256–73; Katznelson, *City Trenches*, 96; Mollenkopf and Castells, *Dual City*, 14.

8. New York City Commission on Human Rights, *Employment of Minorities*, 16; Cannato, *Ungovernable City*, 539–44.

9. Memo from George A. Dalley to Dr. Kenneth Clark, December 7, 1967, box 453, folder 8, KCP.

10. Memo from Elaine Dowe, Assistant Commissioner of Community Development Agency, January 22, 1969, box 24, folder 339, Departmental Correspondence, microfilm 72, JLMP.

11. Petition from MEND Board of Directors to the Council against Poverty, May 13, 1969, box 27, folder 479, microfilm 14, Subject Files, JLMP; NYT, April 7, 1973; ibid., December 1, 1973; ibid., June 13, 1974; *New York Daily News*, March 8, 1995.

12. *Amsterdam News*, January 27, 1968; ibid., February 17, 1968; Jones, *South Bronx Rising*, 174.

13. "Distribution of Council against Poverty Anticipated Funds by Poverty Area for 1967–68," box 11, folder 8, JWJCCR; Julio Morales, *Puerto Rican Poverty and Migration*, 48.

14. Omolade and Falcón, "Black/Latino Politics, Black/Latino Communities"; Jones, *South Bronx Rising*, 168–71.

15. Interview with Cyril Tyson; interview with Leroi Archible by Mark Naison.

16. *Amsterdam News*, December 27, 1969; "Lindsay Admite es Grave Problema Guerra Pobreza," *El Diario*, December 7, 1969.

17. *Amsterdam News*, February 19, 1972.

18. Ibid., December 27, 1969.

19. Ibid., March 14, 1970; ibid., November 27, 1971.

20. Gordon, *Mapping Decline*, 81; Haygood, *King of the Cats*, 323.

21. Press release from the Office of the Mayor, April 7, 1969; and "Mayor Announces Record HUD Grants for Harlem–East Harlem Centers," August 4, 1969; both in box 54, folder 977, Subject Files, Roll 27, JLMP; *Amsterdam News*, July 12, 1969; ibid., August 30, 1969.

22. Gittell, *School Boards*, 76; Podair, *The Strike That Changed New York*, 146.

23. Letters to the Editor, *New York Post*, January 29, 1970, box 21, folder 27, IRF.

24. Memo from Isaiah Robinson to Dr. Harvey Scribner, December 18, 1970, box 12, folder 14, IRF; press release from Evelina Antonetty and Ramon Velez, February 1, 1970, box 21, folder 29, IRF; Katznelson, *City Trenches*, 168.

25. Gittell, *School Boards*, 19, 92, 128; *Amsterdam News*, January 31, 1970.

26. *Amsterdam News*, June 13, 1970.

27. Interview with Hannah Brockington; press release, March 25, 1971, box 25, folder 18, IRF.

28. Babette Edwards, "The Black Professional—Judas in the Living Room?" *Foresight: New Models for Schools* 1, nos. 5, 6 (December 1969), box 24, folder 1, PWP.

29. Evelina Antonetty, "Nosotros los padres," April 1975, box 2, folder 5, UBPR.

30. Letter from I.S. 201 Teachers to Ronald Evans, March 1971, box 25, folder 18, IRF.

31. Letter from Merle Stewart to Chairman of Governing Board, Superintendent of District 5 Mr. Olvin McBarnette, and Chancellor Harvey B. Scribner, April 21, 1971, box 25, folder 18, IRF; letter from Merle Stewart and David Spencer to Chancellor Harvey B. Scribner, November 10, 1970, box 24, folder 16, IRF; letter from David Spencer to Isaiah Robinson, August 17, 1970, box 24, folder 15, IRF.

32. Press release from David Spencer, April 30, 1969, box 24, folder 6, IRF; *Amsterdam News*, April 19, 1969.

33. Press release from David Spencer, April 30, 1969, box 24, folder 6, IRF; AFRAM Newsletter, June 20–24, 1980, box 24, folder 10, PWP.

34. Letter from Hannah Brockington and Babette Edwards, February 5, 1971, box 25, folder 18, IRF.

35. Anonymous, "The Difference in Black," *Forum*, January 1971, box 24, folder 12, UFTR.

36. Edwards, "Trouble in I.S. 201"; NYT, March 23, 1971; *News*, June 28, 1971, box 25, folder 18, IRF.

37. Letter from Merle Stewart to I.S. 201 parents, April 23, 1971, box 25, folder 18, IRF.

38. Press release, United Bronx Parents, May 5, 1970, box 18, folder 38, IRF; Pearl and Riessman, *New Careers for the Poor*, 243.

39. Memorandum of agreement between the Board of Education . . . and United Federation of Teachers, August 1971, box 172, folder 49, UFTR; Sister Gwen Cottman, "Message from a Parent Who Works in a School," *Forum*, February 1971, box 24, folder 12, UFTR.

40. Gittell, *School Boards*, 13, 120.

41. Public statement released by Councilman Carter Burden, April 10, 1973; and letter from President of PTA, PS 107, Rushie Davis, to Community School Board #4, May 1972; both in box 38, folder 20, UFTR; Gittell, *School Boards*, 15; Podair, *The Strike That Changed New York*, 147–50.

42. Fliegel and MacGuire, *Miracle in East Harlem*, 3.

43. Heather Lewis, "Protest, Place, and Pedagogy," 438.

44. Pedraza, "Puerto Ricans and the Politics of School Reform," 81.

45. NYT, July 30, 1972; ibid., November 3, 1974.

46. Flyer from United Federation of Teachers, undated, box 26, folder 23, UFTR; NYT, June 18, 1971.

47. Letter from Gerry Becker to Sandra Feldman, April 2, 1975, box 26, folder 25, UFTR.

48. "Reunión de Padres y Maestros," El Diario, April 28, 1972; "A Threat to Bi-lingual Education," El Diario, May 18, 1972.

49. Letter from Iona Edwards, member of CSB 7, box 13, folder 19, IRF.

50. Interview with Charles Wilson.

51. Del Valle, *Language Rights*, 228; Congressman Fitts Ryan, "Bilingual Education," El Diario, September 16, 1969.

52. Baez, "From Transformative School Goals," 169.

53. Guide to the Records of the Puerto Rican Legal Defense and Education Fund, PRLDEFR.

54. *Aspira of New York v. The Board of Education of the City of New York*, 58 F.R.D. 62 (S.D.N.Y. 1973).

55. Del Valle, "Bilingual Education," 199–203.

56. *Aspira of New York v. The Board of Education of the City of New York*, 394 F. Supp. 1161 (1975).

57. Interview with Pedro Pedraza.

58. Baez, "From Transformative School Goals," 172; Del Valle, "Bilingual Education," 203.

59. Santiago, "*Aspira v. Board of Education* Revisited," 154–55, 163–71.

60. "*Hemos Trabajado Bien*: A Report on the First National Conference of Puerto Ricans, Mexican-Americans, and Educators on the Special Educational Needs of Urban Puerto Rican Youth," May 14–15, 1968, New York City, box 7, folder 8, APP; Sonia Nieto, "Puerto Rican Students in U.S. Schools: A Brief History," in Nieto, *Puerto Rican Students in U.S. Schools*, 20.

61. "*Hemos Trabajado Bien*: A Report on the First National Conference of Puerto Ricans, Mexican-Americans, and Educators on the Special Educational Needs of Urban Puerto Rican Youth," May 14–15, 1968, New York City, box 7, folder 8, APP.

62. United Bronx Parents, undated and untitled, box 2, folder 14, UBPR.

63. Falcón, "Puerto Rican Political Participation," 6; Cruz, "Changing Socioeconomic and Political Fortunes," 49.

64. Andrés Torres, *Between Melting Pot and Mosaic*, 65.

65. *Katzenbach v. Morgan*, 384 U.S. 641 (1966); *Rosa Torres v. Alice Sachs*, 381 F. Supp. 309 (S.D.N.Y.) (1974).

66. The 21st Congressional District later became the 16th Congressional District. After Badillo, Robert García occupied the seat from 1978 to 1990; José Serrano occupied the seat from 1990 to the present.

67. Cruz, "Changing Socioeconomic and Political Fortunes," 68.

68. Santiago-Valles and Jiménez-Muñoz, "Social Polarization," 96, 106.

69. Jennings, *Puerto Rican Politics*, 145.

70. Jones, *South Bronx Rising*, 158.

71. Ibid., 164; interview with Herman Badillo by John Metzger.

72. Green and Wilson, *The Struggle for Black Empowerment*, 87.

73. Jones, *South Bronx Rising*, 229, 258–61.

74. McNickle, *To Be Mayor of New York*, 276; Green and Wilson, *The Struggle for Black Empowerment*, 27; interview with Herman Badillo by John Metzger, 7; Sugrue, *Sweet Land of Liberty*, 523.

75. Freeman, *Working-Class New York*, 256–58.

76. Mollenkopf, *A Phoenix in the Ashes*, 134–42.

77. Ibid., 110–26, 4–5, 142.

78. Kasinitz, *Caribbean New York*, 10, 51, 222–32; Mollenkopf, *A Phoenix in the Ashes*, 89.

79. Koch as quoted in Green and Wilson, *The Struggle for Black Empowerment*, 94.

80. Mollenkopf, *A Phoenix in the Ashes*, 117, 159–60.

81. Barbara Omolade and Angelo Falcón, "Black/Latino Politics, Black/Latino Communities," *Puerto Rico Libre*, Special Collections, Brooklyn College.

82. McNickle, *To Be Mayor of New York*, 149–54; Walter, *The Harlem Fox*, 5, 128–31.

83. Interview with Cyril Tyson.

84. Interview with Dennis Coleman by Mark Naison.

85. Kasinitz, *Caribbean New York*, 236.

86. Glazer and Moynihan, *Beyond the Melting Pot*, xiv–xviii.

87. Ibid., xxv, lii–lxix.

88. Neidle, *Great Immigrants*, 272.

89. Betanzos, "Puerto Rican Professional in America," 147–48.

90. U.S. Senate, *Hearings before the Subcommittee on Bilingual Education*, 544, 551.

91. NYT, September 1, 1989.

92. García as quoted in Kidder, "Early Reaction to 'Urban Enterprise Zone' Bill"; Falcón, "Commentary: From Civil Rights to the 'Decade of the Hispanic,'" 96.

93. Dávila, *Barrio Dreams*, 1–9; Sugrue, *Sweet Land of Liberty*, 503.

94. Marable, *Race, Reform, and Rebellion*, 177; Lang, *Grassroots at the Gateway*, 233.

95. Galvin and Gonzalez, "Reaching Out."

96. "Statement of Purpose of the Coalition of Black Trade Unionists," reel 3, RPP.

97. Pantoja, *Memoir of a Visionary*, 147–53.

98. Meyer, "Save Hostos," 73–87; Jiménez, "Hostos Community College," 101–3.

99. De Jesús, "Here It's More Like Your House," 132–34.

100. "Political Statement of the Puerto Rican Solidarity Committee"; and Minutes of the National Board meeting of the Puerto Rican Solidarity Committee, October 4, 1975; both in box 12, folder 18, EBP; Ransby, *Ella Baker*, 354.

101. Early, "An African American–Puerto Rican Connection," 317.

102. McCaffrey, "Forging Solidarity," 329–39.

103. Wilkinson, "In the Tradition of Revolution," 3.

104. Rivera, *New York Ricans*, introduction.

EPILOGUE

1. U.S. Census Bureau, *The Hispanic Population: 2010*; U.S. Census Bureau, *The Black Population: 2010*.

2. Márquez, "The Browning of Black Politics," 51.

3. Haney-López, *White by Law*, 146; Graham, *Collision Course*, 2, 9.

4. Yancey, *Who Is White*, 10–14; Orlando Patterson, "Race and Diversity in the Age of Obama."

5. Perea, "The Black/White Binary," 350.

6. Rumbaut, "Pigments of Our Imagination," 26; U.S. Census Bureau, *Race and Hispanic Origin of the Foreign-Born Population in the United States, 2007*.

7. Interview with James Haughton, Noel Sanchez, Jorge Padilla, and Ernesto Lago.

8. Fletcher, *Solidarity Divided*.

9. Waldinger, *Still the Promised City*, 229, 240.

10. Center for Latin American, Caribbean, and Latino Studies, "The Latino Population of New York City."

11. Ibid.

12. Reyes, "The Aspira Consent Decree"; Ed Morales, "Demographic Changes Shape Latino Aspirations."

13. Thompson, "Why Mass Incarceration Matters," 703; Alexander, *The New Jim Crow*; Gilmore, *Golden Gulag*.

14. Interview with Lorraine Montenegro.

15. Cartagena, "Time to Walk the Walk," 80–83.

16. Rúa, *A Grounded Identidad*, 96–97.

17. Smith, "Chicago's Luis Gutierrez."

18. Sawyer, "Racial Politics in Multiethnic America," 536; Falcón, "The Puerto Rican Connection."

Bibliography

MANUSCRIPT SOURCES

Albany, New York
  New York State Archives
    State Division of Human Rights
Austin, Texas
  Lyndon B. Johnson Library
    Lyndon B. Johnson Presidential Papers
Boston, Massachusetts
  John F. Kennedy Library
    Robert F. Kennedy Papers
Cambridge, Massachusetts
  Government Documents and Microforms Collections, Harvard University
    Negro Labor Committee Records
    A. Philip Randolph Papers
    Bayard Rustin Papers
Flushing, New York
  Local 3 International Brotherhood of Electrical Workers Archives
Ithaca, New York
  Kheel Center for Labor-Management Documentation and Archives,
      Cornell University
    International Ladies Garment Workers' Union Records
    National Hospital and Health Care Employees Records
New York, New York
  Center for Puerto Rican Studies, Hunter College
    Ellen Lurie Papers
    Antonia Pantoja Papers
    Puerto Rican Legal Defense and Education Fund Records
    United Bronx Parents Records
  LaGuardia and Wagner Archives, LaGuardia Community College
    New York City Housing Authority Collection

Municipal Archives
  Nathan Brown Files
  Seymour Lachman Files
  John V. Lindsay Mayoral Papers
  Isaiah Robinson Files
  Robert F. Wagner Mayoral Papers
Rare Book and Manuscript Library, Columbia University
  Union Settlement Association Records
Schomburg Center for Research in Black Culture
  Ella Baker Papers
  Olivia Frost Papers
  Harlem Neighborhoods Association Records
  James Weldon Johnson Community Center Records
  Edward Lewis Papers
  Richard Parrish Papers
  Preston Wilcox Papers
Special Collections, Brooklyn College
  Puerto Rico Libre
Tamiment Library, New York University
  Local 6 Hotel, Motel and Club Employees' Union Papers
  United Federation of Teachers Records
Union Theological Seminary Archives, Columbia University
  East Harlem Protestant Parish Records
Washington, D.C.
  Library of Congress
    Kenneth Clark Papers

ORAL HISTORY COLLECTIONS

Oral interview with Leroi Archible by Mark Naison, January 26, 2004, Bronx African-American History Project, Bronx Historical Society, New York, N.Y.

Oral interview with Herman Badillo by John Metzger, March 8, 1994, Koch Administration Oral History Project, Rare Book and Manuscript Library, Columbia University, New York, N.Y.

Oral interview with Dennis Coleman by Mark Naison, Natasha Lightfoot, and Harriet McFetters, February 23, 2006, Bronx African-American History Project, Bronx Historical Society, New York, N.Y.

Oral interview with Manny Diaz by Lillian Jiménez, February 16, 2006, Latino Educational Media Center, New York, N.Y.

Oral interview with Manny Diaz by Blanca Vazquez, January 29, 2003, Blanca Vazquez's Personal Papers, New York, N.Y.

Oral interview with Manny Diaz by Gene Sklar, May 19, 1994, box 3, folder 7, Union Settlement Association Records, Rare Book and Manuscript Library, Columbia University, New York, N.Y.

Oral interview with Agnes Louard by Gene Sklar, May 16, 1994, box 3, folder 7, Union Settlement Association Records, Rare Book and Manuscript Library, Columbia University, New York, N.Y.

Oral interview with Dolores Torres by Blackside, October 31, 1988, for *Eyes on the Prize II: America at the Racial Crossroads, 1965 to 1985*, Henry Hampton Collection, Film and Media Archive, Washington University Libraries, St. Louis, Mo.

Oral interview with Ida Torres by Ismael García-Colón, January 22, 2000, Oral History Collection, Center for Puerto Rican Studies, Hunter College, New York, N.Y.

Oral interview with Cyril DeGrasse Tyson by Mark Naison, June 28, 2004, Bronx African-American History Project, Bronx Historical Society, New York, N.Y.

Oral interview with Cyril Tyson by Dr. Noel Cazenave, May 18, 1992, War on Poverty Oral History Collection, Rare Book and Manuscript Library, Columbia University, New York, N.Y.

ORAL HISTORY COLLECTIONS BY AUTHOR

(Unless otherwise stated, all interviews have been conducted by the author.)

Interview with Kathy Andrade, New York, N.Y., May 7, 2004

Interview with Hannah Brockington, New York, N.Y., June 3, 2010

Interview with Juan Cartagena, New York, N.Y., August 15, 2005

Interview with Humberto Cintrón, New York, N.Y., June 17, 2010

Interview with Manny Diaz, New York, N.Y., July 21, 2005, July 28, 2005, and August 18, 2005

Interview with Manny Diaz, José Morales, and José Morales Jr., New York, N.Y., January 22, 2005

Phone interview with Babette Edwards, Cambridge, Mass., January 22, 2007, and September 5, 2012

Phone interview with Luis Fuentes, Cambridge, Mass., October 5, 2005

Interview with Eddie Gonzalez, New York, N.Y., May 10, 2004

Interview with William Hall, Philadelphia, Pa., May 22, 2010

Interview with James Haughton, Noel Sanchez, Jorge Padilla, and Ernesto Lago, New York, N.Y., June 8, 2010

Interview with Hernan LaFontaine, New York, N.Y., December 12, 2005

Interview with Robert de León, New York, N.Y., July 21, 2005

Interview with Stephen Levin, New York, N.Y., December 12, 2006

Interview with Felipe Luciano, New York, N.Y., August 22, 2005

Interview with Joseph Monserrat, New York, N.Y., May 7, 2004

Interview with Lorraine Montenegro, New York, N.Y., June 21, 2010

Interview with Julio Morales, Canton, Conn., December 16, 2004

Phone interview with Pedro Pedraza, Cambridge, Mass., January 22, 2007

Interview with Frank Perez, New York, N.Y., June 4, 2010

Interview with Suki Ports, New York, N.Y., October 17, 2005

Interview with Gloria and Carmen Quiñones, New York, N.Y., June 6, 2010

Interview with Florence Rice, New York, N.Y., June 14, 2005

Interview with Yolanda Sanchez, New York, N.Y., May 25, 2005

Interview with Cleo Silvers, New York, N.Y., August 25, 2005

Interview with Eugene Sklar, New York, N.Y., December 12, 2006

Interview with Frank Torres, New York, N.Y., October 25, 2004

Interview with Ida Torres, New York, N.Y., November 22, 2004

Interview with Gabriel Torres-Rivera, New York, N.Y., August 18, 2005
Interview with Cyril Tyson, New York, N.Y., June 15, 2005, and July 13, 2011
Interview with Charles Wilson, New York, N.Y., October 7, 2005, and May 28, 2010

PERIODICALS

Amsterdam News. Schomburg Center for Research in Black Culture, New York, N.Y.
Community News Service (CNS). Microfilm Collection, Schomburg Center for Research in Black Culture, New York, N.Y.
El Diario. Center of Puerto Rican Studies (Centro), Hunter College, New York, N.Y.
New York Times
The Rican. Widener Library, Harvard University, Cambridge, Mass.

ELECTRONIC SOURCES

Boyd, Herb. "Harlem Legend, Preston Wilcox Passes." *Assata Shakur Forums* (August 16, 2006), http://www.assatashakur.org/forum/afrikan-world-news/20889-harlem-legend-preston-wilcox-passes.html (December 16, 2010).
Smith, Robert L. "Chicago's Luis Gutierrez Preaches Lower Expectations for Immigration Reform." *Cleveland.com* (October 12, 2010), http://blog.cleveland.com/metro/2010/10/a_leader_of_immigration_reform.html (July 19, 2013).

PUBLISHED PRIMARY SOURCES

Clark, Kenneth Bancroft. *Dark Ghetto: Dilemmas of Social Power.* New York: Harper and Row, 1967.
———. *Pathos of Power.* New York: Harper and Row, 1974.
Dubinsky, David, and A. H. Raskin. *David Dubinsky: A Life with Labor.* New York: Simon and Schuster, 1977.
Early, James. "An African American–Puerto Rican Connection: An Auto-Bio-Memory Sketch of Political Development and Activism." In *The Puerto Rican Movement: Voices from the Diaspora,* edited by Andrés Torres and José E. Velázquez, 316–28. Philadelphia: Temple University Press, 1998.
Edwards, Babette. "Trouble in I.S. 201." *Integrated Education* 9, no. 4 (July–August 1971): 23–24.
Galvin, Miles, and Edward Gonzalez Jr. "Reaching Out: New York's Hispanic Leadership Training Project." Ithaca, N.Y.: New York State School of Industrial and Labor Relations, Cornell University, 1982.
Glazer, Nathan, and Daniel P. Moynihan. *Beyond the Melting Pot: The Negroes, Puerto Ricans, Jews, Italians, and Irish of New York City.* Cambridge, Mass.: MIT Press, 1970.
Heifetz, Henry. "Introduction." In *Individual and Group Services in the Mobilization for Youth Experience,* edited by Harold H. Weissman, 13–21. New York: Association Press, 1969.
Hill, Herbert. "Black Workers, Organized Labor, and Title VII of the 1964 Civil Rights Act: Legislative History and Litigation Record." In *Race in America: The Struggle for Equality,* edited by Herbert Hill and James E. Jones Jr., 263–344. Madison: University of Wisconsin Press, 1993.

———. "Guardians of the Sweatshops: The Trade Unions, Racism, and the Garment Industry." In *Puerto Rico and Puerto Ricans: Studies in History and Society*, edited by Adalberto Lopez and James Petras, 384–416. Cambridge, Mass.: Schenkman, 1974.

"An Interview with Hernan LaFontaine." *The Rican: Journal of Contemporary Puerto Rican Thought* 1, no. 4 (1974): 37–43.

Jenkins, Shirley. *Intergroup Empathy: An Exploratory Study of Negro and Puerto Rican Groups in New York City*. Ann Arbor, Mich.: University Microfilms, 1974.

Jones, Hettie. "Neighborhood Service Centers." In *Individual and Group Services in the Mobilization for Youth Experience*, edited by Harold H. Weissman, 33–53. New York: Association Press, 1969.

Katz, Maude White. "End Racism in Education: A Concerned Parent Speaks." *Freedomways* 8, no. 4 (1968): 347–54.

Kidder, Rushworth. "Early Reaction to 'Urban Enterprise Zone' Bill." *Christian Science Monitor*, February 11, 1981.

King, Martin Luther, Jr. *A Testament of Hope: The Essential Writings of Martin Luther King, Jr.* Edited by James Melvin Washington. San Francisco: HarperSanFrancisco, 1991.

Kronenfeld, Daniel. "A Case History of a Block Association." In *Community Development in the Mobilization for Youth Experience*, edited by Harold H. Weissman, 29–43. New York: Association Press, 1969.

Lewis, Oscar. *La Vida: A Puerto Rican Family in the Culture of Poverty—San Juan and New York*. New York: Random House, 1966.

Luther, Beverly. "Negro Youth and Social Action." In *Individual and Group Services in the Mobilization for Youth Experience*, edited by Harold H. Weissman, 151–61. New York: Association Press, 1969.

Martin, Ann W. "Cornell University's Puerto Rican Labor Leadership Project." Paper Submitted in History of American Adult Education. Ithaca, N.Y.: Cornell University, 1995.

McKay, Claude. *Harlem: Negro Metropolis*. New York: Harcourt Brace Jovanovich, 1940.

Melendez, Miguel. *We Took the Streets: Fighting for Latino Rights with the Young Lords*. New York: St. Martin's Press, 2003.

Mills, C. Wright, Clarence Ollson Senior, and Rose Kohn Goldsen. *The Puerto Rican Journey: New York's Newest Migrants*. New York: Harper, 1950.

Montagu, Ashley. "What Every Child and Adult Should Know about 'Race.'" *Education* 66, no. 5 (1946): 262–64.

Morales, Ed. "Demographic Changes Shape Latino Aspirations." *City Limits*, November 28, 2012.

Morales, Iris. "¡Palante, Siempre Palante! The Young Lords." In *The Puerto Rican Movement: Voices from the Diaspora*, edited by Andrés Torres and José E. Velázquez, 210–27. Philadelphia: Temple University Press, 1998.

———. *¡Palante, Siempre Palante! The Young Lords*. 1 videocassette (VHS). New York: Columbia University Station, 1996.

Morales, Julio. *Puerto Rican Poverty and Migration: We Just Had to Try Elsewhere*. New York: Praeger, 1986.

New York City Commission on Human Rights. *The Employment of Minorities, Women, and the Handicapped in City Government: A Report of a 1971 Survey.* New York: New York City Commission on Human Rights, 1973.

——. *The Ethnic Survey.* New York: New York City Commission on Human Rights, 1964.

New York City Planning Commission. *Plan for New York City, 1969: A Proposal.* Vols. 2, 4. Cambridge, Mass.: MIT Press, 1969.

Omolade, Barbara, and Angelo Falcón. "Black/Latino Politics, Black/Latino Communities." *Puerto Rico Libre* 7 (1985).

Pantoja, Antonia. *Memoir of a Visionary: Antonia Pantoja.* Houston: Arte Público Press, 2002.

Patterson, Orlando. "Race and Diversity in the Age of Obama." *New York Times,* August 14, 2009.

Pearl, Arthur, and Frank Riessman. *New Careers for the Poor: The Nonprofessional in Human Service.* New York: Free Press, 1965.

Pedraza, Pedro. "Puerto Ricans and the Politics of School Reform." *Centro: Journal of the Center for Puerto Rican Studies* 9, no. 1 (1997): 74–85.

Ports, Suki. "Racism, Rejection, and Retardation." In *Schools against Children: The Case for Community Control,* edited by Annette T. Rubinstein, 50–92. New York: Monthly Review Press, 1970.

Rice, Florence. "It Takes a While to Realize That It Is Discrimination." In *Black Women in White America: A Documentary History,* edited by Gerda Lerner, 275–87. New York: Pantheon, 1972.

Riessman, Frank. *The Culturally Deprived Child.* New York: Harper, 1962.

Rubinstein, Annette T. "Visiting Ocean Hill–Brownsville in November 1968 and May 1969." In *Schools against Children: The Case for Community Control,* edited by Annette T. Rubinstein, 228–46. New York: Monthly Review Press, 1970.

Seda, Eduardo. "Bilingual Education in a Pluralistic Context." *The Rican* 1, no. 4 (1971): 19–26.

Senior, Clarence Ollson. *Strangers—Then Neighbors: From Pilgrims to Puerto Ricans.* New York: Freedom Books, 1961.

Serrano, Basilio. "'¡Rifle, Cañón, y Escopeta!' A Chronicle of the Puerto Rican Student Union." In *The Puerto Rican Movement: Voices from the Diaspora,* edited by Andrés Torres and José E. Velázquez, 124–43. Philadelphia: Temple University Press, 1998.

Sexton, Patricia Cayo. *Spanish Harlem: An Anatomy of Poverty.* New York: Harper and Row, 1965.

Thomas, Piri. *Down These Mean Streets.* New York: Knopf, 1967.

U.S. Census Bureau. *The Black Population: 2010,* edited by U.S. Department of Commerce. Washington, D.C.: U.S. Census Bureau, 2011.

——. *The Hispanic Population: 2010,* edited by U.S. Department of Commerce. Washington, D.C.: U.S. Census Bureau, 2011.

——. *Race and Hispanic Origin of the Foreign-Born Population in the United States, 2007,* edited by U.S. Department of Commerce. Washington, D.C.: U.S. Census Bureau, 2010.

————. U.S. Censuses of Population and Housing, 1960, Census Tracts, New York, NY Standard Metropolitan Statistical Area. Washington, D.C.: U.S. Department of Commerce, Bureau of the Census, 1962.

U.S. Department of Labor, Office of Policy, Planning, Research, and Daniel P. Moynihan. The Negro Family: The Case for National Action. Washington, D.C.: U.S. Government Printing Office, 1965.

U.S. House of Representatives, Committee on Education and Labor. Hearings before the Ad Hoc Subcommittee on Investigation of the Garment Industry, 87th Congress, 2nd Session. Washington, D.C.: U.S. Government Printing Office, August 17–24, September 21, 1962.

U.S. Senate. Hearings before the Subcommittee on Bilingual Education of the Committee on Labor and Public Welfare, 90th Congress, 1st Session, on S.428. Washington, D.C.: U.S. Government Printing Office, May 18, 19, 26, 29, and 31, 1967.

————. Hearings before the Subcommittee on Employment, Manpower, and Poverty of the Committee on Labor and Public Welfare, 90th Congress, First Session, on Examining the War on Poverty, Part 6, NY. New York, May 8–9, 1967.

Wakefield, Dan. Island in the City: The World of Spanish Harlem. Boston: Houghton Mifflin, 1959.

Weissman, Harold H. "Overview of Employment Opportunities." In Employment and Educational Services in the Mobilization for Youth Experience, edited by Harold H. Weissman, 25–34. New York: Association Press, 1969.

Wilson, Charles. "Lessons of the 201 Complex in Harlem." Freedomways 8, no. 4 (1968): 399–406.

Wirth, Louis. "The Problem of Minority Groups." In The Science of Man in the World Crisis, edited by Ralph Linton, 347–72. New York: Columbia University Press, 1945.

Young Lords Party and Michael Abramson. Palante: Young Lords Party. New York: McGraw-Hill, 1971.

SECONDARY WORKS

Acosta-Belén, Edna. "Ideology and Images of Women in Contemporary Puerto Rican Literature." In The Puerto Rican Woman: Perspectives on Culture, History, and Society, edited by Edna Acosta-Belén, 120–46. New York: Praeger, 1986.

Alamo, Carlos. "Dispatches from a Colonial Outpost: Puerto Rico as Schema in the Black Popular Press, 1942–1951." Du Bois Review 9, no. 1 (2012): 201–25.

Alcoff, Linda Martín. "Is Latina/o Identity a Racial Identity?" In Hispanics/Latinos in the United States: Ethnicity, Race, and Rights, edited by Jorge J. E. Gracia and Pablo De Greiff, 23–44. New York: Routledge, 2000.

Alexander, Michelle. The New Jim Crow: Mass Incarceration in the Age of Colorblindness. New York: New Press, 2010.

Altshuler, Alan A. Community Control: The Black Demand for Participation in Large American Cities. New York: Pegasus, 1970.

Alvarez, Luis, and Daniel Widener. "A History of Black and Brown: Chicano/a—African American Cultural and Political Relations." Aztlán: A Journal of Chicano Studies 33, no. 1 (2008): 143–55.

Andrews, George Reid. *Afro-Latin America, 1800–2000.* New York: Oxford University Press, 2004.

Anzaldúa, Gloria. *Borderlands: The New Mestiza = La Frontera.* San Francisco: Aunt Lute Books, 2007.

Araiza, Lauren. "'In Common Struggle against a Common Oppression': The United Farm Workers and the Black Panther Party, 1968–73." *Journal of African American History* 94, no. 2 (2009): 200–223.

Arsenian, Seth. *Bilingualism and Mental Development: A Study of the Intelligence and the Social Background of Bilingual Children in New York City.* New York: Teachers College, Columbia University, 1937.

Austin, Curtis J. *Up against the Wall: Violence in the Making and Unmaking of the Black Panther Party.* Fayetteville: University of Arkansas Press, 2006.

Ayala, César J., and Rafael Bernabe. *Puerto Rico in the American Century: A History since 1898.* Chapel Hill: University of North Carolina Press, 2007.

Baez, Luis Antonio. "From Transformative School Goals to Assimilationist and Remedial Bilingual Education: A Critical Review of Key Precedent-Setting Hispanic Bilingual Litigation Decided by Federal Courts between 1974 and 1983." Ph.D. diss., University of Wisconsin–Milwaukee, 1995.

Barbaro, Fred. "Ethnic Resentment." In *Black/Brown/White Relations: Race Relations in the 1970s,* edited by Charles V. Willie, 77–94. New Brunswick, N.J.: Transaction Books, 1977.

Barrett, James R., and David Roediger. "Inbetween Peoples: Race, Nationality, and the 'New Immigrant' Working Class." *Journal of American Ethnic History* 16, no. 3 (1997): 3–44.

Bauman, Robert. *Race and the War on Poverty: From Watts to East L.A.* Norman: University of Oklahoma Press, 2008.

Baver, Sherrie. *The Political Economy of Colonialism: The State and Industrialization in Puerto Rico.* Westport, Conn.: Praeger, 1993.

———. "Puerto Rican Politics in New York City: The Post–World War II Period." In *Puerto Rican Politics in Urban America,* edited by James Jennings and Monte Rivera, 43–59. Westport, Conn.: Greenwood Press, 1984.

Behnken, Brian D. *Fighting Their Own Battles: Mexican Americans, African Americans, and the Struggle for Civil Rights in Texas.* Chapel Hill: University of North Carolina Press, 2011.

Bell, Daniel. *The Coming of Post-industrial Society: A Venture in Social Forecasting.* New York: Basic Books, 1976.

Bellush, Jewel. "Housing: The Scattered-Site Controversy." In *Race and Politics in New York City: Five Studies in Policy-Making,* edited by Jewel Bellush and Stephen M. David, 98–133. New York: Praeger, 1971.

Bellush, Jewell, and Murray Hausknecht. "Relocation and Managed Mobility." In *Urban Renewal: People, Politics, and Planning,* edited by Jewel Bellush and Murray Hausknecht, 366–77. Garden City, N.Y.: Anchor Books, 1967.

———. "Urban Renewal: An Historical Overview." In *Urban Renewal: People, Politics, and Planning,* edited by Jewell Bellush and Murray Hausknecht, 3–16. Garden City, N.Y.: Anchor Books, 1967.

Benjamin, Gerald. *Race Relations and the New York City Commission on Human Rights.* Ithaca, N.Y.: Cornell University Press, 1974.

Benjamin, Ludy T., Jr., and Ellen M. Crouse. "The American Psychological Association's Response to *Brown v. Board of Education*: The Case of Kenneth B. Clark." In *Racial Identity in Context: The Legacy of Kenneth B. Clark*, edited by Kenneth Bancroft Clark and Gina Philogène, 231–54. Washington, D.C.: American Psychological Association, 2004.

Bennett, Herman L. *Colonial Blackness: A History of Afro-Mexico.* Bloomington: Indiana University Press, 2009.

Berkman, Barbara, and Peter Maramaldi. "Health, Mental Health, and Disabilities." In *The Columbia University School of Social Work: A Centennial Celebration*, edited by Ronald A. Feldman and Sheila B. Kamerman, 246–64. New York: Columbia University Press, 2001.

Bernstein, Shana. *Bridges of Reform: Interracial Civil Rights Activism in Twentieth-Century Los Angeles.* New York: Oxford University Press, 2011.

Betanzos, Amalia. "The Puerto Rican Professional in America." In *Puerto Rican Perspectives*, edited by Edward Mapp, 147–49. Metuchen, N.J.: Scarecrow Press, 1974.

Biondi, Martha. *To Stand and Fight: The Struggle for Civil Rights in Postwar New York City.* Cambridge, Mass.: Harvard University Press, 2003.

Blanton, Carlos Kevin. *The Strange Career of Bilingual Education in Texas, 1836–1981.* College Station: Texas A&M University Press, 2004.

Blauner, Bob. *Still the Big News: Racial Oppression in America.* Philadelphia: Temple University Press, 2001.

Boris, Eileen. "Needlewomen under the New Deal in Puerto Rico, 1920–1945." In *Puerto Rican Women and Work: Bridges in Transnational Labor*, edited by Altagracia Ortiz, 33–54. Philadelphia: Temple University Press, 1996.

Briggs, Laura. *Reproducing Empire: Race, Sex, Science, and U.S. Imperialism in Puerto Rico.* Berkeley: University of California Press, 2002.

Brilliant, Mark. *The Color of America Has Changed: How Racial Diversity Shaped Civil Rights Reform in California, 1941–1978.* New York: Oxford University Press, 2010.

Brock, Lisa, and Digna Castañeda Fuertes, eds. *Between Race and Empire: African-Americans and Cubans before the Cuban Revolution.* Philadelphia: Temple University Press, 1998.

Brubaker, Rogers, and Frederick Cooper. "Beyond Identity." *Theory and Society* 29, no. 1 (2000): 1–47.

Cannato, Vincent. *The Ungovernable City: John Lindsay and His Struggle to Save New York.* New York: Basic Books, 2001.

Carlton-LaNey, Iris. *African American Leadership: An Empowerment Tradition in Social Welfare History.* Washington, D.C.: NASW Press, 2001.

Carroll, Tamar W. "Grassroots Feminism: Direct Action Organizing and Coalition Building in New York City, 1955–1995." Ph.D. diss., University of Michigan, 2007.

Cartagena, Juan. "Time to Walk the Walk: Vieques and Civil Disobedience in New York with Vicente 'Panama' Alba." *Centro: Journal of the Center for Puerto Rican Studies* 18, no. 1 (2006): 79–89.

Cazenave, Noel A. *Impossible Democracy: The Unlikely Success of the War on Poverty Community Action Programs*. Albany: State University of New York Press, 2007.

Cecelski, David S. *Along Freedom Road: Hyde County, North Carolina, and the Fate of Black Schools in the South*. Chapel Hill: University of North Carolina Press, 1994.

Center for Latin American, Caribbean, and Latino Studies. "The Latino Population of New York City, 1990–2010." In *Latino Data Project*, edited by Laird W. Bergad, 1–61. New York: City University of New York, 2011.

Centro de Estudios Puertorriqueños, History Task Force. *Labor Migration under Capitalism: The Puerto Rican Experience*. New York: Monthly Review Press, 1979.

Chavez, Linda. *Out of the Barrio: Toward a New Politics of Hispanic Assimilation*. New York: Basic Books, 1991.

Clayson, William. "The War on Poverty and the Chicano Movement in Texas: Confronting 'Tio Tomás' and the 'Gringo Pseudoliberals.'" In *The War on Poverty: A New Grassroots History, 1964–1980*, edited by Annelise Orleck and Lisa Gayle Hazirjian, 334–56. Athens: University of Georgia Press, 2011.

Cloward, Richard A., and Lloyd E. Ohlin. *Delinquency and Opportunity: A Theory of Delinquent Gangs*. Glencoe, Ill.: Free Press, 1960.

Cobas, José A., Jorge Duany, and Joe R. Feagin, eds. *How the United States Racializes Latinos: White Hegemony and Its Consequences*. Boulder, Colo.: Paradigm, 2009.

Cohen, Lizabeth. *A Consumers' Republic: The Politics of Mass Consumption in Postwar America*. New York: Knopf, 2003.

Collins, Robert M. "Growth Liberalism in the Sixties: Great Societies at Home and Grand Designs Abroad." In *The Sixties: From Memory to History*, edited by David Farber, 11–44. Chapel Hill: University of North Carolina Press, 1994.

Collins, William J. "Race, Roosevelt, and Wartime Production: Fair Employment in World War II Labor Markets." *American Economic Review* 91, no. 1 (2001): 272–86.

Colón, Jesus. *A Puerto Rican in New York, and Other Sketches*. New York: Arno Press, 1975.

Cornell, Stephen, and Douglas Hartmann. "Conceptual Confusions and Divides: Race, Ethnicity, and the Study of Immigration." In *Not Just Black and White: Historical and Contemporary Perspectives on Immigration, Race, and Ethnicity in the United States*, edited by Nancy Foner and George Fredrickson, 23–41. New York: Russell Sage Foundation, 2004.

Countryman, Matthew. *Up South: Civil Rights and Black Power in Philadelphia*. Politics and Culture in Modern America. Philadelphia: University of Pennsylvania Press, 2006.

Cruz, José E. "The Changing Socioeconomic and Political Fortunes of Puerto Ricans in New York City, 1960–1990." In *Boricuas in Gotham: Puerto Ricans in the Making of Modern New York City*, edited by Angelo Falcón, Gabriel Haslip-Viera, and Félix Matos Rodríguez, 37–82. Princeton, N.J.: Markus Wiener, 2005.

———. "Interminority Relations in Urban Settings: Lessons from the Black–Puerto Rican Experience." In *Black and Multiracial Politics in America*, edited by Yvette M. Alex-Assensoh and Lawrence J. Hanks, 84–112. New York: New York University Press, 2000.

Dávila, Arlene M. *Barrio Dreams: Puerto Ricans, Latinos, and the Neoliberal City*. Berkeley: University of California Press, 2004.

De Jesús, Anthony. "'Here It's More Like Your House': The Proliferation of Authentic Caring as School Reform at El Puente Academy for Peace and Justice." In *Critical Voices in School Reform: Students Living through Change*, edited by Beth C. Rubin and Elena M. Silva, 132–51. London: Routledge Falmer, 2003.

Del Valle, Sandra. "Bilingual Education for Puerto Ricans in New York City: From Hope to Compromise." *Harvard Educational Review* 28, no. 2 (1998): 193–218.

———. *Language Rights and the Law in the United States: Finding Our Voices*. Buffalo, N.Y.: Multilingual Matters, 2003.

Duany, Jorge. "Neither White nor Black: The Representation of Racial Identity among Puerto Ricans on the Island and in the U.S. Mainland." In *Neither Enemies nor Friends: Latinos, Blacks, Afro-Latinos*, edited by Anani Dzidzienyo and Suzanne Oboler, 173–88. New York: Palgrave Macmillan, 2005.

Dudziak, Mary. "Desegregation as a Cold War Imperative." *Stanford Law Review* 41, no. 1 (1988): 61–120.

Dzidzienyo, Anani, and Suzanne Oboler, eds. *Neither Enemies nor Friends: Latinos, Blacks, Afro-Latinos*. New York: Palgrave Macmillan, 2005.

Ehrenreich, John. *The Altruistic Imagination: A History of Social Work and Social Policy in the United States*. Ithaca, N.Y.: Cornell University Press, 1985.

Epstein, Jason. "The Politics of School Decentralization." In *The Politics of Urban Education*, edited by Marilyn Gittell and Alan G. Hevesi, 288–303. New York: Praeger, 1969.

Falcón, Angelo. "Commentary: From Civil Rights to the 'Decade of the Hispanic': Boricuas in Gotham, 1960–1990." In *Boricuas in Gotham: Puerto Ricans in the Making of Modern New York City: Essays in Memory of Antonia Pantoja*, edited by Gabriel Haslip-Viera, Angelo Falcón, and Félix V. Matos Rodríguez, 85–104. Princeton, N.J.: Markus Wiener, 2005.

———. "The Puerto Rican Connection to the Immigrant Rights Movement." *Comité Noviembre Journal*, November 12, 2010.

———. "Puerto Rican Political Participation: New York City and Puerto Rico." In *Time for Decision: The United States and Puerto Rico*, edited by Jorge Heine, 27–53. Lanham, Md.: North-South, 1983.

Fanon, Frantz. *Black Skin, White Masks*. New York: Grove Press, 2008.

Fantini, Mario. "Community Participation." In *The Politics of Urban Education*, edited by Marilyn Gittell and Alan G. Hevesi, 323–37. New York: Praeger, 1969.

Fantini, Mario D., Marilyn Gittell, and Richard Magat. *Community Control and the Urban School*. New York: Praeger, 1970.

Feldstein, Ruth. *Motherhood in Black and White: Race and Sex in American Liberalism, 1930–1965*. Ithaca, N.Y.: Cornell University Press, 2000.

Fernandez, Johanna. "Between Social Service Reform and Revolutionary Politics: The Young Lords, Late Sixties Radicalism, and Community Organizing in New York City." In *Freedom North: Black Freedom Struggles outside the South, 1940–1980*, edited by Jeanne F. Theoharis and Komozi Woodard, 255–85. New York: Palgrave Macmillan, 2003.

Fernandez, Lilia. *Brown in the Windy City: Mexicans and Puerto Ricans in Postwar Chicago*. Chicago: University of Chicago Press, 2012.

Fink, Leon, and Brian Greenberg. *Upheaval in the Quiet Zone: A History of Hospital Workers' Union, Local 1199*. Urbana: University of Illinois Press, 1989.

Fletcher, Bill, Jr., and Fernando Gapasin. *Solidarity Divided: The Crisis in Organized Labor and a New Path toward Social Justice*. Berkeley: University of California Press, 2008.

Fliegel, Seymour, and James MacGuire. *Miracle in East Harlem: The Fight for Choice in Public Education*. New York: Times Books, 1993.

Flores, Juan. *From Bomba to Hip-Hop: Puerto Rican Culture and Latino Identity*. New York: Columbia University Press, 2000.

———. "Pan-Latino/Trans-Latino: Puerto Ricans in the 'New Nueva York.'" *Centro: Journal of the Center for Puerto Rican Studies* 8, nos. 1, 2 (1996): 170–86.

Foley, Neil. *Quest for Equality: The Failed Promise of Black-Brown Solidarity*. Cambridge, Mass.: Harvard University Press, 2010.

Foner, Philip Sheldon. *Organized Labor and the Black Worker, 1619–1973*. New York: Praeger, 1974.

Franklin, Charles Lionel. *The Negro Labor Unionist of New York: Problems and Conditions among Negroes in the Labor Unions in Manhattan with Special Reference to the N.R.A. and Post-N.R.A. Situations*. New York: Columbia University Press, 1936.

Frazier, E. Franklin. "Problems and Needs of Negro Children and Youth Resulting from Family Disorganization." *Journal of Negro Education* 19, no. 3 (1950): 269–77.

Frazier, Robeson Taj P. "Thunder in the East: China, Exiled Crusaders, and the Unevenness of Black Internationalism." *American Quarterly* 63, no. 4 (2011): 929–53.

Fredrickson, George M. *Racism: A Short History*. Princeton, N.J.: Princeton University Press, 2002.

Freeman, Joshua Benjamin. *Working-Class New York: Life and Labor since World War II*. New York: New Press, 2000.

Gallardo, José Miguel, ed. *Proceedings of the Conference on Education of Puerto Rican Children on the Mainland (October 18 to 21, 1970)*. New York: Arno Press, 1975.

Galvin, Miles E. *The Organized Labor Movement in Puerto Rico*. Cranbury, N.J.: Associated University Presses, 1979.

Gilmore, Ruth Wilson. *Golden Gulag: Prisons, Surplus, Crisis, and Opposition in Globalizing California*. Berkeley: University of California Press, 2007.

Gilroy, Paul. *The Black Atlantic: Modernity and Double Consciousness*. Cambridge, Mass.: Harvard University Press, 1993.

Giménez, Martha. "U.S. Ethnic Politics: Implications for Latin Americans." *Latin American Perspectives* 19, no. 4 (1992): 7–17.

Gittell, Marilyn. "Community Control of Education." In *The Politics of Urban Education*, edited by Marilyn Gittell and Alan G. Hevesi, 363–77. New York: Praeger, 1969.

———. *Demonstration for Social Change: An Experiment in Local Control*. New York: Institute for Community Studies, Queens College of the City University of New York, 1971.

———. "Education: The Decentralization–Community Control Controversy." In *Race and Politics in New York City: Five Studies in Policy-Making*, edited by Jewel Bellush and Stephen M. David, 134–63. New York: Praeger, 1971.

———. *Local Control in Education: Three Demonstration School Districts in New York City*. New York: Praeger, 1972.

————. *School Boards and School Policy: An Evaluation of Decentralization in New York City.* New York: Praeger, 1973.

Glasser, Ruth. *My Music Is My Flag: Puerto Rican Musicians and Their New York Communities, 1917–1940.* Berkeley: University of California Press, 1995.

Gleason, Philip. *Speaking of Diversity: Language and Ethnicity in Twentieth-Century America.* Baltimore: Johns Hopkins University Press, 1992.

Godreau, Isar. "Changing Space, Making Race: Distance, Nostalgia, and the Folklorization of Blackness in Puerto Rico." *Identities: Global Studies in Culture and Power* 9, no. 3 (2002): 281–304.

Goldberg, David A., and Trevor Griffey. *Black Power at Work: Community Control, Affirmative Action, and the Construction Industry.* Ithaca, N.Y.: ILR Press/Cornell University Press, 2010.

Goldberg, David Theo. "The Semantics of Race." *Ethnic and Racial Studies* 15, no. 4 (1992): 543–69.

Goldberg, Gertrude S. *I.S. 201: An Educational Landmark.* New York: IRCD Bulletin, 1967.

Goldstein, Alyosha. *Poverty in Common: The Politics of Community Action during the American Century.* Durham: Duke University Press, 2012.

Gonzalez, Evelyn Diaz. *The Bronx.* New York: Columbia University Press, 2004.

Gordon, Colin. *Mapping Decline: St. Louis and the Fate of the American City.* Politics and Culture in Modern America. Philadelphia: University of Pennsylvania Press, 2008.

Gracia, Jorge J. E., and Pablo De Greiff, eds. *Hispanics/Latinos in the United States: Ethnicity, Race, and Rights.* New York: Routledge, 2000.

Graham, Hugh Davis. *Collision Course: The Strange Convergence of Affirmative Action and Immigration Policy in America.* New York: Oxford University Press, 2002.

Green, Charles, and Basil Wilson. *The Struggle for Black Empowerment in New York City: Beyond the Politics of Pigmentation.* New York: Praeger, 1989.

Grob, Gerald N. *From Asylum to Community: Mental Health Policy in Modern America.* Princeton, N.J.: Princeton University Press, 1991.

Grosfoguel, Ramón. *Colonial Subjects: Puerto Ricans in a Global Perspective.* Berkeley: University of California Press, 2003.

Guglielmo, Thomas A. "Fighting for Caucasian Rights: Mexicans, Mexican Americans, and the Transnational Struggle for Civil Rights in World War II Texas." *Journal of American History* 92, no. 4 (2006): 1212–37.

Guridy, Frank Andre. *Forging Diaspora: Afro-Cubans and African Americans in a World of Empire and Jim Crow.* Envisioning Cuba. Chapel Hill: University of North Carolina Press, 2010.

Guterl, Matthew Pratt. *The Color of Race in America, 1900–1940.* Cambridge, Mass.: Harvard University Press, 2001.

Gutmann, Matthew C., et al. *Perspectives on Las Américas: A Reader in Culture, History, and Representation.* Malden, Mass.: Blackwell, 2003.

Hacsi, Timothy A. *Children as Pawns: The Politics of Educational Reform.* Cambridge, Mass.: Harvard University Press, 2002.

Hale, Lorraine E. *Hale House: Alive with Love.* New York: Hale House, 1992.

Handlin, Oscar. *The Newcomers: Negroes and Puerto Ricans in a Changing Metropolis.* New York Metropolitan Region Study. Cambridge, Mass.: Harvard University Press, 1959.

Haney-López, Ian. *White by Law: The Legal Construction of Race.* New York: New York University Press, 2006.

Harrington, Michael. *The Other America: Poverty in the United States.* New York: Macmillan, 1962.

Hattam, Victoria. "Ethnicity: An American Genealogy." In *Not Just Black and White: Historical and Contemporary Perspectives on Immigration, Race, and Ethnicity in the United States,* edited by Nancy Foner and George Fredrickson, 42–60. New York: Russell Sage Foundation, 2004.

Haygood, Wil. *King of the Cats: The Life and Times of Adam Clayton Powell, Jr.* New York: Amistad, 2006.

Helfgot, Joseph H. *Professional Reforming: Mobilization for Youth and the Failure of Social Science.* Lexington, Mass.: Lexington Books, 1981.

Hickey, Neil, and Ed Edwin. *Adam Clayton Powell and the Politics of Race.* New York: Fleet, 1965.

Higginbotham, Evelyn Brooks. "African-American Women's History and the Metalanguage of Race." *Signs* 17, no. 2 (1992): 251–74.

Hirsch, Arnold R. *Making the Second Ghetto: Race and Housing in Chicago, 1940–1960.* Chicago: University of Chicago Press, 1998.

Hirsch, Werner, Joel Hirsch, and Stephen Margolis. "The Effects of Habitability Laws upon Rent." In *Policy Studies Review Annual,* edited by Stuart S. Nagel and Ray C. Rist, 281–85. New Brunswick, N.J.: Transaction Publishers, 1977.

Hoffnung-Garskof, Jesse. "The Migrations of Arturo Schomburg: On Being Antillano, Negro, and Puerto Rican in New York, 1891–1917." *Journal of American Ethnic History* 21, no. 1 (2001): 3–49.

———. *A Tale of Two Cities: Santo Domingo and New York after 1950.* Princeton, N.J.: Princeton University Press, 2008.

Holt, Thomas C. *The Problem of Race in the Twenty-first Century.* Cambridge, Mass.: Harvard University Press, 2000.

Jacobson, Matthew Frye. *Whiteness of a Different Color: European Immigrants and the Alchemy of Race.* Cambridge, Mass.: Harvard University Press, 1998.

James, Winston. *Holding Aloft the Banner of Ethiopia: Caribbean Radicalism in Early Twentieth-Century America.* New York: Verso, 1998.

Jeffrey, Julie Roy. *Education for Children of the Poor: A Study of the Origins and Implementation of the Elementary and Secondary Education Act of 1965.* Columbus: Ohio State University Press, 1978.

Jennings, James. *Puerto Rican Politics in New York City.* Washington, D.C.: University Press of America, 1977.

Jennings, James, and Francisco Chapman. "Puerto Ricans and the Community Control Movement: An Interview with Luis Fuentes." In *The Puerto Rican Movement: Voices from the Diaspora,* edited by Andrés Torres and José E. Velázquez, 280–95. Philadelphia: Temple University Press, 1998.

Jiménez, Lillian. "Puerto Ricans and Educational Civil Rights: A History of the 1969

City College Takeover (An Interview with Five Participants)." *Centro: Journal of the Center for Puerto Rican Studies* 21, no. 2 (2009): 159–75.

Jiménez, Ramón J. "Hostos Community College: Battle of the Seventies." *Centro: Journal of the Center for Puerto Rican Studies* 15, no. 1 (2003): 99–111.

Jiménez Román, Miriam. "Un hombre (negro) del pueblo: José Celso Barbosa and the Puerto Rican 'Race' toward Whiteness." *Centro: Journal of the Center for Puerto Rican Studies* 8, nos. 1, 2 (1996): 8–29.

Jiménez Román, Miriam, and Juan Flores. *The Afro-Latin@ Reader: History and Culture in the United States*. Durham: Duke University Press, 2010.

Jonas, Gilbert. *Freedom's Sword: The NAACP and the Struggle against Racism in America, 1909–1969*. New York: Routledge, 2005.

Jones, Jill. *South Bronx Rising: The Rise, Fall, and Resurrection of an American City*. New York: Fordham University Press, 2002.

Kasinitz, Philip. *Caribbean New York: Black Immigrants and the Politics of Race*. Ithaca, N.Y.: Cornell University Press, 1992.

Katz, Michael B. *The Undeserving Poor: From the War on Poverty to the War on Welfare*. New York: Pantheon, 1990.

Katznelson, Ira. *City Trenches: Urban Politics and the Patterning of Class in the United States*. Chicago: University of Chicago Press, 1982.

Kelley, Robin D. G. *Race Rebels: Culture, Politics, and the Black Working Class*. New York: Free Press, 1994.

Kessler-Harris, Alice. "Organizing the Unorganizable: Three Jewish Women and Their Union." In *The Labor History Reader*, edited by Daniel J. Leab, 269–87. Urbana: University of Illinois Press, 1985.

Kinsbruner, Jay. *Not of Pure Blood: The Free People of Color and Racial Prejudice in Nineteenth-Century Puerto Rico*. Durham: Duke University Press, 1996.

Klor de Alva, J. Jorge. "The Invention of Ethnic Origins and the Negotiation of Latino Identity, 1969–1981." In *Challenging Fronteras: Structuring Latina and Latino Lives in the U.S.*, edited by Mary Romero, Pierrette Hondagneu-Sotelo, and Vilma Ortiz, 55–79. New York: Routledge, 1997.

Kornbluh, Felicia Ann. *The Battle for Welfare Rights: Politics and Poverty in Modern America*. Philadelphia: University of Pennsylvania Press, 2007.

Korstad, Robert, and Nelson Lichtenstein. "Opportunities Found and Lost: Labor, Radicals, and the Early Civil Rights Movement." *Journal of American History* 75, no. 3 (1988): 786–811.

Krosney, Herbert. *Beyond Welfare: Poverty in the Supercity*. New York: Holt, Rinehart, and Winston, 1966.

Kurashige, Scott. *The Shifting Grounds of Race: Black and Japanese Americans in the Making of Multiethnic Los Angeles*. Princeton, N.J.: Princeton University Press, 2008.

Kusmer, Kenneth L., and Joe William Trotter, eds. *African American Urban History since World War II*. Historical Studies of Urban America. Chicago: University of Chicago Press, 2009.

Lang, Clarence. *Grassroots at the Gateway: Class Politics and Black Freedom Struggle in St. Louis, 1936–75*. Ann Arbor: University of Michigan Press, 2009.

Laó-Montes, Agustín. "Afro-Latinidades: Bridging Blackness and Latinidad." In *Technofuturos: Critical Interventions in Latina/o Studies*, edited by Nancy Raquel Mirabal and Agustín Laó-Montes, 117–40. New York: Lexington Books, 2007.

———. "Introduction." In *Mambo Montage: The Latinization of New York*, edited by Agustín Laó-Montes and Arlene M. Dávila, 1–53. New York: Columbia University Press, 2001.

Laó-Montes, Agustín, and Arlene M. Dávila. *Mambo Montage: The Latinization of New York*. New York: Columbia University Press, 2001.

Lapp, Michael. "Managing Migration: The Migration Division of Puerto Rico and Puerto Ricans in New York City, 1948–1968." Ph.D. diss., Johns Hopkins University, 1991.

Lasch-Quinn, Elisabeth. *Black Neighbors: Race and the Limits of Reform in the American Settlement House Movement, 1890–1945*. Chapel Hill: University of North Carolina Press, 1993.

Lawson, Steven F., and Charles Payne, eds. *Debating the Civil Rights Movement, 1945–1968*. Lanham, Md.: Rowman and Littlefield, 1998.

Levin, Henry M., and Harold W. Pfautz, eds. *Community Control of Schools*. New York: Simon and Schuster, 1970.

Lewis, Edward. "The Urban League, a Dynamic Instrument in Social Change: A Study of the Changing Role of the New York Urban League, 1910–60." Ph.D. diss., New York University, 1960.

Lewis, Heather. "Protest, Place, and Pedagogy: New York City's Community Control Movement and Its Aftermath, 1966–96." Ph.D. diss., New York University, 2006.

Lindenberg, Sidney, and Ruth Zittel. "The Settlement Scene Changes." *Social Forces* 14, no. 4 (1936): 461–68.

Lumet, Sidney, director. *Twelve Angry Men*. United Artists, 1957.

MacLean, Nancy. *Freedom Is Not Enough: The Opening of the American Workplace*. New York: Sage, 2006.

Macnamara, John Theodore. *Bilingualism and Primary Education: A Study of Irish Experience*. Edinburgh: Edinburgh University Press, 1966.

Maldonado, A. W. *Luis Muñoz Marín: Puerto Rico's Democratic Revolution*. San Juan: Editorial Universidad de Puerto Rico, 2006.

———. *Teodoro Moscoso and Puerto Rico's Operation Bootstrap*. Gainesville: University Press of Florida, 1997.

Marable, Manning. *Race, Reform, and Rebellion: The Second Reconstruction and Beyond in Black America, 1945–2006*. Jackson: University Press of Mississippi, 2007.

Markowitz, Gerald E., and David Rosner. *Children, Race, and Power: Kenneth and Mamie Clark's Northside Center*. Charlottesville: University Press of Virginia, 1996.

Márquez, John D. "The Browning of Black Politics: Foundational Blackness and New Latino Subjectivities." *Subjectivity* 4 (2011): 47–67.

Márquez, Roberto. "One Boricua's Baldwin: A Personal Remembrance." *American Quarterly* 42, no. 3 (1990): 456–77.

———. "Raza, racism, e historia: Are All of My Bones from There?" *Latino Research Review* 4, no. 3 (2000): 8–22.

Martínez, Elizabeth Sutherland, and Enriqueta Longeaux Vásquez. *Viva la raza! The Struggle of the Mexican-American People.* Garden City, N.Y.: Doubleday, 1974.

Mass, Bonnie. "Puerto Rico: A Case Study of Population Control." *Latin American Perspectives* 4, no. 4 (1977): 66–81.

Matos Rodríguez, Félix V. "Their Islands and Our People: U.S. Writing about Puerto Rico, 1898–1920." *Centro: Journal of the Center for Puerto Rican Studies* 11, no. 1 (1999): 32–49.

Matusow, Allen J. *The Unraveling of America: A History of Liberalism in the 1960s.* New York: Harper and Row, 1984.

McCaffrey, Katherine. "Forging Solidarity: Politics, Protest, and the Vieques Solidarity Network." In *The Puerto Rican Movement: Voices from the Diaspora,* edited by Andrés Torres and José E. Velázquez, 329–39. Philadelphia: Temple University Press, 1998.

McNickle, Chris. *To Be Mayor of New York: Ethnic Politics in the City.* New York: Columbia University Press, 1993.

Mele, Christopher. *Selling the Lower East Side: Culture, Real Estate, and Resistance in New York City.* Minneapolis: University of Minnesota Press, 2000.

Meléndez Vélez, Edgardo. "The Puerto Rican Journey Revisited: Politics and the Study of Puerto Rican Migration." *Centro: Journal of the Center for Puerto Rican Studies* 17, no. 2 (2005): 192–221.

Meyer, Gerald. "Leonard Covello: A Pioneer in Bilingual Education." *Bilingual Review* 12, nos. 1, 2 (1985): 55–61.

———. "Save Hostos: Politics and Community Mobilization to Save a College in the Bronx, 1973–1978." *Centro: Journal of the Center for Puerto Rican Studies* 15, no. 1 (2003): 73–97.

———. *Vito Marcantonio: Radical Politician, 1902–1954.* Albany: State University of New York Press, 1989.

Mollenkopf, John H. *A Phoenix in the Ashes: The Rise and Fall of the Koch Coalition in New York City Politics.* Princeton, N.J.: Princeton University Press, 1994.

Mollenkopf, John H., and Manuel Castells, eds. *Dual City: Restructuring New York.* New York: Russell Sage Foundation, 1991.

Moore, Joan W., and Raquel Pinderhughes, eds. *In the Barrios: Latinos and the Underclass Debate.* New York: Russell Sage Foundation, 1993.

Morris, Aldon, and Naomi Braine. "Social Movements and Oppositional Consciousness." In *Oppositional Consciousness: The Subjective Roots of Social Protest,* edited by Jane Mansbridge and Aldon Morris, 20–37. Chicago: University of Chicago Press, 2001.

Murch, Donna Jean. *Living for the City: Migration, Education, and the Rise of the Black Panther Party in Oakland, California.* Chapel Hill: University of North Carolina Press, 2010.

Murji, Karim, and John Solomos, eds. *Racialization: Studies in Theory and Practice.* New York: Oxford University Press, 2005.

Naison, Mark. "It Takes a Village to Raise a Child: Growing Up in the Patterson Houses in the 1950s and 1960s: An Interview with Victoria Archibald-Good." *Bronx County Historical Journal* 40, no. 1 (2002): 5–22.

Naples, Nancy A. *Grassroots Warriors: Activist Mothering, Community Work, and the War on Poverty.* New York: Routledge, 1998.

Neidle, Cecyle S. *Great Immigrants.* New York: Twayne, 1973.

Nieto, Sonia., ed. *Puerto Rican Students in U.S. Schools.* Mahwah, N.J.: Lawrence Erlbaum Associates, 2000.

Oboler, Suzanne. *Ethnic Labels, Latino Lives: Identity and the Politics of (Re)Presentation in the United States.* Minneapolis: University of Minnesota Press, 1995.

Oboler, Suzanne, and Anani Dzidzienyo. "Flows and Counterflows: Latinas/os, Blackness, and Racialization in Hemispheric Perspective." In *Neither Enemies nor Friends: Latinos, Blacks, and Afro-Latinos,* edited by Suzanne Oboler and Anani Dzidzienyo, 3–35. New York: Palgrave Macmillan, 2005.

O'Connor, Alice. *Poverty Knowledge: Social Science, Social Policy, and the Poor in Twentieth-Century U.S. History.* Politics and Society in Twentieth-Century America. Princeton, N.J.: Princeton University Press, 2001.

Ogbar, Jeffrey O. G. "Rainbow Radicalism: The Rise of the Radical Ethnic Nationalism." In *The Black Power Movement: Rethinking the Civil Rights–Black Power Era,* edited by Peniel E. Joseph, 193–228. New York: Routledge, 2006.

Okihiro, Gary Y. "Colonial Vision, Racial Visibility: Racializations in Puerto Rico and the Philippines during the Initial Period of U.S. Colonization." In *Racial Transformations: Latinos and Asians Remaking the United States,* edited by Nicholas De Genova, 23–39. Durham: Duke University Press, 2006.

Opie, Frederick Douglass. "Eating, Dancing, and Courting in New York Black and Latino Relations, 1930–1970." *Journal of Social History* 42, no. 1 (2008): 79–109.

Orleck, Annelise. *Storming Caesars Palace: How Black Mothers Fought Their Own War on Poverty.* Boston: Beacon, 2005.

Orleck, Annelise, and Lisa Gayle Hazirjian. *The War on Poverty: A New Grassroots History, 1964–1980.* Athens: University of Georgia Press, 2011.

Ortiz, Altagracia. "'En la aguja y el pedal eché la hiel': Puerto Rican Women in the Garment Industry of New York City, 1920–1980." In *Puerto Rican Women and Work: Bridges in Transnational Labor,* edited by Altagracia Ortiz, 55–81. Philadelphia: Temple University Press, 1996.

———. "Historical Vignettes of Puerto Rican Women Workers in New York City, 1895–1990." In *Handbook of Hispanic Cultures in the United States: Sociology,* edited by Nicolás Kanellos and Claudio Esteva-Fabregat, 219–38. Houston: Arte Público Press, 1994.

Osofsky, Gilbert. *Harlem, the Making of a Ghetto: Negro New York, 1890–1930.* New York: Harper and Row, 1968.

Padilla, Elena. *Up from Puerto Rico.* New York: Columbia University Press, 1969.

Padilla, Felix M. *Latino Ethnic Consciousness: The Case of Mexican Americans and Puerto Ricans in Chicago.* Notre Dame, Ind.: University of Notre Dame Press, 1985.

Pastorello, Karen. "'The Transfigured Few': Jane Addams, Bessie Abramowitz Hillman, and Immigrant Women Workers in Chicago, 1905–15." In *Jane Addams and the Practice of Democracy,* edited by Marilyn Fischer, Carol Nackenoff, and Wendy Chmielewski, 98–118. Urbana: University of Illinois Press, 2009.

Patterson, James T. *America's Struggle against Poverty in the Twentieth Century.* Cambridge, Mass.: Harvard University Press, 2000.

Payne, Charles M. *I've Got the Light of Freedom: The Organizing Tradition and the Mississippi Freedom Struggle.* Berkeley: University of California Press, 2007.

Perea, Juan F. "The Black/White Binary Paradigm of Race." In *Critical Race Theory: The Cutting Edge,* edited by Richard Delgado and Jean Stefancic, 344–53. Philadelphia: Temple University Press, 2000.

Pérez, Gina M. *The Near Northwest Side Story: Migration, Displacement, and Puerto Rican Families.* Berkeley: University of California Press, 2004.

Pérez, Richie. "From Assimilation to Annihilation: Puerto Rican Images in U.S. Politics." *Centro: Journal of the Center for Puerto Rican Studies* 2, no. 8 (1990): 8–27.

Perlstein, Daniel H. *Justice, Justice: School Politics and the Eclipse of Liberalism.* New York: P. Lang, 2004.

Plunz, Richard. *A History of Housing in New York City: Dwelling Type and Social Change in the American Metropolis.* Columbia History of Urban Life. New York: Columbia University Press, 1990.

Podair, Jerald E. *The Strike That Changed New York: Blacks, Whites, and the Ocean Hill–Brownsville Crisis.* New Haven: Yale University Press, 2002.

Pritchett, Wendell E. *Brownsville, Brooklyn: Blacks, Jews, and the Changing Face of the Ghetto.* Chicago: University of Chicago Press, 2002.

Puerto Rican Forum. *The Puerto Rican Community Development Project.* New York: Arno Press, 1975.

Pulido, Laura. *Black, Brown, Yellow, and Left: Radical Activism in Los Angeles.* Berkeley: University of California Press, 2006.

Rainwater, Lee. *The Moynihan Report and the Politics of Controversy.* Cambridge, Mass.: MIT Press, 1967.

Ransby, Barbara. *Ella Baker and the Black Freedom Movement: A Radical Democratic Vision.* Chapel Hill: University of North Carolina Press, 2003.

Reyes, Luis O. "The Aspira Consent Decree: A Thirtieth-Anniversary Retrospective of Bilingual Education in New York City." *Harvard Educational Review* 76, no. 3 (2006): 369–400.

Richards, Yevette. *Maida Springer: Pan-Africanist and International Labor Leader.* Pittsburgh: University of Pittsburgh Press, 2000.

Ríos, Palmira N. "Gender, Industrialization, and Development in Puerto Rico." In *Women in the Latin American Development Process,* edited by Christine E. Bose and Edna Acosta-Belén, 125–48. Philadelphia: Temple University Press, 1995.

Rivera, Raquel. *New York Ricans from the Hip Hop Zone.* New York: Palgrave Macmillan, 2003.

Rodríguez, Clara E. "Economic Factors Affecting Puerto Ricans in New York." In *Labor Migration under Capitalism: The Puerto Rican Experience,* edited by Centro de Estudios Puertorriqueños, History Task Force, 197–221. New York: Monthly Review Press, 1979.

Rodríguez-Domínguez, Víctor M. "The Racialization of Mexican Americans and Puerto Ricans: 1890s–1930." *Centro: Journal of the Center for Puerto Rican Studies* 17, no. 1 (2005): 70–105.

Rodríguez-Morazzani, Roberto P. "Beyond the Rainbow: Mapping the Discourse on Puerto Ricans and 'Race.'" *Centro: Journal of the Center for Puerto Rican Studies* 8, nos. 1, 2 (1996): 150–69.

———. "Political Cultures of the Puerto Rican Left in the United States." In *The Puerto Rican Movement: Voices from the Diaspora*, edited by Andrés Torres and José E. Velázquez, 25–47. Philadelphia: Temple University Press, 1998.

Rogers, David. *110 Livingston Street: Politics and Bureaucracy in the New York City Schools.* New York: Random House, 1968.

Rúa, Mérida M. *A Grounded Identidad: Making New Lives in Chicago's Puerto Rican Neighborhoods.* New York: Oxford University Press, 2012.

Rumbaut, Rubén G. "Pigments of Our Imagination: On the Racialization and Racial Identities of 'Hispanics' and 'Latinos.'" In *How the United States Racializes Latinos: White Hegemony and Its Consequences*, edited by José A. Cobas, Jorge Duany, and Joe R. Feagin, 15–36. Boulder, Colo.: Paradigm, 2009.

Safa, Helen Icken. *The Myth of the Male Breadwinner: Women and Industrialization in the Caribbean.* Boulder, Colo.: Westview, 1995.

Sánchez, José Ramón. "Housing Puerto Ricans in New York City, 1945 to 1984: A Study in Class Powerlessness." Ph.D. diss., New York University, 1990.

———. "Puerto Ricans and the Door of Participation in U.S. Politics." In *Handbook of Hispanic Cultures in the United States: Sociology*, edited by Nicolás Kanellos and Claudio Esteva-Fabregat, 110–32. Houston: Arte Público Press, 1994.

Sánchez Korrol, Virginia. *From Colonia to Community: The History of Puerto Ricans in New York City.* Berkeley: University of California Press, 1994.

San Miguel, Guadalupe. *Brown, Not White: School Integration and the Chicano Movement in Houston.* College Station: Texas A&M University Press, 2001.

Santiago, Isaura Santiago. "*Aspira v. Board of Education* Revisited." *American Journal of Education* 95, no. 1 (1986): 149–99.

Santiago-Valles, Kelvin. "On the Historical Links between Coloniality, the Violent Production of the 'Native' Body, and the Manufacture of Pathology." *Centro: Journal of the Center for Puerto Rican Studies* 7, no. 1 (1995): 108–18.

Santiago-Valles, Kelvin A., and Gladys M. Jiménez-Muñoz. "Social Polarization and Colonized Labor: Puerto Ricans in the United States, 1945–2000." In *The Columbia History of Latinos in the United States since 1960*, edited by David Gutiérrez, 87–145. New York: Columbia University Press, 2004.

Savage, Barbara Dianne. *Broadcasting Freedom: Radio, War, and the Politics of Race, 1938–1948.* Chapel Hill: University of North Carolina Press, 1999.

Sawyer, Mark. "Racial Politics in Multiethnic America: Black and Latin@ Identities and Coalitions." In *The Afro-Latin@ Reader: History and Culture in the United States*, edited by Miriam Jiménez Román and Juan Flores, 527–39. Durham: Duke University Press, 2010.

Schneider, Eric C. *Vampires, Dragons, and Egyptian Kings: Youth Gangs in Postwar New York.* Princeton, N.J.: Princeton University Press, 1999.

Schwartz, Joel. "Tenant Power in the Liberal City, 1943–1971." In *The Tenant Movement in New York City, 1904–1984*, edited by Ronald Lawson with the assistance of Mark Naison, 134–208. New Brunswick, N.J.: Rutgers University Press, 1986.

Scott, Daryl Michael. *Contempt and Pity: Social Policy and the Image of the Damaged Black Psyche, 1880–1996*. Chapel Hill: University of North Carolina Press, 1997.

———. "How Black Nationalism Became Sui Generis." *Fire!!!* 1, no. 2 (2012): 6–63.

Scott, James C. *Domination and the Arts of Resistance: Hidden Transcripts*. New Haven: Yale University Press, 1990.

Seigel, Micol. "Beyond Compare: Comparative Method after the Transnational Turn." *Radical History Review* 91 (2005): 62–90.

Ševčenko, Liz. "Making Loisaida: Placing Puertorriqueñidad in Lower Manhattan." In *Mambo Montage: The Latinization of New York*, edited by Agustín Laó-Montes and Arlene Dávila, 293–318. New York: Columbia University Press, 2001.

Sicherman, Barbara, and Carol Hurd Green. *Notable American Women: The Modern Period: A Biographical Dictionary*. Cambridge, Mass.: Belknap Press of Harvard University Press, 1980.

Silver, Harold, and Pamela Silver. *An Educational War on Poverty: American and British Policy-Making, 1960–1980*. Cambridge: Cambridge University Press, 1991.

Simon, Barbara Levy. "Settlement Houses." In *The Columbia University School of Social Work: A Centennial Celebration*, edited by Ronald A. Feldman and Sheila B. Kamerman, 369–81. New York: Columbia University Press, 2001.

Smethurst, James Edward. *The Black Arts Movement: Literary Nationalism in the 1960s and 1970s*. Chapel Hill: University of North Carolina Press, 2005.

Sollors, Werner. "The Multiculturalism Debate as Cultural Text." In *Beyond Pluralism: The Conception of Groups and Group Identities in America*, edited by Wendy F. Katkin, Ned C. Landsman, and Andrea Tyree, 63–104. Urbana: University of Illinois Press, 1998.

Steiner, Stan. *The Islands: The Worlds of the Puerto Ricans*. New York: Harper and Row, 1974.

Sugrue, Thomas J. *The Origins of the Urban Crisis: Race and Inequality in Postwar Detroit*. Princeton, N.J.: Princeton University Press, 1996.

———. *Sweet Land of Liberty: The Forgotten Struggle for Civil Rights in the North*. New York: Random House, 2008.

Sugrue, Thomas J., and John D. Skrentny. "The White Ethnic Strategy." In *Rightward Bound: Making America Conservative in the 1970s*, edited by Bruce J. Schulman and Julian E. Zelizer, 171–92. Cambridge, Mass.: Harvard University Press, 2008.

Taylor, Clarence. *Knocking at Our Own Door: Milton A. Galamison and the Struggle for School Integration in New York City*. Columbia History of Urban Life. New York: Columbia University Press, 1997.

Theoharis, Jeanne F., and Komozi Woodard, eds. *Freedom North: Black Freedom Struggles outside the South, 1940–1980*. New York: Palgrave Macmillan, 2003.

Thomas, Lorrin. *Puerto Rican Citizen: History and Political Identity in Twentieth-Century New York City*. Chicago: University of Chicago Press, 2010.

Thompson, Heather Ann. "Why Mass Incarceration Matters: Rethinking Crisis, Decline, and Transformation in Postwar American History." *Journal of American History* 97, no. 3 (2010): 703–34.

Torres, Andrés. *Between Melting Pot and Mosaic: African Americans and Puerto Ricans in the New York Political Economy*. Philadelphia: Temple University Press, 1995.

Torres, Arlene. "La Gran Familia Puertorriqueña 'Ej Prieta de Beldá.'" In *Blackness in Latin America and the Caribbean: Social Dynamics and Cultural Transformations*, edited by Norman E. Whitten and Arlene Torres, 2:285–306. Bloomington: Indiana University Press, 1998.

Torres-Saillant, Silvio. "Divisible Blackness: Reflections on Heterogeneity and Racial Identity." In *The Afro-Latin@ Reader: History and Culture in the United States*, edited by Miriam Jiménez Román and Juan Flores, 453–66. Durham: Duke University Press, 2010.

Trolander, Judith Ann. *Professionalism and Social Change: From the Settlement House Movement to Neighborhood Centers, 1886 to the Present*. New York: Columbia University Press, 1987.

Trotter, Joe W. "The Great Migration, African Americans, and Immigrants in the Industrial City." In *Not Just Black and White: Historical and Contemporary Perspectives on Immigration, Race, and Ethnicity in the United States*, edited by Nancy Foner and George M. Fredrickson, 82–99. New York: Russell Sage Foundation, 2004.

Vega, Bernardo, and César Andreu Iglesias. *Memoirs of Bernardo Vega: A Contribution to the History of the Puerto Rican Community in New York*. New York: Monthly Review Press, 1984.

Velasquez, Carlos. *The Ramón S. Vélez Story*. New York: Galos, 2004.

Velázquez, José E. "Another West Side Story: An Interview with Members of El Comité-MINP (Movimiento De Izquierda Nacional Puertorriqueño)." In *The Puerto Rican Movement: Voices from the Diaspora*, edited by Andrés Torres and José E. Velázquez, 88–106. Philadelphia: Temple University Press, 1998.

———. "Coming Full Circle: The Puerto Rican Socialist Party, U.S. Branch." In *The Puerto Rican Movement: Voices from the Diaspora*, edited by Andrés Torres and José E. Velázquez, 48–68. Philadelphia: Temple University Press, 1998.

Vinson, Ben, III, and Matthew Restall, eds. *Black Mexico: Race and Society from Colonial to Modern Times*. Albuquerque: University of New Mexico Press, 2009.

Wade, Peter. *Race and Ethnicity in Latin America*. New York: Palgrave Macmillan, 2010.

Waldinger, Roger David. *Still the Promised City? African-Americans and New Immigrants in Postindustrial New York*. Cambridge, Mass.: Harvard University Press, 1996.

Walter, John C. *The Harlem Fox: J. Raymond Jones and Tammany, 1920–1970*. Albany: State University of New York Press, 1989.

Waters, Mary C. *Black Identities: West Indian Immigrant Dreams and American Realities*. New York: Russell Sage Foundation, 1999.

Whalen, Carmen Teresa. "Colonialism, Citizenship, and the Making of the Puerto Rican Diaspora: An Introduction." In *The Puerto Rican Diaspora: Historical Perspectives*, edited by Carmen Teresa Whalen and Víctor Vázquez-Hernández, 1–42. Philadelphia: Temple University Press, 2005.

———. *From Puerto Rico to Philadelphia: Puerto Rican Workers and Postwar Economies*. Philadelphia: Temple University Press, 2001.

Whalen, Carmen Teresa, and Víctor Vázquez-Hernández, eds. *The Puerto Rican Diaspora: Historical Perspectives*. Philadelphia: Temple University Press, 2005.

Wilkinson, Michelle Joan. "In the Tradition of Revolution: The Socio-aesthetics of Black and Puerto Rican Arts Movements, 1962–82." Ph.D. diss., Emory University, 2001.

Williams, Rhonda Y. *The Politics of Public Housing: Black Women's Struggles against Urban Inequality*. New York: Oxford University Press, 2004.

Wrong, Elaine Gale. *The Negro in the Apparel Industry*. The Racial Policies of American Industry, Report No. 31. Philadelphia: Industrial Research Unit, Wharton School, University of Pennsylvania Press, 1973.

Yancey, George A. *Who Is White? Latinos, Asians, and the New Black/Nonblack Divide*. Boulder, Colo.: Lynne Rienner, 2003.

Zipp, Samuel. *Manhattan Projects: The Rise and Fall of Urban Renewal in Cold War New York*. New York: Oxford University Press, 2010.

Index

Abyssinian Baptist Church, 42, 84
Academic performance: and cultural maladjustment, 2, 165; and culture of poverty, 52, 53, 54–55; and demographics, 167; and home environment, 172–73; and language assimilation, 188; and decentralization, 199, 229; and bilingual education, 212, 232
Ace, Johnny, 29
Acosta, Luis Garden, 246
Addams, Jane, 99–100
Africa, decolonization movements, 84
African American churches, 35, 42, 83, 99
African American culture: as permanently damaged, 11; and education, 13; Puerto Rican culture compared to, 106, 108; and community control movement, 169, 170; and Swahili language, 191, 194
African American history, 19–20, 169, 193
African American leaders: and African Americans/Puerto Ricans relationship, 88–89, 108–9, 132–34, 185–86, 214; and grassroots mobilization, 102; and settlement houses, 102, 103; and social workers, 106–15, 129, 252; and youth, 116; and antipoverty programs, 132–33, 163–64, 216, 218–19; and community control movement, 133–34; and African American middle class, 162, 213, 220, 223; and institutionalization of power, 214

African American middle class: assimilation of, 32; social workers of, 113; and African American leaders, 162, 213, 220, 223; and skin color, 207; and community control movement, 211–12, 213; political orientation of, 213–14
African American parents: and community control of education, 1, 166, 167, 172, 175, 176–77, 178, 179–81, 184, 185, 186, 223, 254; and school desegregation, 106, 120; and African Americans/Puerto Ricans relationship, 173, 184–85, 193–94; and African American teachers, 211–12, 223, 226
African Americans: population of, 3, 249; and liberation from multiple systems of oppression, 4–5; as "people of color," 5; racial identity of, 7; political networks of, 11; and black underclass, 15, 250; coalitions with Jews, 17; assimilation of, 22, 31, 250; mutual aid societies of, 35; organized social life of, 42; and poverty and the poor, 42–43, 47, 142, 252; and youth gangs, 51–52; and Commission on Human Rights, 59; and Democratic Party, 83, 84, 136–37, 159, 240; and political representation, 83–86, 93, 136, 213–14, 234, 240; and antipoverty programs, 132–33, 138–40, 142–43; Glazer and Moynihan on, 241–42; as immigrants, 251; incarceration rate of, 253. See also Black nationalism;

Blackness; Black Panther Party; Black
Power movement; Black southern
migrants

African Americans/Puerto Ricans relationship: political alignment of, 2,
3–4, 9–16, 17, 20, 86–87, 88, 89, 92–93,
94, 98, 106, 108, 111–13, 123, 130,
185–86, 246, 254; and ethnic identities, 3, 4, 5, 15, 16, 91–92, 98, 121–26,
145, 183; and racial identities, 3, 4, 8,
15, 16–17, 87–88, 91, 110, 121–26, 130,
144–45, 182–84, 216, 220, 248; and
civil rights movement, 3, 9–10, 11,
12–13, 15, 98, 99, 108, 109, 116–17, 118,
121–26, 214; and political separation,
5, 11, 14, 15, 19, 87–88, 89, 92–93, 108,
122–23, 132, 159–63, 204, 214, 233–34,
238–40, 243, 244; and War on Poverty,
11, 12, 13, 132–34, 255; and school
desegregation, 11, 106, 108, 119–20,
125, 169, 172, 173–74, 191; and antipoverty programs, 11–13, 14, 15, 109,
132–33, 147–54, 156–64, 204, 216, 255,
256; and political independence of
Puerto Rico, 13–14; and labor unions,
15–16, 18, 93, 244; and shared physical spaces, 17–18, 140; and Puerto
Rican migration narratives, 28; and
International Ladies Garment Workers' Union, 65–69, 86–87; and Powell,
85–86, 89; and cross-racial alliances,
86–87, 89, 132, 134, 159, 160, 185, 204,
213, 254; and cultural compatibilities,
87–88; construction of, 89, 90; and
intermarriages, 90; and education,
97, 106, 125; and youth, 116–17, 151,
205–7, 247–48; and March on Washington, 117–18; and social class, 118,
213, 238, 248; and school boycott of
1964, 119–21, 123, 124; and community control movement, 133–34, 164,
167, 169–70, 197–98, 254, 255; and I.S.
201, 181–85; and bilingual education,
191, 193–94, 233

African American Teachers Association,
226

African American women: economic
advancement of, 34; and International
Ladies Garment Workers' Union,
62–63, 66–67; and activist mothering, 97; and tenant organizations, 104;
and community control movement,
196–97; and public assistance programs, 215

African American workers: and labor
unions, 17, 34, 60, 81, 82, 93, 94, 113;
as exploitable, 25, 44, 65; economic
advancement of, 34–35, 113; and urban
renewal, 46, 60; and housing policies,
50; in garment industry, 62, 71, 81, 86;
racial and gender subjugation of, 65–
69; access to political power, 81–87

Afro-Caribbean diaspora, 7, 8, 9, 25, 93,
157–58, 206

Airline Pilots, 77

Alba, Vicente "Panama," 254–55

Albizu Campos, Pedro, 1, 37, 55

Alcoff, Linda, 20

Algarín, Miguel, 247

Alianza Obrera Puertorriqueña, 74–75

Alicea, Víctor, 244

Alinsky, Saul, 103

Alliance for Progress program, 40

Alvarado, Anthony, 229

American Bar Association, 29

American exceptionalism, 170

American Federation of Labor (AFL), 34,
73, 79

American Federation of Labor–Congress
of Industrial Workers (AFL-CIO), 38, 82

American Indian Movement, 208

American Jewish Committee, 110

American Labor Party, 55

Amsterdam News, 88, 89, 123, 124, 219, 220

Anazagasti, Robert, 228, 229

Andrade, Kathy, 77, 78–79

Anti-Defamation League, 110

Antipoverty Operation Board, 136

Antipoverty programs: and African
Americans/Puerto Ricans relationship, 11–13, 14, 15, 109, 132–33, 147–54,
156–64, 204, 216, 255, 256; models for,

97; and white neighborhoods, 116; in East Harlem, 131–32, 136, 147–49, 160–62, 216–17, 218; and African Americans, 132–33, 138–40, 142–43; and Puerto Ricans, 132–33, 138–44; and Wagner, 135–37; and stigmatization, 142–43; in South Bronx, 152–59, 217–21; and participatory democracy, 161–62, 163, 215–16; demonstration districts compared to, 177

Antiwar movement, 209

Antonetty, Evelina: on cultural maladjustment, 1–2; organizing work in South Bronx, 1–3, 153; and People's Board of Education, 2, 176; and antipoverty programs, 152–54; and labor unions, 153; and IQ tests, 165–66; and community control movement, 176, 186, 222, 223–24; and participatory democracy, 196; and youth movements, 203, 207

Archible, Leroi, 218

Area Redevelopment, 272 (n. 13)

Asian Americans: social movements of, 3, 4; and Black Power movement, 4; and liberation from multiple systems of oppression, 4–5; population of, 249; assimilation of, 250

Aspira, 97, 110, 113–14, 127, 128–29, 131, 189, 208, 231, 242

Aspira Consent Decree, 212, 231–33

Aspira of New York, Inc. v. Board of Education (1972), 231

Assassins (gang), 202

Assimilation: and cultural maladjustment, 2; and racial identity, 7, 9; and culture of poverty discourse, 11, 22–23; of Puerto Ricans, 18, 22, 60, 242–43; of Latinos, 18, 250; and cultural pluralism, 22, 30; and European immigrants, 22, 30, 35–36; of African Americans, 22, 31, 250; and race relations cycle, 30; of African American middle class, 32; language assimilation, 188; and bilingual education, 190, 192, 212–13, 229–30, 231, 232

Association of Catholic Trade Unionists (ACTU), 73, 79

Ateneo Puertorriqueño, 143

Atkins, Ruth, 149

Ayers, William, 140

Badillo, Herman: and Council against Poverty, 136; as Puerto Rican leader, 154–55; and bilingual education, 189; and decentralization of school boards, 197; and antipoverty programs, 217, 236, 237; political career of, 235, 236–38, 240–41, 242, 243, 282 (n. 66)

Bagu, Alma, 188

Baker, Bertram, 83

Baker, Ella, 9, 106, 196, 246

Baraka, Amiri, 246, 247

Barbaro, Fred, 139

Batista, Jorge, 231

Beal, Frances, 246

Beame, Abraham, 238, 245

Behnken, Brian, 133

Bellecourt, Clyde, 246

Benedict, Ruth, 31

Bergtraum, Murry, 197

Berman, Marshall, 46

Betanzos, Amalia, 186, 242–43

Bienstock, Herbert, 139

Bilingual Advisory Committee of Spanish-speaking Parents, 191

Bilingual education: Antonetty's activism for, 1; separate civil rights struggles of, 5, 6, 15; and Puerto Rican culture, 13, 189–90, 191, 192, 194, 229; and Hispanic ethnic identity, 15, 233; and community control movement, 169, 170, 171, 187–97, 212–13, 224, 232–33; and self-determination, 187–97; Senate hearings on, 188–89; and assimilation, 190, 192, 212–13, 229–30, 231, 232; transitional bilingual education model, 190, 212, 229–30; developmental bilingual education model, 190–91, 212; and African Americans/Puerto Ricans relationship, 191, 193–94, 233;

Davis, John A., 21
Davis, Juanita, 149
De Bello, Frank, 21–22
Decentralization Act of 1969, 197–98, 212, 213, 221
Deindustrialization, 11, 23, 44, 51, 60, 94, 215
De León, Robert, 26–27, 147, 160
Del Toro, Angelo, 216
Del Toro, William, 205, 216–17, 220, 228, 229
Democratic Party: and white ethnic Democrats, 56, 57; and African Americans, 83, 84, 136–37, 159, 240; and Puerto Ricans, 83, 136–37, 140, 159; and antipoverty programs, 138–39
DeSapio, Carmine, 57, 84
Deutsch, Martin, 166
Developmental bilingual education (DBE) model, 190–91, 212
Diago, Yvette Flores, 85
Diamond, Walter, 236
Diaz, Alice, 96
Diaz, Lisa, 96
Diaz, Manny: migration narrative of, 28–29; and labor unions, 95, 99, 115, 118; and social work, 95–96, 108, 111, 112, 115, 146; and Kenneth Clark, 111, 112–13; and African Americans/Puerto Ricans relationship, 112–13, 121, 124–25, 126; and March on Washington, 117, 118; and school boycott of 1964, 119, 120–21, 126; and antipoverty programs, 138, 141–42, 143, 144, 146; and Tyson, 156–57
Dinos, Carmen, 190
Disease, Puerto Ricans associated with, 25, 41, 51
DJ Tony Touch, 247
Doctors' Collective, 203
Dominguez, Virginia, 7
Dominican migrants, 3, 16, 18, 234
Donaldson, Andrew, 193
Donaldson, Ivanhoe, 176
Donovan, Bernard, 174, 180, 225
Dorfman, Ben, 37

Douglass, Frederick, 126
Drug, Hospital, and Health Care Employees Union (Local 1199), 16, 18, 80, 93–94, 252
Drug use: and juvenile delinquency, 52, 53; and public housing, 104; and medical intervention, 204; debilitating effects of, 253–54
D-Stroy, 247
Dubinsky, David, 62, 64, 71–72, 73, 74, 77, 81, 242
Du Bois, W. E. B., 10, 29
Dukes (Puerto Rican gang), 96

Early, James, 246
East Harlem, N.Y.: demographics of, 17–18, 55, 134, 261 (n. 56); and African Americans/Puerto Ricans relationship, 17–18, 87, 132, 134, 147, 154, 159–60; Puerto Ricans in, 24–25, 140, 159; and public housing, 46–47, 104–5; and youth gangs, 52; public schools of, 53, 166, 173–74; and settlement houses, 95–96, 102, 129, 154, 160, 161; and school desegregation, 106, 173–74; antipoverty programs in, 131–32, 136, 147–49, 160–62, 216–17, 218; and community control movement, 186, 226; and decentralization of school districts, 198–200; and Young Lords' garbage offensive, 203
East Harlem Coalition for Community Control (EHCCC), 186–87, 198–99
East Harlem Community Corporation, 216, 228
East Harlem Multi-Service Center, 221
East Harlem Project (EHP), 102–3, 106, 107
East Harlem Protestant Parish, 52, 104, 152
East Harlem Tenants Council (EHTC), 151–52, 159–61, 202, 216
East Harlem Youth Employment Services (EHYES), 101
East Midwood Jewish Center, 178
Economic marginalization, 25, 34

Female-headed households, 22, 166
Feminists, 40, 127
Festival Bailable, 76
Fight Back organization, 251
Figueroa, Hector, 256
Filipinos, 24
500-Acre Law, 36
Flores, Monserrate, 118, 155, 158, 204–5
Flynn, Ed, 57
Fomento, 38
Fonda, Henry, 33
Ford, Gerald, 246–47
Ford Foundation, 39, 115, 171, 177, 178, 200
Foresight, 2, 223
Forester, Martin, 78
The Forum, 110
Forum, 226, 228
Four Point Program, 40
Fourteenth Amendment, 231
Frankel, Irving, 232
Frazier, E. Franklin, 30–31, 32, 68
Friedman, Bernard, 192–93
Frierson, Sara, 149, 222
Frost, Olivia, 108
Fuentes, Luis, 191–92, 201, 219
Fuertes, Louis Agassiz, 92

Gaines, Edyth, 193
Galamison, Milton, 2, 120, 123, 124, 126, 176, 221
Galvin, Miles, 38, 72
Ganz, Samuel, 163
Garcia, Modesto, 64, 70
García, Robert, 18, 243, 282 (n. 66)
García Rivera, Oscar, 55, 127
Gerena Valentín, Gilberto: and Puerto Rican–labor alliance, 80; and March on Washington, 117; and school boycott of 1964, 119, 120–21, 126; and African Americans/Puerto Ricans relationship, 125–26; and labor unions, 127; and antipoverty programs, 138, 143, 144, 146; and Tyson, 156–57; and youth movements, 203
German immigrants, 56
Gigante, Louis, 218

Gilbert, Jacob H., 190
Gilroy, Paul, 14
Giménez, Martha, 15
Gittell, Marilyn, 276 (n. 19)
Gladnick, Robert, 73
Glazer, Nathan, 34, 35, 44–45, 54, 241–42
Godkin, Edwin, 242
Goldberg, David Theo, 7
Goldstein, John, 181
Gonzalez, Corky, 246
Gonzalez, Eddie, 16, 72–73, 78, 244
González, Fernando "Tony," 203
González, José L., 68
Gráfico, 92
Grassroots mobilization: and African Americans/Puerto Ricans relationship, 13, 112–13, 121–26, 214, 234, 253; and Puerto Ricans, 80, 96, 97–98, 138–44, 253; and settlement houses, 96–97, 99–105; and youth, 97, 110, 126, 128–30; and social work, 106–15; and consciousness of resistance, 115–21; and Puerto Rican women, 126–27, 129–30; and antipoverty programs, 136, 137, 138, 138–44, 153, 164, 243, 254; and social class, 213–14; and Badillo, 237. *See also* Political representation
Gray, Jesse, 105, 119, 151, 152
Gray, Lois, 75–76, 79
Great Cities School Improvement programs, 171
Great Depression, 36, 153, 180
Great Migration, 30
Great Society, 133
Green, Alfred, 163
Green, Helen, 63–64
Green, Roger, 239
Greene, Jerome, 219
Gross national product, 35
Guevera, Che, 203
Guishard de Jesús, Nestor, 255
Gutiérrez, Luis, 255–56
Guzmán, Pablo "Yoruba," 205

Hackett, David, 116
Haiti, 9

houses, 96, 103, 115; and women as activists, 97; and social work, 102, 109, 129; causes of, 115–16; and social science research, 166

Kallen, Horace, 29–30
Kasinitz, Philip, 241
Kate Maremont Foundation, 105
Kelley, Clarence, 237
Kelly, Berlin, 132
Kemp-García Bill, 243
Kennedy, John F., 40, 85, 134, 160, 236, 241
Kennedy, Robert F., 116, 136, 140, 160–61, 163
King, Martin Luther, Jr., 1, 2, 80
King, Sylvester, 225
Kirk, William, 95–96, 103, 147, 160–61
Knock on Any Door (film), 52
Koch, Edward, 15, 214, 237, 238–41, 248, 253
Kochiyama, Yuri, 246
Kornbluh, Felicia, 133
Kornegay, Alice, 162
Kronenfeld, Daniel, 119
Krosney, Herbert, 116

Labor Advisory Committee on Puerto Rican Affairs (LACPRA), 79
Labor unions: and African Americans/ Puerto Ricans relationship, 15–16, 18, 93, 244; and African American workers, 17, 34, 60, 81, 82, 93, 94, 113; and Jews, 17, 68–69, 76; in Puerto Rico, 38; and Puerto Rican workers, 55, 56, 60, 74–81, 93, 94, 95, 113, 117, 244; and Puerto Rican women, 62–63, 66–68, 127; and Puerto Rican migrants, 74–81; white domination of, 81, 82, 94, 99; racist practices of, 82, 84, 252; and civil rights movement, 82, 94; and settlement houses, 100; and wage-price guideposts, 134; and corporate interests, 252. See also specific unions
Lachman, Seymour, 197
Lacot, Antero, 204

LaFontaine, Hernan, 91, 98, 183, 189, 192–93
Lane, Marie, 186–87
La Prensa, 74, 86
Latin America: U.S. relations with, 23, 28, 39, 40, 75; music of, 76; intellectuals from, 92; immigrants from, 98, 244, 250–51; and comparative slavery studies, 122; racial democracy in, 123; Puerto Ricans' identification with, 142, 143; liberation struggles in, 202; anti-imperialist struggles in, 208; civil wars in, 253
Latinidad, meanings of, 4, 6, 249
Latino Justice, 18, 256
Latinos: social movements of, 3, 4; and Black Power movement, 4; cultural identity as mestizo, 5–6; racialization of, 6, 7, 259 (n. 17); ethnic identity of, 6–7; white politicians as advocates of, 15; and labor unions, 16; assimilation of, 18, 250; interethnic tensions of, 18–19, 249–52; population of, 19, 249–50; and American narrative, 20; Puerto Rican self-identification as, 91–92, 251; as immigrants, 249–51; lack of political unity among, 253. See also Hispanics
Lawson, James, 142–43
Leonard, Terry, 181
Levin, Stephen, 204
Lewis, Addie, 104
Lewis, John, 255
Lewis, Oscar, 11, 43, 55
Liberator, 180
Liga Puertorriqueña e Hispana, 24–25
Lincoln Center for the Performing Arts, 207–8
Lincoln Hospital, 203–4
Lindsay, John, 156, 161, 177–78, 202, 215, 225, 236, 238
Lisser, Stanley, 176
Little, George, 10
Little Rock, Ark., 84
Livingston, David, 80
Lloyd, Jean, 181

142; racial harmony fostered among, 9; and War on Poverty, 12, 141; Latinos as largest group among, 19, 249–50; and cult of ethnicity, 34; and culture of poverty discourse, 41–44; and New York City slums, 42; and real estate industry's perception of financial risk, 47; and March on Washington, 118

Mississippi Freedom Democratic Party, 159

Mitchell, Helen, 156, 158

Mobilization for Mothers, 127

Mobilization for Youth (MFY), 97, 115–17, 119, 127, 131, 143, 144

Monserrat, Joseph, 58, 72–73, 86, 91, 122–23, 125, 189, 197

Montagu, Ashley, 31

Montenegro, Binaldo, 152–53

Montenegro, Lorraine, 253–54

Montgomery, Velmanette, 239

Montgomery bus boycott, 84

Morales, Carmen, 64, 70–71

Morales, Iris, 202

Morales, Julio, 108, 109, 114, 127–28, 186

Morales, Pedro, 216

More Effective Schools program, 172

Morris, Aldon, 17

Moscoso, Teodoro, 38, 39

Moses, Robert, 46–47, 51

Mothers' Club, 107, 149

Movimiento Estudiantil Chicano de Aztlán, 208

Movimiento Pro Independencia (MPI), 13, 118, 209

Moynihan, Daniel Patrick, 11, 34, 35, 43, 44–45, 55, 241–42

Multiculturalism, 13

Multiple Dwellings Law, 119

Muñoz Marín, Luis, 36–38, 71–72, 101

Music, 8, 16, 19, 25, 29, 76, 247–48

Naison, Mark, 90

Naples, Nancy, 97

National Association for Puerto Rican Civil Rights (NAPRCR), 80–81, 123, 124, 125

National Association for the Advancement of Colored People (NAACP): self-help efforts of, 35; and Powell, 61; Legal Defense and Education Fund, 62, 195, 231; and Puerto Rican workers, 73; legal approach of, 82; and African Americans/Puerto Ricans relationship, 86, 124; and resistance to racial discrimination, 110; and school desegregation, 120; and youth, 128

National Association of Afro-American Educators, 147

National Association of Puerto Rican Affairs, 155

National Council of Black Studies, 147

National Education Association, 189

National Institute of Mental Health, 115

National Urban League (NUL), 62, 82, 110

Native Americans, 1, 186, 208

Nativism, 30, 86, 88

Navarro, Angel Luis, 64, 70

Nazi Germany, 9, 22, 31

Negro American Labor Council (NALC), 81, 82

Negro Labor Victory Committee, 34

Negron, Frank, 189

Negron, Vincent, 176

Neidle, Cecyle, 242

New Careers, 97, 161–62

New Deal, 57

New Left, 102

Newman, Pauline, 69

Newspaper Guild, 77

New York Association of Black School Supervisors and Administrators, 195

New York City: racial demographics of, 2, 3, 14, 26, 102, 134, 235; African American population of, 2, 25, 83; educational reform campaign in, 2–3; Puerto Rican population of, 3, 24, 25–26, 39, 41, 51, 60, 139, 140; population of black foreigners in, 8, 259–60 (n. 27); black activists including Puerto Ricans as minorities, 9; political radicalism traditions in, 17;

Public school system: and "special" schools, 52, 57, 130, 165; and culture of poverty, 52–54, 57; and culturally deprived child discourse, 53–54, 166; and white Americans, 53–54, 172–73, 186; and racialization, 54; and merit principles, 76, 213, 230; boycott of 1964, 97, 119–21, 127, 128–29, 132, 138, 144, 169, 171; deterioration of, 97, 172; and parent organizations, 153–54; and IQ tests, 165–66; demographics of, 167, 172; and dropout rate, 172, 244; teachers' strikes of 1968, 185, 187, 202; and Puerto Rican teachers and administrators, 190, 191, 192–96, 198, 201, 213, 223–24, 229, 230; and African American teachers and administrators, 195–96, 201, 211–12, 223, 226, 227–28; and community school boards, 197, 221, 228; and decentralization, 197–200, 213, 221–22, 228; and political patronage, 228. *See also* Community control movement

Puente, Tito, 29

Puerto Rican Association for Community Affairs (PRACA), 110, 124, 127–28, 129

Puerto Rican Community Development Project (PRCDP), 144–46, 147, 186, 239

Puerto Rican culture: as permanently damaged, 11; and bilingual education, 13, 189–90, 191, 192, 194, 229; Eurocentric view of, 16; and Puerto Rican Parade Committee, 80; Spanish language as marker of, 86, 125, 128; and African Americans/Puerto Ricans relationship, 87, 125–26; and Hispanics, 92; and submissive culture, 106–8, 233–34, 254; and *compadrasgo*, 152; and community control movement, 169; and naming of schools, 194

Puerto Rican Educators Association, 98, 189, 191–92, 195

Puerto Rican elite: and Harlem riots, 8; and ethnic identities, 14–15, 16, 214; nationalist project of, 28

Puerto Rican Forum, 110, 138, 143, 144, 146, 160, 219

Puerto Rican history, 169

Puerto Rican Labor Committee, 79

Puerto Rican leaders: Puerto Rican-ness as basis for political empowerment, 2, 4; and organizational development, 3; and African Americans/Puerto Ricans relationship, 12, 89, 108–9, 124–25, 132–34, 185–86, 214; and interethnic Latino politics, 18–19; and political representation, 55–59; and juvenile delinquency, 91, 126–27; and stigmatizing labels, 98; and settlement houses, 102, 103; and grassroots mobilization, 102, 108, 110; and social workers, 106–15, 129; and youth, 116; and March on Washington, 117–18; and antipoverty programs, 132–33, 139, 144–46, 147, 156–57, 163–64, 216, 217–18, 220–21; and community control movement, 133–34; and working class, 145–46, 235–36; and bilingual education, 214, 224

Puerto Rican Legal Defense and Education Fund (PRLDEF), 18, 212–13, 231, 232, 256

Puerto Rican middle class: and majority group identification, 8, 118; feminists of, 40; social workers of, 109, 113; and youth, 113–14; and communitarian framework, 114; working-class radicals compared to, 114–15; as Puerto Rican leaders, 146; and community control movement, 211–12, 213; political orientation of, 213–14, 234, 242, 248; growth of, 243

Puerto Rican migrants: in New York City, 2, 25–26, 39, 41, 60; "inferior" culture of, 2, 50, 53–54; and ethnic identities, 7–8, 24; migration narratives, 28–29, 60; and cult of ethnicity, 34, 56, 60, 75; postwar migration, 35–41; and Operation Bootstrap, 38–39; and urban renewal, 46, 50, 51; and public housing, 50–51, 55; and youth gangs, 51–52, 96;

labor organizing of, 74–81; and political resistance, 97–98; as minorities, 99; and public school system, 172

Puerto Rican nationalism: and African Americans/Puerto Ricans relationship, 13, 14, 16, 118, 134, 171, 254; incarceration of nationalists, 55; and radicalism, 56; and Powell, 86; and antipoverty programs, 133, 134, 154–59, 164, 216; and Theater Arts Center, 151; and East Harlem Tenants Council, 151, 160; in South Bronx, 154–59; and community control movement, 168–70, 171, 194, 202, 209; and youth movements, 202, 207; and cultural pluralism, 248

Puerto Rican-ness, 2, 4, 20, 254

Puerto Rican Organizations of Brooklyn, 118

Puerto Rican Parade Committee, 80, 143

Puerto Rican parents: and community control of education, 1, 165–66, 167, 172, 175, 176–77, 178, 179–81, 184, 185, 186, 223–24, 254; and school desegregation, 106; and school boycott of 1964, 121; and African Americans/Puerto Ricans relationship, 173, 184–85, 193–94; and bilingual education, 187–97, 212; and Puerto Rican teachers, 232

Puerto Rican Parent-Teacher Association, 123–24

Puerto Ricans: and Black Power movement, 3, 4, 160, 182; population in New York City, 3, 24, 25–26, 39, 41, 51, 60, 139, 140; political structures of, 3–4, 11; ethnic identities of, 4, 7–8, 9, 14, 56, 75, 76, 91–92, 98, 121–26, 127, 130, 133, 140–41, 145, 160, 163, 189–90, 192, 234, 241, 242, 243, 248, 259 (n. 9); racial identities of, 4, 7–8, 9, 16–17, 21–22, 23, 24, 29, 87–88, 116, 121–26, 133, 139, 144, 174, 205–6, 216, 220, 233, 259 (n. 9); and liberation from multiple systems of oppression, 4–5; cultural identity as *mestizo*, 6, 16, 17; and pov-

erty and the poor, 8, 11, 18, 35, 36, 37, 43, 47, 56–57, 101, 139, 141–42, 144–46, 169; political identity of, 9–10, 11, 15; colonial status of, 10; Mexican Americans compared to, 16, 259 (n. 17); in U.S. racial spectrum, 23–29; racial ambiguity of, 24, 25–26, 27, 29, 87–88, 98, 116, 122, 139–40, 170, 173–74; mutual aid societies of, 35; and culture of poverty discourse, 41–44, 60; and Puerto Rican problem debate, 41–47, 55–59, 98, 102, 127–28; and culture of dependency, 44–45; and political representation, 55–59, 60, 83–86, 93, 136, 213–14, 234–36; and Democratic Party, 83, 136–37, 140, 159; racism of, 87, 220; as Latinos, 91–92, 251; and antipoverty programs, 132–33, 138–44

Puerto Ricans Involved in Student Action (PRISA), 203, 208

Puerto Rican Social Services (PRSS), 142

Puerto Rican Solidarity Committee (PRSC), 246–47

Puerto Rican Student Union (PRSU), 201–2, 206, 207–8

Puerto Rican *tabaqueros*, 75

Puerto Rican women: as power brokers, 12; fertility rate of, 37; and sterilization programs, 39–40; and labor unions, 62–63, 66–69, 127; and patriarchal authority, 68; in garment industry, 71; and activist mothering, 97; and tenant organizations, 104; and public school system, 107–8; and March on Washington, 119, 127; and grassroots mobilization, 126–27, 129–30; and community control movement, 174, 196–97; and public assistance programs, 215

Puerto Rican workers: as exploitable, 25, 44–45, 51, 57, 65; and upward mobility, 35, 88, 113, 114, 163, 199–200, 235; and Operation Bootstrap, 38–41; and culture of poverty, 44–45; and urban renewal, 46, 60; and labor unions, 55, 56, 60, 74–81, 93, 94, 95, 113, 117, 244; in garment industry, 62, 71, 73–74, 86;

racial and gender subjugation of, 65–
69; public and hidden transcripts of,
70–74; access to political power, 81–87
Puerto Rican Youth Conference, 127
Puerto Rico: political independence
movement, 13–14, 75, 126, 133, 168,
169, 170, 208–9, 242, 245, 246–47; and
"whitening of the race," 16, 27; U.S.
colonization of, 23, 28, 35, 36–37, 40,
71, 86, 169, 188, 208, 219, 220, 246; racial exceptionalism in, 27, 28; slavery
in, 27, 28–29, 122–23; overpopulation
discourse, 35, 36, 37, 38–40, 41, 50–51;
unemployment rate of, 36, 37, 41–42;
and Operation Bootstrap, 38–41, 101;
democracy in, 40; and U.S. garment
industry, 71–74; statehood movement,
85; and English as main language, 86,
188
Puerto Rico Department of Labor, Migration Division, 57, 58, 72–73, 76, 78,
79, 86, 155, 189, 190
Puerto Rico Policy Commission, 36
Puerto Rico Solidarity Committee, 208
Puertorriqueños Unidos, 127
Pulido, Laura, 197

Quiles, Anthony (Q-Unique), 247
Quiñones, Carmen, 67
Quiñones, Gloria, 131–32, 149, 205
Quintero, Luisa, 124

Race relations cycle, 30–31
Racial democracy: and U.S. global
image, 9; and U.S. national narrative,
19–20; and cult of ethnicity, 22, 31, 32–
33; and African Americans/Puerto Ricans relationship, 93, 256; and settlement houses, 102; in Latin America,
123; barriers to, 253
Racial discrimination: and African
Americans/Puerto Ricans relationship, 11, 15, 27, 87, 110, 117, 118, 133; in
Puerto Rico, 27, 122; and black southern migrants, 32, 34; minorities' ability to overcome, 42; and International

Ladies Garment Workers' Union, 61–
67, 73, 74, 76, 78–79, 81, 82; and labor
unions, 82, 84, 252; and Powell, 84, 85;
and white social reformers, 99; and
consensus ideology, 108; resistance to,
110; and African Americans' minority
status, 250
Racial domination, and culture of poverty, 41–47, 50–55
Racial identities: and African Americans/
Puerto Ricans relationship, 3, 4, 8, 15,
16–17, 87–88, 91, 110, 121–26, 130, 144–
45, 182–84, 216, 220, 248; of Puerto Ricans, 4, 7–8, 9, 16–17, 21–22, 23, 24, 29,
87–88, 116, 121–26, 133, 139, 144, 174,
205–6, 216, 220, 233, 259 (n. 9); construction of, 6, 8, 29, 256; political deployment of, 6–10; and assimilation, 7,
9; and civil rights movement, 98
Racialization: and cultural maladjustment, 2; and Puerto Ricans as "nonwhite," 4, 6, 7, 8, 11, 23, 25, 91, 110, 139,
170, 259 (n. 17); and African Americans
as "nonwhite," 4, 8, 23; and political
separation, 5; and Mexican Americans
as "nonwhite," 6, 259 (n. 17); and colonization, 10; and culture of poverty
discourse, 11, 43–44, 55, 60; bifurcated racialization, 14, 214; and public
school system, 54
Racial subjugation, 2, 20, 23, 25
Racism: and ethnic identity, 7, 110; U.S.
attempts at erasure of, 9; in Puerto
Rican society, 27–28; cult of ethnicity overcoming, 29–35; Harrington
on, 42; of Puerto Ricans, 87, 220; and
comparative slavery studies, 123; and
culture of poverty, 166–67; internalized racism, 169, 205–8
Ramirez, Julio, 64, 70–71
Randolph, A. Philip, 62, 81–82
Rangel, Charles, 236
Ratcliffe, Delores, 162
Reagan, Ronald, 18, 243
Real Great Society (RGS), 202
Rebels (Italian gang), 96

Reid, Whitelaw, 23
Rent and Rehabilitation Administration, 105
Republican Party, 83
Retail, Wholesale, and Department Store Union (RWDSU): District 65, 18, 73, 80, 93–94, 153, 252; Local 3, 67
Rice, Florence, 63–64, 67, 81–82, 113
Riessman, Frank, 54, 138, 162
Ríos, Carlos, 105, 127
Riots, 8, 161, 202, 234, 241
Rivera, Agustín, 205
Rivera, Lino, 8
Rivera, Melissa, 246
Rivera, Miguel, 205
Robinson, Alfred G., 23
Robinson, Isaiah, 174, 197, 221
Rockefeller, Nelson A., 236
Rockefeller Foundation, 39
Rock, Rock, Rock (film), 52
Rodríguez, David Sanes, 255
Rodríguez, Eugene, 154–55
Rodriguez, Francisco, 152
Rodriguez, Maria, 73
Rodriguez, Pura, 104
Rodríguez de Tío, Lola, 127
Roosevelt, Eleanor, 25
Roosevelt, Franklin D., 36
Rosario, Carlos, 90
Rose, Reginald, 262 (n. 40)
Ruiz, Ruperto, 57–59, 86
Russians, 24
Rustin, Bayard, 117, 119, 120–21, 126
Ryan, Mildred, 104, 105
Ryan, William F., 190

Sabater, Julio, 216
St. Edward the Martyr Church, 152
St. Lucy's Roman Catholic Church, 105
Sanchez, Noel, 251–52
Sanchez, Paul, 79
Sanchez, Yolanda, 108, 124, 127, 146
Sanitation Department, 203
Santaella, Irma Vidal, 124
Santiago Iglesias Educational Society, 79

Scheuer-Nelson Subprofessional Career Act of 1967, 161–62
Schomburg, Artúro, 8–9
School desegregation: separate civil rights struggles of, 5; bilingual education incompatible with, 6; and African Americans/Puerto Ricans relationship, 11, 106, 108, 119–20, 125, 169, 172, 173–74, 191; Kenneth Clark on, 109; and culture of poverty, 166; Charles Wilson on, 180; and decentralization, 198–99; false promises of, 201
Schreiber, Daniel, 173–74
Scott, James C., 70
Scott, Sarah, 178
Scribner, Harvey, 224–25
Seafarers International Union, 71
Seda, Eduardo, 190
SEEK (Search for Education, Elevation and Knowledge), 202–3, 206
Segarra, Arnaldo "Arnie," 202
Segregation: Antonetty's strategy of maladjustment to, 1, 2; Afro-Caribbeans' lack of experience with, 9; Pantoja's experience of, 26; in South, 26–27, 261 (n. 21); de jure segregation, 28; and uniqueness of African Americans' experiences, 32; and public housing, 50; of settlement houses, 99, 102. See also School desegregation
Seigel, Micol, 122–23
Self-determination: and community control movement, 1, 2, 13, 168–69, 171, 180, 202, 209, 211, 221; and African Americans/Puerto Ricans relationship, 13–14, 20, 163, 218–20, 233; of African Americans, 84; and bilingual education, 187–97; and neoliberalism, 244–48
Senior, Clarence, 40, 79
Serrano, José, 18, 282 (n. 66)
Service Employees International Union, 252, 256
Settlement houses: and social work, 95–96, 100–101; and juvenile delinquency, 96, 103, 115; and grass-

roots mobilization, 96–97, 99–105; segregation of, 99, 102; and youth, 99, 115; and indigenous leadership, 99–100, 102–3, 129; and poverty and the poor, 100–101; and participatory democracy, 102; and African Americans/Puerto Ricans relationship, 108, 133, 147, 160; and antipoverty programs, 137, 147

Sexton, Patricia Cayo, 106–7

Shanahan, Thomas, 51

Shanker, Albert, 213, 229–30, 248

Sharkey-Brown-Isaacs Law (1958), 50, 59

Sharpton, Al, 255

Shaw, Clifford, 103

Sherman, Steve, 205

Shriver, Sargent, 137, 138–39, 144

Silverman, Jennie, 69

Silvers, Cleo, 206–7

Simkhovitch, Mary, 100

Sit-ins, 84

Sixteenth Street Baptist Church (Birmingham, Ala.), bombing of, 138

Sixth Annual Puerto Rican Youth Conference, 129

Sklar, Eugene, 103

Slavery: in Mexico, 17; in Puerto Rico, 27, 28–29, 122–23; and uniqueness of African Americans' experiences, 32; black churches developed under, 42; comparative slavery studies, 122–23

Social class: and liberation from multiple systems of oppression, 4–5; and racial hierarchy in Puerto Rico, 27–28; and black southern migrants, 30–31; and culture of poverty, 42–43; and Puerto Rican migrants, 56; and settlement houses, 100; and social workers, 109, 113; and March on Washington, 118; and African Americans/Puerto Ricans relationship, 118, 213, 238, 248; and consensus ideology, 135; and antipoverty programs, 135, 161–63; meaning of, 144–46; and community control movement, 211–12, 213, 223–27; and

grassroots mobilization, 213–14. *See also* Middle class; Working class

Socialist Party, 75

Soto, Willie, 131

South: segregation in, 26–27, 261 (n. 21); civil rights movement in, 82; sit-ins, 84. *See also* Black southern migrants

South Bronx, N.Y.: and African Americans/Puerto Ricans relationship, 17–18, 87, 134, 152, 154, 155, 156, 158–59, 217–21; demographics of, 17–18, 134, 140, 154, 217, 261 (n. 56); and public housing, 46, 47; Puerto Ricans in, 140; and antipoverty programs, 152–59, 217–21; and public school system, 153–54; Puerto Rican nationalism in, 154–59; and community control movement, 176, 193; and Badillo, 237; geographic boundaries of, 271 (n. 8)

South Bronx Neighborhood Orientation Center, 155

Soviet Union, 100

Spain, 23–24, 28

Spanish American Youth Bureau, 57, 86, 91

Spanish Harlem, 8, 29, 55

Spanish language: and bilingual ballots, 15, 235; and labor unions, 76, 153; as Puerto Rican cultural marker, 86, 125, 128; and ethnic identities of Puerto Ricans, 91, 98, 140–41; and Puerto Rican women, 127; and African Americans/Puerto Ricans relationship, 144–45; and Theater Arts Center, 151; and IQ tests, 165; and community control movement, 186. *See also* Bilingual education

Spencer, David, 2, 176, 178–79, 181, 194, 225–26

Spiegal Act of 1962, 104

Stanislaus, Lamuel, 239

Starr, Roger, 237

Stein, Annie, 246

Stevenson, Adlai, 84

Stewart, Merle, 223, 224–25, 227

188, 208, 219, 220, 246; myth of mono-
  lingualism, 187
U.S. Census of 1950, 41
U.S. Census of 1960, 26
U.S. Census of 2010, 249
U.S. Civil Rights Commission, 174
U.S. Department of Health, Education,
  and Welfare, 39, 153, 158, 224
U.S. Office of Education, 31, 244
U.S. Senate Foreign Relations Commit-
  tee, 39
U.S. State Department, 39
U.S. Tariff Commission, 37
United Teacher, 181
Unity Committee, 59
University of Chicago, 22
Upper West Side school district, 177
Upward mobility: and African American
  workers, 34–35, 113; and Puerto Rican
  workers, 35, 88, 113, 114, 163, 199–200,
  235; and individualism, 114
Urban Coalition, 153
Urban League of Greater New York, 120
Urban renewal: and racialization of
  Puerto Ricans, 11; and culture of pov-
  erty, 23, 45; and middle class, 45–46;
  and working class, 45–46, 60; and ten-
  ant relocations, 46–47, 51, 140; and
  tenant organizations, 104; and public
  school system, 173
Urban Task Force, 202
Ureña, Pedro Henriquez, 92

Valle, Marta, 107, 127
Van Arsdale, Harry, 79, 244
Vann, Albert, 239
Vargas, Enrique, 150
Vazquez, Hector, 219–20
Vázquez Calzada, José, 39
Vega, Bernardo, 25, 75, 92, 127
Velázquez, José, 246
Velázquez, Nydia, 18
Velez, Efrain, 129
Velez, Hector, 146
Velez, Ramón, 155–56, 158–59, 204–5,
  217–18, 220–21, 222, 239

Velez, Ted, 108, 149, 151–52, 159–61, 178
Venereal diseases, 41
Verissimo, Erico, 92
Vice, Celia, 118
Vieques coalition, 247, 254–55
Vincent Astor Foundation, 202
Vista, 180
Voting Rights Act, 235

Wagner, Robert F., 58, 59, 105, 135–37,
  140, 236, 238
Wakefield, Dan, 53, 57
War on Poverty: separate civil rights
  struggles of, 5; and African Ameri-
  cans/Puerto Ricans relationship,
  11, 12, 13, 132–34, 255; and minority
  status, 12, 141; and political radicalism in New York City, 17; and material and psychological conditions of
  the poor, 43; and women of color,
  97; precursors to, 116; federal mandate of, 134; and CPC elections, 137;
  and African Americans, 139; and
  Powell, 140; and Lindsay, 156; Senate hearings on, 161, 162; legislation
  included in, 272 (n. 13). *See also* Antipoverty programs
Watts, Mae, 62
Welfare programs: and Puerto Ricans,
  44–45, 56–57, 236; and Antonetty, 153;
  and deindustrialization, 215
Western capitalism, 10, 23, 36, 208, 246
Western imperialism, 10, 14, 208, 246
West Indian immigrants: Caribbean
  identity of, 6; blackness of, 6, 21; political alliances of, 15; Puerto Ricans
  compared to, 22; political representation of, 83; and African Americans,
  93, 239
West Side Story (film), 52
Whalen, Carmen, 44
White, Lee C., 140
White, Randolph, 88
White, Theodore, 35, 85
White Americans: Puerto Ricans' re-
  lationships with, 4; as advocates of